"About 70 years ago, Edgar Cayce began gaining
national prominence in the United States for his uncanny and
otherworldy ability to solve perplexing medical questions,
all while in a state of deep meditative trance.
Today that mantle has been passed to Dr. Douglas James Cottrell
who has demonstrated many of Cayce's marvelous abilities
using the exact same techniques.

The Compleat New Age Health Guide is
the culmination of thirty years of his work in this field.
It represents an awe-inspiring affirmation
of Douglas's finely tuned abilities.
Through this book, Douglas has taken his remarkable
God-given gifts and created the most precious gift
imaginable for all mankind."

~ Richard Syrett
(Radio and Television Host)

The Compleat New Age Health Guide: Volume One

Disclaimer: All information in this book has been obtained through the use of spiritual or psychic sources. All health-related information that may be given is offered for its suggestive and informative value only, and is not to be relied upon as a medical authority. The reader of this book agrees to be fully responsible for the practical application of any and all information contained therein, and relieves the publisher, author, Douglas James Cottrell, his family, and any and all participating organizations from such responsibility.

Cover Design: Douglas M. Cottrell

Photo Credits:
Sarah Eve Cardell (pages 16, 27, 39, 47, 62, 96, 181, 255) www.sarahevecardell.com
Douglas James Cottrell (pages 9, 19, 58, 122, 219). Yoga photos courtesy www.shantiyogainhamilton.com
Douglas M Cottrell (pages 36, 77, 111, 141, 158, 202, 256)
Christine Lobsinger (page 62)

Photo of Douglas James Cottrell by Bob Hill Photo Art

ISBN 978-0-9919795-4-7

First edition

Published in Canada by
Many Mansions Press
www.manymansionspress.com

THE COMPLEAT NEW AGE HEALTH GUIDE

VOLUME ONE

Based on the remarkable
Deep Trance Meditation readings of
Douglas James Cottrell, Ph.D.

Co-authored and Edited by
Douglas Matthew Cottrell, B.A., M.A.

Many Mansions Press
Canada

www.manymansionspress.com

CONTENTS

Looking Forward:

The Mind's Eye View:

ACKNOWLEDGEMENTS

The Compleat New Age Health Guide would not have been published, had it not been for the hard work and expertise of many caring and loving people. To all those who have participated in their special way (and they know who they are), let me express my heartfelt appreciation and gratitude. To be of service without expectation of reward is to give the greatest gift. May God bless each and every one of them.

Most significantly, had it not been for the leadership, dedication and expertise of my son, **Douglas Matthew Cottrell**, this book would not have been produced. From suggesting topics to research, to participating in hours of deep trance meditation readings, to editing and proof-reading all of the material. It was a huge labor of love.

I especially would like to thank:

Robert Appel, who has steadfastly encouraged me for years to produce this book, using the Deep Trance Meditation method. His dedication and support for my work has been unshakable. I am grateful for his guidance and friendship.

Karen Cottrell and I started out in 1974 exploring the mysterious world of D.T.M. Her dedication to our daughter, Cheri, and to her work as my D.T.M. "conductor" is a demonstration of her spiritual strength and love for her daughter. My career as an intuitive would never have been, without her being at my side. For this, and other things, I am deeply grateful.

Tom G. (aka Rammsteinregeln). His dedication in transcribing numerous research D.T.M. readings for countless hours has made this book possible. Without this monumental effort, this book might not have ever been produced.

Louise Cottrell, my daughter, has made this health guide a family effort, and I am so proud of her. Not only has she given me two beautiful grand-children (Ryker and Chlöe), Louise worked extremely hard and transcribed many D.T.M. readings. Much of her hard work has been included in this health guide.

Sheila Gatis and her late friend, **Shirley McKenzie**, started documenting the D.T.M. readings back in the 1980s. Their foresight and hard work to initiate research readings back then was the start of this health guide. I am deeply grateful for their friendship and support of my work.

Karen Birch has worked very hard assisting in compiling the research material, participating in the research D.T.M.'s and coordinating orders. She has tirelessly dedicated herself to the work. Whenever we needed something, Karen seemed to have the magic ability to find it. I am grateful for her friendship and dedication to the work.

Jack Rosen, of the A.R.E.-Edgar Cayce Center New York, has participated in the promotion and validation of the D.T.M. method. His friendship and support are deeply appreciated.

Viengxay Malavong has been an enthusiastic supporter of the work. His knowledge and dedication have been helpful in assisting our research topics. He has encouraged us to push the limit using the D.T.M. source. I am grateful to know him and call him a friend.

Pat Parimi, whose vast knowledge of many things has helped us find our way in producing this health guide.

Daniel Lage has been offering guidance and support of me and my work. When someone volunteers, sees the vision and then carries it out, they are extra special people. I am very grateful to Daniel for his support, friendship, and dedication.

Rebecca Sanford has been a confidant and supporter of the D.T.M. material. Her guidance and suggestions have been deeply appreciated in the formulation of subjects and topics for this health guide. She continues to support my work and I am grateful to all that she has done.

Richard Syrett, radio and T.V. host, has been a long-time friend who has constantly given me the privilege to be on major radio stations in Toronto. I am grateful for his giving me the opportunity to be on radio, so that others might find out about the D.T.M. source and what energy healing is all about. He has become a friend over the last thirty years.

I especially wish to thank the people who have worked so very, very hard in translating my books and making the knowledge from the D.T.M. Source available throughout the world. They have, in effect, "spoken" for me to people in their own lands. To accurately translate anything is very hard to do, never mind an entire book. Translation is not really about words. It's about translating thoughts behind the written word. I am humbled and grateful for their magnificent labour of love: **Mark-Antoine Hachem** (French translation of *The New Renaissance);* **Fernando Schneider** (Portuguese translation of *The New Renaissance);* **Merche Señor** (Spanish translation of *The New Renaissance* and *Secrets of Life);* and **Claude Gillard** (French translation of *Secrets of Life)*. May you be eternally blessed. To say, "Thank you, Muchas gracias, Merci beaucoup, Muito obrigado," is simply not enough.

At this time, I would also like to recognize the following for their support and guidance:

Dr. Steven Meda started me on the path to developing my D.T.M. ability. Without hesitation, he became our family doctor in the early 1970s, watching over my daughter, Cheri, as we applied the treatments Ross Peterson suggested in the D.T.M. session. He, in fact, got me started on the spiritual path.

Dr. Don Viggiani and **Dr. Michael Bodnar** provided the chiropractic care for Cheri, and from them I learned about the subconscious and how the body works through drugless therapies. They were instrumental in their own way in showing me alternatives to traditional medicine. Michael would often validate the accuracy of the D.T.M.'s with clients who took their readings to him. His open-mindedness to explore the D.T.M. source as a source of accurate information encouraged me and gave me confidence to continue on doing the D.T.M. work.

Jim Sinclair, New York businessman, has supported me and my family throughout the years. He has introduced me to people in New York — Susan and Andrew Beer and Amanda Borghese — who, in turn, introduced me to their friends in New York and elsewhere. I am very grateful to Jim. He is my friend and brother. It is a privilege and an honor to know him and his friends in New York.

Seymour Aaron took an interest in my work and helped produce my first book, *Secrets of Life*. He has been a wonderful friend over the years. He arranged for a scientific test of my abilities at a hotel in Toronto. The results of this scientific test proved beyond a doubt that the D.T.M. source could be a highly accurate and reliable tool in finding out the causes for health concerns. I am grateful for his friendship and his guidance over the years.

Everyone has an angel. The **Baroness Uschi von Diegardt** has always been there for me and my family. Since the mid-1970s, I have been encouraged and supported by this angel. Many times, when I was tempted to give up, my angel would encourage me to continue on. At some of the most difficult points in my life, the Baroness would be there with a kind word. I am ever so grateful for her support and belief in me.

The late **Brenda Carlin,** the wife of the famous comedian **George Carlin,** invited me to California in the mid-1980s. **Shirley MacLaine** had written some popular metaphysical books. Brenda introduced me to many movie stars and show-business people. I have maintained life-time friendships with the Carlin family and many of the people I met in California. I am grateful for her friendship and her belief in the D.T.M. method. I enjoyed my friendship with Brenda and George, who were down-to-earth, good people.

Joyce DeWitt, star of television and stage, became a good friend of mine, and I am grateful for the many times we have spoken about metaphysical and intuitive abilities. I am grateful for her belief in me and my work. She is a wonderful spiritual person.

And finally, I wish to thank the three most important people who have helped me on this spiritual path; a path which has led me into your hands with his health guide. My daughter, **Cheri Anne**, and my mentors, **Ross Peterson** and **Rev. Alec Holmes**. If it were not for the sacrifice Cheri Anne made in coming into this world with challenges that ultimately institutionalized her for four years, and if it wasn't for Ross Peterson who gave me my very first psychic reading using the D.T.M. method, I would never have dedicated my life to exploring the D.T.M. source of information for almost forty years. Rev. Alex Holmes showed me how to do spiritual healing or the Laying On Of Hands. Together these three form a trinity that has helped me find my inner way. I cannot express how grateful I am to these three souls. All three have now returned to the spiritual dimensions above, but they live on in my work and in my heart.

Douglas James Cottrell,
Hamilton, Canada, 2014

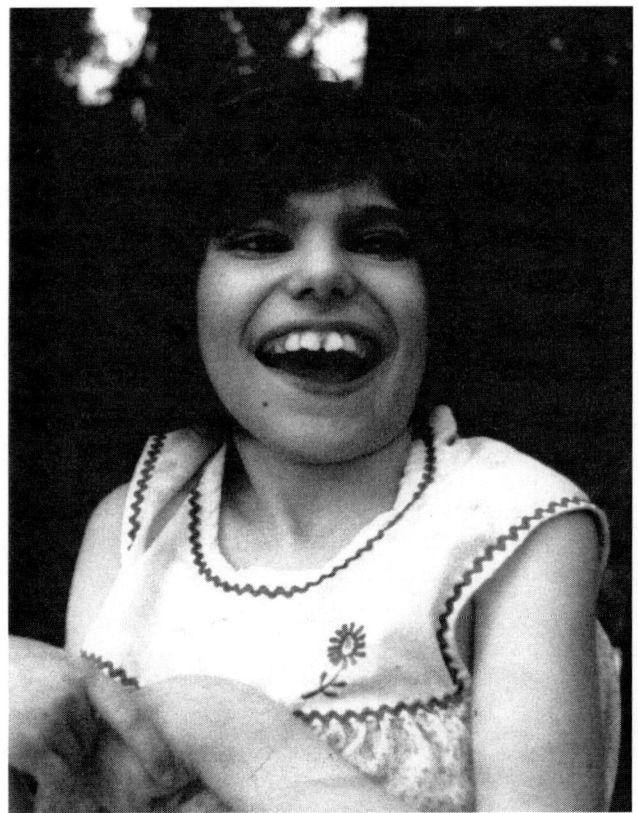

Cheri Anne Cottrell, 1968-2006

FOREWORD BY JACK ROSEN

Edgar Cayce is called "the Father of Holistic Medicine." As a young man, he discovered he was able to enter into a self-induced sleep state, and come in contact with an unlimited Universal Source of information. While sleeping, he could answer questions and give discourses on any subject with authority. Though he had only an 8th grade education, the accuracy of his health readings and the effectiveness of the treatments he recommended made him a medical phenomenon.

For more than fifty years, I have been using the Edgar Cayce remedies and teaching people how to make and use them. As a Cayce Method Educator for the New York Edgar Cayce Center, I have devoted my life to teaching workshops on important concepts from Cayce's health readings. A few months ago, I was teaching a workshop in New York (on Atlantis and ancient Egypt), when I was approached by a young man. He asked if I had ever heard of Douglas James Cottrell from Canada. He gave me some information about Douglas, and soon I was looking him up on the Internet.

I am a firm believer that there are no accidents in life. I had often wondered if there was anyone else who could do readings similar to Cayce, so I was very intrigued. Two weeks later, I drove up to Canada for my own reading with Douglas. A week later, I had started making plans to bring him to N.Y.C. The rest, as they say, is history! He gave readings to over a dozen people, and those I spoke to only sang his praise.

The treatments Douglas recommends in his readings are very similar to Cayce's — castor oil packs , peanut oil, the Violet Ray, etc. Like Cayce, Douglas does not actually heal anyone. All healing comes from God. Our natural state is health, but by our thoughts, actions and karma, we cause our own illness. The information coming through these Sources offers us different methods for aligning ourselves with the Universal Laws, showing us a way to be in harmony with our bodies, and a path for returning to our Father.

The Compleat New Age Health Guide is a treasure-trove of information on health topics. Those who have studied the Cayce readings, as I have, will notice many similarities, but they are not identical. Some of the substances Douglas recommends weren't known in Cayce's day. There are also many topics that were never covered in the Cayce readings, because no one had asked about them 100 years ago. The Cayce information and Douglas's complement each other nicely.

This book will save many trips to the doctor and will teach you how to heal yourself in a holistic way. Besides the Edgar Cayce material on holistic healing, there is no other book like it. I highly recommend it.

"Spirit is the Life, Mind is the Builder and the Physical is the result." (famous Cayce aphorism)

Peace & Love,

JACK ROSEN, A.R.E. NEW YORK,
NEW YORK, NEW YORK, 2014

INTRODUCTION BY ROBERT APPEL

A few years back, I was attending a fairly lavish party given by a good friend of mine, born in China. He was in the process of opening a series of holistic clinics in Canada, based on his family's unique practice of T.C.M. ("Traditional Chinese Medicine") which, literally, spanned generations in his native land.

Without warning, he grabbed my arm and ushered me into a private room where a distinguished, soft-spoken individual, also of Chinese descent, was waiting for me.

My friend explained that the man in the chair was a very well-known M.D. in China, and literally traveled the globe as an ambassador of Chinese medicine, lecturing to Western doctors on the core principles of the millennia-old Asian practice.

My friend had prevailed on the gentleman in question to take a moment to deploy some of these ancient diagnostic techniques on me. My friend knew that I had suffered from a number of health challenges — issues that had dominated my life — since I was a child.

The diagnostic procedure (which involved resting my arm on a small pillow while different pulse points were tested, as well as an examination of the skin, tongue, hair and nails) took less than ten minutes, after which, the visiting physician donned a worried expression, and explained that I had both "blocked chi" and "insufficient chi." Together, this was a very unfavorable combination, and could condemn me to a life of one chronic condition after another.

This, by no coincidence, was exactly the life I had been living.

However, what I remember most about the experience was not the diagnosis (because I had received similar diagnoses from other Oriental practitioners over the many years) but, rather, that this very kind man made it his business to surreptitiously keep an eye on me for the remainder of the party, always watching me from across the room, always with that same seriously-concerned look, as if he feared I would not survive even till the end of the evening.

I went home early that night.

In fact, I do, indeed, suffer from a variety of chronic complaints, and far too much of my life is spent trying to keep them all managed.

That's the bad news.

The good news is that it was specifically these sorts of life-challenges that allowed me to meet Dr. Douglas James Cottrell way back in 1977 and, over time, become friends.

So, you see, every dark cloud does have a silver lining!

In modern parlance, we tend to over-use phrases like "talented," "unique," "extraordinary individual" and — my personal favorite — "needs no introduction" (which, if true, would make these sentences redundant...or, at the very least, superfluous).

I have been privileged, in the past, to have been asked to scribe introductions for other books that Dr. Cottrell has done. In those writings I have tried, with mixed success, to explain to the logical Western mind the "basis" for the extraordinary skills he demonstrates.

In those writings, I have discussed, at length, the notion of the Super-Self (aka High-Self, Oversoul, or Super-Conscious); the Akashic Records or Book of Life; as well as the mysterious and arcane secret that the High Self can only be accessed from the Sub-conscious, and never from the Conscious Mind.

I spent many years reading hundreds of books, and traveling to very odd places, in order to put together these explanations, only to discover that some ninety-percent-plus of those individuals fortunate enough to interact with Dr. Cottrell were really not interested in 'why' he does what he does, or even 'how' he does what he does.

By and large, they were only interested in whether he could, in fact, do what he does; and, furthermore, do it precisely when and where they wished him to.

A subtle difference, but nonetheless a difference.

So, as I soldier on, writing an introduction for a man who, just as the cliché implies, really needs none, let me simply mention the following:

• Dr. Cottrell is considered to be the only man alive who has a proven track record for doing tens of thousands of deep-meditation sessions in the so-called "Edgar Cayce tradition." In fact, Dr. Cottrell has, in his career (started in 1974), done well over double the number that Cayce himself did in his own lifetime. And, as these words are penned, is only lately showing any sign whatsoever of slowing down.

• Dr. Cottrell is mentioned by name in *The Complete Idiots Guide to the Akashic Record* (ISBN 1592579965); and, in summer 2014, was the featured speaker at the ten-day "New York Edgar Cayce" event in N.Y.C., where he delivered both live interactive deep-meditation sessions, and educational seminars to attendees, twice a day, sometimes three times a day, ENTIRELY OVER THE INTERNET. If Guinness had a category for that — they don't! — that would likely be an instant and unbeatable record.

• Although, PRECISELY AS WAS THE CASE WITH EDGAR CAYCE, Dr. Cottrell has the ability to answer questions from deep meditation on a wide variety of topics (spirituality, religion, reincarnation, lost civilizations, hidden meanings in ancient texts, earth changes), over ninety-percent of the requests he gets are heath-related.

As was the case with Cayce, Dr. Cottrell is not a medical doctor, and never touches the questioner during the session. *He is effectively asleep with his eyes closed.* His pulse, blood pressure and respiration are so low he could (and has!) fooled physicians into thinking he was comatose. He simply allows this 'higher mind' to seek the information needed, from the "universal hard drive," and passes it along.

Experts who have studied his work, over the many decades, have concluded that his ability to identify the root cause of a health condition is accurate to a degree that is in the ninety-nine-plus percentile; and, on more than one occasion, he has "beaten" M.R.I.s, C.A.T.-scans, and other modern equipment, both in terms of speed and accuracy (especially because his talent INCLUDES the ability to see a problem "at the cell level" — a skill which, in modern medicine, requires extremely advanced equipment, along with substantial time and expense if, indeed, it can be done at all).

For those kind readers who are still with me, and trying to grasp the un-graspable nature of the phenomenon I am trying to describe, the next logical question would be something like, "If all this is true, then why have I not seen Dr. Cottrell on a major T.V. show, or on the cover of a magazine?"

My response to that?

Thank heaven for small mercies.

I have worked with Dr. Cottrell for almost forty years. In that time, I have, on multiple occasions, seen medical doctors come to him for consultations, but always on the specific condition that the matter remains private. In that time, I have seen many reporters come to debunk him; but, when they realize they cannot do so simply and out of hand, they lose total interest in the story — never quite realizing that a story about someone who can actually perform these feats WOULD BE AN EVEN BIGGER, EVEN BETTER STORY, AND ATTRACT A WIDER AUDIENCE.

In fact, in the decades I have known Dr. Cottrell, I have come to view these many oversights as a *blessing* of sorts, since — *follow my logic carefully* — if Dr. Cottrell had ever become a household word, or found the attention he deserves, he would have been unable to keep up with the demand.

This, folks, is what flat-out killed Edgar Cayce. After a story in *The New York Times* labeled Cayce as genuine, the demand became so great that he had to schedule a third "meditation time" each day to try to catch up. And he paid the ultimate price.

Around the 1990s, there was great media interest in what was then called "Remote Viewing," especially after *Time Magazine* revealed the U.S. government had spent millions on this. Interestingly, the meditations done by Dr. Cottrell *include* this ability, and no fuss is made about it. I used to joke with Dr. Cottrell that he was lucky that no "black van" had ever shown up at his door, containing a bunch of large, athletic, men tasked with the sensitive job of relocating him to the countryside. Permanently.

So, from my point of view, the fact that Dr. Cottrell has been doing this for decades, yet is not especially well known ... that's a G-O-O-D THING.

Bottom line?

For as long as I can remember, I have been nagging Dr. Cottrell to do a book that is one-hundred-percent health-based; a book that both CONTINUES, and ADDS TO, the information that Cayce left behind; *a book for the benefit of everyone who has ever had even one single sick day.*

I have been so relentless in this over the years, so unflagging, in fact, it is a wonder that Dr. Cottrell has not responded with a restraining order!

But, for everything, there is a time, and for everything, there is a season.

After years of nagging, here, finally, is *the* book.

And it is a barn-burner.

Want to **test** this book? Flip to any page at random, read a few sentences, ***and then ask your intuition whether or not the information rings true...?***

Ultimately, that is the only test that matters...
Isn't it?

ROBERT APPEL, B.A., B.C.L., L.L.B.
TORONTO, CANADA, 2014

A NOTE ON THE TEXT BY DOUGLAS M COTTRELL

The information you are about to read was given by Douglas James Cottrell, Ph.D. in a series of intuitive Deep Trance Meditation (D.T.M.) readings.

As its name implies, D.T.M. is a very deep state of meditation somewhere between consciousness and sleep. In this altered state of consciousness, Douglas's respiration and heart rate are slowed, his blood pressure is lowered, and his brain activity changes. As his mind becomes detached from the physical, sensual world, Douglas is able to connect with a greater consciousness which would appear to have unlimited access to all knowledge and widsom.

During a D.T.M. reading, Douglas appears to be asleep, breathing very slowly and deeply, with eyes flickering rapidly behind their closed lids. He is like a computer awaiting instruction. A facilitator gives Douglas the suggestion to allow his mind to go to whom, to where, to what, and to when it is directed, and to give information through the manifestation of truth, intelligence and love. When Douglas indicates he is ready to give answers, the questions begin. He speaks quickly, giving information and using medical terminology with an authority beyond his conscious understanding of the human body.

This book is a compliation of verbatim D.T.M. readings from the 1980s to present. We have provided it in its original question and answer format. The reader will notice that answers are given in the first person plural ("we"). This Source which speaks through the sleeping Douglas is a collective which includes the High Mind of Douglas, the High Mind of the questioner, and any other mind with an interest in the communication. In some traditions, the term "Akashic Records" is used to describe the place from which this collective consciousness speaks. It is a dimension where exists all information, all knowledge, on everyone and everything, from all time.

The information in this volume has been edited for sense and length, but every attempt was made to remain true to the spirit of the original reading. Some of the archaic language (such as "thee" and "thine") has been preserved, while some has been replaced with more modern diction, for ease of reading. In the spirit of the D.T.M. and its timeless quality, we have reflected the older style language in the book's title, by choosing an archaic spelling of complete. We trust you will find *The 'Compleat' New Age Health Guide* to offer timeless information to help you improve your health and quality of life for years to come.

DOUGLAS M. COTTRELL, B.A., M.A.
HAMILTON, CANADA, 2014

[We used this same D.T.M. process to write Douglas's previous works, 'Secrets of Life,' and 'The New Renaissance.' Followers of the works of other seers such as Edgar Cayce, Ross Peterson or Paul Solomon will already be familiar with this concept. For those with an inclination to study the phenomenon of D.T.M. in greater detail, we refer to those sources.]

PART ONE
THE MIND-BODY CONNECTION

Is it correct, as many teachers have said, that physical conditions manifest in the mental before the physical?

Yes, you would find between the mental and emotional states a correlation: what is held in the mind is manifested in the body. The emotions are both the constructive and destructive forces in the body. Are they separate? Nay. They are similar, and they are yet distinct.

Here, an attitude along with an emotion is attached. These two - the attitude being the directive, the emotion being the constructive or destructive influence - cause either the body to be diseased or the body to be builded up. You would find in memory there is evidence of this linkage; as you would think of some pleasant memory in the past, the body would feel pleasant. There would be a recall of the event in the past, as well as a recall of the feeling and the emotional attachment of that event at the same time. Also, if you would look at a distressful point in time, the same memory would provoke the same attached emotion, and the body would feel ill at ease or diseased. This is evidence of what is taking place in the mind itself.

Therefore, when an unpleasant situation comes into the mind, there is an acceptance of this unpleasant idea, and then the mind dwells on the same. Remember, dwelling on something, focusing on something, or being extreme and staying focused on that thing causes - to that same degree - the emotions to amplify. Of course, if they are pleasant (such as being in love), the body is filled with creative influences. If it is adverse, then the body is filled with destructive influences.

Every cell within the body possesses its own consciousness; yea, its own soul. Yes, the cells in the body possess their own consciousness. If you would take but one cell, you would find within this cell the memory of the complete body. The body is the macrocosm, the cell is the microcosm; but together they are the body. They are worlds apart, yet they are of the same universe.

To understand this, understand thought: as a thought is committed, the cells in the body respond. If the thought is detrimental, some lose contact and begin to degenerate.

Research shows that the placebo affect, the sugar pill, can actually cause changes in brain wave activity. Would you please comment.

Of course, anything that a person believes will cause changes in the brain activity (which, of course, changes the outcome of the body's acceptance or rejection of what is offered); as the mind is the builder, and the mind is the way. There is not significant understanding of the function of the mind (and we do not mean the brain). The placebo, being given to an entity who believes it is medicine, sets up a certain receptive nature in the mind itself. The thought form behind the placebo that this is going to now trigger some

healing, or a certain effect on disease in the body, in part, gets the mind, the thought, the entire body and the involuntary aspects (or subconscious mind) functioned and focused towards some healing of some specific - call it here - origin, disease, or part of the body-mind that needs to be corrected.

The very idea - the very thought - is contained in the placebo; likewise in the medication given to the body also. It has a certain - call it here - purpose, a certain ideal, a certain expected reaction to being ingested into the body. One triggers the body chemically, the other (the placebo) triggers the body psychologically. That is why suggestion given to a suggestible mind is so profound. Here, you border on the body's own ability to focus on a problem and to put into play its natural healing forces, systems, techniques. For is it not the body, in the end, that cures itself?

Understand that medicine (chemicals taken into the body) only affect the chemical side of the body. They do not affect the other aspects that make up the healing reinforcement or restorative, rebuilding, rejuvenation, or growth cycles of the body, you see. They do tend to affect symptoms, rather than causes. But, again, the medicine taken into this body works with the body in a profound way, for the body is in need of sufficient medicine or chemical therapy. The body accepts this and works within, you might say. This is the "sledge-hammer effect" of working with the body. It gets the body's attention very quickly and, indeed, fills in the gaps that the body needs or requires for better health or improvement over disease.

The placebo is, likewise, as dramatic in certain instances, but they both function with the body; the placebo affect causing the body to believe it is going to be healed and, therefore, the healing process is triggered. Then the body simply carries out the belief, you see?

Do certain thoughts affect certain cells?

Indeed, as they would affect certain organs in the body itself. Those of criticism would affect the stomach and small intestine. Those of resentment, the large intestine. Those of anger, the heart. Those of timidness and stifling, the lungs. To the joints (specifically, the spine), rigidity of thought. Yes, those thoughts that affect the body affect the cells and organs, whether they are individual or groups. But understand this: no organ is an island unto itself.

Some intuitive people say they can "see" disease in someone before it manifests in the physical body. What is this process?

The aura might be considered an energetic field that is influenced by the generating forces in the body. There are chakra points or (you would call these) the spheres of the inner self, relating to the emotional states of the body. These chakra points, from reproduction urgings in the lower body to the ability of intuition or the soul mind at the higher, would seem to broadcast what is visible light. This visible light is a combination of actual vibration in the body; vibration, taken to the higher levels, is seen as different colors. The color would correspond to a different rate of vibration, if you will. Like sunlight divided into the seven rays of the rainbow, each color has a slightly different vibrational rate; and that is why it is seen or perceived by the human eye as different in color (but, in fact, it is simply a minute difference in vibration, you see).

The aura radiating from the body is the vitality of the physical body; the vibration, if you will, of each cell of the body giving off a certain hue of light. It is changeable, because the mind itself fluctuates (as do all things that are alive in nature, and move through nature) and the fluctuation causes the aura to change its hue or its color. Anger and reproduction urgings tend to promote a red or rouge color. Cerebral or intellectual thinking (or what would be creative thinking) tend to produce more of the golden and lime-green colors. These are presented as a desire to acquire information or association. Moving forward to the light blue colors and upward to the dark purple or indigo, these are colors when the mind is focused at understanding the law or attempting to find some truth, or seeking answers to some question.

Understand the colors can be quite pale or they can be quite intense; a mind might have light inquiry at first, and then severe concentration. It is like looking at a scene through the window, on one hand, then a magnifying glass, then a telescope. The mind can fluctuate between these three levels of activity and, as such, the human aura can fluctuate through the different colors; very quickly and also very slowly.

The aura demonstrates the very thought of the mind, you see. It is also a sensing mechanism. It is also a communicating mechanism as well.

Are people aware of one another's aura?

When two people stand close together, often it is said they "get a vibe" (or vibration) from one another. Some might say they get a "good feeling" or a "bad feeling" from someone. Others may say "I felt something from him" or "I felt something go out of me to her." They always use the term "sense" or "feel," for the aura is - let us say - an expanded sensory about the entire body; three hundred and sixty degrees around the body, and three hundred and sixty degrees vertically about the body. This area expands and contracts.

As such, being a communication device, one can become telepathically closer to another by actually feeling or sensing these thought patterns that are contained within the aura. Now this is to say, when one is at ease, or in a very peaceful mode, the aura is expanding. Likewise, when one is secretive, or fearful, or is engaged in some difficulty in life, the aura immediately contracts and is very close to the body. As it moves out and expands away from the body, it can be considered beneficial and normal. Withdrawn and kept close to the physical form, it would be considered abnormal and it is adverse to the physical body.

This wave or tidal effect fluctuates greatly, as the moods or the attitude change within the person itself. The aura can be influenced by air, or moving through the Earth's atmosphere, and also within the magnetic effects upon the body, for the aura is influenced magnetically as well (amongst other things).

Can you boost your own aura?

If the body is well, if the body is exercised properly, if the movement of the body is correct and all things are working, the aura expands. Celibacy (or abstaining from carnal influences) also affects the aura itself to expand. Looking away, or looking at clouds, or concentrating with the eyes causes the aura to deplete as well. Therefore, the intention is to attempt to make the aura move like a cocoon about the body; the eyes not giving energy away, the body at ease and peaceful, keeping its own energy close to itself, not wasting the influence. And, finally, attempting to keep the mode, mood, or thoughts pleasant and peaceful (loving, if you will). All other thoughts cause the body to be depleted and, as such, the physical effect is disease or tiredness; most usually, leading up to intense difficulties.

What affect does music have on health?

Again, it is the vibration rather than the tone that affects the centers. That which is of the sharp, high pitch (currently seen in jazz and what would be considered punk rock) is affecting the reproductive centers primarily, and stimulating or bringing forth the beast within the physical body. Look to the base drums and other implements that would bring about the lower vibratory rates. Those of the upper vibrations (the symphony, or the woodwinds, the flutes, the violin) deal with the soothing aspects of the brain and cause secretions of chemicals, or enzymes, or hormones that would calm and soothe and heal the body. Now those instruments or music-ranges between the drum and the flute would affect the mid-portion of the body, the thorax portion.

As there would be the scale - *Do, Re, Mi, Fa, So, La, Ti* - there would be, from the testicles or vagina upwards, effects through the body, taking into account the corresponding organ with the corresponding note. Striking a note can cause stimulus to that particular area of the body. Music, the sound itself, is not heard; it is the vibration of the music that is heard, and the body hears it all over itself, not just the ear drums. The feet, the hands, the chest, the earlobes, the nose, the top of the head all hear the music through vibration. As such, the emotional states that correspond with these organs are stimulated.

Do the colors we wear affect our health?

Usually the colors worn reflect the attitude of the entity itself. However, yes, the colors can be chosen in order to affect the attitude or feeling; and, if this is done, this affects the health indirectly.

For instance, if one is feeling extremely anxious or excited, we would recommend the colors of blue or green to be worn, for this would cause the entity to slow down, to become relaxed.

However, if an entity is normal in its attitude, feeling comfortable, and it begins to wear plenty of green and dark blue, it becomes depressed, for it relaxes the body too much.

For those who would wish stimulus, the wearing of the color yellow stimulates the mind and makes the mind more articulate. For those who would wear brown, it makes the body more comfortable, for it is an earthy color. Red challenges, fires up, motivates.

Yes, it affects the attitude; but more often than not, it is a reflection rather than a deliberate choice. But by choosing the colors, the color itself vibrates and the body's vibration could be matched (or, at least, affected) by the color worn.

Could you describe how best we can overcome our emotions?

Firstly, it would be to understand that the emotional state itself is not to be overcome. It is to be harnessed, it is to be used as a force that would be considered constructive.

How do emotions affect health?

Be it a constructive application or destructive application of the emotional forces (which are the constructive and destructive forces within the

body), there can be perfect health reigning within a body, or there can be ruin reigning within a body. The choice is the individual's. What would you think of? Would you think that which would be harmony and content, or that which would be disharmony and discontent?

Try the following experiment. Think of the self in the most exalted high, in what you would call the most perfect ability of self. And repeat it three times in your mind with a degree of sincerity. Notice how the body feels. Does it not feel elated? Does it not feel comfortable, relaxed? Do you not feel good with yourself? Indeed.

Now, reverse this, and attempt to think of that quality, that criticism that is most painful to self, and repeat it also three times. Notice the body sags. Notice the hollow feeling within self. Notice the weakness within the body.

With this understood, the question would be more perfectly asked, "How can better health reign in the body through proper attitudes, and, as such, emotional expression of that attitude?" Repeat again the quality that would be most liked, most relevant in self. What would you like most about the self? Repeat it now, at this point, and feel the difference, again, in which the body would soar like an eagle; as such, restoring the energies to a constructive force within the body.

Are emotions the greatest inhibitor, in regards to spiritual growth and perfect health?

The emotions are the inhibitor or the propeller. It is through the mind, in choosing these emotional states, that selects the destiny or direction, retention or advancement of any and all. It is a simple matter of choice. But understand: the only constructive emotion is love.

Would you comment on fear?

Fear itself does not exist. We would ask: give us a handful of fear, show us fear. Fear, in the physical sense, cannot be done. It can be done by the demonstration of the activity or actions of an entity, a beast, or a plant. It cannot be, in itself, encapsulated.

To understand fear, it is the mind expecting a destructive fact. It is what would seem to be the individual becoming self-reliant to the point of reliance upon self's own capabilities, and then being taken out of this comfort zone. This position becomes fear. The comfort zone is in what would be considered control of the action, or event that is taking place. Yet, if one would understand: with the proper attitude, in harmony, no harm can come to anyone.

Overcoming fear is, in a sense, becoming more faithful, more vulnerable, yet assured that no harm can return to self. For as the attitude of constructive activity is cast forward, and the expectation that there will not be difficulty, the result that is desired (the absence of fear) will be produced.

Fear itself is a state of confusion in which one would be out of control over an event or an action, expecting a destructive or negative aspect to take place; usually to themselves and those they would hold near and dear.

Would you comment on anger?

Anger is an expression of the emotions in a narrow vein, in which there would be the explosion, in which the energy built up within self would not be contained and would be used in what you would call destructive energy or release.

Now, there is justifiable anger, make no mistake. Anger is an emotion that can be used justifiably to release the accumulation or build-up of energies within oneself. Should it not be released, it would work adversely against the body. Here, anger unexpressed first begins to disrupt the circulatory system, affecting the veins and arteries within the body, eventually affecting the heart and coronary, affecting disruption (or attack, as you would know it).

Fear, on the other hand (being of the same vein of physical disharmony) would affect the pancreas, you see, and the nervous system. These would be the physical expressions of the emotions that would be considered negative, in the physical sense.

The expression of anger, in the positive sense, brings to a head the difficulty, the emotion, and the event, thereby restoring harmony to the disruptive event or action; constructively, done without condemnation of another (without sin, you see), it allows the body to be healed from the hurt.

Would you please comment on jealousy?

Jealousy is simply one of the emotions that would be brought forth in relationship to selfishness (the original sin). Here, it is a possessive state. It is the emotion of supremacy and possession. It is also amalgamated with fear, you see; the fear of loss. It is an emotion that is produced in which there would be negative connotation. You would find there would be disruptions to the entirety of the physical form. Amputation of the gall, the appendix and cysts or growths would be the outcome in the physical body of this emotion. The constructive emotion would not be jealousy, but it would be confidence and pride.

Would you please comment on hate?

Hate is sin, for it is condemnation of another. You would take the strongest emotion and apply it with a destructive manner to another. Woe be to that one who would hold hate or grudge in the heart towards another. For there, in themselves, they would feel the full repercussion in which there would be disruptions, primarily with the head, the sinuses, the throat, the voice and the reproductive centers. For hate itself is condemning and it should be avoided, for hate in itself cannot be demonstrated either. It is a produced state of action, willfully done. It is not triggered, but it is the creation of intensity in what you would call disruption of thought towards another, towards a thing, towards a beast.

Would you please comment on greed?

When an individual would accumulate to themselves all things more than they would need. Whatever they would see, they would covet, and they would gather toward it. They would retain for their own welfare. Greed is taking away from others, also from themselves. For greed is a falsehood, you see; for, in the end, all that they would possess, all that they have accumulated will be set aside. Even the physical body will be set aside also. They will have exactly what they started out with: themselves.

Greed is attempting to hoard, be it any thing or any wealth. True wealth lies in knowledge. And knowledge with experience combined produces wisdom. A Man is a truly wealthy Man when he can walk with his possessions in a bag over his shoulder. Greed is hoarding for selfish purposes and the application of selfishness.

What is the meaning of happiness?

The meaning of happiness is simply: it is an end result of that which has been done or carried out by one.

Could you please talk about unconditional love?

It is complex, and it is simple. Understand it is simply this: under any and all experiences, seek the best in another, know the outcome will be favorable, and know that there is good within the experience or the entity you would meet.

In learning to practice unconditional love, it can be summed up as learning to love those who would be your enemies, who spit in your face, who defile your form. If you can truly learn to love these who would commit the most heinous crimes, knowing within them there is that spark of good, there is that spark of life, that hope of humanity, then you will truly learn to love. You would not utter a condemning word, a judgment, a criticism. You would only utter praise.

You do not have to associate with one in this position, but then again, you do not have to condemn them either. This is where the indifference, lovingly, is practiced. Love is simply seeing the best in all that you would meet; caring for another as you would care for yourself.

PART TWO
A HEALTHY SPINE, A HEALTHY BODY

What is the value of keeping the spine flexible?

You would find that keeping the spinal column flexible is immensely beneficial to any physical body. You will find it will have a degree of benefit that will incur longevity in the physical body; for through the spine travel the nerve impulses. These come from the brain itself and are (what you might call) electro-magnetic impulses. As such, they travel through this pathway, this highway of the nervous system to their various junctions or branch points. Then, they exit from the spine to those areas, tissues, or organs that are designated as their territorial or regional abode. You find here, that the spine itself becomes the pathway for all information going in two directions; from the brain to the organ, for instance, or from the organ through the body (the spine) to the brain itself.

As such, the beneficial aspects of a flexible and supple spine are that the pathway is not impeded. There is the continuation of the impulse from the brain to the physical area in the body. This is the highway or pathway of the body, the communication center of the body. As such, reflexes, as well as direct commands come from the spine and that which is within - the spinal column or what you would call the cord within the spine itself.

Now, should the spine be condensed, compressed, injured or made rigid, then immediately this pathway is directly affected (adversely, of course). As such, the nerve impulses are somewhat hindered in their function or proper mechanical order. As such, the communication between the area or region of the body (or organ) and the brain become somewhat distant. Thus, although it is not completely shut off, there is an impairment that occurs within the area of the body that is impaired within the spine itself.

You can compare it to a garden hose which has water travelling through it; water comes from the tap and is directed by the nozzle. When there is a bend in the hose or a squeezed and compressed area, what comes from the nozzle of the hose is somewhat less than what the pressure was at the tap, such as a trickle that would occur at the end of a nozzle. Likewise occurs the message from the brain to the body.

Here, there are two communicating systems in the body. The central nervous system compares to the conscious and voluntary aspects of the body (although it does enter into the subconscious mind in what you might call the involuntary aspects of the function of the organs and tissues in the body). However as the communicational aspects through the nerves are impaired or reduced to a trickle, so is that which is all-important to the conditioning, timing and function sequence (and other normalities of an organ or tissue) retarded or otherwise affected in a negative sense.

Combined with the circulation of the body, which is the second form of communication in the body, the organ can survive well and can function for many years. Yet, as the organ would function for this time, there would be a slow degeneration and ultimately here, the organ would cease to function sufficiently, and that which is usually operated upon is the organ itself, rather than the spine.

If the spine would be manipulated, massaged or made correct in its alignment, then the tunnel which is created within the spine (that which is the cavity for the spinal cord) would be more in line with the other vertebrae within the spine, and the communication would readily increase. Although it would take some time for the spine to align and hold this, we find the increase in communication would be greatly enhancing the function of the organ that it ultimately reaches (or any other region or part of the body).

In short, remove the restriction in the spine and you feed the area of the body that is needed or - as you would call it - that is in communication with the brain itself. The benefits are immense here, as can be understood. This allows for regeneration of cells, proper function in the area or part of the body; and also, with good communication, there is the ability for longevity for the body to remain.

For, you see, as the body ages, there is the imperfect replacement of cells in the tissue, or organ, or the region. This imperfect replacement is called the aging process. As the entity progresses in the constantly continued replacement of the old cell by the imperfect cell, the body speeds up in its aging process. Look to those areas of the body that are not massaged, stimulated, or utilized, and you would find sluggish activity. As such, the imperfect replacement of these cells would be quicker. An organ can break down due to what would be called old age, even if the body is not of an old age. Keeping the spine healthy and flexible prevents this.

Having a flexible spine ensures the communication is perfect throughout the body and that the brain (which is, to some degree, the switching process or mechanism) does continue to function and keep in touch with, and otherwise communicate with all aspects of the body. The body then retains a healthy and youthful atmosphere, condition and existence. The exercises that would bend and stretch the spine would be most appropriate in keeping the body youthful.

What happens during adjustment of the spine?

As those who would force the spine into alignment - the osteopath, the chiropractor or others who would use the same manner of physical effort - you would find that there is a degree of stimulation at the nerve center in the area of the body as well as the brain itself. As there would be the alignment of the spine, there is the manipulation of the entire endocrine system. As such, this affects the organs in the body. One organ is not an island unto itself, as any are not organs unto themselves. Whether it is believed or not, whether it is understood or not, any who manipulate the spine manipulate the endocrine system itself.

As such, there is an alignment, compensation and otherwise balance within the major organs of the body. As well, it releases muscle tension or stress, should the vertebrae be in relation to a muscle region in the body. Aches and pains are alleviated, for the balance of the body is returned to more perfect.

When there is more perfect alignment in the spine, there is a spread or (as you would call it) a balance of body weight, evenly upon the skeletal system or what you might call the framework of the body that allows, here, proper weight distribution and function to all sections or areas of the body. It is somewhat like building blocks, one upon the other, and in the midst, moving one slightly to the left or the right. The upper part is somewhat wavering and tightens, as in a muscle structure, to compensate for the shaky imbalance point that has been reaped in the mid-portion of the stack. The lower compensates also to balance the upper portion (as the shoulders against the pelvis, you might see it). Thus, a scoliosis can develop, creating further difficulty.

Pain and disease can occur in the body with the slightest point in the spine being out. These types of ailments, however, are more located in the base of the spine than the midpoint, but for an example, it is easily understood.

As one would adjust that particular point, or manipulate, or stretch it back into alignment, a solidifying effect occurs and, as such, a benefit of balance is given to the entire body. Muscles then release and compensate back to a normal position. Most importantly, from that point that you might call a kink in the back and there on down becomes more in touch with the switching centers in the brain itself. This allows perfect function of the organs, regions, and tissues in the body to, again, occur.

At the manipulation time, there is a surge of energy that comes from the upper region of the body, down through the lower portion of the spine and into the organs themselves, stimulating or giving them what you might call a "shot in the arm" of energy; and, as such, a compensating balance occurs so that there is not an over- or underactivity of the organ or region. This is done rather quickly.

As we have given, at the time of adjustment there is a balancing, not only to the muscle and skeletal sections, but also to the glands, functions, and secretions and other systems improved in their function.

During an adjustment of the spine, what happens to the nervous system?

Understand that as the position might be called imperfect, the nervous system itself would be somewhat stretched or strained; in particular, that point of injury or kink in the spine. As there is the adjustment backwards to the more perfect position, there is elasticity within the spinal column that allows the normalcy or (what you might call) the retention and, as such, positioning of the spinal cord to be more perfect; and, as such, it is resilient to that degree.

However, immediately, there are fluctuations of information or impulses from the brain to that kink point and beyond, as we have just given. What occurs is a degree of energy transferred and the electromagnetic field of the entire body becomes more balanced also. All points - even those that would be considered reflex points in the body - are stimulated by the adjustment. For, you see, several times a second there is communication flowing forward and back to the area and brain regions.

As such, when there is a manipulation, the nerve system is greatly shocked at first. Then, as it begins to balance, it reiterates the communication and, as such, relief is brought about, primarily in the conscious levels of the mind, and also in the voluntary and involuntary sections of the body itself.

To what extent are the glands affected by an improper alignment in the spine?

They are greatly affected, as you would understand it in the analogy of the garden hose. There is somewhat of the understanding that the nerves themselves are but receivers of sensations and, as such, transmit what they receive to that area in the brain that is corresponding. There is not the understanding that there is a nerve flow. It occurs forward from the brain to that point in the body emanating at the nerve ending or terminal and, as such, a return of information backward to the brain itself. Now, this can be in conjunction with the wall, or abdomen of the body, and also, here, to the kidney and stomach. For, you will find here, that as a trunk line from the main spinal cord emanates outward to one side of the body or the other, it begins to branch off. As such, several areas of the body (although the same region of the body) are along the same nerve center, and thus are greatly affected when there is an injury to the spine itself.

Now, if one would take the lower region of the back, including the pelvic girdle region, one can find several systems and organs in the trunk line, as we have given. If such an injury occurs to the spine, then there is not the control over the bladder and kidney and what can be considered the pelvic region, extending here even to the reproductive organs. All begin to shut down. Within the body, as one system is affected, it tends to spread throughout the entirety of the system. If one kidney is affected, then you would find there is difficulty in the entirety of the urinary tract (call it infection beginning in one and spreading throughout). As such, multiply this, by understanding that as one system is affected, it readily affects another system. The urinary tract affects the reproduction tract. The reproduction tract affects new cell production in the body, in accordance with old cell removal through the spleen.

As such, you find here several systems are already (as you might call them) affected "en masse" by one particular system being out of whack. Thus, the communication through and into these particular systems (and what might be considered intercommunication between systems) is drastically affected. It continues to get worse. No organ is an island unto itself in the body. Likewise, no system is an island unto itself. Both must strike a balance. This can be readily seen as a sore knee and a corresponding difficulty would be a sore elbow, diagonally across the body; right sore knee and left elbow soreness or strain. Why? Because they are corresponding reflexes within the body and, as such, diagonally attempt to balance the injury in the body itself. Teeth can be compared here. One tooth is gone on the right side, there will be a corresponding difficulty on the left side, possibly in the lower, if the original would be in the upper. The body is not a haphazard organism. It is a highly complicated, sophisticated and critically balanced mechanism.

However, to understand the flow between the two is to understand much about the body's line of communication. As this would be understood, there would not be asked the question of why difficulty occurs in the body; why there is the question of nerve flow as opposed to nerve sensing. This is basic kinesiology and any who would study the body would find its reflex points, would find that the systems are intricate with one another. As such, when there is one problem in the spine itself, it affects virtually all other systems in the spine itself. That is why it is necessary to be wise to have a spine that is supple and in line.

How helpful are spinal adjustments in assisting the body to heal itself?

Most helpful. It is like clearing a traffic jam from a highway; as there would be the removal of the obstruction, then the body can naturally be in communication with the injured region or affected system. As such, the body can then bring about a degree of balance. All in order, all in good health with a little patience, with a little persistence, that which can be taken into the body (good foods) and also that which would be emanating from the body (good thoughts). If good thoughts are held in the mind, and good food or nutrient is taken into the body, and the nerves are in communication with the areas in the body and the brain, then the body can heal itself most perfectly, most dramatically.

Yes, it is most important for manipulation or alignment here, for this allows the body to clear away the obstruction and thereby give itself a clear understanding of the situation at the injury point (or when there is disease in the body) and to utilize the many protection systems, agents and otherwise healing processes that it has at its disposal; and, as such, to activate them. In most cases this is why there is disease in the body; when there is a shutting off or lack of communication of a certain area or region in the body, where there is not the ability of the body to compensate and, as such, bring the healing forces to bear. This is seen with the mind as well as the body itself.

Would spine adjustments be helpful to older people as well as children (or infants)?

Yes they could be considered beneficial to all; for even as there is the protrusion of the cranium from the womb itself, you would find here that, with some, there is a difficult birth or a little tugging is necessary. As such, separation can easily occur, cranial slippage upon the atlas and axis bones can occur. Rotation or misalignment of the cranium to the neck (or head to the neck, as you would know it) can occur. Even that one who is but a few moments old, to a few weeks, or a few months can have the realignment of the upper spine or neck (and in almost every case find it necessary). As this would align the neck, then the body would begin to continue its further development and to understand the various functions and systems within itself.

As the mind (or, as you know it, the brain) would become more familiar with these mechanical switching processes, it, too, can develop farther. Assimilation of food, for instance, is one of the most difficult for the body to handle at the time of birth and thereafter. For as it begins to ingest food within itself, there is not the highly-developed and sophisticated set of mechanisms for, first of all, enzyme secretion, breakdown, or digestion of foods; and, as such, the assimilating process itself, and then the eliminating process thereafter. As one would have obstruction in the neck, how could the organs themselves function perfectly and continue to develop as they normally do, through a manner which you might call obstruction in the nerve passageways?

As manipulation occurs in the youngster, yes indeed, this system is helped and, as such, development can be considered more normal. If a child does have problems in these areas, check in the upper portion of the neck or the base of the skull, and you would find here the localized misalignment in the usual situation. In the other, where you would find difficulty with stomach and elimination, check the base of the spine, the lumbar region, and you would find the pelvis could be tilted or rotated here. As this would be brought into alignment, simply and easily, then elimination would be more perfect, as might assimilation of foodstuffs.

To the very old, we would suggest as the manipulation would be taken upon the body that it be accompanied primarily with a degree of massage and heat. The muscles have aged, you see, bones have worn, and, as such, the spine has formed its comfortable resting place; what you might call its familiar stance or position. The massage would allow the muscles to release and allow some give to the spine. As such, the peanut oil, camphorated oil or castor oil that would penetrate would allow the bones to slip more easily. Now, when one has degrees of deposit between and on the vertebrae, it is most difficult to cause movement within the same. However, as the body would apply the oils to itself on the spine, and as there would be manipulation slowly and easily, you would find the muscles would release their pull or hold and allow the spine to function more perfectly by having, first of all, the proper alignment.

It is best to proceed cautiously with the aged. For as alignment of the spine would occur, so would the nerve impulses, and you might have over-stimulation of certain organs, systems, or tissues in the body. Immediately, with this over-stimulation there would be degrees of illness brought upon the physical body. For instance, the stimulation of the kidney might unlock a degree of discomfort, or dis-ease, or infection that has been secured and held within the body until that point of stimulation. Then, it proceeds to expose itself within the body, so that it might be eliminated from the body.

As such, any who would approach the aged, or those who are ailing and somewhat older should do so cautiously so that there is not the initiation of several symptoms and several disrup-

tions within the body's normal function. They should also proceed, here, with massage of the spine and stimulating, paralleling the spine, the chest and facial regions (or what you might call the lymphatic system). This helps to prepare the body to eliminate more readily the toxins and the sluggish function of the lymph; the poison mucous systems within. In short, it begins to prepare the body for the removal of discomfort or dis-ease that would come about with the manipulation of the spine.

How often should children be examined and adjusted in these younger years?

We would recommend periodic adjustments arbitrarily by any in authority, as the parent might be. Once every three months would be a good time for a check-up. However, as a child is more active, and as a child may be more physically abusive with himself, then it is beneficial after any injury or discomfort to the spine that the child be immediately taken to the osteopath or chiropractor. For unusual injuries, falls, or other injuries to the spine, it is beneficial to have it compensated immediately and thereby allow the spine to function more perfectly.

As an overall rule, once every three months for a normal child, more regularly for a physically active child. However, no more than once or twice a year would be considered acceptable also. It depends upon the activity of the child. The more physically active, then the more cautious the parent should be with the spine. This can be done simply by having the child disrobe, stand at ease, and face away from the parent. The parent can check the alignment of the shoulders to the pelvis. As such, look from the side and see, again, if the shoulder is rotated a little or the pelvis rotated a little. Then, as the child would progress in age, this would be easier to see as the child would establish good posture. For then, the parent could see if one shoulder was lower than the other, or one side of the pelvis was higher than the other.

Another form of checking the child at home would be to have the child lay on its stomach on the floor. Then have the child bend its knees and bring the feet to a vertical position and examine the height or the equality of the length of the legs. This again, would point out whether there is injury or alignment difficulty in the spine. One leg may be considerably shorter than the other. As such, this would allow time for the professional to have the examination.

Please give other methods that would be helpful to keep the spine aligned and flexible.

Any who would engage in those exercises that would bend and stretch the spine would find themselves quite easily healthy. Those exercises that are Eastern in nature, such as yoga, are beneficial. Any who engage in this form of exercise first challenge the mind. As the mind is brought around, in control, the body naturally follows. But, do not overdo the exercise. Yoga should be properly done; the mind and the body cooperating as one brings the body to that point of stress, or taxing, or limit. To go beyond this only serves to disrupt the body. If the body is taken to that point every time there is a bend or a stretch, and then it is released and compensated with a bend or a stretch in an equal and opposite direction, then you would find the body would cooperate in its loosening and flexibility; its healing.

There is no need to be extravagant or bend the self into a pretzel; but use those exercises that would bend and stretch the spine in an easy manner. This would be most beneficial for the average individual. Utilizing the steam bath, or sauna, or heat lamp is also helpful prior to the exercises. Swimming and running are beneficial, for they affect the cardiovascular system as well as the spine. Jogging tends to disrupt. Any form of sudden and choppy movement tends to disrupt.

Stretch the spine. Stretch the legs, the neck, the arms. Stretching in equal and easy manner, only for a few seconds, then releasing the body and repeating it in an equal and opposite direction would be considered by far the best exercises that can be done. Observe the animals in nature: the dog, or the cat. Upon rising, they stretch, first one way, then the other. Likewise should the physical body be stretched.

Are concerns about the safety of spinal adjustments valid?

Indeed, to some degree, they are valid. For, you would find incompetence exists in all theaters or forms of medical or health practices. You will find, however, that, on occasion, they are over-done. Any cannot rise above any other and say they are the best, their form is safest, and all others are at fault. You would not find any heart specialist who says that they have cured through health, heart disease. You would not find any who would make such a claim. You would not find any kidney men standing and saying they have cured kidney disease. Not a one (we are speaking of total cures and wiping it out, obliviating the disease from Mankind.)

Therefore, we find that any who stand above another and say that their discipline in the health field is better than another - whether they be the massage person, the chiropractor, the radiologist or the chemist - none holds the key to perfect health. Indeed, in manipulation of the spine, it is necessary to seek out a competent individual: one who has the ability with the hands to manipulate the spine and to avoid any difficulty (that is to say, critical difficulty, such as paralyzing or injury to the spine).

One who is competent can take the body and place it back in more perfect alignment of the spine and, as such, bring a degree of health that is far faster and more direct than those who would attempt to treat the body with stimulants, chemical procedures, or otherwise artificial means of attacking the same problem in the body. For one discipline affects the symptom, the other affects the mechanical organism or situation in the body. Sometimes, it is necessary to incorporate several disciplines in order to remedy or bring health to a physical body; massage, chiropractic, and supplement from chemicals (or what might be considered the concentrated form that Mankind uses so often). As such, this brings about health.

However, overexposure to X-rays can be done by the osteopath, the chiropractor, the M.D., or the radiologist. Care must be taken not to overexpose the body. This concern can be shared by all who incorporate this type of machinery and all who undergo such exposure. Thereby, it is up to the patient, again, to take the responsibility to prevent overexposure. Become familiar with the thing, you see. Utilize the shields when it is necessary.

However, we find the risk in any theatre or any discipline of medicine or healing art is the same. On occasion, we find this can be considered most difficult, but, we also find, on occasion, that it is the only therapy that does remedy a situation in a body. Alignment of the neck so that it can support the head can only be done with the vertebrae in the neck being aligned. It cannot be done with chemicals (or drugs, as you would know it). It can be artificially accomplished with the support of a brace. But, again, the head is not being supported by the neck or bones, as it should have. It is temporarily being supported by an outside implement. There is only one alignment and therapy for this alignment, and if it happened to be osteopathic or chiropractic, it amounts to the same thing: the physical manipulation of the vertebrae in line with the other vertebrae in order that the head might be supported upon the neck in a natural fashion.

A podiatrist cannot claim that they would have the remedy for neck problems and we find it, on occasion, ridiculous for others who would have skills in other disciplines of medicine or therapy to claim that theirs can remedy the entire body, and theirs is the only form of acceptance for health in the body. Nay, we find the body is made up of several components, several systems and features. As such, diet, exercise and mental attitude, all being correct bring perfect health to the body. The surgeon's knife is necessary and should be utilized when it is necessary. None should attempt to avoid surgery by the manipulation of the bone or the massage of the muscle when it is not warranted. All are important.

When you find the medical arts becoming scientific, you will find that the medical sciences will be incorporating all forms of therapies. It will include from massage and diet, to the chiropractor, the surgeon, and the psychiatrist. All will be utilized to incorporate a good mind, a good body and, as such, a healthy mind and body.

Is there such a thing as too many adjustments?

Anything that is done in excess can be considered derogatory to the body; therefore, yes, too many adjustments can be considered difficult and even harmful to the body. As such, when one finds the condition persists, then one must look past the physical and evaluate the emotional and mental states of an individual. Example: if an entity keeps returning with stress symptoms such as hard muscles in the shoulders and back, and extending to difficulties in the second, third and fourth dorsal region of the spine, between the shoulder blades, and every week the entity returns for adjustment (or every other day in severe cases) and there is not improvement, then one must look for other forms of additional therapy to be brought about to bring relief. Massage would be first chosen, for it would tend to relax the muscles, increase the blood, and allow the spine to be more easily manipulated and brought in line. If this does not work, then we should look to the emotional and mental states and find out what is causing the stress in the entity's life. Remedy this and then the body itself would adapt or remedy itself through the manipulation of the spine and massage.

However, as one would continue to affect, massage and adjust the spine, and there would not be benefit, then there would only be continued force used upon the spine and possible injury. Too much, here, would be considered repetitive adjustment without any result. As long as there is result (even a little) then there can be considered the safe adjustment and, as such, the continuation of this should persist. If an entity seeks every day an adjustment, of course, again, there is some difficulty that should be looked at in the emotional and mental states. For understand, the mind is the builder. The mind is the way. Seek the attitude of the entity. As such, you will find the key that will unlock the hidden difficulty or disruption in the body itself.

Was Hippocrates considered a manipulator of the spine or a medical doctor?

He utilized all forms or practices (as you would know it) of therapy. There was massage of the feet, there was massage of the sinus regions, there was massage of the eyes and the utilization of colored glass and the peering through the glass towards the sun in order that there would be a selection of rays (or what you might call colors) that would emanate into the eyes and cause some improvement in the physical body. The entity was aware of vibrations or frequencies upon the physical body as having some effect. He was also engaged in homeopathy, naturopathy, massage, chiropractic, osteopathic and was highly skilled in the diet and different herbs. He can be considered the father of medicine for, here, there were various concentrations of herbs recommended for ailments in the physical body that worked well. He would be considered the father of health; for what you might call modern-day medicine, if they would combine all their skills and treat the body with the mind and not try to separate the two. For this entity did interview the patient before there was the treatment. On occasion, he even asked the entity to bring forth its dream, so that, through the dream, there might be interpretation of the perplexing problem in the physical body.

Yes, the entity used all disciplines here, and taught the same. We do find polarization or specialization has led to what would be considered derogatory health care (as you would know it in the present form); not to say that it is not good, or to say that it is not bad. It is simply to say there has been separation. Although there would be understanding of the physical body (even in the finite mind, in the dissection of the same), there is not the understanding of the importance of the attitude. For, those things that are held in the mind affect the physical body. What is held in the mind does manifest in the physical body. This one, the father of modern medicine, understood this. It is why the different disciplines were utilized in bringing about healing.

Please give any further information that would be helpful and beneficial on this topic.

The best that any can engage in is a degree of exercise, combined with proper diet. As these two are combined, it is attempting to seek through the mind that which is building and healthful for the body. For you see, the mind is the builder, the mind is the way. The body is the receptacle. If there is stiffness in the mind, there will be stiffness in the body. As there is a desire for health in the mind, then health will become the order of the day. A flexible mind breeds a flexible spine. Utilize those exercises easily that would affect the suppleness of the spine. Seek out the professional help when it is needed. Engage in the massage from time to time. Steam baths would also be helpful here, in allowing the spine to function more perfectly. It would allow the body to detoxify itself through the skin. As such, that which is seen as the manipulation and flexibility ingrained in the spine itself can add years to the life and make the latter years more enjoyable. The aches and pains will not come upon the body as quickly (or may even be avoided) if there is a persistent and consistent working towards a flexible spine.

PART THREE
ASSIMILATION AND ELIMINATION

It is said that the artificiality of the Twentieth Century environment is a major contributing factor to disease. Would you agree or disagree?

Yes, for it allows the body to become weak and over-toxify itself. Rather than the body, which has been programmed by the Creator to handle poisons and toxins and eliminate them from the system, the artificiality (as you call it) is causing the retainment of these foreign particles within the body. As such, the body, which is incapable of handling these foreign particles, overloads itself, over-toxifies itself and, as an automobile or vehicle that would transport cargo would be overloaded and ultimately break down, so does the body.

There are warning signs, but few listen to these, the indicators upon the physical condition. Pain is an indicator. It is a healthy feeling; for when there is pain, it is an indicator that something is attacking a healthy organ or point in the body. Most disregard this, take the capsule or the pill, deaden the nerve endings in the brain, and ignore the symptom that something is wrong in the liver, or the stomach, or the heart. They effectively shut off their warning system. As such, they continue with their practice, be it poor diet or poor thought, and the organ that is being affected continues to be affected until such time that it is so overloaded it breaks down completely.

The body must be kept cleansed. This is by the urinary system, the elimination of physical congress, the circulating system of the blood, the lymphatic system (which removes the toxins through the body), and the skin. Here, washing or bathing the body is seen as being helpful. Does it not make sense to wash the body on the inside as well as the outside? Each and every entity could use the enema therapy (colonic therapy, as it would be known). No one -- repeat, no one -- could not be helped by this. Everyone could be. See?

However, that which is taken in -- the grease, the oil, the high bread content, and that which is termed "fat" tend to overload the system; calcium overload, cholesterol overload, some phosphorous overload.

Eat a good salad each and every day with plenty of olive oil and this would allow a degree of cleansing on the inside of the body; and, as such, the body could then be healed within its own self. For, like the mechanic, it can do what it needs, but it must be given a helping hand. The carbonated drink is most destructive here, to the body. Should one take a little, the body can tolerate; but should one become an addict, and hold the soda pop in the hand continuously drinking, drinking, drinking, ultimately the diaphragm, the valves within the stomach, and even some toxins in the liver break down the ingestion system. The body cannot handle it, you see. As an example, it is better to drink water pure than water that would be filled with gas carbonated.

What is the value of colonic hydrotherapy?

First of all, the colonic is that which is imposed as intestinal hydrotherapy or a cleansing of the large intestine (the colon itself). In that which is understood: as the body would require bathing on the exterior from time to time, would it not be logical to bathe the body internally? For the female of the species here, douching is most important and, indeed, most helpful in removing toxins from the area of the feminine parts (the reproductive center, you see). Likewise for what would be more to the cleansing of the toxins or (as you would call it) accumulation in the colon itself. Would it not be best to cleanse this, from time to time, in any way, any manner that would be considered beneficial? For, you see, it is only logical to cleanse the intestine to remove the residue, the fecal matter that has adhered to the pockets in the colon itself; that which would lie within the colon for long periods of time.

As such, in what would be termed a colonic, it is necessary to cleanse the colon by flooding the colon, the large intestine, with different fluid mixtures. These fluid mixtures would be most helpful in removing simply the residue from the colon wall and, as such, preventing the reabsorption of that which would be considered vile to the body: the toxins. As such, this would remove it from the body, you see.

Simply, a colonic is an intestinal hydrotherapy procedure. It is, in fact a simple cleansing of the intestine, which is the body's natural organ for holding and then expelling from the body those excrements that would be toxic and harmful if they remained in the body.

A colonic is a procedure that is utilized by several. In the ancient times here - yea, as far back as the Egyptian - you would find this procedure was accompanied here with the manipulation and the massage of the bone and the muscle in the body. Some would call it osteopathic or chiropractic or massage therapy. This was in conjunction with anointing the body with several oils that would be found beneficial to the maintenance of the cells themselves. However, the integral part, the cleansing of the body internally was considered a most important rite or ritual.

From the Egyptian, we find this was carried through even to the present. You will find reference to this in the ancient Chinese, as those who would induce the herb or other mechanical means to remove matter (physical congress) from the colon itself.

You will find it brought forth from the early Christian also here; those who would engage in the cleansing of the mind and the cleansing of the body. There was a degree of fasting which would be helpful in removing the intake, and thereby, in a time lapse, allow the body to cleanse itself of all food particles; or, at least, the attempt to remove most of them that would be taken in, digested, assimilated and carried forth to the colon, and, as such, eliminated. Fasting was considered most important for spiritual (if not intellectual) reasons, to allow the mind to be clear thinking, for there was a greater awareness that the body itself does work very, very, very, very hard when food is ingested. If you would only know how hard the body works, there would not be many who would gorge themselves before there would be the sleep state induced. For, you see, the body works during this state, and sleep is not as restful.

However, as fasting would be induced in the early Christian state, also there was engaging in the cleansing of the other end of the tract, as the enema, the colonic. It is a simple procedure;

it is a simple result to remove the residue, aiding the body in a mechanical manner or fashion to remove the toxins and the matter (physical congress) in this area.

Now understand this was also given with a degree of herbs and there was musk, or (as you would call it) grape juice taken with the meals. This musk, or grape juice - no sugar added, pure - is that which is beneficial, for first it affects the pancreas and, in turn, the thyroid, and what would be the bile to be secreted here, allowing for more perfect easement in elimination. Of course, this was done on a daily basis, either in what would be the red wine or what would be the grape juice. You would find ingestion and, as such, elimination in most would be improved speedily and readily.

However, more to the question itself: as there would be the cleansing of the colon itself, then the vibratory rate of the body would increase in (what would be considered) more of a helpful and healthful rate. As the body would be cleansed, then you would find it would take on a degree of brightness or illumination; energy, some might call it, vitality others may call it. You would find that healing procedures in the body would be greatly enhanced.

Again, the colonic, in co-operation with other treatments, or (as you would call it) remedies or procedures, you would find the body itself would be cleansed from both ends, from the stomach on down through the intestinal tract, and from the anal upward here into the large intestine itself. This would take approximately three days, as we see it. As it would be done once each day, allowing the body to cleanse the lower colon, mid colon and upper colon, then, as the food in its natural progression through the body would march through the colon, it would be easily removed from the same.

Now many would say that their eliminations are normal, meaning that they "go" once a day. Let us clarify this. Normal would mean once after every meal. As such, three to four times a day would be considered normal, for this would allow the body to remove, in a speedily fashion, that which is sluggish, that which is vile and disruptive. For you see, the longer there is this waste product in the body, the greater the chance for reassimilation. For the organ of the colon has no consciousness of what is right and wrong. It simply absorbs into itself that which is in it. For you would find, here, one-sixth of all blood supply would be either around the colon, at that point in time, and in the intestinal tract also, you see. There is great transition both ways, or in both directions (as you may call it); nutrients going into the body, excrement or waste out of the body, and this assimilation and elimination are closely related here.

Now in regard to polyp or other swelling in the pockets or difficulty in the movement of the colon, or what you might call a stretch or twist in the colon, or what you might see as difficulty through the membrane in the diaphragm and (you would call it) the sheath that surrounds and separates the organs - all can affect the positioning of the colon and, as such, elimination would be considered even more difficult. For unless there is the natural colon shape, unless there is the natural diameter, unless there is a natural secretion or function (the manipulation of the muscle, you may call it) in conjunction with those fluids that would aid the matter to make the transportation along the colon; unless these are perfect, the body becomes sluggish and, as such, death truly begins in the colon, for the body cannot eliminate that which is harmful to it, and, as such, it manifests other ailments, difficulties.

In the physical body, there is evidence, here, of simple disruption in the colon itself. Therefore, the simple procedure, on a regular basis, combined with a proper diet and proper intake of fluids - not to underestimate the function of the bladder, the liver and the kidney - the colon itself can be considered (if it would be actively pursued to be maintained in a healthful state) "the fountain of youth" in the body, or that which would be considered the delaying of the physical wear and tear in the body, or (as some might call it) death in the body.

Now this can be done in several manners. However, to the question itself: you would find that, as there has been considered simple water with a degree of temperature that would make it comfortable for the body, it can be utilized here in a simple enema fashion. Cleansing the colon would allow the body itself to be greatly enhanced, the life itself to be extended, to cause a vitality and a youthfulness that would stretch well into the years that some would call "golden." See?

During the three-day colonic cleansing period, could you please give the fasting diet and quantities that would serve this purpose fully?

If there is the intent to cleanse the colon, it is best to understand that this procedure should be ongoing. Proper diet is most helpful. That which would be considered roughage in the diet is extremely beneficial and does aid in what would be the movement of this, the waste product through the intestine. It actually cleanses, to some degree, see.

As there would be a cleansing diet, we would understand that as the body would engage in the cleansing procedure, there would be certain chemical and physiological changes taking place in the body. It would be first necessary to engage those - you would call - laxatives, or those herbs or those foods (even if it would be the chemical) that would induce a degree of easement in elimination (physical congress). Any laxative is better than none, you see.

However, as the diet would be primarily light, and as it would be tapering off over the three-day period as the fast itself, you would find this would be beneficial. However, we can go a little previous to this and suggest that upcoming to the fasting, upcoming to a colonic cleansing, upcoming to any treatment upon the body, do so in an easy manner. Do not force the body here or there. It is attempting to cleanse itself and it should be done under enjoyable circumstances, rather than under forced, tyrannical, martial law dominating what the body will or will not do. So you see, why be hard on the self'? Why not be relaxed and loving and comfortable, and allow the body to function even more perfect than it is at present? For, you see, harshness with the body tends to negate that which is desired and tends to cause omissions and ultimately deterioration to the point in which there is no commission of the cleansing process whatsoever.

However, as there would be the approaching this period of cleansing, we would suggest that there be the eating of the apple for three days; raw apple made into any form that can be ingested: sauce, chunks, or from the core, as long as there is the eating of at least half a dozen of these apples per day (more if it is desired or needed). Combine with this, on the first day, seven or eight large tumblers of water (more, if it can be tolerated). An ounce from the spoon of olive oil should be taken in the morning of the first day. This helps the colon get the matter mov-

ing (so to speak), to cause secretions here, in elimination that would be considered necessary or pertinent to that which is attempting to be carried out in the body.

On the second day, another teaspoon (or ounce) of the olive oil would be helpful. Another half dozen or so apples (up to ten or so) would be a good range, and, again, more water. Allow the water to be taken in, you see, for the apples act as a catalyst (so to speak) or as an agent that allows the kidney to function more perfectly in elimination. The water, of course, is the means in which the fluid is carried out through the body, as the elimination that is necessary.

On the third day, as much olive oil that can be taken; an ounce or two in the morning would be helpful, and then the apples. On the third day (yes, even on the second day) there would be a noticeable increased removal of what would be considered unwanted and poisonous secretions (physical congress itself).

We would suggest then a lapse of time of approximately seven days to ten days, in general terms (as you would call it), then the colonic therapy should be commenced for a three-day period. Here, the diet leading up to the same should be one of grapes, purple or green, seed or seedless. Grape juice itself - two ounces of pure grape juice mixed with two ounces of water - would be a good solution (as you would call it) and, again, a little olive oil can be taken.

If one is having difficulty with the colon - if there is a bend in the colon, if there is a stretch in the colon - then it would not be pertinent to engage in too much activity that would be considered physical. For we find if one would be a lumberjack or would engage in much bending or lifting with the abdominal muscles, the colon would tend to be set in place and would tend to function naturally and more perfectly through this form of exercise. However, as one is not engaged in this, and there are disruptions that can be seen with the X-ray or with the mind (if it would seek out, in its own records, the indication of this condition in the colon), and again, not too much physical exercise (for here, you wish not to cause difficulty in the colon) but massage should be instilled here. One who would be skilled in the same would engage in the descending colon, come across, then upward, so to speak, to the traverse portion of the colon, and then on the third and final massage to the ascending portion of the colon.

However, upcoming to the treatment, this can be done by that one who would be the recipient of the treatment and can be induced by itself. However, as the intestine would be lubricated (so to speak) from the grape juice, from the grapes that can be taken as a snack or as a whole meal, we would find that the intestine would be ready to eliminate; yea, it would have a softening effect on the residue, you see. And, again, if one is having difficulty with the colon, more exercises are necessary. If one is, however, in good shape or in good form in the colon, then a degree of bending exercises can be considered acceptable - sitting upon the floor, bending the head over towards the knee, those type of exercises. Sit-ups may be done, although it would be better to raise the legs rather than lift the head, in this form of reverse sit-up. And any form that can be seen as massaging and flexing the stomach muscles corrects the abdominal muscles, you see.

Then commence the program for three days. Try to engage, at the same time each day, the treatment of the colonic. It is not to be too severe to the body; that is to say, it is not to be too much of a shock to the body (for it will be a shock to the body). As such, do it gently, do it easy, allow for the natural processes to take place; and, here, the mechanical aid, the colonic therapy itself would be most helpful in aiding and removing the residue that is collected in the large intestine. This would be done the same time each day and, as such, for those that can do the exercises, continue these over the second and third days. For those who cannot, have someone engage in abdominal exercises or massage (as you may call it), pressing neatly and gently into the intestine with the fingers and with the knuckles, rolling back and forth (but not so much that it causes pain) to those areas, as we have given; descending portion, traverse portion, and then the ascending portion of the colon, or (if you will) the left lower side of the abdomen just below the breastbone, above the navel in the traverse portion, and then to the right side of the body in a vertical position (the ascending portion of the colon).

The colon itself, for those who are not familiar, is in a C-shape (or should be in a C-shape) commencing at the right side of the pelvis, going up to just below the rib cage, across the body to the other side of the pelvis, and then down towards the groin and, as such, heading backwards to the back of the body, to the anus itself. Follow this path in massage. Again, this could be done at the time of the colonic, prior to the colonic, but not so much after, you see (although it could be done after also, to aid in faulty elimination).

As for the diet, it would be light. Do not tend to eat too many vegetables that would be roughage. Eat more of the oils (the olive itself). Now the oily olive - dark green or dark - can also be taken by those who cannot take the oil from the spoon. That which is of the Greek variety would be best. Both come packed in the olive oil itself, you see, and are most helpful.

These can all be taken prior to the three-day engagement or the treatment. But eat of the grape, and drink the grape juice, and if this is not too helpful for those who are chronically constipated or have difficulty (diarrhea also), then engage in what would be considered the laxative or the massage; whichever would apply. Those laxatives that are commercially available (either in pill or bar form) should be taken. It is better that a laxative be taken every day than the body be congested or constipated - even for one day.

How often should a colonic cleansing occur?

It depends on when it is commenced in the life. It is better to be persistent and consistent in anything than to be haphazard, and then to commence and then forget. As one would be a child itself, you would find, even from the early stages (the newborn), that a short enema is helpful. Understand the body is not fully developed in the digestive and elimination processes in the body; and, as such, a short enema, given from time to time, would help; not so much that it would make diarrhea, but that it would allow the body to cleanse itself and to aid in elimination, even from the very first few days of birth, you see.

However, we find in this particular culture in the Canadian and American areas, that this process has not been widely accepted and, as such, we shall approach the explanation for those who have not had a colonic or have engaged in any type of enema therapy. From this, then, it would be necessary to engage in, for the first three months, one treatment every month; that is to say, one series of treatments every three months. A series should be for three days, for this would tend to allow the body to naturally eliminate from the small intestine to the large intestine itself also. As such, you would take approximately this length in time for the body to eliminate that which has been ingested into the body, as the length of the intestine is several meters.

From this three-day series, here, engaged once a month for three months, then it would be better for every other month for a treatment or two or extending the full three-day cycle. Now it can be done every other day, or weekly, or whenever there is a degree of headache, dizziness or fatigue felt in the body. It is not necessary to engage in a full-blown type of colonic, but rather a simple enema bag with a needle insert would be sufficient. The fluid would allow the body to aid or (you would call this) loosen and ultimately remove from the colon that residue that is congested here.

It would also be helpful for an entity to engage more in the joy of life and not to hang onto resentment and to retain hostility; for this is seen as also the emotional retention. It affects the physical retention and, as such, if one can release the anger and seek more the joy of living, then this would be helpful also.

But to the question, the indication of when this would commence: we would suggest at least four times yearly that any entity would engage in cleansing of its intestine. We would suggest fasting in between, from time to time. Take a day in a month in which there would be given the body physical rest in which you would not undergo a degree of bombardment from food. And as this would be done, this would be helpful leading up to those treatments of the colonic itself.

Now, can it be overdone? Indeed it can be. However, do not do it so much that the body loses its ability to eliminate on its own. But if there are those who are serious yet not zealous about this, this can be done on a weekly basis until there would be the cleansing of the colon itself. Our examination has been with those who are having a little trouble in their elimination but are not presenting the serious conditions in which there would be ulcer, anal infection, polyp, exaggeration of the pocket or the colon itself, some difficulty in peristaltic movement, cancer of the colon or other ailments.

We are pertaining our inspection primarily to those who would be relatively healthy (so to speak) and would wish the cleansing process. For those who are in that category that would be difficult, then it would take one who would be skilled, one who would be knowledgeable to apply the correct pressure, the correct amounts of water and other fluids - coffee enema, Glycothymoline, or any antiseptic, alpha-iodine, chlorophyll - these all can be utilized in their specialized areas. But for our inspection, it has been primarily to a little antiseptic (Lavoris or Listerine would be good) in water and applied to the body.

Would you please give us a specific solution and time frame for those who would wish to clean the female organs?

If this would be done, nine to ten ounces would be a sufficient amount here; a little Lavoris, Listerine, or an antiseptic which would be general and safe in a solution. Time frame would be whatever it takes to engage in this. If there would be mucous or phlegm or (as you would call it) discharge, then there would be the necessity to place into this coffee grounds. Take the water, strain them through the same, then use this in what would be the douche itself. Again, eight to ten ounces would be a good range. This would allow cleansing of the same. Understand, if there is a discharge in the feminine aspects, it is largely due

to congestion in the colon itself, you see; as such, it would be much better to cleanse the colon in combination with the douching of the physical body. For is it not logical that the body does bathe itself inside as well as outside? Yea, it does.

As to what would be after each cycle of the menses, this would be a good time to cleanse the same. Or, again, depending upon the intercourse activity and, indeed, the number of partners, then, of course, it would be needed to be increased, see. For here, infections or viral conditions, irritations in the urinary tract, all would play an important part in the activity. But on a general basis, for one who would be considered light or periodic in the sexual function itself, then after each cycle, once a month, would be considered acceptable. If it is increased to once a week, or once every other week, then this would be even better.

But, again, if there would be several partners, and if there would be some irritation, then it would be necessary to increase this; yea, after every partner (so to speak) or more to a few days; every third or fourth day, if there would be infection or virus here.

Please give any further information on this subject that would be helpful or beneficial.

Simply and easily, understand the indicators. Look

to the skin of the body. Is it rough or is it dry? Are there cracks and wrinkles upon the same? Look into the eye. Is it listless, or is it bright? Look to the tongue. Is it coated, or is it pink? Look to the breath in the morning (halitosis or bad breath, some may call it). Is it prevalent in the body, or is there none? If there is, then there is difficulty in the intestine. If there is roughness or dryness to the skin, then there is trouble in the intestine. Is there headache or dizziness about the body? Is there a degree of congestion or constipation in and about the body? Is there migraine in the body? Yea, is there susceptibility to virus and mucous conditions? This is where the body has had the assimilation of the toxins into itself and these conditions exist.

Look into the physical and see how the body functions. Is there stiffness in the joints? Is there stiffness in the fingers; yea, in the spine, in the pelvis? Is lubrication in the body at the major joints a problem? All these come from difficulty in the colon itself. Cancer is also allowed to manifest in the body, and, as such, if the body could eliminate those cells that would be toxic, irregular - indeed, harmful - then they would not have the greater opportunity to be lodged in the flesh or in the tissues of the body.

You cannot have a condition that is evident that does not first begin with the body's inability to remove it from the body itself. Yea, this is true. Each condition that is seen in the body primarily could have been removed from the physical body, if there had been more perfect function in the colon itself.

Understand, death truly begins in the colon. Keep the spine flexible and you have youthful appearance. Keep the colon in good shape and function, then you have the youth for life. For most of the life, even into the aged years, most important, you see, is that which is simple but is overlooked by most would-be authorities - those who would be healers - in this day, in this age, in this country.

Headaches and acidity in the body and other ailments are directly related to the condition of the colon itself. You see, in any body, if there is cold, bronchitis, mucous, or any other form of virus, it is largely due to the body itself having a high degree of acidity, and this has been allowed to manifest in the body through poor diet (but primarily through poor elimination). Allow the body to be cleansed, and most illnesses can be eliminated.

But understand also, the emotions are the constructive and destructive forces in the body. Whenever there is consternation, criticism, adversity, resentment, what is it that happens to the abdominal muscles and the intestines? Do they not tighten up and become rigid with tension? Indeed, they do, and no cleansing procedure can exist properly when it is restricted in its function. Understand, it is better to have a good belly laugh each and every day than it is to take medicine. Understand that it is good that you seek the joy in others as well as yourself as it is to contemplate disaster. Understand as there is a well-being state in the mind, then the physical body will have a well-being state, in the physical sense.

For those who engage in the healing procedure, bathe the outside of the body religiously, and do the same for the inside of the body, for it is more important to cleanse internally than it is to cleanse externally. For those who wish light and life, let them choose what would be light and life. For each has before it doubt or darkness, life or death, and the right to choose.

PART FOUR
KEYS TO LONGEVITY

To increase longevity, some people are practicing a form of diet very similar to starvation, with a bare minimum of calories. Please comment on this.

Would this make sense that one should starve themselves that they may live longer? Nay. We find that there is some determination to attempt not to over-work the body, but let us examine this. Is it not true that as the body works harder, the harder it works, the stronger it gets? We see this to be more natural. As the body would be given foods for its maintenance, or for its body-building, or for longevity (if you would call it that), then it would be more important to work in harmony with the body so that the body would be given what it needs at any particular given time. The body should always be on the slightly heavier side, or plump side, or slightly in a preparation or preparedness stage, you see. For if one needs to call on physical strength, it would be best to have it when one calls upon it (gained previously) than it would be to attempt to call upon something that is not yet there. Would this not make sense?

As such, to the question itself: those that would be limiting the body are themselves attempting to limit and control the physical form, not realizing that longevity begins in the mind. The mind is the builder, the mind is the way. Attitude is most important, above all things. Longevity is a life-long, daily pursuit, and it cannot be done simply by the diet. It must be done by all aspects of the self. But begin with the mind and how the mind and body react so that the emotional states are utilized, for the emotional states are both the constructive and destructive forces in any body, regardless of diet.

We do not see this as a good idea to closely starve the body, for when one does this, one takes away from the body. It would be better to give to the body in excess a little of all things than to simply eat in excess of a few things which tend to fatten the body, or poison the body, or thin the body, or deny the body. Longevity is a daily pursuit. Learning what to give to the body on a given day is best for longevity purposes. Keep the body healthy; keep the body balanced (as well as the mind and the lifestyle or environment in which the body is kept). Then you would have a formula for longevity, you see.

We would suggest, to this question, that simply denying the body in order to prolong its life is not fool-hardy, but may be considered impractical if done independently of all that we have just stated.

Can you please discuss the factors that contribute to longevity?

Indeed, that which we have just given would be appropriate for the answer here. We would add that there should be a balance in each and every day for items. There should be a time for worship, a time for sleep, a time for work, and a time for play. The more closely the balances of all these sectors can be proportionate equally, then the greater chance the body has for longevity. Let us assure you, the worry-wart or those who are in a state of anxiety or stress are not in harmony with all four aspects, and they are more imbalanced in a singular direction; therefore they are dis-eased in their mind and in their emotional states.

The body, which follows the mind in emotional states naturally, follows into a state of imbalance or disease, you see. Let us assure you that any invasion or infestation in the body physically has first happened in the mind. The emotional states, which are the constructive and destructive forces, have allowed the body to be weakened to such a point that the infestation, the invasion of bacterial or viral forces, or sedentary and other disruptive forces has begun and is allowed to continue.

Therefore, to the mental and the emotional states, above all, the attitude is important. One should always have an optimistic and hopeful attitude. One should always do those things that would keep it in a state of peace. One should realize that stress and anxiety are natural states to be in, but one is not designed to be in them for long periods of time. Again: for long periods of time.

Worry is a great disruption, a great disease that affects the mind, and emotional states bring great disruption in the physical body. One should find a vocation or an activity that one can play at, and, therefore, the work and the play would be the same; but, in fact, in this life, one would never work, but would always play. This would allow enthusiasm, which is the great elixir for longevity, to be prevalent each and every day of the life. Joy, expectation, enthusiasm all bring about longevity in the body.

Worry, fear and anxiety are evils in the body that rob the person of the life. They eat up the longevity, if you will. Therefore, proper diet is but one part of the entirety of the entity. There should be a mind-washing to remove all aspects of adversity and negativity. This can be done with entertainment, or joy, or meditation. There should be a commune with the higher self and all the spiritual forces - or the dimensions that lay beyond - in which the self can gather information to solve all concerns of human nature, problems, and difficulties, you see.

And then there should be the preparation in the practical aspects of life that there would be sufficient material resources to sustain and maintain the life. For humans (as you know humans) usually believe they need a lot more than they usually do. Being in harmony with what is needed to sustain the self is the key here that will not embellish or cause worry, or make the self a slave to material assets. Play should always be incorporated into everything that is done. This changes the attitude, it lifts the spirit, and it allows the body to live longer. For indeed, which automobile would function longer: one where either the accelerator is pressed to the floor or the brakes are pressed to the floor (and sometimes both are pressed to the floor at the same time); or the automobile driven with a light touch, an easy-going forward and a gentle stop? Likewise, treat the body, treat the life, and treat the mind as you would the automobile that would be gently used, with constraint, putting limits on desires, and, under all circumstances, looking for what is the good side of things, you see.

Would drinking alkaline water assist this?

Primarily it allows the body to fight off viral and

mucous conditions that would invade the body, for any virus or bacteria would have difficulty in catching hold in the body. Understand that disease enters the body through one of the gates in the body, and as these gates would be protected, or would refuse entry of bacteria or virus conditions, then the body would not be affected. But when such an invasion, or penetration, or inhabitation occurs by the virus or bacteria, it must reside in the body somewhere, like a gang of thieves looking to find a hide-out in the body. The alkalinity within the body provides closed doors and denies access; as such, in this denial it encapsulates the viral and mucous or bacterial condition and eradicates it before it can take hold in the body.

Are there any other longevity enhancers in the same class as alkaline water?

Fresh vegetables grown in the vicinity and region in which the body resides are a good source of alkalinity here; plenty of fresh air and the discipline to properly breathe. We would suggest the visitation of both high and low altitudes, especially what would be sea level. This would be better for the body. Attempting to keep the arteries and veins flexible is also good, and therefore oils need to be taken into the body or smeared directly on the body. They would have the effect of keeping the artery and the veins flexible or taut; that is to say, it would not allow blood to be puddled up in the vein or artery, you see, or become restricted or so hard that blood would have difficulty squeezing through the same.

Understand blood pressure needs to be increased and decreased regularly, in order to keep plaque off the artery and to keep the artery supple, so that more blood can be pumped through the artery and called upon when the body is more physically active; or when the organs must call upon more blood to function as they should.

Digestion and elimination are areas that need to be practiced for balance or perfection. Eliminations need to be more perfect and more complete. Washing the body on the inside is just as important as washing the body on the outside. To assimilation, let it be gentle to the body, never stuffing the body to such a degree to cause hardship, and never leaving the body to starve (or fast, if you will) for long periods of time. While fasting is good for the body for two or three days, the body should not be forced into longer fasting than that, save for willful or purposeful means for spiritual or religious purpose, you see (and only when the body is in good condition).

And, of course, plenty of good, fresh, clear water given to the body. These would be the elements. Iodine, protein, fat, minerals (especially iron) need to be given to the body, in order for the body to exist as well as the forces of light. These combined would allow the body to improve or enhance its longevity. Eating of those foods that would come from animal or plants that would have longevity in them also is helpful. From turtle egg to the hibiscus tree, or the aged eucalyptus, you see; all have a tendency to improve. For remember, what is taken into the body: the body absorbs both the physical mass and also the vibration of the same.

Edgar Cayce said the combination of water, salt, soda, and iodine constitutes the fundamental requirements of the body. What was meant that the body only requires these four elements?

It should not be understood that it is only with

these building blocks that the body can exist. Rather, these are the elements that would harness all aspects that would be given to the body to maintain it. For instance, sunlight (or light) and sound are very necessary for the body also. These would not be ingested, but the body should be exposed to them (especially the sunlight itself). Breath would also be necessary to sustain the life. With this broader understanding then, these elements that would be given should be considered necessary elements that, if they were denied from the body, or if the body would be deplete of these substances, then the body would be in jeopardy, become ill at ease, or even cease to exist as a living form. These are necessary elements, for they affect the atomic structure. These are the ingredients that keep the machinery working, so to speak (grist for the mill, you might say). But they are very important to keep balance within the body; a harmony within the balance of the body.

Understand the form is such that the body is exposed to all the elements, all the physical influences of the world. Constantly throughout physical life, the body is accepting and rejecting things that are affecting it, placed on it, or placed in it. If you look upon a physical body and you think of it, there are things that come into the body, but there are at least four ways to reject or remove things from the body, including the pores, the exhalation, and the body's filtering and rejecting or discarding mechanisms through the bowel and kidney. These require a large amount of activity or energy to be used in the body. Why? Because the body is exposed constantly to detrimental elements or influences that cause it to be ill, or to cease. And yet it continues to grow, become strong, procreate, and exist for many years. The planet is a hostile one. The influences are provided to balance the body between what is derogatory, and what is complimentary. These elements are the four (there are actually five) bases for existence and for life. Understand that if a body is in perfect harmony, and works at longevity (even from a young age), then the length of life would be more than ten times the age at which puberty is reached. However, longevity is something that needs to be looked upon every day of the life.

To the question: the body cannot exist only on these elements, but the body cannot exist without any of them. The denial of these, even in small amounts, causes imbalance in the life and physical health of a body, generally speaking.

What is the fifth element?

Iron.

Could you describe the dosages and general routine of how to use the four elements?

Understand these are found in foods, or minerals, or items that the body would put into itself, orally, or topically upon the body, or even by just laying against certain elements, or touching or handling them; they would be absorbed into the body. Gold itself would be good to handle (or even to ingest). However to these trace amounts, a little each day, or taken into the food or put onto the food would be good. For instance, the sodium bicarbonate could be taken in a drink or it could be found in water - placed in water, or found in water naturally. Sea salt would have a combination of iodine that would be easy to ingest, plus this type of salt would have the elements, including the sulphur and the chloride and nitrogen that would be necessary to build a body at the cell level. Therefore sprinkling this on food regularly (if the food is without salt) would be a good idea. At least once a week, a pinch of salt would be a good idea, depending on the type of weather (more in warm weather where the body perspires than cooler weather where the body does not perspire). But used as a spice in cooking, or added to water, or placed on food, at least a healthy pinch of salt each week would be a good rule of thumb in moderate climates. Iodine may be taken simply by a few drops of Atomidine* under the tongue. This should be done monthly, three to four drops. Where bodies are lax or have difficulty in thyroid function, then a few drops each week would be good, until the body loses the mass and (let us say) shrinks the body to what would be a more normal appearance.

All elements should be taken in small amounts, and if found in water or with a high degree of mineral content in the water, like zinc, or that which would be found in nuts, like zinc (almonds especially), the body can reduce the amount given directly to itself. Otherwise, the amount should be at least weekly, a pinch of salt, a few drops of iodine, or sodium bicarbonate added to the water.

What is the action of the four elements in the body over time?

The body will be easier in its function. It will be (let us say) more youthful. The aging effects will be delayed or deferred. The body will be able to remain healthier and ward off any attack or invasion of disease; viral or bacterial, you see. The body's skin will heal faster and the bone will heal faster, if broken. The bone itself will be stronger and remain more elastic or flexible, as would be the arteries. All disease begins in the body when the elimination is impaired or slowed down somehow. The eliminations would be improved and the functions of the electrical or magnetical influences in the body would be kept at an optimum level.

Each cell has a filament and vibrates at a certain frequency. Above or below a correct frequency, disease sets in, and the body would be either hyperactive or hypoactive, and, as such, these imbalances breed dis-easement physically in the form. The elements would allow the body to remain strong: better teeth, better eyesight, better color of skin, fewer warts and blemishes appearing on the skin. Eliminations would be optimum and the sexual influences would be normal or high, the appetites of the body in general would be good. The body would wish to be more active, more outgoing and there would be a certain excitement for life. Depression, or fatigue, or even laziness would be minimized or nonexistent.

Are there risks with long-term consumption of sea salt, sodium bicarbonate or iodine?

None that we can see, unless, of course, they are taken in excess. For all things taken in excess can be difficult for the body, but taken in moderation (as we have suggested) as a rule of thumb - a pinch here, a few drops there, a mixture with water - with balanced diet and movement or exercise of the body, the functions would allow the body to be improved or more accepted. For, you see, assimilation is more about what is accepted, than what is given. For if the body has poor assimilation, even the best of the best that is given to the body will be useless (or practically useless), for it will not be properly assimilated. To have good assimilation, therefore, the body will continue to accept, and as it accepts, it grows stronger, grows more youthful, more alive.

But if taken in excess, then the body would tend to be almost as if poisoned, but it would not be by error at any particular point. It would take prolonged and willful exaggeration of these amounts taken into the body to cause any impairment. For there is a saturation point reached, and if that saturation point is reached, then the body will over-react or become unresponsive to what else would be given. It is better to be moderate than to have a "feast or famine" approach with any elements. But to these three, using common sense and a good rule of thumb, one can assess what the body needs and what it does not need any more (or may need a little more of one and a little less of another). However to the question: like sugar, a little is helpful, but a lot is unpleasant. The elements can be taken in moderation and on a long-term basis. We do not see any impairment or difficulty; again, taken in moderation.

If a person could only use one supplement for general health and longevity, what would be the most effective choice?

Assuming there are different shortages in the world itself, salt, of course, is the best supplement that the body requires or needs. Iodine would be the next.

For each of the major organs and systems in the body, please provide an overview of supplements that would be beneficial for better health and longevity. First, the brain.

Primarily, the brain itself is benefited by vitamins that would be taken into the body, and also oxygen. Therefore, breathing is most important, especially fresh air; not stale air, or recirculated air in a vehicle or household, but to be outside. Breathing is most beneficial to put oxygen into the blood, to affect all of the organs, but, in particular, the brain. To invert the body so that there is increased blood supply to the brain is also very helpful as a form of exercise, but it is more mechanical; not to stand on the head, but to invert the body, to have most of the body higher than the brain or the head, like a shoulder-stand, or laying on the floor with the legs on the bed (so to speak). This form of inversion easily allows more blood flow into the brain.

All vitamins taken into the body would be helpful, but the B-complex would be extremely helpful. The saw palmetto and serrapeptase would also be helpful for the brain (as well as other parts of the body). Gold would be helpful to other parts of the body (as we have given) and it would be helpful to the brain.

Any form of sprouting seeds or bean sprouts would be most helpful to the brain itself. Keeping the blood supply in the brain is paramount to improving the brain's health. Those foods that would be helpful would primarily be seeds and beans, lentils and small fishes that would be captured in the sea itself (although fish in general would be helpful; more specifically the fish oil).

The ginkgo biloba is helpful to some, but not all. Any tea that would be helpful for the gut or the stomach (like the slippery elm) would also be beneficial for the brain itself. Sugars should be avoided, save for cane sugars or sweeteners like honey (these would be helpful to the brain itself).

Iodine is most helpful for the area of the motor skills (medulla and cerebellum). The basic elements that are to benefit the center or controlling part of the body - such as salt and vitamin A - are good, and any source of zinc would be good.

Those oils that would be from the fishes (as we have given) would be good, although oil obtained through plants would be helpful, too.

The main ingredient that would be helpful would be any herb or product that would increase the blood supply through the brain itself or increase the oxygen content in the body. Iodine is most important for the brain. Most are deficient and, indeed, increasing the iodine allows the brain to function more correctly. Low grade infection in the brain, or the neck, or the body itself does allow deterioration of brain cells, you see.

Proteins on all levels should be given to the body, whether it is from animal or plant; high amounts of protein are most helpful and effective in maintaining good brain function.

Whether there is brain damage from concussion, or striking of the head (bruising of the same), the brain does not readily accept healing (shall we call it), and, indeed, increasing the fluid in the brain cavity (the skull or cranium) can put pressures on the same. Indeed, in the middle portion of the brain, in the lower back, increasing the temperature, or pressure of air, or atmospheric pressure can help remove sediments through the tubes that connect the inner ear and the drainage in the lymphatic system. That which is benefited in the drain of the lymph is also beneficial in the draining of the central ear, or the middle and lower back portion of the brain itself.

Berries of all sorts would be helpful for the body, from the blueberry to the cherry to exotic berries of all sorts. Those foods that would have enzymes in them, like papaya or even cacti, would be most helpful to the brain itself, and there are a variety of products we see available, in taking the cactus juice (or the meat from the same) and applying it to the body.

Silver is a good benefit to the body as

well. However, eating more of the zinc would be helpful, generally speaking, than any other.

Please provide an overview of supplements to aid the colon.

The large intestine can be seen as basically a bag in the body. Its function is most important, inasmuch as it removes from the body waste material. Blood supply to the intestine is important, and so are bending and stretching exercises that allow the intestine to function more correctly in its movement or its contracting and flexing, inasmuch as it removes from the body through these mechanisms the physical congress. Washing the body on the outside is a good practice. Occasionally washing the body on the inside would likewise be a good practice, and whether it would be called the colonic, or whether it would be enema therapy given to the body, occasionally, it would be most helpful.

Tension held in the diaphragm tends to affect the colon, and when there is a hiatal hernia, the colon itself is stretched or is incapacitated. Keeping the proper shape in the colon, which would look like a C laying on its side (so to speak), is good practice for the colon itself. This can be recognized by examination by a physician. Agricultural experts look at the feces of animals and they make this a prime diagnosis on how healthy the animal is. Little in regard to the human examination of this would be seen; therefore, understand that the stool can tell a lot about what is taking place inside the body, in particular in the colon itself.

The colon should function not once a day (and certainly not "occasionally"), but it should function two to three times every day. When a meal is taken in, the colon's natural function (or reaction) to digestion is to eliminate. Any form of stimulation through elimination is beneficial to the colon, as the colon eliminates and removes toxins and waste materials out of the body. The emotional correspondence here in the colon is resentment, or the retainment of anger, or injustice. Here, to impose upon someone may cause the colon to reduce its function, and those who are imposed upon (or bullied) usually develop some congestion in the colon itself.

However in peering into the body, the colon itself should be kept functioning and not allowed to deteriorate to the point where it begins to leak, or to the point it begins to be congested (that is, constipated), or to the point it is overstimulated with too much bile secreted (diarrhea in the body, you see). Somewhere in the proper order, keeping the bowel functioning is very important.

Taking a spoonful of olive oil, on occasion, would help the function in the intestine. Flushing the body will stop the development of polyp and sediment being captured in the sedentary or concave folds in the colon itself. Infrared light or heat on the outside to increase the blood flow to the colon is a good idea. This can primarily be done by sun tanning the body and keeping high amounts of vitamin D in the body. This would be good for all of the organs, in particular the thyroid (of course), but it does affect the middle part of the body (or the colon itself).

Any purple vegetable, including eggplant, would be good for the body in the colon itself. Nuts can be taken, but they should be well chewed and even made into powder or paste. This would be helpful for the colon, as it would not be irritated (or even cut) on the inside. Although it seems to be very tough, sharp edges can cause minor bleeding in the colon itself.

Foods that are green in nature are good for the body, therefore salads made from all sorts of vegetables would be good, and at least a bowl of salad or roughage would be beneficial to be taken every day.

Porridge is also good for the colon, as it helps to flush or cleanse the same, and this gruel, or porridge, or rolled oats would be good to act as a cleansing agent in the colon. Therefore, have a large bowl occasionally, and this would act as a cleansing agent. If the body is sedentary, dried fish should be given.

Pork or pork products should be avoided in a body that is not active. Therefore, if one is physically active - in other words, if one makes a living through sweat, or physical exercise, or exertion - then sometimes the body would be requiring pork (or it can benefit from the same); otherwise, a little crisp bacon would not hurt on occasion, but all other aspects of the hog should be avoided by most who are sedentary.

Any food from the sea would be most helpful for the colon, save for those bottom-crawlers or those scavengers that would exist on the floor of the ocean, as these should be avoided. However, eels, herring, and sardines would be very good for the colon itself.

Salts of all types should be given and they would be helpful to the body. Sea salt in particular is beneficial to the body and, here, in the colon it is most helpful.

Juices from green plants are most helpful.

Dairy products, including cheeses from the cow, would be most derogatory in a lot of different bodies. Rule of thumb would be to eat more of the goat cheese than cheese from the cow (however, in moderation).

Beneficial for the secretion of bile (and, therefore, the function of the colon) would be grapes and grape juice, and/or red wine. Smaller berries such as cranberries, raspberries, blueberries and cherries would also be beneficial to the colon.

What was the original purpose of the appendix?

Call it a place for poisons to be put. It would be a filtering place to trap stones or seeds or impurities that would be in the diet.

Please provide an overview of supplements to aid the gallbladder.

The gall itself accumulates like a secondary cleansing organ, in conjunction with the liver. Keeping the gallbladder functioning would be to maintain grapes or grape juice in the diet, to stimulate the thyroid, the pancreas, and, in turn, the bile to be secreted. Chickpeas, grape seed extract would help the bile; also taking Swedish bitters to kick-start the digestion. Cherries and berries would be helpful. Take the orange peel and shred or scrape it. Taking some of this occasionally would help remove any stones or collection points in the gall. Eating the orange peel by grating a little off would be a good tonic for the body.

Calcium, magnesium and copper lactate in a combination would be helpful to the gallbladder. Taking large amounts of mineral water into the body would be most helpful, also.

Castor oil packs applied to the general area would be helpful as well. The gallbladder can be stimulated, the same as the liver.

Getting proper sleep at night, especially entering into the deep states of sleep, is most helpful. It allows the liver and gall to function in a more connected way. Supplements that are most helpful to this would be those obtained from the roots, such as parsnip and other white vegetables.

Now, in particular, that which can be given to the body would be soups and broths made from the bones of animals (the goat, the fowl, or the fish), where the bones would be broken or exposed and then stewed. As such, the residue from the same (the broth) would be most helpful in affecting or stimulating the gallbladder itself.

Apple cider can be taken, on occasion; even the fermented type, you see. This would be helpful indirectly to the gall, you see. However primarily the grape seed extract and the saw palmetto would be helpful to stimulate the gall.

Please provide an overview of supplements to aid the heart and blood vessels.

Making sure the body eliminates is most important. Now, either the body assimilates or it eliminates; it does not do both functions at the same time. In the middle is the digestion and assimilation process, and for most bodies there is a difficulty in assimilating. This is why the body begins to deteriorate, for it does not matter how many vitamins, or proteins, or minerals are taken into it, the body simply does not absorb. As such, even on occasion when the body is being given plenty of food, it starves (so to speak), for it has the lack of ability to assimilate. As we have already given, those beneficial aspects would be to cleanse the body internally.

Swedish bitters can be taken to kick-start digestion. As such, the body would assimilate a little more efficiently (shall we call it), as it would be breaking down the food through the digestive process, and assimilation would be advanced. Gelatin or gelatin powder also can be added to help the assimilative process. This helps the vitamins taken into the body to be assimilated and, therefore, to affect the circulatory system.

All B-vitamins affect the circulatory system. Proteins in the diet affect the circulatory system. Serrapeptase (or serraflazyme, as it might be called) tends to remove plaque from the arteries. The best form of health for the arteries and the heart is to increase the internal pressures so that the arteries are expanded, and the blood supply radiates out to all the small areas of the body (including the surface of the skin). This can only be done through exertion exercise, or bending and stretching exercises. Yoga is most helpful, for, in this form of exercise, as the mind is brought around in control, the body naturally follows.

However, any form of cleansing of the arteries is helpful, and this means that the elimination systems in the body should be optimized: plenty of water, plenty of eliminations, plenty of excretions, so that there is removal of waste material. This is the place to start for betterment of the arteries and the heart.

Keep the weight as lean as possible, for, here, fatty tissue in the small intestine and fatty tissue in the heart leads to poor circulation and disease starts in the heart (including edema, or water around the heart, in the sheathe that surrounds the same). This becomes dangerous for the heart.

Iron is most helpful in the body, for all of the organs but, in particular, the heart itself. High amounts of iron in a good body keep the body strong and avoid fatigue in the body. Assimilation of oxygen through the lung itself directly feeds the heart and the remaining circulatory system. Placing the body in hot baths, like hot springs with plenty of minerals, or a hot mineral bath would be most important to the circulatory system and to the heart itself.

That which is stimulating to blood supply in the leg would be, perhaps, a little red wine and some dark rye bread. This would help to produce red corpuscle with plenty of iron in the body itself. When there is deficiency of iron and iodine, the body does not produce the red corpuscle as productively and as steadily (as strength-oriented), and the body deteriorates and ages prematurely.

Keeping the body more alkaline, of course, is a necessity for good health in the circulatory system, as well as at the heart. As we have given, those enzymes made from the silkworm are most helpful (like serrapeptase) to remove plaque from the same.

Carrot and cabbage juice mixed (two ounces of each) is a good way of absorbing mega doses of vitamins that directly affect the heart and the circulatory system (in a secondary way).

Keeping the arteries flexible avoids the so-called hardening of the arteries; this means, keeping the body flexible, keeping movement in the body through those exercises of yoga, tai chi, qi gong, or other forms of isometric exercise. See?

In a general way, what we have given would be helpful for the artery, but it is the amount of vitamins that are assimilated that is most important. Take all of them, but, in particular, vitamin E would be good for the heart and the arterial (although there may be some resistance to this). Vitamin D absorbed from the sun also would be most helpful to the circulatory system in general, and to the heart in a connective way, see.

Please provide an overview of supplements to aid the kidney.

In part, the kidneys are the most important organs of the body itself. Here, the kidneys act as a cleansing agent for the blood itself. Blood supply to the kidneys and nerve flow to the kidneys is most important. Castor oil packs on the kidneys occasionally are very good or helpful, especially for those kidneys that are under duress or would be worn. Anger in the body that is suppressed and kept within the body (shall we say) adversely affects the kidneys and causes them to reduce their functionality and their capability of removing sediments, poisons, and toxins from the bloodstream. It is most important to maintain health in the kidney above all other organs (in the narrow view of removing diseases from the body). Blood supply to the kidney is most important, especially through the small arteries that feed the kidney. The adrenals that sit on the kidney should be addressed as well.

Emotional states of fear and prolonged states of anxiety, or stress, or fear adversely affect the kidney through the secretion of adrenaline in the body, directly causing the kidneys to be in a high state of alert or function, which causes them to wear out sooner rather than later. For the kidneys, that which would be beneficial, therefore, would be that which would improve the blood. Keeping the body more alkaline (as we have already given), for the same reasons, would be best.

Castor oil packs will soothe, and relieve, and somewhat aid the kidney in a reduction of inflammation.

However, for the kidney itself, assuming it has good blood supply and good nerve flow, those herbs that would be helpful would be those that would be prickly like the stinging nettles, and the chamomile tea. Such herbs, combined with any other supplement that would increase blood flow, like the saw palmetto, would be most helpful. The serrapeptase supplement could also be given where there are small arteries feeding organs, you see. These, too, would increase blood flow to the organ, and would enhance the blood flow through and around the organ itself.

For the kidney, copper lactate is good, and calcium, to some degree (but not extensively so). Licorice root would be good, and any source of gold or silver taken into the body would be helpful, especially gold itself. This can be taken into the body through sources like carrots or other orange-colored vegetables. The gold itself can be found in confectionary toppings or decorations, or gold that has been beaten to a very thin, thin consistency. A pinch put on the tongue occasionally would be very helpful to the kidney itself.

Keeping the function of the kidney, therefore, is the strength of the kidney, in keeping the muscle strong, but also in keeping the poison away from the body and allowing the body itself to be purified. Grapes, grape juice, grape seed extract also affect the kidney (as we have given) and the liver.

We would find that, on occasion, the oil from spicy or hot peppers or sweet peppers - those that would be considered in the hot areas - would be very helpful for the kidney. This can be done occasionally, not on a regular basis, unless one would be from those areas that maintain peppers in the diet.

Burdock root, licorice root and, on occasion, St. John's Wort herb would be helpful.

Ginseng would be most helpful to the kidney, and we would find other such roots similar to ginseng (whether it is the hot or cold, red or blue variety) would be good.

Truffles also would be helpful for the kidney, and, to some degree, mushrooms, especially those that grow in the forest (wild, rather than those which are fostered upon) and there seems to be a variety of these).

Fishes of all sorts would be most helpful as well; in particular, those that come from the deep parts of the ocean, see?

A little or a pinch of sulfur taken into the body on occasion would be good for the kidney and the liver. The liver and kidneys are tied together in their function, see?

Please provide an overview of supplements to aid the liver.

To understand the organ itself is to understand it is a filtering organ. It removes from the body those sediments as best that it can; and, as such, it also produces bile that is required, and there is somewhat of a metamorphosis that takes place in the creation of the bile. There is supposed to be a transition of sediment into the bile and, as such, it is eliminated. However, any particular food that would stimulate the liver would be acceptable. Grapes, for instance, and oils of all kinds, from fish oils, to flax seed or grain oils, to olive oil, these are beneficial for the liver itself.

Also certain vitamins, in particular vitamin C would be good. High dosages of vitamin C or ascorbic acid are very good to cleanse the body and, as such, aid the liver itself.

Germanium would be a good mineral.

There are several other elements and teas that would be helpful. Instead of naming them, we would say those herbs that have spikes or would be somewhat fluffy or furry on the outside, like the stinging nettles or like the burdock root.

Almonds, of course, would be good, and so would the apricot seed, see? Grape seeds or grape seed extract are also good for the liver. Any seeds, like pumpkins, sunflower, and watermelon would be good for the body, directly and indirectly.

The liver needs to be flushed and, therefore, any form of improvement here would be helpful. Understand the liver dumps (if you would call it that) sediments or waste material through the body up to the top of the body and into the bloodstream itself, which is supposed to carry the sediments out of the body. The liver is complex. It is the organ that is, itself, most important to the body to eliminate and remove from the body unwanted, unpleasant and unnecessary sediments and what you would call dis-easements. There is no simple element here, but by keeping the organ healthy, the body will be improved and the life prolonged.

Castor oil packs over the liver are exceptionally good for the liver, and should be done occasionally for those over the age of twenty-five (at the very latest, after the age of thirty-five).

The diet should be one that is more fruity, especially in the morning. This would help the liver function with natural sugars. Honey is also good for the body and for the liver. That which would be best would be the unpasteurized or pure honey, for it contains certain elements of peroxide that would be good for the body.

Any form of stimulation to the liver would be good, but understand that blood flow through the liver is most important. Heat lamps or increasing the body's temperature by exercise, or by placing it in steam baths would be exceptionally good. It increases the blood flow through the liver by dilating the artery itself, and as the arteries are expanded, so is the blood flow increased.

Sea salt or salt from the sea is good for the liver, as is kelp, or iodine itself.

This would be sufficient to understand the complexity of the liver, giving the various functions that it performs. However, the liver is like a filter bag, like a vacuum bag. If it collects the residue or the sediments, not only should it be emptied, it should be shaken or cleaned (so to speak), like the bag. The residue over long periods of time causes the liver to lose its vitality. In association with the small intestine, and, in particular the Peyer's Patch organ, if the body is balanced or maintained in these three, the liver should function correctly, that it should be perpetuating its own cleansing and its own health, see?

Of course, not poisoning the body is good. Refrain from stimulating drinks that have caffeine. Remove from the body carbonated drinks, for they tend to poison the body. Remove from the body those foods that would be manufactured. Eat more of the natural way, and, in particular, drink plenty of water. Diseases hide out in the liver. Therefore, attempting to keep the body more alkaline would be priority, for in any body that is slightly more alkaline than acidic, disease cannot exist.

The organs hold part of the soul. The organs hold part of the well-being of the body. Like seven servants, they have their role to play. Each organ has within itself a response emotionally. Keep the liver optimistic by keeping the outlook optimistic, and by living life fully. Any suppression of the life, like incarceration or dominance over the self (let us call it) or feeling hopeless and unloved adversely affects the liver as well.

Please provide an overview of supplements to aid the lungs.

The lungs themselves are best kept healthy with breathing exercises that expand the same. To avoid a build-up of edema or fluid conditions in the lower portion of the body, iodine given to the body would help the diaphragm which tightens and releases, causing the lower part of the lungs to expand or breathing to occur. Germanium as a mineral would be good; gold would be good; iodine would be good, and we would find even silver taken into the body would be good. The lung tissue itself is sensitive to collecting sediments (the little cilia in the bronchial and extending into the lung). Keeping these sediments and mucous out of the lungs is most helpful or beneficial by breathing (as we have given), causing the diaphragm to contract and expand through deep breathing techniques. This would be one way of increasing the general health to the body, but specifically for the lungs.

Attempt to keep the breathing atmosphere free of sediments like molds, mildew, and dust; this, of course, is common sense and should be maintained. Remove dairy products from the body and eat more of those foods like celery, asparagus, and any long-stemmed vegetable. Also we would find that corn is good for the lungs, and sunflower seeds, you see. Seeds of all sources are good, but we would find chickpeas and sprouted seeds or beans to be very good for the lungs indeed.

Good health in the body for the lungs would be to eat vegetables that are purple in color, and also kelp or iodine-rich foods, you see. Soft tissues in the body tend to collect toxins and poisons easily. In the lungs, take care not to take soot into the body, else it tends to burn the same, to cause explosions or interruptions of cells.

We would find that any bulb plant like onions and garlic would be good, you see. Honey (as we have given) is good for the body, and for the lungs in an indirect way. Those fishes that are in shells would be helpful; escargot would be good for the lungs, see. Sea eels, especially those that are electrically charged, would be helpful to the lung, as are fishes of all sorts (especially those that are of the deep sea variety). Octopus and squid seem to be acceptable, also. Again, the juices of the vegetable would be helpful.

To be in the sun and to breathe deeply would be the best exercise. To build up the tissue, the iodine and iron should be taken into the body and, in particular, to have good blood supply to the lungs itself.

Please provide an overview of supplements to aid the pancreas.

As we would examine the emotions, they are most affected in this area. Fear overrides the function of the pancreas, and, therefore, keeping the body in an emotional balance point would be most helpful. The pancreas requires stimulation in a positive way. Removing fear, or sensitivity to criticism, or worry would be most helpful in this, the pancreas itself.

The pancreas itself is in coordination with the thyroid. Iodine would be good for the pancreas. Keeping the pancreas healthy is a matter of keeping the thyroid healthy. Grape seed extract would be good for the pancreas also.

A reduction in artificial sugars or sugar from the sugar bowl is helpful.

Again, iodine affects or benefits the pancreas. Iodine and omega oils would be helpful. Flax seed oil would be helpful here.

Foods that are purple in nature would be good, as are grape seeds or grape seed extract, horse radish, and horny goat weed (as it might be called). Serraflazyme also.

PART FIVE
PAMPERING THE BODY: THERAPEUTIC MASSAGE

Edgar Cayce was a proponent of massage. Of what value is it?

That which is known as massage, the ancient art itself, is most soothing to the body. Through the physical touch, there is transfer of endearment, transfer of emotion, transfer of care. As such, in that which is seen as the therapeutic massage, that which is designed to bring comfort to the aching and sore body, it is to understand the procedure of massage is most beneficial even at its most basic level. The massage relaxes the muscles of the physical body and restores the creative force that manifests itself through the circulation of the body and delivers such curative and creative force to the various parts, areas or sections of the body, as may be required, through the direct physical touch. The benefits are many.

In understanding massage, it is to bring about an increase, primarily in the circulation of the body. It is also designed to indicate to the body the need for relaxation of a certain muscle or groupings of muscles. Most importantly, it is allowing the body's own elimination systems to be stimulated, the lymph node and anode system, attempting to remove the toxins from the body through the natural elimination systems. Also, other sections or organs of the body benefit greatly from the added benefit of massage and in the various techniques.

The liver or the kidneys can benefit when there is oil applied to these particular areas of the body and this oil (castor oil, for instance) is massaged into the body to bring about a lubricative, restorative and healing effect, internally in the body. You would also find, here, that the nervous system is also greatly enhanced and improved with a degree of massage. The electromagnetic impulses that flow in and about the body are benefited from the soothing natures of the massage itself.

Bones can be lubricated by the application of peanut oil on the same. As there is increased flexibility or relaxation through the spine, then the nerves can react more favorably and function better. Thus, all systems of the body we have outlined can be greatly affected in a curative and beneficial manner. Through the simple massage, whether it is grasping one's palms and rubbing them together, or the squeezing and rubbing of the muscles of another's body to bring about a degree of relaxation, it makes little difference. The soothing effect is highly beneficial.

Please explain what happens to the body during massage.

First of all, you would find, assuming one is relaxed and prepared for a good time, that the body, in the respiration and the heart rate, begins to lower. If one is running a little high in blood pressure, this tends to be lowered, when one is relaxed. As the massage takes place, you would find that between that person who would be the client or the recipient, and that one who would be the giver or the masseur, there is a rapport that takes place. Through this rapport, the soothing, caring, loving touching that is natural in nature occurs first. The body responds to this pampering in a most positive and soothing fashion. All systems begin to function more freely or perfectly; as in the bladder and kidneys, there is relaxation; as in the colon or large intestine, restraint relaxes and there is ease in the body's major elimination system.

Blood flow is usually increased to the specific area in which massage is being applied. Again, the electromagnetic activity in that particular area is increased. However, the body is put in a position of relaxation and, as such, restorative and curative energies then begin to focus and work at the various levels or systems in the body. The nerve system becomes more sensitive. The body becomes aware of itself more fully, and this is a major undertaking. As such, the attention of the body's regulatory systems can then direct more specifically that which is needed to a specific area. You would find that a degree of cleansing takes place by stimulating the lymph system and, to some degree, the cleansing of the arteries is aided here, through simple massage.

What takes place is that the mind itself is put in a secondary position of control and the masseur becomes the prime control of a specific part of the body, aiding it, pampering it, increasing its activity and, above all, soothing it.

How important is the rapport between the massage client and therapist?

It is most important, for as one would relax and allow a degree of trust, the bond of trust to be shared between client and masseur, there is a natural sharing of energies through the simple, therapeutic touch of massage. When one is soothing, both in word and manner, this primarily sets the tone for the entire massage and, as such, can be considered constructive. Of course, the reverse is true if one is irritable and snappy. Then, of course, the massage would not be successful to a higher degree, as the recipient would be on guard, unable to relax and be, perhaps, abused by the masseur, by the lax attitude.

Therefore, it is extremely important that this rapport is one of trust and pampering and an expectation and fulfilment of this pampering is in the mind of the recipient concerning the massage, from the outset. It is extremely important.

You would also find that through the touch, the masseur is led to the specific area in the body and a degree of giving through the body's life force itself, or what you might call the healing force through the hands is emanated here.

How would one select a compatible massage therapist?

It would be to, first of all, meet with them personally. This feeling or rapport would be immediate. It is also beneficial to have one who is recommended and who has proper credentials or has a good clientele. Then, it would be easy to understand that they are good at what they do and are being of service and, indeed, are providing some need in human nature.

On the first encounter with the masseur, it is best to "feel them out." By conversing with them, you would have things in common or you would look elsewhere. It is by simply meeting, as we see it.

At the first massage, there would be an indication whether or not to return. The first indication of massage should not be a painful experience, but rather a light and easy experience, with some degree of a "getting to know you" attitude. There should be a degree of soothing and relaxation ensuing from the treatment. If this does not happen, best to go elsewhere.

How might a body benefit from self-massage?

The affects are immediate and are directed to the area of concern almost instantly. For example, if there is a cramp in the foot, one massages the foot immediately. Of course, the pain is reduced, the blood flow increased and, as such, it has been a curative process.

Self-massage is difficult, but to the lower extremities of the body and, indeed, to some areas in the thorax portion or mid-portion of the body, and also in the facial regions, massage is extremely helpful and, indeed, beneficial. It can be done most any time to a specific area in the body. Facial massage restores lustre to skin that would have been a little lax and, by massage, elasticity comes back. Also applying different herbs and ointments to the face improves the circulation and, thus, the texture to the face and forehead. This can all be applied by the self.

However, for those areas between the back of the head and the buttocks and also the rear portion of the legs, it is best to seek out a second person for this process.

However, to the question: the benefits are endless here. As we have given, it can be done in private, it can be done specifically for that portion of the body that is in need of massage. Cold feet should be massaged most vigorously, by rubbing the hand forward and back (or a combination of hands forward and back) to create a friction-like massage, to increase the heat in a specific area, and thereby increase the circulation.

The benefits again, without being too technical, are extremely helpful.

What value is massage therapy in removing disease from the body?

The value is great for anyone who is not "actively active." By that we mean for one who has more of the passive occupations, rather than that of the laborer's occupations; or if one is not as sports-minded as one used to be, then you would find that the massage is extremely beneficial. For, specifically, it affects the lymphatic system in the body. This is often referred to as the "lazy lymphatic" elimination system. The reason for being termed lazy is that this specific system does not readily have a peristaltic movement or other contract and relax movement of its own. It relies totally on the body movements for the stimulation and pumping of fluids, toxins and those substances to be eliminated through the body. While they may be considered a pump that would be paralleling the spine as a lymphatic pump, it is specifically in the chest and throat regions we are speaking. As there is a degree of stimulation through the chest and throat fluids internally (specifically affecting the hearing) throat, nasal and sinus regions are indirectly (yet directly) mechanically benefited through the increased activity of the massage and, thus, increase of the activity of the lymph system itself.

As for the increase of the blood flow to various centers, it is most helpful also. Through the blood is delivered those that would be considered the restorative and growth substances of the body. You would also find here, with a degree of massage, that which would cling to the internal portion of the arteries (plaque, as you might call it) is, to some degree, stimulated to be exited from the body. It loosens it up (so to speak) in the arterial and then it is simply handled by the body in its natural manner.

How often should a person have a regular massage?

As has been given, as one is inactive themselves in a passive occupation, then it would be regular; once monthly or whenever there is stiffness or lack of physical exertion on a regular basis. However, as any would combine a degree of physical exertion (or exercise, as you may know it) with the massage, then it would be necessary for partial massages to be done on a regular basis; that is, the lower portion of the body, or the arms and chest region, and then the neck, head and shoulder regions on another occasion. This type or manner could be done here, once a month also. If one is extremely active, then, depending upon age, it can be spread out, here, over a few months at a time.

Simply, as one takes more responsibility for themselves and increases their physical activity, then spaces between massage visits can be expanded. This is so, unless, of course, there is a degree of difficulty and the body has been overtaxed. Then, massage should be immediate. However, there are different forms and what we have been speaking of is massage through the hands of one individual to another. But here, again, it is often used in sports complexes, the hydrotherapy tub, and in this manner, it is usually done each and every day. There is no harm in this and, indeed, if one, through ability can afford a massage like this once each day, it would be extremely helpful for a brief time; four to five minutes is all, you see.

What are the effects on the body of the different intensities or depths of massage?

First we shall deal with friction massage and the movements of the hands in a clockwise and anti-clockwise manner. These are primarily designed to use the elimination system (the organ of the skin) directly to bring about increased toxins to the pores or exit areas in the skin and, as such, remove them. This type of massage is usually accompanied with a forward and backward motion (or friction, as it is called). This increases heat in a specific area and thereby increases the blood flow in that area, thereby increasing the curative results. This is the commonest, lightest massage and is relatively safe. Used in and around delicate areas - for instance if the spine is in pain, then the back can be massaged on either side without too much threat of difficulty or injury.

A light pressure or squeezing motion with the fingertips can be considered the second depth of massage. This is beneficial to increase those systems that are near the skin itself: the lymph and the veinous system in the legs and arms. You would find here also, massaging the soles of the feet and the palms of the hands with these light pressures to be extremely helpful. This would bring about unlocking of some muscle groupings, smaller muscles in the back, shoulder, the scalp and the rear of the head.

A deeper massage or (as you might call it) a grasping and squeezing type of massage is enhancing to the layers of muscles deep below the surface and enabling them to relax, allowing the blood flow to be stimulated on occasion through these dormant and stagnant areas. Although the blood is not fully stopped, it is sluggish. You would also find that this type of massage is utilized to stimulate the organs and various centers in and about the endocrine system itself.

With a rather rigorous and full depth massage, the internal organs are, to some degree, massaged benevolently and, on other occasions, brutally. However, to this particular area, internal sections of the body are affected most beneficially and, to some degree, emotional responses can be attributed to this deep massage itself. Not only does this affect the nervous system, it affects the circulatory system and, indeed that gland or section of the body that is under direct pressure. This particular massage is most helpful in relieving deep-seated problems or anxieties in the body and can also be considered restorative to the posture of the body itself. It is primarily used to unlock emotions that are causing, here, the stresses to occur in the muscles of the body itself.

This would be a brief outline of the various attempts of massage.

Please give the benefits of Shiatsu.

This is in conjunction primarily with various systems in the body and here, in conjunction with the time of day or cycles, this particular massage can stimulate or tranquilize various systems in the body. As such, its benefit can be considered enormous. Through the simple massage of a specific area, a mood is set, or changed, or altered and, consequently, the body's function can be dramatically affected. Its primary benefit, of course, is to take the body's own healing energy from one vibrant place and transfer it to another system that is slacking somewhat. In this transfer, the body, using its own life force, becomes more healthy.

Please give the benefits of Rolfing.

This, primarily, is a degree of massage designed to get at the emotional states within the mind. The emotions are the constructive and destructive forces in the body. This form of rather intense depth massager tends to unlock the emotions that are, here, stored within the various centers of the body itself. This form, simply and easily strips away that shield that has been encrusted around the hurt and, as such (as we have given) emotional response usually occurs. But this is stripping away of what you might call a barnacle. It allows the body to function more perfectly, more honestly and brings to the surface those emotional situations which have been locked deep within the physical body. If you will, Rolfing is the key to unlocking the inhibitions of self.

Please give the benefits of deep muscle massage.

This is primarily to affect various groups of muscles in and about the body. The technique is to bring about elasticity and tone, while at the same time, relax. As such, this can be stimulated to various centers in the body and the pressing here, rather vigorously at certain points and muscle groupings, tends to relax very well these muscles in the low back upwards to the scapula, upwards to the base of the neck itself. It tends to stimulate and, indeed, relax those muscles that are normally not handled by other forms of massage. If you will, they are too deep within the body to sense or feel any soothing, rubbing here, taking place to those muscles that are in need, you see.

Please give the benefits of European style massage.

These forms of massage tend to stimulate and excite the nerve endings in the body. As such, you would find this tends to be an exhilarating attempt at massage done on a regular basis. Here, to some degree, it shocks the body, but, to some degree, it soothes the body and in this manner that which is commonly seen as European massage, the body system (in particular the perspiration system) is called upon to secrete poisons and toxins out of itself; out of the skin, you see. Its primary benefit is in removing the toxins from the skin and restoring more perfect circulation in and about the surface regions of the body itself.

How should an individual prepare for a massage that would obtain the greatest benefits?

Indeed, a certain amount of preparation can be evoked here. Have the body immerse itself in water; hot or cold makes little difference, but if it can be alternated, it would be most helpful (for example, cool one time and warm the next). This allows a degree of improvement immediately to the circulation and, to some degree, allows the muscles to relax. In particular, it cleanses the body of those toxins that are at the skin level, at what you might call the pore openings; and through the hot and cold technique, you would find that these pores release great amounts of toxins and poisons. As such, this bathing or showering - showering would be better - tends to be extremely helpful prior to the massage, for it simply gets the outer layer of dirt off the body. Then, as the oils are used upon the body, they can be absorbed more readily into the pores or through absorption into the skin and to those various centers or places that the oil will be of greatest benefit.

We would also suggest the body temperature to be slightly raised and the feet should always be kept warm, even if it means keeping socks upon the same, or the feet wrapped in a large terry cloth. The body should always remain toasty warm throughout the massage. But just prior to the same, the body should be in this position. Of course, all the garments should be removed from the body, so there can be a degree of breathing through the skin as well as the respiratory center. A degree of relaxation or freedom is necessary for this type of massage itself. The preparation, therefore, is to keep the body warm and clean and to keep the outlook relaxed and passive.

Would a steam bath prior be helpful?

This would be another form of cleansing the pores. Yes, this would be helpful to most, save those who would have a tendency to become light-headed and restrictive problems with the circulation; in particular the throat and head region. Then, it would be better not to utilize this form of cleansing.

Which lubricants or oils should a massage therapist use?

Indeed, there are many varieties of oils that can be used here, depending upon the technique. In particular, the oil for the bones or lubricating would be those that penetrate extremely quickly into the skin; that is to say, peanut oil would be an excellent oil. Camphorated oil, combined with a little olive oil, peanut oil and, indeed, castor oil would make a good all-round tonic for this kind of massage; in particular affecting the skin and the bone, as well as the blood. Creams made of aloe vera are most helpful and restorative to the body; in particular to the abdominal and intestinal regions. However, any oil that tends to be absorbed into the body tends to be handled by the body, for it absorbs through the flesh into the circulatory system itself. Therefore, it is necessary to take the oils that would be considered natural in nature; those that have been secreted from the bean or the pod or the nut would be most helpful. The list is endless as we are examining, it. Almond oil, most helpful; wintergreen, witch hazel, all beneficial as you would know it.

When would it not be beneficial to use oils?

When there is a circulation problem near the skin itself, and when there is some degree of reaction to the oils upon the skin. When one has an extremely oily complexion and there is congestion in the intestine, it would be better not to place more oils upon the skin, only to affect an overdose of oil in the skin region, you see. When there are degrees of difficulty, as given, by allergy or irritation to the body, and when there is some degree of circulation problems and restrictive natures, it would be better to use the teas (mullein) to aid the arteries rather than oils. When basically there is need for circulation in the surface of the skin, then a degree of friction massage can be used and oils can be put aside.

Please give a general massage technique that would be beneficial for most.

Simply and easily, it is to always massage towards

the heart. If you are at the foot, move up the leg towards the heart. If you are above the head, then move from the crown of the head down towards the heart. Technique should be simply one that is in clock-wise and anti-clock-wise movements, making, here, with the right hand, clock-wise and with the left hand, anti-clockwise movements in a forward motion - say, from the knee to the thigh - would be an exceptionally good manner of massage. Degrees of pinching and pulling can be utilized also, and those points that can be considered specific or localized points, where a muscle is locked can be squeezed or pressed upon along the muscle and let the muscle relax completely. However, for the massage of oneself, it would be extremely beneficial to utilize these rather simplistic modes of massage. But, when one massages another, then it is beneficial to be somewhat knowledgeable in the art of massage.

When should massage not be used?

When there is a degree of threat of blood clot or varicose vein or other ailments in the body that would he considered congestive to the circulatory system. When there is some degree of blockage in the intestine, either gas or substance itself, massage can be used here, but, very carefully; primarily, not to use the same, you see.

Please give any further guidance on massage that would be helpful.

Massage, in itself, has been a practice utilized here, from the beginning of Mankind. It is a social indicator. It is also an act of endearment. Simply rubbing the brow of one individual, one who is dear to oneself, causes many positive and soothing reactions within the recipient of such a caress itself. There are many attempts to stimulate and bring pleasure to the physical body, and massage can be used for both therapeutic improvement and to bring pleasure to the body itself. These types of massages, combined for an overall purifying and creative manner, can be considered most helpful in bringing about the body's own mechanisms, own techniques to stimulate the growth and the removal of those cells that are considered diseased in the body more easily and with more fluidity.

Massage itself is a technique that can be self-administered, but, here, under the hands of another, is added to a pampering mode with restorative and curative properties (as well as what we have touched upon). Massage is something that can be given freely as an act of love or as a manner of employment. However, the result is to utilize the body's own capable systems to bring about a youthful appearance and to keep the systems functioning more perfectly to eliminate, beautify and rectify the body's various portions, cells, systems and, indeed, sections. Massage is that which can be utilized by most without harm and difficulty. As such, if any would fear arthritis, they should have a good peanut oil massage once a month.

PART SIX
HEADACHES AND MIGRAINES: WHAT YOUR BODY IS TELLING YOU

What is the cause of the common headache?

In that which is known as "headache," you would find that there are many areas of the head that pertain to this particular condition: in the frontal regions (the forehead and temples), into the top, or crown of the head and pertaining to the base or back of the head itself. Now the neck and shoulders also bring on degrees of influence into the head itself with the result of headache. However, to understand the headache itself, you would find there are several reasons for this, the head to ache.

In the first instance, you would find that a degree of congestion in the intestinal tract (the colon itself) would allow an increase of toxins in the blood. You would find this is in conjunction with some degree of difficulty in elimination (physical congress) or also extending to a degree of constipation in that regard, you see. In either case, this particular indication would be toxins in the blood affecting the upper regions of the brain itself in blood supply and return of blood in the arterial and venous. It is usually felt in the sinus, frontal, and temple areas of the head itself. It is simply that the arteries are overloaded and toxins are bringing about the pain in the area described.

Pain in the upper portion or crown of the head relates to the nervous system. You would also find degrees of tension in the body - difficulty in the stomach or in the groin region, or extending to even cramps in the legs - would also bring about degrees of pain in the upper region or the crown of the head. You would also find a degree of imbalance in the glands of the body (the endocrine system) and, as such, this imbalance in those glands that would secrete the timing mechanisms in the body (known as hormones) would bring about aches in the head pertaining to the thalamus and hypothalamus: the controlling center in the brain itself. This is in conjunction with the pituitary and pineal glands in the brain.

That which is felt in the lower portion or in the back of the head would be primarily due to tension held in the neck and shoulder region, and also some degree of misalignment in the spine itself; in particular, the neck. This would affect the motor skills area of the brain, the medulla, and the balance system, the cerebellum. These two portions of the brain would suffer from degrees of restriction. The restriction would be muscle tension pulling the skull (the cranium, as you would know it) downward here, and placing pressure on those portions of the brain (as we have given).

Degrees of sluggish activity in the fluid that is in the lower portion of the brain itself will be felt as ache in the head. This particular difficulty would be brought on by disharmony within an entity - within the entity's values of what is right and what is wrong - and also in the action of omission or what can be considered a commission of action (either procrastination, or going against the self). Attitude will affect this difficulty in the neck and shoulder primarily as tension, and then indirectly (yet directly) in the low portion of the head itself, in the back.

In the next instance, you would find degrees of difficulty or blockage in the sinuses and affecting the chest regions and the lymph glands (paying attention to the nodes and anodes, you see). Here, a degree of pressure from the blockages in the lymph system can be felt. This would be readily seen in the sinus areas, above the eyes and below the eyes. Also you would find some degree of congestion in the inner ear region, and also some phlegm or fluid in the throat itself. This is strictly due to a degree of acidity within the body, causing the mucous conditions to be formed in the sinuses, and this poor drainage from the elimination system of the lymph results in pressure; headache felt in the regions we have just outlined.

Now you would find there are other reasons - growths or tumors that can be seen - and these would be felt as a degree of pressure internally, as if there is insufficient room in the skull for any interior pressure. This would be brought about by any swelling of the arteries also.

You would also find a condition that would cause the arteries to pulsate. They would first lose pressure (that is to say, the blood supply would be sluggish) and, as such, there would be a collapsing somewhat (minute in its measurement) of the arteries. Then, as the blood flow would be increased, there would be the expansion of these minute arteries in the brain and that expansion would cause a feeling or sensation of great internal pressure; headache, as you would know it.

These would be the general reasons for headache, not pertaining to any outrageous and rapid growth of cells or other indications of chemical imbalance in the body (although these would be legitimate causes for headache, as it is seen). In what would be described at this point, the headache results from several different physiological states, but these are connected to the attitudinal states also.

Please explain the causes of a migraine.

You would find this has a condition of pounding and, indeed, battering of the cells in the brain itself, causing what would be continual and almost unbearable pain; not necessarily to the brain itself (for, you see, the brain does not feel pain) but to what would be considered the nerve endings here, in what would be the corpus callosum or the central nervous system. This would be in conjunction with the arterial flow to the frontal lobes of the head itself.

You would find, in almost all instances, there is a degree of congestion in the large intestine, or the colon itself. This congestion would be in accord with what we have just given - a degree of toxins being assimilated back into the blood system, and being delivered to the brain itself. You would find degrees of sluggish activity within the peristaltic movement of the colon of polyps or other pockets within the colon, causing (or at least the opportunity to cause) this retention of the fecal matter within, and, as such, the absorption of the toxins and poisons back into the system, and, as such, the pain is felt in the head itself.

This is in a strictly difficult and dirty colon activity. The cleansing of the colon would right the situation almost immediately. The taking of olive oil in large doses would also aid in the cleansing of the colon.

However, you would find that, in some instances, it would be found that those who wear glasses tend to bring on a degree of migraine headache also. Now understand that vision is poor due to a degree of sluggish activity in the fine arteries and veins within the eyeball itself and, as such, this does fractionalize the light, and does blur the vision. Again, here, this would be seen by dirty arteries in the body itself, stemming originally from the colon's inefficiency to eliminate, and also the liver and the kidneys must take some of the blame. But in the body, it is dirty arteries that are affecting the vision. As such, the corrective glasses that would be worn could, from time to time, be incorrect, depending upon how much dirt (call it plaque, or scale, or sediment within the blood, as it would more likely be known) is in the arteries. As time would indicate, the vision would be impaired and this would cause a degree of imperfect focus and a degree of difficulty in depth perception. As such, impairment in the vision would cause the nerve endings themselves and the eye (which would be warring with the lens itself) to have signaled to the brain degrees of pain that would be felt primarily not in the visionary sense (as to behind the ear) but primarily in the upper region of the sinus and the temple area. This can be remedied, of course, by simply removing the eyeglass and allowing the eyes to rest. If this be the case, then the simple manner of correction would be to increase the lens upon the eye, or decrease the lens upon the eye, in order to allow the vision to be more perfect. However, if it tends to fluctuate, then the greater cleansing of the blood must occur, as this would then remove the sediment, toxins and plaque from the arterial. Then the eyes would not fluctuate so much in their fractionation of light, and the vision would be more perfect.

Now, you would also find for those who have difficulties in the low portion of the spine (the low back, at the pelvis, or what is known as the lumbar portion of the spine), whether it is a degree of curvature that is lately increased or enhanced from what it should be; or when there is a degree of compression upon the bones; or when there is a degree of rotation of the bones, here, this particular difficulty affects the brain itself, and brings about a degree of migraine pain. This would affect the elimination centers of the body, of course, but it would primarily affect the brain. By allowing the body to be massaged, or heat to be given to the lower portion of the body, or by using the services of the osteopath or the chiropractor about this portion of the body, then the migraine would be treated and could be eased.

In what would be the stomach itself, you would find any who have a tendency to be "in a stew" (or worry) tend to secrete digestive juices, and these digestive juices in the stomach and the intestinal tract tend to bring on a degree of imbalance in the chemical content of the body. You would find this is most common with those who suffer from insomnia (lack of sleep, you see, or the inability to gain sleep when it is desired or demanded). This portion would have a degree of increase in the enzymes in the activity of the stomach when it is considered to be bare or barren. As such, this chemical imbalance would bring about a degree of migraine, usually felt in the center portion of the head, primarily above the ear, on either side. This particular difficulty, of course, is directly psychosomatic in a true sense, in really bringing on the imbalance chemically in the body, causing to some degree, the secretion of adrenaline into the system, causing the affects of the adrenaline in the brain itself (restriction of blood flow, *et cetera*).

You would also find lack of oxygen in the blood as a cause of migraine headache itself. This is primarily found in those who would have a degree of tension within the mind, worry or anxiety, or hypoglycemia, pancreas difficulties, and also extending to the stomach wall. This would cause the diaphragm to pull tighter, tighter, tighter more to one side than the other, and this would pull the sheath beneath the skin more to one side than the other. This would affect, in turn, the thyroid and the pancreas. As such, the assimilation of oxygen into the blood would be very light. If there would be a sample of blood taken from any artery (not vein) and all oxygen content examined, it would be found this particular condition would show dramatic decrease of oxygen content. This would be the cause of the headache felt in the brain itself, for the migraine would be directly due to the brain screaming out for more fuel (for more oxygen, you see). And, as such, the brain, in conjunction with the nervous system, would cause the heart rate to be increased, and more blood would need to be pressured into the brain in order to assimilate more of the oxygen in the working of the brain, you see. However, the more blood that is pumped, the faster the heart. The faster the heart, the more the anxiety, the more the headache. The more the headache, the more blood is needed, and on and on in the circle it goes.

Any would need a little iodine in their diet to organically bring about a degree of control in low oxygen content, for it would begin to release the diaphragm itself. Now any can do the same with a degree of hydrotherapy or deep breathing exercises, to increase the oxygen content in the blood, yes; but also to begin to relax the diaphragm. Here, if the mind (which in most cases, usually, is a highly creative and imaginative mind) can be controlled, can be utilized, here, in a constructive manner, then this energy would not be wasted and the body would heal itself.

When one is aware of a migraine coming on, what may he or she do to prevent it?

As we have indicated here, depending upon the condition itself, yes, there are those that could be given. The enema can be given immediately. This would be given to relieve some of the condition of assimilation of toxins within the body itself. This can usually be felt at the stage when there is a beginning of the headache. But as there would be the enema given, there would be the ability for the body to eliminate more perfectly and cease the assimilation of the toxic substances back into the blood.

Also might be given would be a degree of alcohol (for those who can tolerate a degree of alcohol). This would tend to thin the blood and would be seen as a suppressant or tranquilizer, without side effects (for it is found in nature itself).

You would also find those who would eat of the slippery elm would begin to be affected positively in the degree of coating the stomach, in preventing increased worry symptoms (increasing the secretion of the digestive juices) as this would be protective against the stomach.

As there would be those who would visit the chiropractor or the osteopath, when they have a feeling of difficulty, primarily due to the low back pain or low back misalignment (as we have given) in conjunction with the migraine, there are those that can utilize the Coca-cola syrup; a teaspoon to a teaspoon-and-a-half in a glass of cool water, sipped slowly. This would begin to relax some of the body symptoms. This can be done in order to suppress the conditions as they would begin to come to the body.

However, those who suffer from these conditions of headache should engage in a program, as we have outlined, depending upon their specific cause for the headache in the first place, and then they would not feel it coming on, for it would not have the potential to come on the head itself, as a pain in the head; and, as such, it must be a preventative and a maintenance situation, rather than a curative one, as you would know it. See?

Pertaining to a diet, and the cleansing of the colon, those who would eat no artificial colors and no spicy foods, but would remain on a simple diet that would exclude sugar from the sugar bowl, and would be primarily of the vegetable and some of the meats (the fish, the fowl, or the lamb would be good, baked boiled or broiled) would align themselves more in their diet to that which would be helpful; that is to say an unsophisticated but not bland diet. There are many wonderful dishes that can utilized here, with a degree of sauces and preparations and combinations of the same.

Those who would keep the spine supple and straight would also be beneficial in preventing migraine. And those who would attempt to bring about a degree of improvement in their emotional states would lessen the probability of migraine; for, here, anger and also condemnation of another brings about a degree of pressure at the heart. Also worry over things that are out of the entity's control still brings on further the migraine itself. As there would be temperance, as there would be a middle-of-the-road attitude in the emotional states (that are the constructive and destructive forces in the body), then you would find this balance, this temperance eliminates the migraine itself.

In a general way, a balanced and nutritious diet, combined with a balanced and (you may call it) hopeful outlook in the mental and emotional states, in conjunction with proper body maintenance and lubrication (pertaining to the spine) will greatly reduce any migraine situation.

But understand the migraine is the warning. It is not in itself the problem. The problem is usually found elsewhere in the body; and, indeed, in the attitudinal states of the body and the mind, then this condition (or conditions) will be eliminated and the warning of headache or migraine will no longer persist, for the body will have righted itself, will it not?

Please give any herbs and/or other supplements that would be helpful also.

That which would be helpful would be a degree of vitamin supplements that could be taken here; in particular vitamin A and E. These would be beneficial. B-11 and B-12 can also be taken. These would be good just prior to (or just after) any form of attack of migraine or headache itself.

Grapes and grape juices should be taken on a regular, daily basis, either as a snack, or taken in what would be two ounces of grape juice with two ounces of water, fifteen to twenty minutes before food is ingested into the body. This would affect the thyroid, the pancreas, and, in turn, the bile to be secreted, and will allow for the lessening of the sluggish activity in the colon itself. We have given that olive oil should be taken; a spoonful or two daily. This would begin to keep the cleansing of the colon more perfect.

We would find alfalfa sprouts would also be most helpful to the body. Goldenseal can be taken. Burdock and mullein can be taken also, as teas or eaten (in some instances) raw (but we find it is better to take it of the tea itself, you see). Yellow mustard can be taken in the capsule. Castor oil, of course, would be helpful also. Garlic itself, cayenne pepper, and onion, to some degree (in some instances cooked, in others raw) would be helpful. These would be, in particular, in cleansing the blood. They would also be beneficial in reducing the headache in what would be a preventative mode. Raspberries can be taken also, and seen as a helpful and reductive form or treatment of migraine itself. Any of these would be helpful, as we see it.

Please give other foods and drinks that should be avoided for this condition.

Here, it would be food prepared with (you would call these) additives, spices, or artificial food colorings. For even this causes a degree of hyperactivity in some, you know; and, as such, the diet would best be more plain than it would be sophisticated. Salts and peppers could also be avoided. Those foods that tend to bring about the acidity in the body would be the plums, the pineapples, and the meats (the red meats in particular). Pork should be avoided, for it tends to congest the intestine itself and indeed the enzymes continue to thrive here, after there has been cooking, you see (these, again, affect the migraine, you see).

Do you have any further information or guidance on this subject?

Understand that pain in the body is a warning system. It is an indicator that there is something in the body. Pain in the head does not necessarily mean that the problem is in the head. It means the problem is stemming elsewhere, perhaps, in the body, and, as such, is affecting the pain. As we have indicated, in these different areas of the brain, it could relate to different portions of the body itself.

However, primarily speaking, headache is seen as high acid states in the body, combined with degrees of sediment (or toxins, as you would call it) in the blood, and these are felt in the head. But the indications all point to the blood itself, and the large intestine. If all these would be cleansed, both the blood and circulatory systems and the natural elimination system (the large colon) in conjunction (or in line) with the blood, it would allow for more perfection and the reduction of acidity within the body itself. For no virus or mucous condition can exist in a body that is not acid, but is more alkaline. See?

Make the body alkaline. Understand that the mind itself is not in control of the emotional states and a degree of humor or entertainment is most helpful to reduce the stress or tension felt in the muscles of the body. And as there would be a degree of humor brought into the life, there would be those secretions of platelets and other substances in the brain that would be seen as a healing mechanism to the body itself. See?

Pain in the head is a warning that there is difficulty in the body elsewhere, pertaining to both the physical as well as the mental and emotional states. Therefore, keep the emotions constructive. Seek the joy of life. Chase worry out of the house, and replace it with joyous expectation.

PART SEVEN
AILMENTS AND REMEDIES

Acid and Alkaline

Please comment on alkalinity and acidity in a body.

Each body possesses a line that would be perfectly balanced, and it is between the alkaline and the acidity within the system. Now, when a body is balanced perfectly, there is no disease within the body; it is perfectly healthy. But understand, the absence of disease within the body does not necessarily mean the body is healthy. However, any can test themselves to see if there is more acid or alkaline, and which side of the line they are on. Take the litmus paper itself. Place it under the tongue. If it turns pink or red, there is too much acid within self. If it turns blue, there is more alkaline. The darker the blue, the more alkaline.

Now a body which is more acid than alkaline tends to allow the viruses and the mucous conditions to exist, breed and multiply more easily within it; for the acidity within the system allows, harbors, incubates these virus and mucous conditions (for these are exceptionally good breeding grounds for the viruses and micro-organisms). However, a body that is more alkaline than it would be acid (above the center line, you see) cannot - repeat, cannot - allow virus and mucous conditions to be formed within it; for the alkaline destroys the virus and mucous condition, the micro-organisms, you see.

It is, therefore, more feasible for anyone to have the body more alkaline than acid. Now, each body would fluctuate as a pendulum would swing from one to the other, but attempting to maintain a balance within the two states would be perfect. Very few can do this, due to the thought patterns and the dietary habits. However, as they would attempt to keep the body more alkaline, they would enjoy a dis-ease-free body, rather than one that is susceptible to any and all communicable and virus conditions; for the body would seemingly be protected against them. That which is without the body cannot be harmed within the body, if the body is prepared.

Each body is constantly, through the assimilation of food and water, vacillating between these two extremes. To keep the body slightly more alkaline than acidic is to ward off viral and bacterial influences which cannot exist within the alkaline state. Bacterial influences simply cannot exist in a state that is alkaline; it is somewhat poisonous to them. If you would examine those who are somewhat long-lived, you would find that usually their water source has a predominant alkalinity content.

As such, acidic states within the body tend to promote viral and mucous conditions. A sick body, one that is filled with mucous, ammonia or other forms of mucous, would largely be seen (if there would be given a pH test) to be high in the acidic, or high towards the acidic levels. By quickly adapting and bringing the body towards the alkalinity, the body would repair and heal itself, for the viral and bacterial conditions would be reduced, and then eliminated from the system.

Does a relationship exist between the pH of the mouth mucous and susceptibility to colds?

Yes, the relationship exists, but it is not that it can be proven in all conditions. For colds, you see, are indications of stress within the mind and body of an entity. When the body becomes stressful, it begins to hold onto toxins. It begins to produce mucous in the lungs, the sinus, and nasal passage-way. As such, this build-up occurs. As we have given, Man is more than a physical machine. It is a mental, emotional and physical entity, and, as such, all three must be seen to be balanced; and, as such, the pH and the cold can then be rationalized. For when the body itself has more phosphorous and the acid within itself (and a degree of calcium also) it would be more susceptible. But until then, it is in a mental state. And this is where the confusion is taking place.

With reference to acid and alkaline bounds, would you please discuss a diet suitable for most people?

In that which would be more to the alkaline in the diet, it is true that the body swings from alkaline to acid as a pendulum in its different states. But here, eat of the lowly vegetable, for the diet should he approximately eighty to eighty-eight percent vegetables. These should be grown in the vicinity in which the body resides and be of the freshest variety. The fruits would also be taken. Some fruits (such as plums) contain too much acid and should be held to a minimum, but the body should be more to the alkaline state. For as there is alkaline increase (as you would call it) over the half-way mark more to the alkaline, you see, no virus or mucous condition can survive in a body that is more alkaline. For acid states allow a breeding ground for the viruses and mucous conditions; alkaline destroys the mucous and virus conditions within the body. The diet should be mainly of the vegetable; partly cooked or eaten raw. This would be best.

How can two different types of foods such as baking soda and then vinegar produce the same alkaline reaction?

Indeed, understand the sugars that are taken into the body turn into the acids. That which would be acids taken into the body - such as citric acids - turn into that which would be the alkaline. It is the body's conversion, the baking soda and the apple cider vinegar. It is the body's own process and how it uses the chemical reactions within the stomach, how it affects the same.

Acid Reflux

Why has the condition known as "acid reflux," which was unknown a generation ago, reached epidemic proportions?

It would be considered something else to start with. There would be considered such things as indigestion, and, along the way, Swedish bitters, or bitters given after a meal would be one way of dealing with this digestive difficulty. Let us say it is more like a mis-diagnosis, or it was mis-termed. However, due to certain investigative procedures, there can now be seen the stomach twisting or being pushed upward, and, as the surgeons become more skillful at removing the gallbladder, and becoming aware of the sedentary forces (that normally would sit in the gall, now sitting in the intestine) their investigation has gone beyond this and found that the digestive fluids, which normally would be moving through the body, are now pooled up in the stomach. In the past, this would be for any who would indicate the acidic irritations; they would also have been diagnosed as, perhaps, having stomach ulcers. It is a clarity of the diagnosis situation in the body function that now there would seem to be an epidemic, but, in fact, it is just something that is now more known and provable than it has been, in the past (that is, from the diagnosis perspective).

However, what is going on in the minds of people most of the time these days? Fear! Fear of death, fear of loss, fear of sickness, fear of disease. Each day, more and more. Those who have left the farm and have migrated to the city have, to some degree, lessened their resistance to disease by moving into a lesser-challenging environment in the city than in the country. In so doing, they have also left their ability to adapt or be strong in the greater outdoors. Now, they are also moving away from a sedentary and more peaceful lifestyle, to one that is filled with more stresses; in particular, timetables and deadlines. The clock rules the life. Their pressures internally (in their mind) are constantly increasing, and what is held in the mind or the thinking is readily connected to the conditions in the stomach.

Therefore, when the mind is constantly on edge, constantly being challenged, constantly being bombarded with fearful thoughts, news, and information, it is only natural that individuals would live in a heightened state of anxiety or fear. The body responds in kind, and fear tends to make the organs (the stomach at least), of course, function overly so, and digestive fluids or acidic levels rise in the body, for the body is always churning, as the mind is always churning. See?

Digestion is an acidic process of breaking down whatever is put into the stomach. Now, outside of this acid consumption (so to speak) the tissues further down from the stomach are not readily prepared to handle the high degree of levels of acid that are produced and are flushed (shall we say) along the intestinal tract. The body is capable, to some degree, but is not capable of this forever! Stopping the production of acidic fluids building up over these digestive processes would be the place to start, and the place to start this is in the mind; that the mind is not constantly churning. The mind is not like a seagull, aimlessly flying, looking for more garbage to put into its gullet. The mind must be distracted, from time to time (we speak of playtime). Therefore, as a distraction occurs , the body can divert its attention, its focus, and a feeling of wellness, humor, love, or play readily ceases the production of the destructive tendencies of the adrenals and the stomach (and the secretions in the glands themselves). When one is in a state of anxiety, they are in a state of fear; this is a flight-or-fight mentality. No one can be (nor is it designed that they should be) in this state of mind for long periods of time.

Acupuncture

There has been a movement or direction in the field of acupuncture to replace the traditional needles with electronic pulses. As you see it, are these pulses or probes as effective as the traditional needles?

It depends on the applicator and the amount of stimulation through the pulse. We would find that they are about equal, but the post or needle put into the acu-point can be considered more specific to that point; whereas the other, the electrical, tends to broadcast a little, as we see it. But, in essence, we find the stimulation of the needle would be similar to the electrical pulse, you see. We have little or no difference as we would compare them.

Would you please discuss how acupuncture differs from reflexology?

Reflexology uses nerve endings in the feet, but there are other nerve endings throughout the entirety of the body - entry and exit points. These could be seen as whorls of energy located in and around different points within the body. Acupuncture (or acupressure) stimulates these meridians at their entry and exit points. Reflexology stimulates, in groups, the area that is being affected or reflected, corresponding to the foot and the part of the body. Generally speaking, reflexology affects a specific area; acupressure or acupuncture reflects a specific area.

In the study of kinesiology, the entire nervous system is linked. It is one massive communication process system. The flows through the nerves themselves can be greatly affected and, as such, affect the brain and the organs simultaneously. However, the function of the nervous system is not understood by many. There is part knowledge here and there. Examine the points on the meridians or (as you would call it) the acupuncture / pressure points of the body, and examine the feet, and you would find energy that would enter and exit from these points; for the body is an electrical-magnetical and chemical combination (concoction, you might call it). Reflexology deals with the electrical-magnetical impulses. Acupuncture would deal primarily with the electrical application; acupressure, electrical and magnetical.

Stimulating the endocrine system tends to cause the secretion of hormones, enzymes, in and around the various organs and systems, for no part of the body is an island unto itself. This is seen to by the nervous system. If you have a headache, pressure on the big toe would seem to be ludicrous, yet let us assure you that the big toe, massaged and soothed, would remove the headache, for the body is connected; it is within itself, separated and yet whole. Massage the toe and the head feels better. Where you would doubt (and we find there would be some), burn the finger with a match. Notice the perspiration on the soles of the feet. Now, is the body not connected? Is it not affected? Indeed it is, for pain would reach out though the entirety of the form, not just the finger. We could go on and we could write volumes and volumes and volumes of the nervous system function.

Addiction and Drug Abuse

Please discuss drug abuse (prescription as well as illegal) that affects the minds and bodies of many in our society?

Illegal chemicals and influences, those on the black market (at the street level, as you would know it) are becoming (and have become over the past) quite predominant in the usage and provocation of usage, to those who would be youngsters as well as adults. There are also those individuals who have acceptance and control over prescribed medication or drugs (what may be called hard drugs).

As such, there is a tendency, for the frailty of the human is weak, to become involved in those drugs that would be somewhat mood conditioning or to bring about emotional states. As such, when an entity is stressful, they tend to dampen the aggressive spirit and make it somewhat benign or harmonious. As one who would be somewhat depressed, it can speed up the metabolism and allow an increase in what would be the production or out-goingness of the entity.

As such, as one begins to affect their physiological and emotional states by intake of these concentrated forms, then there becomes dependency, and, as such, a selective dependency upon those particular conditions that are sought; and, as such, one loses their will-power and becomes enslaved to that which is known as drugs.

The abuse, in either case, comes into that which would prey upon the condition in the human form to avoid, alter, or change their perception of an experience or that which would be an experience about to take place. As such, it is an immediate way to avoid a situation. Some would use these as they would be somewhat frail, nervous, or tense, in order to avoid that which would be considered the condition of uneasiness that they would feel or sense.

As such, all tend to damper the spirit, tend to alter the physiological as well as the mental and emotional states in any entity who abuse these conditions. They selectively bring about feelings of gratification to the physical form. Abuse of drugs is a selective process in the beginning to bring about moods, feelings, or conditions of pleasure. Some utilize these drugs in an abusive manner to bring about a feeling of euphoria; some, a sexual sense or feeling of sexual gratification. No matter how simple it may be seen, the ideal is to alter the present status or the present prescribed status and bring about a degree of prescribed change. This is done artificially through those who would utilize the drug; for this causes the changes within the physiological states, producing the psychological changes that are perceived by the user, you see. Therefore, abuse is an attempt to maintain an artificial emotion or state.

Understand some drugs are helpful here, in bringing the body a degree of correction in the physical states, as well as the mental and emotional states, thereby allowing the spiritual influence or effect to come about. However, to the abusive manner, you would find here that those who abuse the drug tend to push themselves into artificial states of ecstacy, rather than those who would, through a natural process, bring about a natural state of ecstacy; a time when all is in harmony in the mental, in the emotional and in the physical states. Only then, when all three are in harmony, can there be touched upon ecstacy of the soul which would be perceived as pure love.

This status can be artificially-induced temporarily by those who would utilize those things that would heighten their artificial acceleration or ascension to the soul level, or to those dimensions that would be between the soul and the self, to touch upon the true sense of love. Those who would use and abuse these drugs would not attain (nor would they be released in order to obtain) those natural states. The affect of the soul would be to separate, rather than to enhance. On occasion, it is acceptable to utilize the senses and those items that would be promoting relaxation in order for the soul and the flesh to become one. However, in most instances, it tends to be a road block.

Can the obvious damaging effects from drug abuse be corrected?

In some cases, yes; in some, no. In most cases, however, depending upon the usage of the drug, that which can be related to heart rate, blood pressure, kidney taxing, bladder, and the reproductive centers being affected by abuse - all can be, to some degree, remedied. But in the cerebral, where there has been the negating of cells in the brain itself, in most cases, this cannot be regenerated or reassociated to other levels (or other states of mind, as you would call it).

How may an individual overcome the influence of the drug dependency?

First and foremost, it is to understand that, within themselves, they have created a dependency. This dependency has usually been to artificially avoid a circumstance or situation. As such, they must then reverse themselves in their path and seek out what originally was the reason for the drug abuse. As this would be conquered, then it would be helpful in order to regain ground that has been lost.

However, those who would "go cold turkey," you would find this would be the harshest and most abusive method of attempting to revert or cleanse the self; although it would be the quickest method, we find, again, it is the most severe. As such, it would be necessary for any to attempt to reduce, gradually, the abusive amounts that they are engaged in. As such, you would call this weaning themselves from the drug, if they are in that condition or state and are able to do so.

For instance, let us use the cigarette as a method. One uses twenty cigarettes per day and they decide to stop using these cigarettes. Then they use fifteen in a day and, for a week or two, maintain this level. Then, after that, they go to ten. Again, a week or two passes with the maintenance of ten a day, and then they cut it back to five. And from five to one. And from one to none. As such, a period of time has elapsed and they have weaned themselves from this condition or use. The body has also been given time to make chemical adjustments, as well as other energy levels and conditions (you would call these nerves, as well as circulatory adjustments) to this particular condition; and, as such, they can leave it alone. With the will power, yes, with a degree of compassion, the entity has weaned itself from the use of the drug, and this can be done for many that are termed soft drugs; what you would call marijuana, or cannabis, and other items that are used, such as hashish itself or hash oil.

However, to the hard drugs leading up to heroin itself, the method of cold turkey must not be attempted. This would be most devastating to the body and would be like opening the self up, removing all veils of protection, and then having a locomotive drive over the self. No chance! As there would be the reduction, bit by bit, then a substitute (methadone or other chemical) must be used here, in order to bring about the less taxing forms upon the body, and allow the body to gain ground. Only after this usage and the continued weaning from this that would take some time (again, depending upon the amount of abuse that the entity has given itself), by bringing about a degree of calmness and harmony can there ultimately be the curtailment of the use or abuse of drugs (as you would know it) that are called hard. Both matters would work.

However, the decision to overcome the drug must first be in the mind and the use of the will; for the will is a far greater source of power than anyone usually gives it credit for. As there is the understanding of the will power, then there is understanding of true power. Overcoming any condition in the body is possible.

As one who would begin to withdraw, by entering the states of meditation, they could come in contact with their center, the core, or the soul (as you would know it). Then, rather than being isolated, there is an effect that self is working with self in harmony on the subconscious levels; the states that can be the controlling states of the involuntary muscles and organs of the body. And, as such, this would speed up the process for the body to unlearn the dependency upon the drug and bring about a dependency upon its own usages of chemicals in order to bring about a normality in the mental, emotional and physical states.

Thereby, for any who attempts to engage in a withdrawal program, it is best not to go cold turkey; better to be loving and kind to the physical body and attempt to taper off. This would not fault the systems, and would give the body some chance to regain, constructively, its status, prior to the use of the drugs. Then there must be the attempt to conquer the condition that brought about the abuse of drugs in the first place. This would be a different matter. However, it must be overcome, else there will be the slipping back into the dependency, artificially avoiding the problem.

Please give suggestions for family and friends of a drug user that would be helpful to understand and assist him or her.

Upon the first realization that a friend or family member is abusing drugs, understand that they are trying, first of all, to escape from something. It may be the weather, the responsibilities of life, it may even be meeting new people. As such, there is something lacking from the character or personality of the individual. Do not condemn or abuse, coerce, or otherwise argue with that one who is abusing the drug; for, you see, they are abusing the drug in the first place because they have some perceived weakness in their own character and they use it as an escape mechanism.

The first action is to be a friend, not to worry about the abuse of drugs, or that which they would do to themselves, or to fear for their lives (as suicide); but be their friend. Be there, time, and time, and time, and time, and time again, when they need you to pick them up, bail them out, or protect them from themselves perhaps. But be there, always willing. It may take ninety-nine times before they come around, but they will come around. Others may take nine times and they will come around.

Therefore, it is necessary to not condemn and to be patient in the handling of those family members or friends. Do not become self-righteous, or do not appoint the self as the protector and overseer for your friend or family member. But, rather, be encouraging and attempt to be helpful. Wait until they come to that period, that point in the life that they, themselves decide that they wish no longer to be enslaved to the drug. As this would be done, then you will have the greater opportunity to help and the higher probability to see that they would be helped and maintain a status of drug-free (or, as you would call it, no abuse).

As you would be there, again, it would require a degree of consistency and discipline, in order to be there at their worst times and help them overcome or go through those circumstances that would be related to drug abuse. But be there, patient and ever willing. This would be the best way to approach the situation. As they would be helpful (that is to say, in disclosing what they are attempting to run from) then attempt to help them, through a method of conversation and support, never letting them down, although they might let you down. When they come to the state of believability that you do genuinely care, then the door will begin to open, and they will allow you to see within themselves and, as such, the problem will ultimately be bared and they will overcome themselves. They, themselves must overcome. You will do nothing but give support and reflect that which they, themselves would be able to understand or recognize that is taking place within themselves in the first place.

Another, yet faster method would be to take a photograph or, even better, video movies of them in their stupor or their exposed, exaggerated, abusive state and, as such, the viewing of the same will allow them to come to some conclusions of just how terrible they look, and how enslaved they have become. This would be best given to one who is willing to accept how they look and appreciate. Do not force it on any, else they will, for spite, refuse to accept that which they see. This can be done only in sessions, or group sessions, or therapies, or those who would be the afflicted person willing to overcome their condition. This would be seen as a secondary, yet primary state to self-awareness.

As s a friend or relative, as one does feel for their friend, your heart goes out to them; understand it is they, themselves that have put themselves in the position of abuse in the first place. If you can find why, then you will have done much. If you can attempt to help them understand why, then you will have done much more. But do not force or coerce; it will only drive them into deepening the states of resistance. See?

Be supportive of them, and continue in your own life, not that you become greatly involved, and not that you would allow them to perceive your feeling sorry for them, but do so at a fifty-fifty level. Go fifty per cent of the way. If they come their fifty per cent, then continue. If they do not show signs of interest, then leave for the time, always bearing in mind there will come a day in which they will come about.

The abuse usually (as we have given) stems from some need. If you can meet the need and be aware of it, then you will have the greater opportunity of expediency. Give them much love and much attention, even if they do not return it (even if they are abusive).

Pray for them. The prayer should be: "Dear Lord, I pray for my son (or my daughter, mother, father, or friend) that they will come to the understanding of what they are attempting to show themselves, and the sooner the better. Amen." This prayer, with visualization of sending love, with the demonstration of love, of tolerance, of faith, of patience is the best manner that one can help. One can help only when the afflicted person is willing to reach out and receive it. If it is not that way, if you do not offer help and they receive it, by attempting to receive it on their own, then you would be considered waste.

Therefore, reach out and attempt to grasp that one who is in need. But allow them the opportunity to remain dignified and to keep their pride, in order that they might reach out and accept your help and, as such, use it to alleviate themselves on a permanent basis, see.

Any who abuse drugs tend to allow themselves to be put in situations in which there would be satisfaction to the carnal or the physical, but any who attempt to overcome the drug, to bring about a degree of improvement in themselves have surely taken the spiritual path; for temptation is the root of all evil. Execution of that temptation is demonstration of weakness; restraint from that temptation is a demonstration of strength. For the strong do not condemn the weak; for the weak reach out for the strong.

As such, understand that drug abuse and the gratification of the physical self is nothing more serious, more difficult than any temptation or any sin that inflicts others in the world. It can be overcome, through will, through desire, through prayer. As it is overcome, the challenge has been met and the soul can win. For overcoming self is the greatest task any individual can attempt to take. Those who do it deserve many compliments, for it takes super-human strength to overcome their weakness. See?

Ajahuasca

Would you recommend the sacred drink Ajahuasca as a way to expand the mind?

It would be similar to the use of peyote. We would find that any mind-enhancing stimulant would be temporarily beneficial, but it would not be suitable. It would all be artificial (so to speak), in the end, for the intention is to allow the mind to merge and advance to the higher dimensions without breaching its consciousness with intoxicants or hallucinogenic substances, you see. For this, in a way, limits the ability to open the door yourself (so to speak), to view the higher realms, through the electrical-magnetical stimulation in the frontal lobes and the pineal and thalamuses. To some degree, it can allow the mind to sense a reality beyond the reality created, expected, and lived in (or the illusion of life, as you would call it). It does work in getting past these levels, allowing the self to clearly see the dimensions you would call spiritual, and the beings that would re-

side on these frequencies, or levels, or dimensions. But you would be like a drunkard; at peace and able to see things, but the trust or the clarity would not be evident as the influence of the personality would adulterate what is being seen or created in the mind's eye (as would any such hallucinogenic or artificial, provocative substance).

Now, in small amounts, or used initially (once or twice perhaps), it would open the door and show the mind that there are other dimensions. But if one is aware of the same, one need not have a door-man, or an assistant do the things that the self is capable of doing: peering into the great portal of the Akashic, or looking through the present moment to an array of time, past, present, or future, with detachment, of course, setting aside the personality and the daily distractions.

Allergies and Food Sensitivities

To what extent do people's allergies or sensitivities to food contribute to their ill health?
To the same extent as their thinking does (as you would know it), for allergies are nothing more than the body being unaware of the irritant within itself. As it is irritating itself, then it only has itself to blame. Most allergies are caused by a fear embedded within the thinking. Fears of cats or dogs cause one to sniffle, sneeze, and itch when they are close; for it is a nervous reaction buried deep within the mind that emanates as physical discomfort. Once they leave the animal alone, there is no illness, there is no allergy. It is through the mind and the states of the mind that allergenic conditions, in most cases, affect the physical body and, therefore, set up disease within the body, to that extent, it affects.

Alzheimer's Disease

It was once said by this Source that if you would examine the cause of Alzheimer's disease as a pie, aluminum would be the largest slice of that pie. What are the other factors?

These would be other substances taken into the body and maintained or retained in the body (lead, for instance). Chemicals that are primarily associated with farming, especially pesticides that are both used at the farmers' level (in other words, where there would be open exposure and breathing in of these chemicals or pesticides) and also pesticides at the consumer level that would be ingested when the fruit is not properly washed, you see, the pesticide is taken in and builds up in the body. You would find also certain degrees of chemical from aspects of pets, you see. Whether it would be their aroma or their scent or the smell of the animal, but it is largely the oil and influences of pets - whether it would be their droppings or urine or whether it would be from their coat or their saliva. These can affect the body, if taken in the form or body itself. They may cause other conditions in the body, you see.

What can one do to lessen the risk of contracting Alzheimer's Disease?

One should be mindful of what they put into the body itself; what they would take in through the gates of the body, you see. All food should be properly prepared when there would be fruit involved. Washing should be done thoroughly. Scrubbing of grapes, for instance, would be good. Remove the white powder or what has adhered to the fruit itself. If fruits are to be taken in, one should be knowledgeable of where and how they were grown. For remember, what is put into the root of the plant is developed and stored in the fruit of the plant. As there would be the washing of the fruits that would have sprayed-on pesticides, if there would be detoxification of the blood through chelation therapy or other attempts to purify the blood (this can be from oxygen therapies through to more aggressive blood cleansing, as chelation would be, directly with intravenous effect) and then in the middle ground would be the use of foods that would be blood-cleansing here, usually the body can survive when fresh fruits and vegetables are given to itself (and they can be, on a regular basis, ingested and they would remove the sedentary forces from the blood). Teas and herbs that would be blood cleansing would be also given. This would be seen as any tea made from a spiky or furry plant or root, you see. And, as such, this would be a good rule of thumb, you see.

But the body should also engage physically its natural ability to cause the body to perspire, either through exercise or though a sauna or steam room, you see. Allow the body to eliminate through the skin, for the skin is an organ and it is designed to eliminate, you see. Also, it would not hurt to invert the body or to have blood into the head itself on a regular basis. This can be done by inverting the body on an angle board, or placing the lower end of the body higher than the upper part of the body. Proper manipulation of the neck, either through neck roll exercises, massaging the neck and shoulder muscles, or traction (pulling the head a little away from the shoulders), all would enhance blood flow into the brain. The oxygen which is able to be extracted from the blood (and therefore is good for the brain) allows it to function more correctly. Also the blood is able to remove sedentary forces that are found in the soft tissues of the brain more readily. With increased pressure, by inverting the body, the arteries and veins in the brain expand and contract more normally, and this would be very good for the body and for the thinking as well, for it would enhance the electrical activity within the brain itself, you see.

Take care of the teeth as well. The teeth should not have mercury within them, of course; but also the body should have within itself good teeth. For as the teeth are removed, this causes difficulties, or brain cell cessation, or damage, you see. There is a direct correlation between the teeth and the brain, you see. As such, good teeth, good gum activity definitely reduces the amount of difficulty in the brain tissue, you see.

Encourage more blood circulating through the cranium or the cavity (the skull, you see). This can be done by a variety of ways. Laying the body down, massaging it, giving it traction, putting it on vibrating beds, whatever. By head and neck exercises, by heating the body up and cooling the body off, by placing it in whirlpool baths, steam rooms or saunas, by swimming exercises, or by simply inverting the body on an angle or inverting it one hundred and eighty degrees (depending on the capability of the person, you see), all would prevent mental illness, leading up to the condition of Alzheimer's, you see. The brain tends to be a little bit of a sponge for metal and toxic chemicals, you see (as does the liver and the spleen).

Animated Ash

One of the least explored remedies from the Edgar Cayce readings was the ingestion of an-

imated ash which was made in a very special way, according to directions in the reading, and required skill followed by UV light. Is this still useful for cancer today?

This would have an effect upon cancers in the liver, and in the stomach; also upon the eyes and somewhat upon brain disorders or cancers, you see. The effect here is to alter or change the soft tissue, especially what would be a brain tumor. The tumors would look like paper rolled up tightly, see, and the light and ash would have a tendency to dissolve the paper-thin tumor itself. It works best on tumors that are like paper (or very thin) that have a sheet-like effect or look. For those that are more like a ball tumor, that would be a hard core, it does not tend to work so effectively. But as we see it, it has a disintegrative effect as it eats away at these thin layers of tissue.; again, more to the brain tumor than any others. The light and the activated influences of the ash act like a disintegrating substance, see, almost like an acid in the body.

What percentage of cancers would this successfully treat?

As we have given, those that are like wafers, or that would come rolled up like a newspaper, or like sheets of paper rolled up, see? Any of these forms, it tends to work best. Therefore, a small but significant amount of cancers.

Is it correct that the UV light portion of the treatment is not to be put onto the tumor, but onto the spine?

As we observe this, we would find that this would be somewhat effectual in both areas. However, if it is put on the softer tissues, as we have given, it does not appear to be given directly to the tumor or wafers or wafer-like tumors. Therefore, affecting the nerve system, it would appear to be the best placed on the spine itself, see? Affirmative.

Apple Cider Vinegar

Apple cider vinegar is being touted as a cure-all. Is it possible that it is being over-used by the general public?

Apple cider vinegar should be used infrequently; perhaps less commonly than expected. It is better when condensed to a powder form and used to cleanse the colon itself. The acidic levels of the vinegar can easily bring about movement or improvement in elimination, and help to remove congestion from the colon. As it is used in the morning with a little honey or water, it acts as almost what you might call an astringent here; but, in fact, it is not. It is a good tonic to the body, but it should not be taken in abundance, but rather sparingly, you see. Taken with apples, it helps in removing toxins that live and hide within the kidney. Primarily, it tends to counteract virus and bacterial content in the body, and helps to direct their physical removal from the body itself. It can also be used to force the body to vacate the colon. We also find it has an ability to remove or affect viral and bacterial conditions such as hepatitis and herpes itself, you see.

Should apple cider vinegar be used in conjunction with the apple diet?

It can be used in conjunction with this, in the morning especially; yes.

Apple Fast

Please summarize the apple fast recommended by Edgar Cayce as well as this Source.

Eating apples for three days and large tumblers of water, along with the apples each and every day. A spoonful of olive oil may be taken on the first and second day, and, on the third day, about an ounce of the oil as well. This would act as a catalyst with the kidney and remove imperfections and impurities from the blood.

Could you explain how this works?

Apples alone for three days causes, in a sponge-like way, the ability to pull out of the body a degree of toxins and sedentary forces. They also tend to stimulate the kidney and remove toxins from the kidney and the liver. Raw apples act as a cleansing agent, working in harmony with the kidney, spleen, bladder, liver, and pancreas. They also affect the hormonal structure, and they do affect the bile secreted in the body as well. They activate it, you might say. They bring the elements of the body's purification system, especially the urinary, to the forefront. They remove disease-bearing material, especially that which has been trapped in the cavities of the colon itself, especially in the ascending portion.

Arteriosclerosis

Can you please comment briefly on the cause of arteriosclerosis and the best focus of treatment?

To some degree we have touched upon this, the hardening of the artery. Both the artery is blocked, and plaque is allowed to adhere to the wall of the artery. The blood flow is restricted, and the artery wall itself becomes thick and loses its elasticity. It is no longer supple, although the body (as you would bend the arm) would still bend the artery, and it would simply not curtail blood flow to the lower part of the limb.

However, in order to keep the artery functioning correctly, the diet or intake into the body of all foods and all things that would be taken into the body should be balanced, or limits put on desires, so that there is not an imbalance of any particular food or any particular thing in the body; but rather there is a balance within the body of all things coming into it. Those things that would be taken into the body as a cleansing agent are incorporated into the routine of the body itself. Again, washing the body on the outside; it is very helpful if the body is washed on the inside as well. To the arteries, washing the same can be done by those elements that are put into it. For remember, the blood carries all things about the body. Only the lymphatic system (which can be considered as a parallel circulatory system) carries things within it like unto the artery itself. Therefore, the herbs or the teas that would be blood cleansing should always be taken or maintained. The body should be given of heat and cold to expand and contract the muscle and the artery. The plaque in the body can be removed if there is proper exercise, and what is given to the body would not be high in animal meats or products, you see, and that the green vegetable or the lowly vegetable is taken on a regular basis.

However, plaque-removing herbs should be taken (and/or chemicals, if they are necessary) but, most importantly, the body should always be taxed, physically. It is good to work the body so that it becomes tired each day. The extremes of lowering and increasing the blood pressure internally by a natural means is very good for the arteries that they would not harden. For any who cause the body to perspire for a length of time causes the temperature to go way up and the blood to flow outward from the artery to the smaller arteries or capillaries, out to the finer arteries that would cause the redness on the skin to occur or appear. This will allow fresh oxygen to be distributed to the extreme of the artery itself. This, therefore, will keep the artery itself better or more flexible and longevity will occur. See?

Arthritis

See also Cherries

Why has arthritis reached epidemic proportions in the United States?

Primarily it is the lack of taking water into the body. It is the poor diet we speak of (the North American's diet); the affluent, you see. It is the introduction of food that has been processed; what has been put into a box, or can, or frozen. The food value has gone way down, you see, and there is a difficulty in the body extracting what would be a balanced form. For food should be of the freshest variety and grown in the vicinity or region in which the body resides. However, with the physical form becoming less and less active, an imbalanced diet, usually higher in saturated fats, and improper combination of foods, and sugar, fat, and salt in high proportions, then the body naturally becomes more lopsided (shall we say) in its ability to function. The body cannot function without proper fuel taken into it. The body is battling exaggerated amounts of sugar and fat. Compared with the inactivity, then this, in conjunction with anger, fear, financial woes, depression, loneliness and other anxieties of the society, the natural output (of course) would be for the body to be imbalanced.

Anger is a primary emotion to be considered, here, that triggers the arthritic conditions in the body. For understand what is manifested in the body is first held in the mind, and the emotions are both the constructive and destructive forces in the body. As there is much anger in the world and there is much fear in the world, and as the world is more stressful, naturally there would be the increase of the disease or dis-easements that would affect the body. Anger causes the muscles to clench, the teeth to grit, knees and shoulders and elbows to grit.

Understand that this particular ailment is nothing more than irritation at the bones, at the joints. For here, you will find that dis-ease in the joints of any human body (arthritis itself) tends to be an irritation or a reddening (an infection, you may call it) taking place at the bones itself, in the joints.

Understand that there is a degree of substance or (as you would call it) toxins, secretions, or sediment that the body itself does store in these most suitable places, into the small joints between the fingers and the toes, into the larger joints in the ankles, the knees and the hips, and in the shoulders and the elbows; also (of course) into the neck downward here, through the spine to the pelvis itself. Every nook and cranny that is at the joints, you would find is a suitable place for the body to store irritants, toxins, and waste materials. For here, they can be placed on a shelf (so to speak) out of the way from the blood vessels and from the most important organs. Unable to secrete or eliminate from itself these toxins and waste substances (as physical congress), then the body does the next best thing in order to protect the heart, liver, kidneys, lungs, thyroid, pancreas, stomach, and upward into the brain itself; by taking these substances and placing them, even sealing them within different joints.

As this would be seen, the joint is but a ledge, and waste material is placed upon the ledge. It tends to adhere and harden into the bone itself and encase the joint itself. As more waste material is subsequently placed in this, in an irregular fashion, you have what could be considered rheumatoid or that which would continue to enlarge as rheumatism (arthritis, you see) and continued here, into bursitis. As such, you would find that the joints themselves tend to swell, and as they tend to swell, they are sometimes misaligned from one joint to the next, due to the constant compacting, stuffing, and placement of these waste substances; so much so that, at first, there is the restriction in the movement of the joint and a little stiffness is evident; very little pain is seen.

As it continues, as the body continues to eliminate secondarily the toxin and the waste material in these cracks and joints of the body, there continues to grow within the body more pain through the manipulation of the joint, until eventually the finger that has the arthritis between the first and second joint can find itself greatly warped or twisted, pushed out of shape, causing severe pain. The same pain is felt as if one would grab the forefinger and twist a corkscrew or attempt to make a fifteen or twenty degree bend in it, at the joints. Slowly and steadily this does occur, causing severe pain, severe difficulty.

Of course, loss of mobility in the joint itself occurs, and, as such, loss of the dexterity in the hand and, indeed, other usages of the limbs of the body, you see. As it would continue to deteriorate in the body (say, in the spine itself) even the restriction at the cord could cause, in some cases, paralysis. But in most instances, it is simply that the body is irritated as an irritation of the bones, at which the joints are adjacent here.

This would be a description and, to some degree, an understanding of arthritic conditions itself. It is the waste substances not being placed out of the body but, rather the body's own protection for removing these harmful substances from the vital organs in the body itself, you see; and, as such, there is the arthritis condition seen here in the joints, in the bones; for it carries with it arthritic pain, yes, but also the dis-ease or destruction of the very bone itself in the joint, you see.

What can individuals do to overcome this condition and attempt to restore themselves to more perfect health?

It would be to first understand that the mind is the builder, the mind is the way. The mind is, and has been, that which is seen in the physical body in the present: the master of the illness, or the disease, or the health in the physical body. Very seldom, you know, is the disease first contacted in the body, and then the attitude or state of mind of the entity changed to cause the illness. It is usually that the state of mind or the attitude is first that which is held in the mind and, as such, the illness or adversity in the body simply manifests around that attitude.

To understand arthritis is to understand it is a stiffening dis-ease or discomfort in the body. Any who are stiff in their mind, any who are guilty of rigid thinking - unyielding - then they have a tendency to find their body growing in rigidity, see. As one would be extremely critical or stubborn of others, and hold onto their judgmental natures, then this form of rigid thinking tends to overspill into the body itself. For you see, nothing ever thought or any function of the mind does not isolate itself. For with every thought there is a physiological response.

The puritans, for instance, those that would be the judgmental, the righteous who proclaim themselves as self-righteous, all have this and are guilty of arthritis itself. As they would attempt to be more flexible in their minds, their words and their deeds, then they would find that the conditions in the body could relinquish, you see; and, as such, the irritation at the bones could dissipate (yea, even disappear).

However, that which could be considered organic to aid the difficulties: it is best to understand that there are conditions in the body that can be set up, that do affect the physical states. For instance, through the eyes in the daylight hours, there is absorbed degrees of ray from the sun. These ultra violet rays, or a portion of the sunlight that is taken in through the eyes tends to stimulate the thalamus, hypothalamus, pituitary and pineal sections in the brain itself. This, in turn, produces chromosomes or the lubricating forces within the body; as such, this allows the bones to move, to be manipulated without undue pain or damage. Much as a machine would be in need of oil to carry out its function smoothly and efficiently, so would the joints in the body (with the body's natural secretions of these chromosomes, so to speak). As such, the body would be lubricated, stimulated from observing the sunlight through the eyes itself, affecting the centers of the brain.

Now also you would find that if one who wears glasses continuously or drives in a vehicle, or for the most part is working in the night-time hours (in which there is not sufficient daylight), or one who is behind glass doors or windows, these all have a tendency to filter out or not allow the existence of the ultraviolet spectrum of the sunlight itself. It is therefore necessary for any who wear glasses to use that type that would allow the ultra violet to penetrate the glasses worn to affect the eyes and, therefore, those centers (as we have given) to produce lubrication forces in the body. Those who work nights should attempt to bathe themselves in the sun from time to time without sunglasses *per se*; without a shield of any kind. Look in the direction of the sun, but not at it. This will allow the greater intensity of the rays to be absorbed through those centers through the eye, as we have given.

The cleansing diets and the colonic (intestinal hydrotherapy) would also be a good place to start. But it must be maintained, you see; it cannot be hit or miss. The diet or the on-going eating habits must be altered. Good rule of thumb would be: one vegetable from below the ground and three from above, and of the three from above, two should be of the leafy variety, one of the bean or the pod. These should be the freshest variety and grown in the vicinity in which the body resides. Red meats and meats cooked in oils should be avoided; the hog or pork should also be avoided. Fish, fowl or lamb, baked, boiled, or broiled would be best. As the entity would engage in more vegetables, semi- or partially cooked, retaining a crunchy nature high in their vitamins and mineral status, these would all affect the body in cleansing the same.

We would also suggest that an amount of olive oil be utilized from time to time, in order that there would be the continued cleansing through the intestinal tract. Now also it would be necessary once there has been the cleansing of the large colon or large intestine, the application of the olive oil internally to aid in this, and some change in the diet more toward that which would be considered a poverty diet (and by that we mean simple foods that do not cost a lot of money and are relatively easy and simple to prepare); no spices, no flamboyance with the palate but simple, easy, lowly vegetables. You will find much improvement in the condition seen, as the arthritis.

Then you would find it is necessary for a degree of improvement to stimulate the circulation of the blood and the lubricating effects of peanut oil. This can be massaged on the joints and can be easily absorbed through the skin. It would affect the joints or the lubricating areas that are in need, you see; and, as such, would be found to be quite a lubricant itself in allowing the movement more freely and without much stress or pain, for those who are in such conditions with the application of the peanut oil. This can be done by the self massaging into the joints, or it could be done by one who is skilled in the same.

Now in a general overview, we would also suggest that which is called Atomidine* or Atomic Iodine, and this iodine can be taken in general - three to six drops would be sufficient - in order to allow some degree of improvement to the joints itself. As this would be given or attempted to be given, you would find improvement or you would find not. But best to understand that in this attempt to remove the residue in the muscles and in the arteries (but, in particular, in the joint itself, you see), these basic remedies: diet, cleansing, and the iodine would be helpful in a general overview. However, it is necessary for more specialized treatment to be given for what would be considered a "hard case," you see.

Should the atomic iodine be taken forever?

Three to six drops in a glass of cool water, taken for five days to some seven days would be sufficient. Then leave off for a period of equal time. If it is used for five days, leave off for five days, and then commence again. We would suggest this be done and, indeed, olive oil be taken from the spoon, for this type of iodine tends to dry out the intestine. And, as such, it could be continued until there would be the lessening of the arthritic condition, or until there would be felt the tremble in the arm or the foot, and then this would be a signal that there is too much iodine in the system. However, as the body would continue to negate itself of the arthritis, then this could be left off completely, you see.

Please give specific advice on how one might overcome the condition in the mind.

In understanding the mind, it is quite like attempting to understand the universe. There are set places or points of reference, but there is a void between each of these references that is not widely travelled or known of. In the mind itself, such is the case. As one would attempt to have a degree of self-respect and a degree of patience, these would be most helpful. But, in general, it is the words that are cutting; the words that tend to negate, rather than support. As any would attempt to alter their thinking, then they would have a very difficult job on their hands, indeed. Yet for all, it would be best to engage in this attempt to conquer oneself, for this is the spiritual way.

As they would first begin to relax their control, so to speak, and to not hang onto a degree of adversity or difficulty, it would be a good place to start. Humor is that which is the best medicine for this disease (and is for most) for it does affect the body's own secretions that would tend to make it immune from those that would be considered disruptive to others (such as arthritis, such as any form of disruption). But humor, or watching humorous shows or individuals, all tend to affect the body extremely positively, you see. As they could attempt to seek a little joy in the life, and to put worry back where it belongs, out of the life area, and allow a degree of the laughter and humor to come in, this would tend to allow a degree of flexibility; and, as this would be given, further flexibilities, until such as there would not be any difficulty at all within the mind, at all within the body, you see. For as times change, so do attitudes.

Would you please give any other herbs or supplements that could or should be used with the condition of arthritis.

Indeed, in what would be first of the tranquilizing affect upon the body, alcohol would be good to use in small amounts, to relax the physical body itself. You would find the slippery elm would also be utilized here. You would find also those teas that would be cleansing to the arteries - mullein, burdock, camomile - all would be helpful. You would find other herbs, those that would affect the intestine - the licorice and the wormwood - all would be helpful also in removing residue or difficulty from the colon itself.

However, as one would eat the apples for three days, nothing but apples in any form that is desired (but raw would be best, sliced or diced makes little difference), and with these three days of apples, take seven to eight large glasses of water. This would act as a catalyst in aiding the kidney to cleanse the blood itself. On the first day, we would suggest a teaspoon of olive oil. The same on the second, and on the third, a couple spoons or three, or as much olive oil as can be assimilated. This would, in fact, improve eliminations and would be the place to start, you see. The raw apple (or the apple diet, as it is known) can be taken with tea or coffee (black, no sugar or milk), and can be repeated on a monthly basis, or every other month, or quarterly, or whatever is decided by the self, you see.

There are those herbs such as the dandelion, kelp, alfalfa and even chlorophyll that can be taken in allowing improvement in the intestine. The idea is to understand that the body must reverse the process of toxification, for here, in the first place the body stored these toxins in the joints, in order to protect its vital organs. As there is an attempt to cleanse the body internally, through the colon in particular and the urinary system, then the body begins to reverse the process, by taking the deposits and attempting to pass them back into the colon, and therefore eliminate through the system itself. This could and would be done slowly, and would require a degree of patience and love, rather than anger directed at oneself.

Does the herb devil's claw have an effect on arthritis?

As of the herb taken into the body, it would have an effect but it would be a passive effect; it would have a tendency to work in coordination with the kidneys (somewhat like a catalyst) but also in collecting and removing the sedentary forces that would be irritating to the bone, and having them compensated or removed at the joint or on the bone and they expeditiously carried out of the body. Therefore, it has an effect on the disease by improving the body's ability to filter sedentary forces that would otherwise end up in the nooks and crannies of the body through the elimination through the kidney. This would be like sand in the lubricant of any machinery, you see; it tends to remove the grit from the lubricating forces in and around the bone, affecting the inflammation (or inflammation-causing substances), you see. It has a two-step purpose. However, the body must consume plenty of water for this to take effect or be effective, you see.

How does adding iodine to the diet benefit arthritis?

Iodine is one of the substances that is essential to the cell level itself. To some degree, it thickens the wall of the cell, making it more resilient or durable; more elastic, flexible (we speak of soft tissue, of the membrane in and about the area of the joints and also the fluids in the body). These are affected by the iodine itself. The intention here is that the body communicates from cell to cell and this speeds up the process of the functions of the body to remove the irritants or inflammation at the joint or joints in the body, preventing further adulteration or (you would call it) filling up of the sedentary forces in nooks and crannies of the body; but also to the direction of fluid that would ease through the membrane and would cause a reduction of friction, first on the membrane, then on the bone itself or into the joint area or region. Also, it causes some degree of elasticity or contraction-releasing (so to speak) of the muscle itself. For as the muscles pull tighter together, the joint naturally seizes or rubs tighter, one surface upon the other.

Recall that the form has, through evolutionary resources, come from the sea in the first place and this particular substance is an essential element in the body. However, for the general understanding, it does affect the cell at the cellular level; particularly the wall of the same. It improves communication between the different systems or the cells within the systems, you see, and it does cause the secretion of lubricating forces to be more prominent, as well as causing the muscles to relax, or allow the muscle fibers to extend or stretch easier, and thereby allowing the counter-produced contraction of the muscles at the joints to ease, stopping the friction or compression of the joints themselves.

What is the best way to help someone who has arthritis?

It would be, first of all, to bring about a degree of reassurance and affection, patience, and understanding. Attempt the person who has the affliction to see the goodness about herself or himself and attempt to aid them in their thinking to not rise so quick on the emotional level to this or that; but attempt to have the affirmation "Live and let live." Also it should be given, over and over, "I am becoming more flexible in my body, for I am becoming more flexible in my values, and I am becoming more flexible in my attitudes. As such, I am more flexible in accepting things as they are, rather than the way I think they should be." And in this form of affirmation, said again and again (although lengthy) any who would aid in this affirmation would tend to speed up the process.

Now there is a fine line between being cynical and being discriminatory, but there is no need to be judgmental; therefore, attempt to bring into the life different sets of values. Attempt to tolerate all things; for you see, in Japan or China or in any of the Orient, burping and anal gas are considered compliments to the chef itself, while in the West, both at the table (or any other misdemeanor in that regard) tend to be embarrassing to the person emanating the sounds, and could be insulting to the host or hostess. Yet, what is taking place? Same individual in a different country would get applause from the host or hostess, you see. It is the point of view. It is the value. It is those who consider themselves just, or those circumstances that are considered right.

Let us assure you, there is not a human in the world itself who is right. They are all wrong, yet they are all right. None is perfect. And as the Master said, "Let he who is without sin cast the first stone." Likewise here, attempt to be, in this circumstance, easy-going and not so rigid as to what is right. Do not become too over-zealous in the self-righteousness, you see. Live and let live. Any who would assist any who would suffer from arthritis (no matter how slight), let them live and let live. For you see, that which you see in another is that which you recognize within yourself. Whether it is amplified in respect, or whether it is squashed and disseminated in violence or (you would call it) disrespect, it is still within the self. For if it was not, you would not recognize it, and it would not bother you.

However, as it would be seen in self, attempt to be loving, kind with the self, and be patient. It will require much strength both in that one going through the attempt to transit or grow in its attitude, and those who would be aiding or helpful to the same. Be patient, seek humor, seek the joy of life, and above all, live and let live.

Can you offer any further information on this subject that would be helpful and beneficial?

You would find there are several types of arthritis and difficulties that affect the bones and the movement or swing in the joints. But understand it is to "the bones that are within the mind" that the amplification and initiation of the healing should commence. As any would attempt to live and let live, as any would attempt to be more flexible in their thinking, then you would find there would be an easement in the body's natural eliminations, and there would be easement in the body's movements; as such, there would be improvement to any condition that would be considered arthritic, even though it would be considered chronic.

The place to start would be in the mind and, following that, the intestines, and then direct application through massage, or even through the adjustment of the spine itself to engage in what would be stimulation to the nerve centers by the osteopath or the chiropractor.

Arthritis need not be within any body. Take a good peanut oil bath once a month and you never need fear arthritis for the rest of your life. Utilize the soothing, massaging waters of hydrotherapy to increase the blood flow, and this would enhance the body. But what is really being done is the pampering of the body and relaxing the mind. Relaxing the mind is putting joy back into the mind (peace into the mind, you see) bringing it back to normality (or improvement, as you would call it) in the physiological states.

It is much better to have happy thoughts and a happy body than it is to have negative thoughts and a negative body. But each has its own choice. Each has light and life, or death and darkness in front of it. Choose that which you will, but as for ourselves, we would choose light and life. Even in the most adverse and most difficult situation, there is always humor in it, there is always a blessing in it. Seek to find the humor and the blessing in life. Live and let live. See?

Asthma

Please comment briefly on the cause of asthma and the best focus of treatment.

Primarily, asthma can be located as a deficiency in the nerve flow of the lung and the controlling center of the sympathetic-parasympathetic trunk lines to the thalamus or hypothalamus (the controlling center for any body). The messages are not emanating from the brain to the organ and the organ back to the brain. In short, there is impairment here, usually located in between the shoulder blades of the spinal column. This is the entry point for these trunk lines or nerves that radiate from the spine to the lung itself. Compressive forces, injury to the spine, rotation of the vertebrae or other impairment to the nerve flow are the initial difficulty for the asthmatic reaction or difficulty. It is the nerve not being able to function or communicate directly between the brain and the organ that can be considered (as a rule of thumb) the initial cause.

There are other conditions: the diaphragm spasm, there is edema or fluid in the lung, there is poor blood supply in the lung, there would be forces to the rib cage itself that would extend the difficulties mechanically to the body. Primarily this is a difficulty affecting the nerve communications between the brain and the organ or lungs. Also it would be a state of mind, or anxiety, or stress that would be in the mind of the entity itself, in which there would be a heightened state of alarm, adrenaline secreted into the body, and tension held in the diagram. As each body is slightly stronger on one side than the other, it would pull the sheath that surrounds the organ to one side, thereby causing a squeezing or compressing force on the lung. As a rule of thumb, those who are susceptible to this condition usually are poor breathers and do not breathe deeply enough but breathe with only the top of the lung. Training the self to breathe with the full extent of the lung, from the diaphragm, would be a good way to combat anxiety, to increase oxygen in the blood, and thereby allow the body to be blood-oxygen enriched, and therefore not prone to fainting or lightheadedness. As such, this would not allow the condition to precipitate or, here, to be a self-fulfilling condition, you see; difficulty in oxygenating the blood, causing the body to be difficult or dizzy, and causing the asthmatic attack.

How can this be prevented?

If there can be a calmness in the stomach, slippery elm as an herb would be a good beginning point. If there would be a calmness in the diaphragm and if there would be a correction in the alignment of the bone and the vertebrae, thereby allowing the nerve flow to move more fluently, chances of an asthmatic attack would be very low in one who is susceptible to the same. Acupuncture may be used, in particular during the tenth hour in the PM to rectify any asthmatic condition. It would allow the chi energy or the nerve flow/life force energy to re-enter the area of the lung itself (which are very important to the body). All would have the effect of increasing the nerve productivity, or nerve flow, or energy flow (if you will) between the organ and the controlling center in the brain.

We would also add to this: the causes of the fluid or condition of asthma being found from the mucous being builded up from the dairy products, you see. One who would be susceptible to this should avoid all aspects of milk from the cow.

Attention Deficit Disorder

What causes attention deficit disorder?

Primarily it is an imbalance between the chemical nature of the body and the activity within the brain itself (what would be electrical-magnetical impulses, you see). Sometimes, pressures of the skull, where the brain has not flexed, or is not manipulative is at fault. Sometimes the artery within the skull or the brain cavity is not full or (we would call this) capable of moving the blood through the same. There are restrictive natures within the body, in the neck itself, affecting the pressures of the artery. Diet is of major concern to the effect of attention deficit disorder.

However for a single cause, or a single point of view, whether it be the palate, or the shape of the teeth, or the compressing forces within the neck, there is usually a hormonal imbalance; a glandular function or imbalance where the glands are not in harmony with one another and the natural exuberance or (call it here) livelihood, the physical expression into the child itself, as all children would be more physically expressive. Therefore look at what would be at the other end of the body, as any compressive forces in the lumbar; the imbalance in the stomach and the stimulation effect between the thyroid and the pancreas, you see. There is no single cause, but it would be to look in these areas, you see; glandular malfunction or excitement even to the pineal and pituitary, affecting the thyroid and pancreas, you see.

Depending on the cause, the best treatment would be to examine the spine to correct any pinched or compressed forces in the spine itself, to look for traction in the neck and to the shape or misshape of the head itself. Notice the shape of the skull with certain individuals. Manipulating or flexing the bones in the skull at a younger age would allow the pressures of the brain to be released. And look to the function of the endocrine system itself. Notice the effect of sugar, preservatives and artificial foods. Look to give a child who would be overactive a bland diet, a diet that would cool the same, rather than excite the same.

Therefore, examine the spine. Examine the nervous system and the gland, and how they function with each other, and what is put into the body (the foods itself, you see). If these preliminary examinations are unsuccessful, then examine the teeth, the palate, and the blood supply into the brain.

Autism

Autism is a condition that affects many children. Please explain the causes and suggest the best form of treatment.

As we would examine the condition itself, we would find there is some erosion or destructive influences given to the brain. These would be foreign substances given or injected into the body. Live bacteria or virus given to the body would attack the brain stem, specifically, at the base of the brain. Here, it would fester, and it would be like a log split into splinters. The infestation would cause the brain stem to appear like roots of a tree, rather than the trunk of the tree; splintered or with holes in the same. This causes difficulties to the controlling centers of the body; it can cause the brain to segment or isolate certain parts of brain functions. In other words, instead of having an amalgamated brain, it would be like having several little brains, or sections of brain that are isolated and do not communicate with each other like they should. In a homogenized brain, there would be communication up, down, left, right and all around. With this particular malfunction in the brain, it is like having gobs of brain that are connected by thin strands of nerves. Estranged from the central or mass of the brain, these segments or bits of brain do their best, but they are functioning independently or without a homogenized collective, you see, like satellites (so to speak) around a central intelligence.

This attack on the brain stem can occur by viral infestations where high fevers are given to the body. Certain viruses and bacterial influences can exist for some time, even under the high fever temperatures which are designed to eliminate it. On other occasions, injections into the body can right away affect those bodies that are disarmed or have not built up, in their immune systems, sufficient protection in the body. It is somewhat cynical and erroneous to give a healthy body strands of disease, especially if there are multiple diseases given at the same time. For then mutation takes place in the body and the host body, especially in the base of the brain, can be or irreversibly altered.

Now, also there is, on occasion, malformation of the brain due to malformation of the skull and the pressures internally. During the progression through the birth canal, the head has been squeezed to such extent that the palate is pushed out of place. There are compressive forces on either side of the head that give the head a narrow appearance (or front-to-back, and the forehead is sloped and the back of the head is raised). These malformations or misalignment can be easily corrected soon after birth with simple pressures of the hands. The bones of the skull or cranium would move freely and, with some pressure, aligned into a more rounded head or skull form. One who would be skilled in the same should be consulted.

Also, there is, during the process of birth, a stretching of the spine, especially if the body is breaching in birth, or there has been some difficulty and forceps need to be used to extract the body. If the head is pulled too severely, then a stretching of the brain stem occurs. This, too, causes disruption, and there is difficulty in the movement of nerve flow through the stem itself. On occasion, almost a detachment of the brain stem occurs at the base of the brain. This affects the motor skills area of the brain and affects the logic and reasoning aspects consequently. These are mechanical disruptions or injury to the body that may or may not be preventable, due to the birthing circumstances. But corrective measures should be taken soon thereafter to align the vertebrae and the cervical and to position the skull upon the head properly, using those modalities, of course, who would be skilled in the thing.

As to what is given to the body, by inoculation or injection, this should not take place for at least several years until the child has been able to build up its own immune system. Then there should not be any multiple injections of disease at the same time, for they cause mutations in the body, giving them strength and completely undermining the purpose for which they were given. The healthy body needs not be given disease to make it healthier. Rather, keeping the body slightly more alkaline than acidic would be far more preventing of colds, flus and disease in the body than most anything else. Proper diet, nutrition, breathing good air, drinking good water, and movement activities or exercise would be far greater preventative functions than injecting disease into the body.

Now, for those who are susceptible to virus and bacteria, after the age of five or seven, perhaps some weak strand, given as a vaccine, would be acceptable, and would not cause such alarming disturbance into the soft brain tissue, especially the brain stem area. This particular disease affects not only the brain stem, but (depending on circulation) can deposit itself in the brain and causes (as we have given) separation of the brain components. You might see it as compartmentalizing the brain itself, and then difficulty in communicating with these different compartments.

These are some of the conditions that would relate to the condition you would call autism. There is also the stimulation of the nerves (as we have given) that causes them to be highly sensitized to the point that there is too much information being given to the brain. This, too, causes the condition of autism. For when there is too much information, then there is little accepting, recognizing or even contemplating and managing the information. Therefore, you might call it information overload. The system breaks down and numbness occurs. Combined with the emotional states of fear and anxiety, this drives the personality into seclusion or inwardly. As in some of the other conditions we have given where the brain is compartmentalized, the personality can be locked away in the depths of isolation, for its own protection, you might say.

In this, where there is overstimulation, then the body can be given pressure all over its body, to deaden or stop the constant array of information being given to the body. Like wearing heavy clothes, or putting the self under some heavy weights, the body desensitizes over time. You might see the body as being wrapped up or finding itself in a cardboard or wooden box even, where it is compressing on each side and all around. This desensitizes the body or it loses its overstimulation, like wearing a heavy overcoat, see? It stops the invasion or invasive thoughts and stimulation. See the body as having receptors all over it, signals being given, and no central way to discriminate as to what is important and what is not. Another way of seeing it is that many people are talking in the same room, and the self is attempting to listen to one conversation, but instead hears them all and is muddled. It cannot hear any conversation. This is a crude example, but this gives the idea as to what is taking place.

Once the body has been calmed down, then there could be some order given, or some activities or play-time that would not be too stimulative, but more a singleness as to purpose: rolling on the ground, for instance, or batting a balloon in the air; simple things. In time, the body's assimilation and organization will allow the nerves themselves to be somewhat cohesive and the brain will collect itself; the satellites will join up with the main brain, so to speak. There will be a healing and there will not be a de-compartmentalizing, so to speak. We trust we have given the idea or picture to understand what is taking place.

Now, therapy, play-therapy, repetitious movements of the limbs imitating swimming or walking, having the entity reason out its behavior or stopping the enormous amounts of information coming into the self all lead to controlling the self. As we have given, care should be taken in examining the spine, for usually there are compressive forces in the neck and there may be also compressive forces in other parts of the spine, including the lower end or lumbar. One who would be skilled in the thing in manipulation of the spine (an osteopath or chiropractor or even a masseuse or masseur) should be consulted and considered for possible success for use of the same. Any form of reasoning with such a mind should be done step-by-step, getting the child's mind to trust and then to come out of this isolation that it has put itself in, or allowing the mind to reach out and to amalgamate with itself. To physically manipulate the body, the palate, and the bones in the skull all align or improve the thinking process. Removing any kinks or stimulation of pain in the nerve systems is paramount. Then, have the body stimulated with pleasure. Then indeed, allow the creative forces to manifest and the body can overcome its condition. Repetitious movements like imitating swimming or crawling re-educate the brain and grow new pathways, helping the brain to amalgamate and communicate with itself as a whole unit, rather than one that has been segmented into four or five pieces. See?

Bipolar Disorder

Please explain the cause of bipolar disorder, and explain the best form of treatment.

In understanding this condition, it is to understand that this is part and parcel of what would be the mental attitude and the behavioral aspects of an individual. This would be seen as the emotional responses that would be positive, and then negative, or constructive and then destructive, or what would be cooperative and charming and what would be overbearing and demanding; hence the term bipolar. It means that the emotional states polarize towards one point or the other, between happy and sad, between optimism and depression. It is a complicated emotional variance, but it is to show that extremes in the emotions are encountered. Now, this can come from a variety of causes, and we will include some here that would be a little unusual.

In a normal understanding, the emotional natures are governed by the timing devices or hormonal secretions in the body. The body chemistry determines how the body feels. This would be seen in the organic sense, and therefore when the body is in good health and optimistic, the body feels good. When the body is ill, and feels pessimistic, then the body is in a destructive or depressed mode; opposite in feelings or senses. The cause is the secretions in the hormones. The emotions are both the constructive and destructive forces in any body, for they affect the very health of the body; as the metabolism functions, when it is in a favorable, optimistic level, it builds up the body. When it is in a pessimistic, depressed or derogatory emotional status, it tears down the body even to the point of bringing disease into the body.

Having this as an understanding, then as one can regulate the hormonal structure of the body, or as one trains oneself through the attitude and personality, or habits, one can overcome despair, sadness and depression willfully. Those who have this extreme polarization cannot. They have very low willpower in this regard, in selecting their emotional states, and preventing themselves from being triggered to an emotional response by outside influences.

Moving from the chemical reaction and the ability to willfully control the emotions, those who are susceptible may be also from historical influences. An abused child has the habit of enjoying or experiencing abuse, giving it to others. The abused child grows up to become the abused adult or parent, because it is part of the personality, habit or inner being. As children living with schizophrenic parents, the child may not be schizophrenic, but it learns to polarize its emotions. Fears, anxiety and abandonment or isolation can cause the polarization of the emotions. There is nothing worse than to be a child in a family where no one is paying attention and someone close - a relative, or a neighbor, or someone trusted in the family - is plaguing the child with abuse, and abuse would mean sexually touching, bullying, verbal abuse, threatening, or sexual activity, all against the will of the child. Also, compounding that, would be the child's religious perspectives or understanding. Knowing that something is unjust, immoral, or incorrect, and yet no one would believe it, then the child assumes it is sinning against God or against nature. This, too, tends to set the emotions into polarization. Relief of the abuse and the response is positive, optimistic, and enthusiastic, then the abuse occurs again and the child become pessimistic, isolated, and has guilty feelings. Therefore, the history in the life can dictate how one experiences the emotions as a child. No balance means extremes, and therefore the emotions as they are experienced in the child, become the habit, become the personality, and become the reactionary aspect that polarizes the person as an adult, to their emotional expressions, unfortunately.

There is an intention to do right even though the self is feeling very alone, isolated, and incapable; it does things it does not wish to do. Usually it chastises, is critical, and can go on and on for hours criticizing those around it, those who would be his or her loving or meaningful members of the family, friends, or close circle. In public, it is even worse, for there is no restraint. In a position of authority, they become black or white; very critical and tyrannical, or very loving and convincing. The influences can be as simple as the person's personality, being the sum-total of all the experiences so far. There is usually a sense of injustice, of being abused, of being overworked, or somehow being disbelieved and unprotected by its family, its parents, or anyone else. The person becomes an individual and reacts through flight-or-fight. As such, the person learns to be charming, convincing, very seductive and soothing, can be well-liked, and even charming to strangers as well as those who would be meaningful or close at hand. And on the other hand, it can be to the other extreme: demanding, tyrannical, critical, always right, and everyone else wrong. These are the levels of cause for the emotional and mental imbalance that you would call bipolar. It simply means that, depending on the circumstance, the individual responds without checkpoint or balance, but responds to the extremes. When they are attempting to be liked, they are very sociable, very talkative, very charismatic. When they are to the other extreme, they can be very independent, isolated, angry, and mean.

To these extremes, therefore, these would be the circumstances that would lead up to the emotional imbalance. The remedy is love. The remedy is an introspection, to find out where the injustice took place in the background, in the previous time, in this life; t revisit those times in which the self felt injustice, felt betrayal from its father or its mother (usually from its father), and then to revisit it as an adult, attempting to take responsibility but not feeling obliged that it was causing the effect or the circumstance. This can begin to slowly unlock the polarization or reaction to the extremes, and as such, it can find some middle of the road between the two extremes. They no longer find themselves at fault, ugly, bad or evil, or the cause of their own suffering. They learn not to judge themselves. See? They then associate responsibility with others, and are able to distance themselves from the event through this understanding. Therefore they are at peace and they can understand when little things go wrong, it does not mean that the whole world is falling apart. They can deal with these little traumas, difficulties, slights, irritations and criticisms in an emotionally-mature way, or with balance, or compassion and understanding.

Getting a person who is extreme in their emotional responses, one has to be skillful and it will take some time, for usually they are very clever, intelligent, and they have come to this extreme behavioral difficulty by being trained to do so by their parents, their teachers, those adults and associates for whom they formed opinions of being important or meaningful, and then they felt betrayed. Getting the trust back, getting the sense of justice back, getting them to see the world not from extremes, not in black-and-white, but to see it with a little grey area would be the key. This would have them look inward and come to the conclusion that they can feel something, they can trust something, without having to be demanding, mean or nasty, but rather they can be kind and compassionate and deal with disappointment in a benevolent way.

They should eat good diets and have good food. They should attempt to surround themselves with people who are loving in nature and, in time, they need individuals to talk to. Usually they select their friends and complain in the most intimate detail of what is most bothering them. It would be better to have a therapist deal with them than a friend who might be a little annoyed and simply give them advice to get rid of them. "Yes, yes, you are absolutely right." This form of complacency works temporarily, but then the burden is that they are required to take responsibility. When they do, the responsibility should be such that it is of themselves but not for other people. They do not have to fix things. They do not have to be responsible to an overbearing state for anyone else; in particular their own children.

This leads to the balance point in the mind. This balance point, coming to a point of futility almost, leads them to understand that they need not be extreme in their emotional responses, that they can check themselves at a certain point so there is not a little thing that goes wrong, taking them to the nth degree of catastrophe, but it takes them only to the point of a little thing gone wrong. Disappointment and despair, disillusionment by betrayal can be set aside. They can deal with life in a more general, perfect way. They need not put themselves in positions of great responsibly in their vocational aspects. They can be in a state of harmony. But, again, their purpose is to find a balance point. To this end, this would be an inconclusive answer, but to find what would be a balance point, would be to find love, and to be loving. Those who are in this position usually want life on their own terms; the reason they want it this way is: it is predictable, they understand it, there are no surprises and they are not to blame for anything that goes wrong. Any extreme in life is still an extreme.

Black Seed Oil

What are the benefits of taking black seed oil?

Any intestinal disorders, any infections, and any inflammations in the body; primarily inflammation, you see. It seems to affect the bacteria in the intestine; it negates what would be growing or

spreading bacteria or affecting infestations or parasites in the body. It does seem to clean the intestine out (so to speak), lubricating and cleaning, but also removing any appendages, attachments or disease that would be found inside the body without harming the body itself. It does seem to quell the body. It coats the intestine, and speeds up the delivery of digesting food as it would, thereby preventing any infestations to lodge in the body. Too much of this and diarrhea would occur, but it would be seen then as a purging of the body. Too little and the stools would be large or hard, but it would seem to scrape away those areas that would be compacted in the intestine or would be difficult in removing.

Body Image

Could you please comment on the condition of poor body image, and suggest a way to overcome this way of thinking?

There is a brain wave recognition difficulty. The more there is starvation in the body or the more there is poor nourishment in the body, the more this attitude or opinion persists. As we look towards any who would see themselves as too thin or too thick, in the area of the imagination, this is somewhat a perplexing perspective or attitude, for it is self-deceptive, see?

Those things that would wake up this mind, would be anything along the lines of those enzymes like what would be in coconut or papaya or even cacti. The system is lacking sufficient oxygen, and there is additional fatty tissues or substances in the body. This causes the image to be blurred in the mind, and the recognition of the self, opinion of the self is usually derogatory, from one extreme to the other. Waking up the self to see clearly, this is somewhat difficult, for you are attempting to touch upon the lower, animalistic levels of the self that are borne out of what you would call logic; self-deceptive thoughts or denial, see?

This is a thyroid-pancreas condition in conjunction or combination with some recollection in the mental faculties. Usually vitamin D would be the carrier for improved vision. Increasing the blood flow in the center portion of the brain would help to relieve the condition. The diet should be of a very low fat or no fatty substance in the diet itself. Combined with some sulfur - either a pinch on food or ingested by dipping the finger into the sulfur and then putting it on the tongue - this will wake up the body (so to speak). Lower levels of selenium allows this to be maintained in the body (as does low levels of zinc). These things given would attempt to bring the recollection in the moment, to those who would be of various sizes.

Body Odor

What could you recommend as a good way to reduce or eliminate unwanted body odor without commercial deodorants (which contain aluminum)?

Understand that body odor is the organ of the skin functioning as it ought to, in the removing poisons and toxins that have been absorbed from the blood. They are now being excreted from the body through the pores of the skin. The basic improvement is to increase the eliminations on the inside in the normal fashion. Drinking plenty of water is a basic solution, for it aids the kidneys that give the body substance to dispose of those substances that are unwanted or being rejected by the body. Keeping the body regular (physical congress) is also a necessity, for any form of congestion or constipation will lead to the body's odor increasing. Here, the body is attempting to rid itself of these sediments or toxins in any way or form that it can. This includes pimples in the skin. Whenever pimples are evident, it is the intestine that is having difficulty eliminating, and the body is becoming overly polluted. The poisons or toxins that are circulating through the arterial, naturally through the small arteries in the skin are deposited in certain points in the lymph system or in the small sacs attached to the lymph, that require the body to form reservoirs or places of storage for these poisons or toxins that are not otherwise being eliminated from the body. Of course, the pimples being extracted, remove the pustule and the toxin itself. Boils and cysts are of the same, see?

The primary solution, then, is to give to the body enemas or colonic irrigation or those substances that would have the body eliminate more regularly and more fully. Olive oil from the spoon would be assistive and helpful. Any laxative would be good to keep the body regular. But having a better diet begins the process of removing poisons and toxins from the body. Of course what goes into the body should be monitored strictly. Avoid carbonated drinks. Avoid sugars that are excessive. Avoid fried foods or deep-fried foods. Avoid things that congest the intestine, like cheeses. There is no mystery here. The odor of the body may be directly proportionate to the constipation, congestion, or the retaining of poisons and toxins in the body that might otherwise have been eliminated. Water is the basis for good eliminations. Exercising the intestine as well as giving to the body those things that are constructive or nutritious is one way of improving physical eliminations from the body.

But, the body needs to perspire, for it is a natural elimination system in the body that, for most people, might be considered something different, and not recognized as an eliminating organ; an organ to eliminate toxins and poisons from the body. It is very beneficial that a body enters into hot rooms to perspire, like a steam room (steam would be better than the dry heat of a sauna). You may wrap the body up in extra clothes or blanket or wrap itself in plastic. The heat generated causes the body to perspire; the perspiration allows the poisons or toxins stored up in the body (all over the body) to be removed. When they are removed, the body can be repaired.

Therefore, understand that perspiration or sweating is a very good thing to help remove the poisons that are resident within the organ of the skin. Simply take a hot bath occasionally or put the body in a whirlpool, sauna, or steam room. Then, the body may be rubbed with purifying herbs, or rinsed and washed thoroughly. Make sure the body is rinsed prior to cooling, for as the body cools in temperature, the pores would close, trapping the poisons or toxins within. As the body perspires, the pores open, and what is within is excreted to the outside or can be washed away. This is the purpose.

Placing onto the body a good soap and water and washing those areas under the arms and in the groin (for instance) is essential. Indeed, putting deodorant on the body is unnatural and all deodorants only mask the problem; they do not remedy the problem.

Breast Enlargement

Could you recommend a way for females to naturally augment or increase the size of their breasts?

Any stimulation whatsoever would be sufficient. Eating a little more fat in the diet would affect the tissues. Increasing the circulation through the mammary itself can be done, by either vitamins, massage, heat packs, or wearing blankets and plastic around the chest. As the blood flow is enhanced throughout the area, the mammaries usually enlarge themselves. But look to this as fatty tissue or fatty substances that should be taken in.

Any stimulation whatsoever to the breasts will bring some benefit. This can be massaging the breast in a professional or amateur way. This can be bouncing on a rebounder, or taking the body up and down a staircase.

Any particular acupuncture that would affect the body that would be strength-building from the shoulder-blades to the shoulders, to the mammary itself, can be given. This would heighten and increase the lymphatic flow through the general region itself. One who would be skilled in lymphatic massage could also be utilized here to increase fluid flows through the breast area.

Now, it is an attempt to remove toxins or sediments that we are speaking of, not to increase blood flow and lymphatic substance flow through the same for the sake of just having it move quickly through the mammary itself. See? What would be most important would be iodine and honey. The iodine may be put on drops on the tongue. The honey may be taken a spoonful at a time, and there can be honey smeared on the breasts as well. The breasts have a certain absorption nature to liquid or fluids. Then the rest would be the building up of fatty tissues in the mammary. This can be done by diet.

The movement of the pectoral muscles or the stimulation in a physical way, once this is done, it allows the body itself to begin to shed excess weight, and to strengthen the mammary as if one would be improving the muscular structure, for support and for flexibility in the chest region or area.

Increase in the diet more protein and a higher fat. Engage in those exercises and those massaging effects that would stimulate the breasts, in a pleasurable, pleasing and therapeutic way. Keep the lymphatic fluid moving and the body should respond very quickly.

Bursitis and Tendinitis

Could you please comment briefly on the cause of bursitis and tendinitis and the best focus of treatment?

These would be primarily a rusting of the body, or a lack of fluid or substance that would lubricate the body itself. Here, inflammation is formed at the areas near the joints of the body. As such, the body becomes stiff, temperature in the area is usually lower, and blood supply is usually diminished in the region or area. Understand the body as being an intelligent machine that has to deal with garbage and pollutants. The garbage is usually disposed through liquid and/or physical conduits in the natural functions of the body. But, in this case, as a machine, little sediments or interfering pieces of debris must be swept up and disposed of in a normal machine or factory setting. The body accomplishes this by taking these sedentary forces, sediments, toxins, irritants and it buries them in the nooks and crannies throughout the body. In some occasions, the body is doing exactly that. It is taking these threatening sedentary forces or irritants and placing them at the far ends of the body.

To decrease the condition of bursitis and arthritis condition, we would find that increasing the circulation to the local area is paramount. Then a degree of stretching and manipulation of the muscle, then body-building the muscle with exercise would be a good rule of thumb or place to start. Now, as the body is slightly more irritated (and usually aged a little) then it would be also to pay attention to the kidney. Acupuncture can be given to the kidney to stimulate the same. Diet changes are usually necessary, in which there would be a blood cleansing diet: those foods that would be taken into the body, or teas or herbs that would remove sedentary forces, elements, irritation from the body. Inflammation would be reduced greatly and the body's flexibility or ability to use the muscle and/or the joint would return.

Hot and cold baths, or hot and cold water should be used to bring about blood changes. First, to flood blood to the area with the warm water, about sixteen minutes in the same, as hot as the body can stand, then to drive the blood deep into the body about six to eight minutes in water as cold as the body can stand. Then repeat three or four times and, as such, the body would relieve itself greatly with new blood flow to the localized area.

Now, aspects of cleansing the blood can also engage chelation therapy, enemas and colonic therapy, massage therapy, and supplements such as glucosamine given to the body. But none would be better than the actual manipulation of the blood flow in the general region. For this would be able to bring the curative and restorative forces of the body to bear on these tender points.

But see it as a piece of machine with plenty of debris, sawdust, grit or grime clogging up the fine belts and gears of the machine. A sweeping clean of this debris is necessary. The body can do so through the diet management, the manipulation, and the water therapy, you see. Otherwise, the bones may be scraped and chemical therapy may also be given to help relieve or block the pain in an attempt to remove the inflammation.

But inflammation is simply evidence of what is irritating and should not be there. A good peanut oil massage throughout the whole body monthly and none would fear to be arthritic or suffer from this condition; nor those oils that would be restorative or curative to the body: lanolin, castor, peanut, olive oil, sassafras oil, sesame seed oil, camphor oil. These, in equal parts or individually, along with eucalyptus oil as well (and maybe add Absorbine Jr. or wintergreen as part of the elixir or oil) and this would allow the body to be restorative or regenerative in its own way.

The energy fields that would radiate from the body itself would be enhanced and the aura fields would be seen more clearly, almost as if the body would glow, you see. However, understand the emotions as well. Those who would be embittered, those who would be angry, those who would have feelings of suppression or dominance over them by a spouse or a parent or by their employer or employment facility may suffer this as an indication of hanging onto poisons and toxins (and also deep-seated anger that is unexpressed). The emotions should be catered to, as well. Whether it is forgiveness, or it is justice, or it is revenge, or witnessing "just due" to the perpetrator that has commenced the oppression against the individual; it makes little difference (save there is some resolve or justice, and this would remedy the condition, as we see it, as well).

Caffeine

Can you recommend an alternative to caffeine as an energy stimulant?

We would find the stimulation in nuts; also, in certain elements like zinc, and we would find them in certain elements that would be found in eucalyptus oil and some perfumes that would incorporate insect venom or juices, you see (sometimes even their bodies). The stimulation is, therefore, more towards the adrenal, like iodine. This would be a stimulant that might also be perceived as a suppressant, but it would be predominantly the iodine or sea salt, you see. There seem to be plenty of berries and nuts that would be seen as stimulating, you see, without caffeine. Now, these would be natural sugars in some part that would be seen in their reaction to cause the thyroid to fluctuate and the heart to increase in its beat; not that they are poisonous, but that the body would react to the same (like bee venom, you see).

Cancers

Tumors, Types of Cancer, Breast Cancer, Skin Cancer, Parasites.

Can you please comment briefly on the cause of cancer and the best focus of treatment?

We would start with the emotional states, for

those who enter into this state of "hopeless disease" usually have the hopeless attitude itself. There is a genuine feeling of being unloved or incapable of being receptive and receiving love. Individuals usually have themselves in such a state that they are feeling unwanted or unloved in some way, that there is no hope for their condition or predicament, or that they are being placed in a situation that they would rather not be, because of circumstances, duty, responsibilities, financial obligation or outright being bullied, forced, or coerced. In any of these cases, the end result is such that there is a state of no joy, depression and even a longing for death to occur. As such, the cancer begins to develop. This is not, of course, for all cases, but it is a general rule of thumb. As there would be a state of emotion that would bring to some determination of joy, some degree of hope into the body, then the body's natural forces - restorative, curative, replenishing of self - can be more functional in removing this influence in the body.

That said, you would find that cancers usually are, again, the body storing some toxic substance in the body, and then cocooning it with flesh or with what would be considered a tumor. Fibroids are those that have builded up, protected around certain soft tissues. Those that would be benign tumors are such that they would be cocoons in which the internal pestilence, parasites, disease, or bacteria has been encapsulated but has not considered its capsule a host and attempted to grow and break out of the host, as what would be in the rapid and outrageous growth of cancer. Cancer refers to the body's inability to replenish cells which then run amok, creating excess amounts of cells that are rogue cells: deteriorated, misshapen, or an abrasion of what would be the normal function of cell growth, you see; the replicating of cells being replaced in an orderly fashion gone amok, you might say.

In these different regards, you would have some idea that there is poison in the body and, therefore, the body is suffering from the cancer; that there is pestilence or parasitic influence in the body, and the body is attempting to capture and hold it within. And finally there would be a state of anxiety that would bring about the body's normal outrageous and rapid growth of cells, usually from what would be held within; an outrageous anger that has been contained, and, once spread in the body, would spread rapidly throughout.

Now there are different forms of this in the body that would be different from cancer in the liver, or the blood flow, or the bone, or the flesh and soft or hard tissue. That which would usually form in the lymph would be a demonstration of the body holding onto toxic substances, poisons, parasitic influence, or garbage. That which would be seen in the muscles or abdominal region - the intestine, anus, in the filtering areas of the body - usually would come from parasitic influences, viral and bacterial influences that have been encircled or encapsulated in a tumor. At some point in the physical body, the cause has been an influence, but the body has not been able to handle it, usually because of the state of depression, or anxiety, or anger, or that the body itself is handling the cancer but is losing the battle; for as the pestilence or parasitic influence would attempt to grow out of the tumor or spread, the body would build up another layer and the tumor itself would grow.

Poisons that are currently given to the body should be given in small amounts that they do not weaken the entirety of the constitution of the body or bring into impairment the function of the body's lymphatic system, or filtering device system in order to handle toxins or poisons. Rather, small amounts given directly to the center (or the point of origin, if you will) in the tumor would be such that greater accomplishment or remedy would occur.

As to the tumor itself, in order to curtail that, or to eliminate all aspects of what is contained within, there can be simply a tying off, a disruption in blood supply to the tumor in any way that it can be accomplished; whether it is poisoning the blood supply, whether it is a noose around the tumor, or whether it would be the collapsing of the blood supply (such as what is accomplished with hyperthermia). All would have the same affect. The tumor would turn acidic because it would die and would not have a blood supply to it, you see; and what would be encapsulated internally would also diminish or die; and, as such, the tumor would be successfully removed.

Surgical removal of tumors is often necessary within the brain itself. Also, when surgery occurs, you see, growth hormones kick in, and the tumor usually is re-stimulated, as the wound would be naturally brought about to heal. Therefore, the surgeon has the dual problem of attempting to suppress the body's natural growth hormones, or healing process, while, at the same time, hoping that the body heals from the surgery (which is usually major upon the body). If any would maintain a state of alkalinity (high amount of alkaline influence in the body), then the bacterial influences would not exist in the body, and this would be as a rule of thumb and any tumor or cancerous substance would be curtailed. Any embellishing of this idea through to the removal of blood supply to the tumor (as we have given) would suffice to remove the baggage of the garbage cells of what would be intruding and invading forces within the body, such pestilences or parasitic influences. A good rule of thumb is treat the body first as being invaded by parasitic influences, however.

Are parasites to blame for cancer?

It is not parasites themselves that cause the outrageous cell growth or cancer, but, rather, as individual organs succumb to the disease process and blood flow stagnates, blood becomes thicker and darker and oxygen levels decrease. This creates an ideal environment for parasites.

You mentioned there were several types of cancer. Can you please give more detail regarding the causes of the different cancers and how they should be treated?

As we would examine the disease cancer, we would find that there are several different types, as many as eighteen or more varieties. There are also diseases that are treated similar as (or in the class of) being cancerous but, in fact, they are not. In answering the entirety of the question, we are attempting to find the cause for the cancer or those that would be considered tumors, growths, or rapid and outrageous growth of cells in the body. Look to both the organic aspects in the physical form, as to the body's function primarily at the growth hormone or growth system within the body and also the mental and emotional states. Understand cancer as cells that are growing outrageously, rapidly and without - call it here - unity, structure or form that would be healthy. Therefore, this unhealthy form would be considered a rogue growth of cells manifesting in the body. However, if you would look primarily into ordinary tumors themselves (if there would be such a term for this), then you would find that a tumor itself is little more than a mass of cells, or the body growing into a mass, or developing some mass of cells that are forming a large lump, or a growth of cells that are attempting to overtake healthy cells, healthy systems, and healthy organs in the body. By so doing, they disrupt the body and become self-destructive, in that the tumor, along with the body, dies.

Therefore, it should be understood that the body's ability normally to heal or to remedy disease in the body is somewhat confused; the body itself does not seem to recognize cancerous growths within its form, its parameters, or the limits of its own physical existence. This confusion is seen not that the body is ignoring the problem, but that, in fact, the body is attempting to do something about the problem.

The problem would be to understand that cancerous cells are misshapen. They are rogue themselves. But what makes them such? For the basic understanding of a tumor, it is that the body attempts to grow a cocoon, a case, a box (if you will) in which the disease is encapsulated. This could be parasites being contained within the body, isolated, not eliminated, you see. The proper way to remedy all diseases in the body is to eliminate them from the body. Of course not allowing the disease into the body in the first place is correct and preferred. But humans (as you know humans) tend not to pay attention to the gates of the body and disease can invade the body, be invited into the body, or allowed to enter the body through these gates or orifices in the body.

That said, however, as the body would attempt to eliminate them, and there would be difficulty in eliminations (for whatever reason), the body then imprisons the invading disease, parasite, or irritant in a tumor. As such, the way to combat or to remedy cancer, on this level, is to simply eliminate or terminate the cause that is deep within the tumor itself that is causing the body to develop the tumor.

The size of the tumor is equal to, or in relation to, the parasitic influence or the disease inside the tumor attempting to increase its physical dimension, or size, or numbers and break out of the cocoon or the box. As it is in a situation of growth or situation of blood supply for nutrients and oxygen, you see, the body, attempting to cocoon the disease, in fact provides an environment that the disease can be fostered, you see. As such, attempting to go to this center of the tumor, so to speak, and eliminating the life forces of the parasite or the bacteria or the virus is the key.

Taking away from the parasite or bacteria its environment or its livelihood would be easy and best. Therefore, two ways to overcome cancerous cells or cancerous tumors are such to eliminate or attack the virus or the parasitic implant in the first place with some toxic material, or to cause the blood supply to be terminated and allow that which is within to starve to death (so to speak). Surgery, of course, is well practiced and is usually seen as the first line of defense. Surgery in removing the tumor and that which is within, of course, is usually successful.

However, that which would be non-intrusive can be the application of heat in the tumor. Heating the body up to some forty-six degrees Centigrade causes the blood vessels to dilate and then collapse; and as they collapse, blood supply to the tumor and all that is within ceases. There is a structure in which any living force inside would starve to death (so to speak) from a lack of blood supply and, as such, this then would end the body's need to continue expressing some form of cocoon, or cage of the virus. As it would attempt to break out, the body's tumor would grow bigger. This endless cycle is terminated as there is no need now to allow the virus, parasitic influence, or disease within to escape, for it has been terminated.

The application of poisons or radioactive patches or other forms to terminate that which is within the tumor can be done if there would be more exact attacking of the tumor internally rather than affecting the entire body (by poison or chemotherapy, as it is called) but that it attempts to be isolated in and about the tumor. This would be the next best, as also there would be an effect at the cell level.

That which would be developed soon would be the areas of magnetic resonance and the effect that frequency, sound, or light has on the body (or the tumor more specifically). It will be found that the very high vibrations tend to cause flesh to deteriorate and with some degree of - call it here - direction of the frequency that is controlled, then the disease can be, with the right vibration, eliminated or terminated; and this life force, therefore, terminated within the tumor or the body allows the body to be disease-free.

Surgery ultimately simply removes a large block of cells and then hopes the body does not have the growth hormone activated, which usually occurs, and therefore indirectly causes the body to again build a tumor, you see (only this time it is usually rapid and indeed outrageous in its growth). Attempting to keep the body's T-cells, growth hormones and chemical balance in check is difficult, for the body seems to respond robotically. However, understand that once the cells are disturbed, it is like bees in a beehive. The cells swing into action and they do what they are innately able and directed to do, even at the body's expense, you see.

Therefore, attempting to overcome these diseases once in the body should be done with heat, light, and sound, as opposed to the first offering of surgery - although in some cases, especially with brain cancers or tumors, surgery is immediately required so that there can be the regaining of the space in the cranium cavity itself, and the elimination of such material is, by necessity, expedient through surgery, you see. We speak of larger and fully-developed tumors in the body itself.

To the preliminary or the beginning stage, attempting to remove what we call cysts and soft tumors, these can be done by proper eliminations. Elimination of the body is always the key to removing disease within the body. Also keeping the body slightly more alkaline than acidic helps to prevent any viral or bacterial influence in the body from taking hold and causing disease in the body itself.

Therefore, these become preventative measures, as well as rescue or curative measures, for those types of cancers that would be in the soft tissues, especially. Again, the body may be given treatments of heat where the area around the tumor would be heated to over forty-six degrees Centigrade for a length of time that would require the blood vessels to dilate and collapse, starving the tumor and therefore indirectly (or directly, depending on your point of view) starving the disease or the cancerous problem within the tumor.

Secondly, poisoned and radioactive patches are usually given to the body in great quantities, much more or much greater than the body would require. Less is better, and more specifically-targeted would be the tumor, rather than the entire body. A combination of what would be hyperthermia, the heating of the body, and the radioactive patch or chemotherapy in small doses would, indeed, be successful in great amounts of time.

However, in keeping the body alkaline more than acidic, the body would be able to eliminate the parasitic or cancerous influence in the body in the first place. Eliminations (physical congress) in keeping the body active through lymphatic stimulation, and also by engaging in much drinking of water, the body can normally eliminate toxins, sediments, parasitic influences, bacterial and viral influences in the body in the normal way. Therefore, there is plenty that can be given to the body in the beginning, in the attempt to keep the body healthy.

However, pollutants, environmental influences, strong chemicals all tend to enter and reside in the body. Mercury, pesticides, poisons, heavy metals, all these that are taken into the body are placed in the soft tissues or in certain parts of the body in order that they would be, again, encapsulated if they cannot be eliminated. Therefore, in any environment, or any vocation, or profession in which there would be an inhaling or the ingesting or the contact with toxic substances, the body needs to be extra special in the eliminations, either by sweat baths, saunas, steam baths, enemas, colonic therapy, foods that would tend to draw out of the body conditions of pollution, and, of course, the cleansing of the blood, which is seen to be done by chelation therapy and, to some degree, chemical therapy or herbal therapy.

Above this, stimulating all organs, the ductless glands, the liver organs, you see, the endocrine system itself needs to be paid attention to, for here is the life force in residence within the body; in particular the kidney and the colon itself. These organs or systems are not separate and distinct, but are indeed distinct and (if you will) similar or conjoined. These need to work in unison to keep the eliminations of the body in top form.

Therefore, the causes of cancer, in a very general way, can be seen as we have given. The remedies can be specific, and the preventative activities need to be consistent and specific for the type of environment or the activities one carries out in the daily life. Of course, ingesting lead, or toxins, or poisons through the pottery or cookware or other such ingestion of metals and mercury - the placement of mercury in teeth or the chemicals placed in water (the chloride) - all have an effect upon the physical body. The relationship towards the obtainment of cancer is the exposure to these particular elements, including the ingesting of soot in the lungs through smoking, you see.

The root of the healing of all dis-ease affecting the body is the cleansing of the internal organs of the body and proper diet in which the body can cleanse itself. The body can - and is capable of - healing all that is within itself. Look to the *Book of Corinthians* in the writings of Paul the Apostle, and ye would find here that it is stated that Man is more than a physical machine. Man possesses an intellect and a soul. Those things of the outside or external forces cannot harm Man, for they are outside. Those things on the inside are controlled by Man. As such, the body is controlled and can control itself through all forms of attack by the virus, the mucous condition, the disease, the biological malfunction, the micro-organisms, and so on. It is within Man as a whole being that there is the regeneration process, for how is it that they are grown? How is it that cells reproduce? How is it that the body, when it is wounded, heals itself?

Examine this, the most simple thing. Cut the finger. Do not run to a medical person, a healer, seek the chemical, or seek the diet improvement or the exercise, but look at the finger. See the blood begin to clot, and as the clotting takes place, the scab will form. The body is healing itself and it is protected. Where did you learn this process? Was it taught to you by the parents? The teacher? From where did you gather this information? None could answer, but we would give: it is the body's own knowledge, and the body's own function to heal itself, even with the simplest wound, the scratch. This principle, being accepted as truth is evident right through the body itself.

Mankind is possessed of emotion, intellectual thought, and reality (the body itself). The cure lies within self, for any disease, any cancer, any difficulty. It is the body's own knowledge that it can prevent dis-ease in the physical being. But disease, if you would examine it, begins in the mind, and mind itself is the builder. This is where all cures, all analytical explorations of disease will begin. For it is beginning and is evident within the Earth at this point even now, the power of the mind over the body, the use of the mind over the physical improvement for health. Ye would also find that there is within the Earth a degree of fasting, colonic therapy, intestinal hydrotherapy (or cleansing, you might know it), nutrition or dietary alterations being more to that of the Oriental style of eating (steam, boil, broil, little meat, plenty of vegetables grown in the vicinity in which the body resides, and of the freshest variety). This is what the body needs more of: plenty of fiber. Seek towards the primitive races here, in which there is a high fibrous condition in the diet, and you would find that the cancer, heart and stroke difficulties are far lower. But unless the mind has been altered, unless the hopelessness in the mind has been relieved, the "hopeless disease," the cancer, cannot be dispelled from the body. The attitude first must be altered permanently; then the body would be healed permanently (until it would die or expire, you might call it).

What steps should be taken to prevent infection by parasites or viruses in the first place?

Primarily by keeping the body's mechanisms of elimination highly efficient and correct. This means internally washing the body (the colon itself). This means making the body sweat, perspire and to secrete the poisons that would be locked within the skin itself, or more or less stored as they would be attempted to be removed from within. A pimple is such a storage, where some toxic substance or some product is needed to be eliminated. It is pushed into the skin when it cannot be pushed out of the body in the colon itself, or eliminated through the natural means of the urinary system.

As such, to the question more specifically: keeping the body's eliminations at peak form is a necessity. Keeping the body physically active is also a necessity. Give the body the proper nutrients through a balanced diet or a balanced amount of food (different varieties, you see) taken in, and eat food that is good and wholesome. Food that is prepared or food that has added to it great amounts of sugar, salt and fat are impairing the body's ability; overloading and polluting it, you might say.

Therefore, keeping the body more alkaline and preventing parasitic influences or the invasion of diseases (both bacterial and virus, you see) is, of necessity, a method of keeping the body resilient and protective, for no viral or mucous condition can exist in a body that is slightly more alkaline. These two steps of improved eliminations in all the manners in which the body eliminates and of keeping the body's balance slightly more alkaline by ingesting foods that are alkaline-producing (or efficient in the first place) can be considered preventative for the body itself against any forms or attack of cancer.

Those nuts that also have within them the attempt to spur the body's development and the ability to eliminate at the cell level (such as almonds, you see) would be good as a preventative. An almond a day would be best to take, rather than an apple a day to keep the doctor away.

Therefore, if one is involved in an environment of smoke or metal, or pollution, keeping the body protected is, of course, paramount. If there is extra activity in these areas, then there should be the extra attempt to keep the body purged of any influence that would invade the body in the environmental influences.

And above this, mental attitude is, indeed, most important, for the body itself either has high morale or low morale when it comes to diseases in the body. When the body is depressed, when there are feelings of foreboding, or guilt, or regret (or any form of suppressing emotions) the body becomes more apt to contract disease in the physical form. For the hopeless disease of cancer - hopelessness, or having no hope, having no belief that justice will be served to the self, or if there is anger that is built up but not expressed - these are the emotions (and emotions are both constructive and destructive forces in the body) that are destructive and tend to permit (if you will), provoke, or provide an environment in which cancer can sweep into the body.

A body that is full of laughter, full of enthusiasm, and full of great expectation or hope usually overcomes any and all diseases rather easily or efficiently and effectively. Laughter, therefore, can be considered good medicine to any body that would be in jeopardy, or in disease, you see. Emotional states are the constructive aspects. They release the chemical natures of the body to combat the irregular cells and the conditions of invasion or intrusion in the body. The hormones in the body carry out the timing or signaling devices in the body that cause the glands themselves to produce more hormones, more chemicals or more procedures to keep the body clean and healthy and purged of invading influences; while at the same time attempting to reflect positive, wholesome cell production, whether they replace the skin on the body, or the soft tissue in the organ, and all areas or systems in between. Keeping the body optimistic keeps this production positive and healthful, as well as youthful, you see.

Meditation and entering into states of avoiding wrong thinking (if you will) or incorrect thinking allows the mind to, once again, revisit its creative center and to bring forth renewed invigoration of the cells itself; that is to say, all cells within the body, especially those in the organs of the body, you see.

What properties in the almond make it a good cancer preventative?

You would find there is zinc and other trace elements in the almond that would have the ability to be absorbed into the body rather easily; also the ability to break down clusters of cells which would amalgamate at the atomic level. This can be seen as a spacer that would separate the cells that would be irregular or cancerous in nature and allow them to be discarded more easily. It can be said that almonds identify cells that are irregular and assist in their elimination. The almonds themselves may be raw or roasted, but not fried or deep fried.

You would also find similar cancer-fighting properties in apricot kernels, for they have the ability to affect cells that would be related to the T-cell family. They would migrate along with, and attempt to affect any cocooned condition or cocooned irritation in the body. This is largely seen as the center of a tumor. They tend to penetrate and destroy that invading force or that parasite that the body would normally wrap up in a cocoon or cell package.

Within the almond is a secretion. If you would take the almond and make it into a juice itself, you would find within the almond there are agents here, that cause the cells of the body to be realigned with zinc and other minerals found within, causing the body to respond in a more attuned nature with itself. When there are irregular-shaped cells (the cancer, you would call it), here the almond prevents this. Whereas there would be the single cell that would malform, the almond in the mineral cell would allow the body to attune. You might call this dealing with the forms of magnetism around and in the body. It keeps the cell harmonious in its vibratory rate.

Would three almonds a day for the average person be effective?

Two to three for any who would be fearful of contracting the rapid and outrageous growth of cells (cancer, as you would call it) and the various forms of the same. Two to three would be sufficient, yes.

Can you please explain the link, if any, between radio or microwaves and cancer?

Certain frequencies, as we have given, cause the body to deteriorate. Certain frequencies, or the exposure to radiation in the body (which, in the future, will be found to be beneficial) are, at this point, seen as detrimental to the body. The problem is that the body is bombarded with too much of the frequencies and, as such, these tend to weaken the cell structures, change the filament in the cells themselves, and cause the cells to become rogue, misshapen and rapid in their growth, you see. Therefore, with the stimulation of frequency upon the body, like all things, a little is acceptable; too much is detrimental, you see.

One who would be skilled in pathology, one who would be skilled in metallurgy would be able to direct the confinement of frequencies that would build up the cells, but they would be reproductive, healthy, vibrant cells. In other words, the cell frequency would be speeded up to its proper vibration level. On the other hand, if they are taken above the vibrational level and the frequencies are much higher, then the cell becomes self-destructive and a contaminant to the cells all around it. And, like a rotten apple in the barrel of apples, the poison or rottenness spreads to other healthy cells that would be nearby the cancerous.

Are some people more susceptible than others to cancer?

Indeed, some have a weaker constitution. Those who work in environments in which they would breathe in, absorb through their skin, or by some other means take into themselves those toxic substances - whether they are gases and fumes or metal and soot - these would be, by virtue of exposure, more susceptible, you see. Those who tend to be fearful and worry, or those who have suffered some injustice as a child (or even as an adult) or those who have swallowed great amounts of aggression or anger and cannot get it out (because they are shy, or because of their religious points of view, or whatever reason) all these conditions tend to be susceptible to the disease taking hold of their body.

Would you please explain the cause of breast cancer, and give the best form of treatment.

In what would be found in the mammary would be cyst, fibroid tissue, and cancerous outrageous cells in their growth. Usually this is poor eliminations in the body leading up to deposits through the lymphatic system that turn the sediments, poisons or toxins in the body into cyst, fibroid tissue, or tumor. Also, there are degrees of parasitic conditions in the body that may lead to tumors in the breast, or in other soft tissue.

Keeping the body healthy by good eliminations is the place to start. Colonic irrigations, washing the body in the feminine aspects, and keeping the body clean outside as well as inside, usually keeps the body from developing substances, tissues, or cells. The lymphatic system, which is designed to take away poisons or toxins, collecting it from the body after the body has been worked or put to effort, where those cells that are no longer wanted should be discarded is the sewage system in the body (you might say). As this is maintained, as the health of the body is maintained, the lymphatic system no longer becomes a collection point in the nodes or anodes; it becomes like it was before; a system to rid the body of toxic and noxious materials. Throughout the life, the body should be cleansed from the inside-out, and on the outside-in. The skin is an organ that discharges poisons and toxins through the perspiration and through the flaking of cells from the skin. Therefore, keeping the skin healthy helps the body to eliminate from its largest organ itself (the skin, see).

However, to the question: one who would be skilled in lymphatic massage should be consulted regularly after the point in which the body has become more sedentary than active. For being active, the lymphatic system itself functions, and through this function it eliminates those by-products, cells or sediments (as we have touched upon). Keeping the attitude in the body is most important as well. If there is hopeless thinking or hopelessness in the life, then usually the physical result is some form of hopeless disease. Remember, the mind is the builder, the mind is the way. The emotions are the constructive and destructive forces in any body. Therefore, putting the self in positions that would bring on hopelessness, sadness, depression, or an overall sense of sadness, leads the body into certain types of cancer; resentments and anger lead into bowel cancer, for instance. In the breast, it is largely due to emotional feelings of sadness or being taken advantage of, or being underestimated and under-appreciated. This is speaking to the emotional nature that brings about the derogatory aspect of disease into the body.

But there are other forms of cancers or disruptions in the cells caused by electronic apparatuses, cell phones, and radiation from computers as well as what would be the ingestion of soot from smoking or being involved in an environment in which the air quality is poor, poisonous, or noxious. The collection of these airborne sediments through the lungs, into the lymph, can cause cancer in the breast as well as other areas: the throat, esophagus, stomach, but usually it is through the lungs and through the area of the lymphatic system itself. Therefore, keeping the self in a good environment, away from such pollutants, away from such radiation, and removing the cell phone from breast pockets or brassieres, or packages around the neck - holdings or bags, you see - any form of electronic device that gives off radiation, like a cell phone, like a GPS or other transponding influence, should be kept away from the human body, at least a safe distance. See? This begins the place to improve the body.

As to increasing the lymphatic flow, massage techniques, putting the body in water, swimming, or exercise, any form of movement keep the body youthful; especially isometric exercises, running, all forms of athletic activities. Bending and stretching the body with those exercises that are Eastern in nature keeps the lymphatic system flowing and removes the sediment. Poor diet, toxic environments, emotional difficulties or despair all lead the body to a position of great despair and difficulty.

There are other forms of irritation here. The solution would be to eat those foods that would be healthy to the body; plenty of vegetables, plenty of fruits. Those supplements that would be taken would be almonds, nuts of all kinds, and massage techniques that would empty the lymphatic system. The breasts need to be massaged thoroughly, even simple squeezing to dislodge the cyst, the sediments, or those areas in which they have suffered deposits from the body's own lymph system or circulatory system. The more the breasts are restrained, the less they are benefited, for they do not move, and the more they become collection points for toxins and mucous conditions, and even bacterial and viral conditions, see? Using massage oils or those that would be oils and liniments, the breasts should be massaged regularly to speed up the lymphatic system moving through them and also to increase the blood flow through the chest, throat, abdomen, and even to the back and shoulderblades.

Spinal manipulation should be regular in keeping the spine functioning correctly. The nerve systems going through the same will also function regularly and naturally, which would bring the healing forces to the area of the breast and the surrounding tissues, membranes, muscles and bone. This should be done on a regular basis. However, the cause is primarily poor eliminations in the body, a sense or feeling of being trapped, unappreciated, and even being criticized or bullied. Sometimes injury to the breast - a punch, a strike, an accident, a lace ration - these, too, can bring upon the opening up of the cells that would repeat or duplicate in a rapid or outrageous manner. But first, the stage is set with the body being toxic; that is to say, with the body requiring to be changed slightly more to the alkaline side than the acidic side.

The body purging itself on the inside as well as the outside of those toxic substances, and to the lymphatic system being stimulated so that it might better carry out and carry away those toxic substances would be a place to start. From eating wheatgrass juice and improving the small intestine, through to eating a balanced form of little in the way of carbonated drinks, little in the way of sugar or deep-fried foods, this is a subtle way of keeping the intestine functioning correctly. A good diet, a good form of exercise or movement, and good exposure to the outside air and light can remedy any condition of difficulty in the skin or in the soft tissue. Take those substances that are alkaline-producing over those that are acidic-producing and the body should respond quite well.

What causes skin cancer, and what may be

done to remedy it?

Anything that is in the skin is usually demonstrative of the inability of the body to eliminate the toxins and poisons from within. The skin can be affected by radiation, bright lights, or abundance of UV radiation; likewise, microwave activity or what would be high frequency sound generation devices or frequencies, you see. The low frequency causes bone to grow. The high frequency causes skin to deteriorate. Therefore, cell phone devices, hand-held devices, or any other form of radiation coming into the body regularly and consistently in the same place can cause a disruption at the cell level. Those cells that are disruptive mutate, and the mutation can be seen as cancerous in the skin itself.

Therefore, remove from the self any radiation, any light that is harmful, but do not be afraid of sunlight. Sunbathing the body before the eleventh hour in the morning or after the second hour in the afternoon should still allow the body to absorb sunlight in a healthy way or manner. However, at the mid-day, this is when the body might have too much or direct radiation that is destructive through the ultraviolet rays (so to speak); the visible and invisible levels of light.

However, as we examine the condition, increasing the body's elimination, removing toxic substances from the colon, the liver, and having the bladders of the body work more correctly or in a balanced way, this should usually remove any toxic substances that are being deposited in the skin itself. The blood, being polluted with sediments and toxins, carries these through the body. The lymphatic system attempts to remove these through its filtering processes. The kidneys and the liver attempt also to remove these substances from the soft tissues and from what is taken into the body.

As eliminations are enhanced and colonics are used, vegetable juices may be given to the body and sprouts from beans and seeds may be given. This would give high nutrition to the body and, although the volume of food is decreased, the body's assimilative process of nutrition is maintained and strengthened. At the same time, the elimination factors are increased in their activity. They remove disrupted cells or cells that have lingered and have not been culled, isolated or removed from their location in the body. The body is constantly removing cells and replacing them, and the disrupted areas or cells in the skin can be quickly affected or removed (healed, if you will) by such replacement activity.

The body needs to be in a healthful way, highly alkaline in its balance between alkaline and acidic, highly healthy in its circulation being increased throughout the body or the affected area. It also needs to be highly motivated by the body's increased eliminations, removing pollutants, toxins, and substances or sediments from the blood, the lymph, the liver, and the kidney itself. Any form of stimulation in the urinary would be helpful. Toxins in the blood may be removed through teas, the apple diet, or fasting. Also, the consumption of wheatgrass juice and other green substances like *spirulina* would be helpful to aid in removing skin cancer in the various types, conditions, or intensities.

Specifically look to the liver and the kidneys and their function. The bladders themselves are secondary but they, too, with toxins and sediments in the body, may become susceptible. Keep the body eliminating. Keep the acidic levels lower. Keep the body moving. This should remedy the conditions that you would call skin cancer.

Examining life in the Twenty-first Century, is there any other substance which we can add to the list of cancer-fighting foods?

To avoid cancer, do not put tainted food into the body, but do eat a diet that would be more fruits and vegetables, natural sugars rather than artificial, and keeping the spices of the body, and the metals that would be taken in, regulated; that is, not to follow any one specific dietary direction all the time. This would be the subtle way.

We would find there are other influences that would help the body. Drinking alkaline water every day would add years to a life, for it would remove the basis of attack through the parasites and through the viral and bacterial conditions in the body.

As for anything better, understand that anything that aids the removal of poisons, parasites, and makes the body insulated against viral and mucous conditions would be the best. Understand the process of cancer. Any toxic substance could trigger any tumor or cell that would then appear layered or thickened, because it has enveloped a parasite or a germ within it. Eliminate the cause, and you eliminate cancerous cells. To some degree, the almond facilitates this, as we have given. The pursuit of alkalinity would be the best source, the first line of defense, as we see it.

Do you have any additional comments on the topic of cancer at this point in time?

It would best be to understand that the body does not betray the self. The body is not an extension of something else. It is, indeed, the extension of the self and those conditions that are held in the mind. The mind is the place to start. The attitude shifting from despair to enthusiasm to optimism is, indeed, a good start. But one cannot simply wish away that which is. One must have a plan. Be practical in the application of that plan. Look at the body and find out what is wrong, and attempt to find the emotional key (so to speak).

Releasing the emotion in the mind that is spurring on the condition of disease in the body can quicken the results. Forgiving the self, as well as others, seeking the help and assistance of others to pray for the body to be better, are all ways and means or things that can be done that have an effect. But most importantly, it is that there is a desire for the body to get better in the first place, and that, once the body becomes better, that the self will be put in a better environment and will not feel trapped or imprisoned in its circumstance.

Then, as this would be commenced, a true believing that something good is going to happen, and that the self can remove the burdens that are upon the physical, mental and emotional selves will allow for the body to become resilient and to overcome the effects of any pressure, or any disease, or disease-ment, you see. For in fact, as it would be understood, if it were believed, disease begins in the mind. Harboring resentful thoughts, thoughts of anger, frustration and worry, all tend to lead the body to states of poor health; whether it be a runny nose or whether it be a cancerous tumor in the stomach depends upon the intensity of the mind and just how expressive the emotional aspects of the self are, you see.

Cancer is a disease that can be overcome, as all diseases can be. All that is necessary is that the person look for the remedies and the cures. Then there can be some action taken, some resolve to overcome the problem in the body, rather than to simply lay down and accept what has been given as a death sentence. For remember always that God is a loving and just God. There are no injustices in the world, as you know it.

Candidiasis

What is the cause of the medical condition known as candidiasis?

This would be seen as an imbalance in the body, that the body is more acidic than alkaline in its imbalance. The primary difficulty in the body is imperfect eliminations. Where there is constipation (or even diarrhea) in the body, then you would have all of the above conditions taking place in the body. Like dominoes, you might say, the conditions mount. Each condition is dependent on a different domino, beginning with the acidic levels or difficulty in the body. These conditions mount or propagate themselves, you see.

Carbonated drinks are usually the basis for acidic buildups in the body; although it is not, of course, the only cause. As far as causal effects in the body, it is that the body produces mucous when there is slightly greater acidic environment in the body. If the body is slightly imbalanced towards the alkaline side, then the body is unable to produce viral and bacterial or mucous conditions within the body. Discharges from the genitals and irritation in the palate are linked (but not in the same manner, or way, directly). The discharges are usually due to the body's inability, because of the acidic levels, to remove the mucous substances that are accumulating in the organs themselves.

What would be upon the tongue is an indication, indeed, there is difficulty in the sinuses, in the palate or throat, the bronchial, and in the lymphatic system in and around the upper part of the body. There is mucous in the esophagus and it advances upwards (not downward) because of poor eliminations in the body. For understand that the ingestion of vitamins is one thing; the assimilation of the same is another (and the delivery of the same is yet another issue). Water and the moisture in the body is the medium upon which the vitamins are transferred, assimilated, and utilized to and at the cell level, for water is the conduit of the body. As there is assimilation in the body, then the vitamins can be directed to the specific cells. There is a specific direction of vitamins to specific areas in the body. This is unknown, or unseen, or unthought of that the body has the ability to direct vitamins to where they are needed or utilized.

Therefore, in understanding further, the conditions in the body can be also seen as a lack of proper digestion (but not because of food having some difficulty in the stomach, too much acid, or bile, or digestive juices, you see); understand it as the mucous higher up in the esophagus not being properly moved or eliminated in the body. Notice the salivary glands, the lymphatic glands, those about the mouth, those that secrete saliva and those that drain the saliva or mucous away. On occasion, these are overworked. They are congested. As such, they build up in the breast or arms (these would be nodes, you see), and, as such, are temporary deposit points for what would be considered garbage or sediment in the body. The intention, here, is to have them erode, dissipate, or flow into the elimination tracks.

The remedy, therefore, is to take that which would be helpful to the body on these several levels or planes. Grapefruit seed extract has the ability to rectify candida or mucous conditions. It also has the ability, in the mouth, to affect candidiasis and remove this from the throat and palate. It can stimulate the lymphatic system and, to some degree (although it is not harsh) to stimulate the bowel itself. This can be taken to remove toxins from the mouth or the other parts of the body (male or female, you see). It also assists mucous movement in the large and small intestine (but primarily in the large intestine). Therein there should be also given to the body enemas or colonic irrigation. This would assist quickly and dramatically what is to be removed from the body, in the physical sense. More water should be given to the body; the more water in the body, the more absorption is capable from cell to cell. For what is placed in the body to be helpful (food, nutrients and vitamins) would be carried to the cell level, bringing the body back in harmony.

The intention is to remove the acidic levels from the body to keep it more alkaline. Any food that is alkaline in nature should be eaten more, and acid-producing food should be taken less (or avoided). This does not necessarily mean that citrus fruits would necessarily produce acidic levels; nay, it would be the opposite. But any carbonated drink would imbalance the body quickly and greatly to the acidic levels. Therefore, eat those foods that would be more of a natural diet. Eat mono meals, or ones that would consist of one or two foods. More than one food at a time confuses a body that is already confused with acidic states, and enzymes are not properly secreted, leading to difficult or partial digestion.

Humans are affected by the emotional states (which are the constructive and destructive forces in any body). When there are stresses brought about in the body, the hormonal systems in the body are imbalanced, but so are many glandular systems that secrete the hormones themselves. Stress, worry, and fear have physical effects in the body. This understanding should be seen that those with thyroid conditions need more iodine in the diet and also more measures to calm the body, whether it is taking slippery elm as a tea or kava kava as a tranquilizer. The idea, here, is to bring the body back in balance. The emotions that are best are those of being in love and loved (and also humor); the feeling of easement to be in the company of others that are social and not threatening. To be in this environment and, indeed, to be happy is the point at where life should be lived. Very few, however, look to this. There is always a searching, a hunting, a scourging, a predator or fearful attitude held within the minds of most. Who would be happier: he who would live in a mud hut, or he who would live in an apartment in New York with all the conveniences? In all probability, he who would live in a mud hut. Humans are strange in their logic, their thinking and usually they do the right thing for the wrong reasons.

The conditions in the body can be altered, in an organic sense, by simply keeping the body more alkaline. Wash the body on the outside. Let the body be put in warm rooms (steam rooms) to purge the poisons from the pores or cells of the skin. Let there also be the washing of the poisons from the inside; that the enemas or colonics be given on a regular basis. Consuming plenty of water also assists the body in its natural need to eliminate, and to utilize the moisture for all the beneficial systems in the body.

There should be a little "brain washing" as well, to wash those thoughts from the mind of fear, or anxiety, or depression, or loneliness. Meditation is a good practice, and is necessary for the body; so is proper rest or sleep. To this end, the body needs to purge those worries from its mind, so it is not distracted. For though the mind looks like it works in chaos, it has an order to it. If the mind is thinking on any one fear for too long, then the mind becomes singular, or pointed, and out of balance. Let the creative forces be random and chaotic. Let the mind be distracted by those things you would call play or entertainment.

The body needs all aspects of work, worship, rest, and play in order to be properly balanced (as well as washing away those influences, attitudes, arguments, slights, or uncomfortable thoughts). Wash these away once per day, whether it requires listening to pleasant music, surrounding the self with pleasant fragrances, or having the additional touch upon the body. Allow it to be soothed, pampered or babied, you see. The feeling of love or intense love is a curative force which can speed up the body's natural healing ability and processes, you see.

Cannabis

The use of cannabis or marijuana oil, for health purposes, is very old. There is a theory now that the properties of this plant would be a very effective treatment for different types of cancer. Could you please discuss this.

In examining this particular plant there are several intricacies, in the use of the plant. From the leaves, to the root, we find the entire plant can be utilized, as in all things found in nature. Nature has within it the medicine cabinet or storehouse for all medicines (as you would know it). In the plant form, the different arrangements, or usages of the parts of the plant are quite complicated, complex and sensitive. When they are synthesized, or taken from nature and copied, there is a loss in this, the complexity. The complexity of the plant is necessary for the metabolism or the assimilation of the plant into the body.

This particular plant has abilities that would affect the blood. It does affect the controlling centers (thalamus and hypothalamus). It does affect the soft tissues, like the eyes, the thyroid, the liver, the bladders, the spleen, kidneys and adrenals. Therefore, this particular plant is beneficial in that it isolates those cells that would be rapid and outrageous in their growth (cancers). It also has as tendency to cocoon illnesses and diseases in the body. It tends to hydrate the cells of the body, and also it breaks down the shell or meniscus of bacteria, see? For viral conditions, it tends to isolate, encapsulate and then eliminate from the body; it sort of scoops illnesses, you see.

However it has a primary tendency to convert matter; what is in crystalline form can be softened or made into gel or then liquid form. The condition is evident in the body that this is a plant that has been used historically to affect thinking, brain function, skin conditions, and the eliminating aspects in the body. By being absorbed into the blood, it affects an array of soft tissue centers (as you would know it).

To the question: there is some benefit for this in aligning the body, making it more healthy, and removing these sediments that have mounted and are consistent in any body, see?

How best should this be taken into the body?

This can be ingested. The fumes of the same can be inhaled also, but to be ingested would be the assimilative way. Oils made from the plant can be dabbed on the skin or the tongue and this would be assimilated into the tissues of the body quickly. Made into vapor, there is some loss of benefit, but this would be equal to the same loss used in digestion when it is ingested in the body. It may be made into teas, or brews, and this would tend to be much more compatible or easy with the body. Of course, the leaves may be eaten raw, like a salad, but this would be a different effect. When there is some change in temperature, there is a chemical change that activates the properties within the plant itself. Therefore, either baking, ingesting or producing it into an oil base or form causes these chemical alterations to take place and, therefore, it is used for different reasons or has different strengths to be used in the body. One of its base properties is primarily to be used as a tranquilizer or such that would bring a soothing, relaxing, tranquilizing effect to the body. Then it would affect the glandular secretions, to allow a certain hormonal balance to occur. This would be a minor balance. As we have given, ingested and put into the blood, it does have an effect, not as a hallucinogenic, but what would free the mind from certain worries and allow a certain alignment within the glandular secretions and the controlling centers in the back of the brain (medulla and cerebellum) and the center of the brain (thalamus and hypothalamus), see?

Canker Sores

What is the cause of canker sores?

Too much acid within the body, expressing itself in the sensitive saliva areas of the mouth and the tongue itself, see?

Carbonated Drinks

It has been suggested that carbonated drinks acidify the body and should be avoided, especially if one is trying to keep an alkaline diet.

Would you please comment?

Indeed, carbonated drinks are not natural for the body. It is the ingestion of gases within the system that can, indeed, plague the body, causing disruption within the intestinal tract and also affecting the body's filtering devices adversely. For understand the gas itself has been compressed. As it is ingested into the body, it expands in its normal state. This causes internal pressures that affect the stomach, the esophagus, the valves at the upper and lower end of the stomach, you see. It causes difficulty in the intestine and can produce flatulence here in the intestine or adds to the fermentation process and production of methane gas and other substances in the body itself. Indeed, it is stressful to the kidney (as it would be to the body itself) as there would be an absorption of the gases in the blood itself, you see. It can turn the body acidic if there is extensive consumption of the carbonated gas. This causes cysts and tumors, cirrhosis of the liver, destruction of the living cells in the liver as well. It can also place pressures at the heart, you see.

The condition here is not radically dangerous to the body, but if endured for long periods of time and consistently, it can be considered as poison into the body itself, you see. Why would one put into the body gaseous substances that are not conducive to improving the breathing, you see, to improving the vitality of the body, to improving the metabolism itself, you see? The blood is saturated if there would be continued drinking. It does wear the body down, as it would be slowly poisoned, you see. But if the body has vitality and is alkaline, it would take a considerable time before there would be any noticeably adverse affects. However, if there is alcohol here, as well as soda pop and some water that is artificially carbonated, then, over a period of time, the body, indeed, would be acid and would lose its resistance to viral and mucous conditions, you see.

Castor Oil

What causes the Edgar Cayce-style castor oil pack to offer help or health benefits?

The pack itself is the delivery or the applicator for castor oil. The castor oil pack is an application to allow the greater amount of absorption of the castor oil, sometimes in Latin (Roman) called *Palma Christi* ("the hand of Christ") referring to its curative and healing affects. The pack itself allows the oil to absorb greatly into specific areas of the body. The oil itself is in harmony or in sync with the tissue of the body, causing a regeneration of new cells where wounds have been found and softening scar tissues, for it works with (and in harmony with) the cell itself, helping it to knit together.

For organs, especially the abdominal areas, it allows regeneration of new cells and healing focuses to be brought into play through the oil and the heat generated by the pack. It allows the oils to penetrate deep into the abdominal cavity; a sort of weeping rain of oil, you see, into the intestinal areas, into the walls of the abdominal area, and this affects both organically the cell and also the delivery or the controlling substances of the nervous system as well. It affects and improves the chi energy moving through the meridian lines of the body as well. It is like putting a warm blanket on the body, and with the body's natural healing forces, it works in harmony with them, stimulating the organs and the systems that they might function more correctly.

Castor oil is a substance that works with the body to remove impurities, to fight off infections for it can be considered anti-inflammatory as a substance, you see, and also as a lubricating force in the body. It allows the cells to move about more comfortably in the subatomic level, you see. At the same time, it allows them to carry and keep the healing forces, nutrients and substances, chemicals otherwise in the general region or area of the body. To burn victims, it would soften any scar tissue which would add as an oily blanket (so to speak) keeping infection out, while allowing the body to knit together, to rebuild in an accelerated way new cells that would be curative or (you would call this) would be healing to the wounds in the body.

Are the packs useful during times of good health or only illness?

What is good health? Is there good health when there is not dis-ease within the body? Yes, in what would be the conditions as a maintenance, they would help the body maintain its health, thereby improving its vibratory rate, specifically for kidney and intestinal uses. Yes, this can he used (and should be used) on a regular basis. It would be seen as a preventative, and it would be seen as an improvement of health to better health.

Is there any way that the traditional Edgar Cayce castor oil pack could be improved to get out even more of the sedentary material that adheres to the wall of the colon?

It is a matter of absorption into the body, and the castor oil would be helpful in removing inflammation and, to some degree, affecting the body with - call it - a lubricating effect. But here, understand the castor oil pack is to allow the oil to be absorbed into the body; therefore longer periods, or more frequent periods of application of the pack would, of course, be more advantageous. If the body is heated up, placed in a warm room, or wrapped in blankets, or placed in a steam room for a brief time, this naturally causes the pores in the body to open and the passage of the oil through the pores would be enhanced or improved. See? It is a simple, mechanical process; no mystery here. But if the body is warm or if infrared light is used, this assists the oil to be applied, absorbed and distributed in the body itself.

Cataracts

Can you please comment briefly on the cause of cataracts and the best focus of treatment?

These would be the body's cell production gone wild, you see. For it should be understood that all cells in the body are replaced. There is a belief that this is done within a seven-year cycle or period. It is true that every cell in the body is replaced at one time or another. This is how the body maintains itself. Old cells are dislodged, removed and are exited from the body. New cells are grown in place of the old cells. Now whether it is the toenails or the fingernails, or the hair upon the body, or the sputum, or whether it would be the flaking of the skin off (as dandruff might be), or any other form of elimination, the body does regenerate, replace and eliminate the cells constantly.

The tissue or cell structure in the cataract (or tissue in the eye) is the same as the roof of the mouth. The body has different replacement rates, depending on the part of the body. The cells of the mouth are every few days; the eyes are a little longer. But it is the growth of what would seem to be a shield, or a tissue, or a replenishing of the lens cover (if you will) of the eye.

Deterioration of this can be done by the use of simple saliva from the mouth of the individual placed in the eye. It would tend to ward off or reduce the cataract itself and, as such, the cell production. For you see, the recent cells are produced more readily in the mouth than, for instance, the soles of the feet because of the high acidic levels of the saliva. Therefore, if this is used in the eye, we would find great success in removing or diminishing the cataract altogether, as the saliva would be a natural way of eroding any excess growth of the eye itself in the pupil or eyeball, you see.

There are other forces or influences that can be done, but this would simply be the body building up that there are no readily-used toxin elimination systems, for kidneys, constipation, or poor elimination can be seen as part and parcel of the body's build-up of difficulty here in the eye; but also the wax build up in the ear, and the lymphatic system being sluggish or slowing down, and the sinuses of the body not draining properly or becoming stagnant. Again, breeding grounds, collection points for garbage cells that should otherwise be eliminated. Understand: the same influence that makes the fingernails grow makes the cataract grow.

What would be best would be to have these cataract cells, prior to becoming cataracts, be removed or eliminated in the body's natural way. Again, it is to have the body perspire, to have movement or physical exercise that would be tiring to the body to allow for the removal of these cells through the stimulation of both the circulation and the lymphatic system itself. We would find that stimulation of massage with healing oils (or stimulating oils) would be a little stimulating to the body, and a good sweat or cleansing of the pores in the face would be a good deterrent to this, as well. As a general rule, the body's elimination should be highly maintained, and stimulation of the lymphatic system paramount, you see.

Cerebral Palsy

Can you please explain the cause of cerebral palsy, and explain the best form of treatment for the same.

You would find difficulties of blood supply into the brain itself, affecting the thalamus and hypothalamus. You would find also that, hormonal secretions in the body being irregular, the thyroid itself would be somewhat imbalanced. It would be hypoactive and/or hyperactive, or a combination of the two extremes. Manipulation in the neck and spine should be done in such a way that this would allow the brain to increase in its blood flow, the skull to sit more firmly on the neck (Atlas and Axis, you see), and for the body's chemistry to be somewhat balanced. For there usually would be hormonal imbalances taking place here, and the hormones should be examined and balanced, easily.

As to what would be the difficulty in the brain, usually there is some swelling internally, and the need for manipulation of the bones in the head. A cranial-sacral therapist can be accommodating, and may prove, in a large percentage of the time, to relieve the pressures in the brain or in the cavity itself, in which the brain resides.

Chelation Therapy

It is theorized that called chelation therapy (intravenous injections with EDTA) is beneficial to most, and with enough treatments, can even reverse dementia. Please comment.

The use of the combination, depending upon the cleansing process in the body, if it is removing plaque (which it is occasionally credited for), this allows invigorated blood flow into various parts of the brain. With increased blood flow, there is increased delivery of oxygen and, indeed, thinking would improve; perhaps removing conditions of dementia, or inoperative synapse fluctuation or excitement. Brain tissues functioning correctly would allow thinking to return to normal.

In this regard, depending upon the circumstance in the human body, this process of chelation therapy, designed to remove sediments such as heavy metals in the body, can, of course, have continued benefits; they would help to remove congestion in different organs, different parts of the body, as it is carried through the body by the blood system. It encapsulates residue or foreign objects, sediments and therefore delivers them out of the body in the normal process of elimination.

We would agree, this has benefits, which should not be relied upon as a sole cure-all for the body, but it does have benefits for those who have been exposed to, for instance, workplace chemicals. The one who has a sod farm is exposed to chemicals even though he is in the open air (although sometimes in sheds where it is being mixed). It can easily adulterate the body with poisons. Nervous system attacks, emotional disorders and even slight dementia can occur, because there is poison in the body. This process, this method can remove the poisons quickly and efficiently and the body can respond very quickly. The same for those who would work in places or factories where they are exposed to the inhalation of metal - welders, grinders, foundry workers, steel mills - those who work with mercury and other chemicals can easily be exposed and absorb the same. In these cases, the body has the intelligence, using the chelation chemical or process, to remove the sediments. We would agree, therefore, it has capabilities that would be mildly effective in the body. Simply removing sediments, toxins and poisons makes sense.

For those who have plaque in the blood, would the process of EDTA not be as effective for those who are not exposed? The argument has been made that the chelation process undoes the building blocks of plaque everywhere, regardless of how it got there.

We would agree with this.

Does EDTA taken orally through the digestive system have the same effects, or near the same effects, as the EDTA taken intravenously?

When it is taken orally, it tends to degrade, for it has to go through the digestive process and it is somewhat damaged, but there is still some benefit here. That which is injected tends to be more potent, but it can be somewhat hard on the body. That which is taken orally would have a tendency to feel easier on the body. One is passive, one is aggressive. However, taken orally, it would tend to be slower but more correct in the processes of the body. It would affect the intestine adversely at first, and then complimentary later. It would affect the assimilation of food into the body by making that part of the body a little sluggish, you see. However, to the question itself: the pill, this would appear to be acceptable.

What other supplements, herbs or compounds act as a chelating agent if taken orally to the same degree, or better, than the EDTA?

It would appear that any of the plants that tend to be furry or have hooks or barbs on them or prickly surfaces would be the ones to ingest, you see. They have a tendency, in their complex makeup, to affect or attack many levels of sediment within the blood. It is this wide array, this complexity that makes these cacti, or herbs, or plants so effective as a remedy, you see, for they work in harmony with the body.

Please give a specific example.

Chickweed.

Chemtrails

Consider the phenomenon known as contrails or chemtrails, where airplanes in Western nations dump chemicals into our atmosphere. What effect are these operations having on the health and immune system of the population at large?

As any would-be elements secreted into the atmosphere, there is a residue effect that is negative or adverse; as such, this affects respiratory conditions in anyone who is breathing the same. It also affects the libido, and can indirectly affect conception possibilities. It affects the reproductive centers in the body (diminishes the same) and, if one is exposed to this type of pollution consistently and frequently, there can be the destruction of brain tissue itself. The purpose here, however, is to affect primarily the respiratory centers in the body. The body would be filled with these droplets or these aluminum-based elements, which is stored in the nooks and crannies and in the soft tissue of the body (including the brain, in particular). This is the result of these substances that are carelessly secreted into the atmosphere. Unfortunately they are entering into the water tables and they do not go away; for, once created and secreted or released into the air or water, these types of elements remain forever. Temporarily residing in one body and then returning to the Earth, they are released, and they find their way into another body.

What can people do to minimize the negative effects?

It would be to have simple air filters in their dwellings where the air would be circulated through some sort of a filter or screen. It would be to avoid exposure to these elements or these secretions, by simply being inside; understanding that water droplets attract these elements and, therefore, having any form of fountain, water sprinkler or other substance around the dwelling would be helpful. But we see that the best would be a filtration device that would clean the air. If there are plenty of trails in the vicinity in which the body resides, then perhaps relocating to a different location would be appropriate. If the air is still, then stay inside or vacate the region in which the body finds itself. If there are high winds, and these are at high altitude, then this would be dispersed over a wide area and would not necessar-

ily have any effects in a concentrated form,. If there are stationary trails above the self, then indeed, close the windows and doors and have some filtration device within the dwelling that would clean the air, ever remembering not to have air pumped in from the outside directly.

You may also put copper screens, around the area in which the self resides. In extreme cases, these could be embedded in the ceilings and walls of dwellings, hidden under the wall board or plaster. These would have a tendency to negate other influences of microwaves and other waves of light and frequency. However, this would be used in an extreme situation only.

Take into the self plenty of iodine and flush the system with eight to ten tumblers of water each day. This would be a good rule of thumb to maintain any cleansing of any exposure to these elements that might remain in the body for the rest of the life. This would seem to be beneficial, from our perspective, as we examine this at this point in time.

Cherries

Cherry juice is often recommended for cases of gout to deal with excess uric acid. Could you please describe the mechanism involved?

Consider gout as a bunch of fibers. They mash together; they build up and expand. They are like little needles here, and they dig into the tissues. They register or are deposited, usually in the right foot first, farthest from the heart, in the nooks and crannies or in the bone crevices of the body. Cherry juice tends to dislodge the fibers, surround them with a coating, cocoon them (you might say) and have them removed. For, as the body sends them out through the circulatory system, the condition of difficulty is to be found in the migration from the arterial system and into the venous. If this migration can be prevented, then these fibers can be removed or eliminated while still in the arteries of the body, while still flowing away from the heart. Otherwise they can become lodged, build up, block the flow of blood, and become very painful indeed. The cherries tend to disintegrate, isolate, surround, and otherwise extricate these fiber-like substances that would be considered sedentary or gout.

Does it follow that people with a tendency to arthritis should drink lots of red cherry juice?

Yes, black cherries, cherries, all juices from the cherry trees or cherry family. Understand that different folks have different reactions and, therefore, cherries of all types should be consumed, but it is the black cherry that seems to have the best effect; although all cherries may be taken in season, and plenty of them, by all types of people. Yes, it makes sense, but do incorporate other types of cherries as well.

Chiropractic

How frequently should a healthy body have a chiropractic adjustment?

If it would exercise itself properly (which would be the bending and stretching of the spine itself), there would be no need for the manipulation by another, unless there would be the injury. But should there be a degree of lack of physical energy or bending or stretching (as you would call it) of the exercises of the spine, then we would suggest the periodic maintenance be continued here; once or twice a month would be sufficient. But this cannot be considered a constructive form of healing. Any chiropractor worth his salt would recommend a degree of exercise; the bending and stretching of the spinal column in accord with his adjustments (taking into consideration we are dealing primarily with healthy bodies). Those who would not be as healthy would need specific exercises and, as such, specific adjustment. But generally speaking, the movement of the spine through exercise is the best form of exercise. Yoga is an excellent way to gently - repeat, gently - bend and stretch the spine.

Over the years, there have been a number of changes in chiropractic manipulation. Consider one such system, which is typical of the group, Network Spinal Associates. Instead of forceful changes all at once, the patient lies facedown for a period of time and enters a near-meditative state, while the therapist makes small, almost subtle changes to the body, very gentle pulls and pushes, coming and going over thirty minutes. Does this work?

Yes, if the therapist is both skilled in the thing and simpatico with the one being worked on. If you would watch the subtle or energy bodies, you would see this makes them shimmer or pulse. There is no bruising or force, no trauma or shock to the body, and indeed, if done correctly, the benefit would be longer lasting for the one being treated.

Chlorine

For most of the population in North America

or the Western environment, are we absorbing excess amounts of chlorine through the showering process?

Yes, or through the drinking water itself.

What are the symptoms of excess chlorine intake?

If a person does not smoke, then the first symptom would be that the teeth would be soft or the wall of the same would weaken; also the luster or shine of the enamel would be diminished.

Dr. Hulda Clark believed that common chlorine bleach, which is used in most households, is especially dangerous to be exposed to. Do you see any unusual harm or danger in chlorine bleach exposure?

Could be; chlorine was used for gaseous substances and can be disruptive. The same might be said of salt, to a lesser degree. However, to the question: depending upon the temperature and confinement of the bleach, it could be considered dangerous in breathing the fumes. It could be poisoning the body. Yes, to the question.

Chocolate

Some have said that milk chocolate is one of the worst foods to ingest. Would you agree or disagree?

It is not a "bad food," and it can be taken on occasion; but for the purpose of the comment, it does tend to leech calcium from the system and produce mucous in most bodies that are susceptible to viral and mucous conditions (especially those who have difficulty in digesting dairy products, especially milks, creams and cheeses from the dairy cow). The chocolate itself has a high level of sugar and caffeine, on occasion. Therefore, it can have a roller coaster effect on the blood sugar level within the body, causing disorientation, causing upset in the metabolism itself. It does tend to slow the body down for most of the activities (including the thinking), but it tends to speed up the emotional responses, you see. These can work both for, and against, the body. However, largely due to the leeching of the calcium that leads to softening of the bone, this can lead to damage within the longer bones of the leg, as well as producing excess amounts of mucous that would affect the lungs and create a condition of edema, a fluid condition within the same. It is also hard on the kidney and the spleen and, on occasion, it can also drive the adrenal glands to be overactive, you see.

Is dark chocolate any better?

All tend to be of the same source. The dark chocolate itself can be a little richer in stimulants for the body. The dark chocolate itself does have, on occasion, fruit within the same and the molasses, as opposed to sugar.

Chronic Fatigue Syndrome and Low Energy

What causes chronic fatigue syndrome and what is the best treatment?

It is both a combination of toxicity in the blood increasing, and a decreasing of oxygen in the blood. Simply put: the body produces too much waste or toxic substances within the blood. The body becomes polluted (you might say) and, as such, the body becomes tired; as such, there is less and less room for oxygen in the blood itself. The oxygen, of course, is what would be given to the blood in the hemoglobin itself; the oxygen surrounding the blood cells itself, you see. The body's hormone system, the regulatory glands in the body, the thyroid, the pancreas, the liver, as well as the kidneys, become imbalanced and, as such, the body becomes sensitive to extremes or conditions and this sensitivity causes the body to become tired, or constantly tired.

The remedy for this is simply to improve the oxygen taken into the body. Put the oxygen more into the arterial, or what would be the red blood, as opposed to what would be the darker or the blue blood in the vein, you see (to give some comparison).

Next would be for the body to remove the toxicity and the influences that are weighing it down or holding it back. This can be done by breathing exercises: forty to eighty deep breaths in the morning and in the evening (or any time the body feels sluggish or tired when it ought not to, you see). There can be the introduction of oxygen bottles or oxygen supply. Again the intention is to overcome the air quality/pollution effects primarily; but to allow more oxygen to be given into the body and, as such, building up the blood, hemoglobin or kinetic energy within the same. The body should be forced to move, to exercise until it perspires. Whether this is done by heavy lifting of weights, or whether it is done by simple stretching or slow moving exercises is, of course, dependent upon the level of fatigue. However, the body should be builded up, should be put on a regime of body building.

There should be plenty of good water taken into the body and plenty of good food taken into the body.

Chelation therapy might be helpful for this immediately to remove the sedentary and toxic forces (in most cases).

Plenty of water taken into the body and, indeed, some forcing, either of increasing breathing exercises, increased exposure to oxygen (an oxygen mask or oxygen therapy) or even the hyperbaric chamber can be used to increase oxygen in the body's blood and the body should respond very quickly.

It will need to maintain an active physical life thereafter, however, to maintain the positive effects. And, of course, air quality or pollution effects from the work-place or the environment in which the body resides (or in the occupation that the entity resides) should be considered as well. Farmers who deal with chemicals (sod farmers, people who work in orchards) are particularly susceptible to a build-up of poisonous influences, including factory workers (as we see it) that would be masking the condition of chronic fatigue, when, indeed, the body has been simply poisoned, you see.

Certain people complain about chronic tiredness and lack of energy. What would be the prime cause of this?

Lack of oxygen within the body; over-toxification of the body also. Poor eliminations would be the first indicator. Light breathing, or breathing through the mouth and expanding only the upper regions of the chest would be a second cause.

Where to correct? Breathe from the diaphragm through the nasal passageway. More fiber in the diet, and a three-day enema program would allow any body to begin to turn itself around and feel more lively, more enthusiastic, more energetic. We would recommend a fast every now and then to give the poor, old body a break, see?

The mind is the builder. The mind must be in control. For who is the master: the belly or the brain? Each and every entity should fast at least once a week to allow a degree of mental attunement and strength to be derived, yes; but to give the poor body a break. If you would only know how hard it works, there would not be any excess food taken in. There would be just enough to get by. But the plea for the palate, the body suffers; a few brief moments of pleasure and hours of toil. Is it worth it? Nay, we see not. But habits are habits.

Colds

When one feels a cold coming on, what is the best method of stopping it?

Rest in bed, plenty of fluids and think warm, loving thoughts. Here, the added baking soda - half a teaspoon in a glass of warm water taken every two hours - can prevent, for it tends to remedy the alkaline balance of the body.

Colloidal Silver

Do you agree that, for the average person, colloidal silver (taken as an internal drink in water) has the ability to kill parasites, bacteria and fungi?

Affirmative. We do.

Is there any side-effect to this, or is it a relatively safe modality of treatment?

Too much causes congestion. The body is a vehicle that has a saturation point. Going beyond the point causes difficulty. For instance, putting a piece of wire on the arm, and bending the arm, and bending the wire single-strand is easy at first. But if more bands of wire are put on top of each other, or bound together, then you have a rigid, inflexible brace rather than what would be a flexible, cooperative alignment. Similarly, too much silver causes a build-up or residue to exist in the body. Therefore, less is better, or a tincture is better than a maximum amount. Like iodine, methods to find out where that point in which the body has reached its saturation limit would be necessary to verify each dosage as correct.

Colon and Digestive Issues

Diarrhea, Flatulence, Irritable Bowel, Laxatives

Please comment on the causes of diarrhea and what you would recommend to treat it.

Diarrhea in the body should first be seen not as something that is derogatory, but is, in fact, a natural process in the body, expediting that which has been given to the body that needs to be eliminated from the body quickly. To understand diarrhea is to understand the process in the body. When there is congestion or constipation, there would be a building up of bile and other fluids in the colon in order to assist the dislodging of what would be congested (physical congress, you see) in the colon itself. On occasion, there is the stool removed, and there is then a series of loose or fluid-like matter that is exited from the body. This is the body's natural mechanism to remove from itself matter that needs to be rejected.

On other occasions, there is what would be poisons, or toxins, or even bacterial or virus that would be in the small intestine, and it would be passing through to the large intestine. These substances, those derogatory influences in the body are being removed from the body quickly, for they are a danger to the body. They are somehow impeding the body's natural function.

To understand that which would be chronic diarrhea is, therefore, to pay attention to the position of the intestine (small or large), for there can be a fold or twist in the intestine and the body is now using this mechanism (diarrhea) to remove physical congress (that which has been obstructed in the body). Therefore, not to always think that diarrhea needs to be stopped is our point. Natural processes in which there is an ease in elimination through diarrhea is the body's natural reaction to something that is derogatory, yet natural in the body.

When things are chronic (and this would be for more than three days), then the body should be examined for some of the conditions we have described. When there is disease in the body (especially what is found in the small and, perhaps, the large intestine) it is a serious situation. The body is attempting to remedy the same, and medical attention, or therapeutic attention, or the person's personal attention should be focused on the condition.

Parasites within the body (worms and other invading influences in the body) can be eliminated, in part, from the body being expedited, or diarrhea being utilized. When it is not, then there needs to be something within the intestine that would coat the intestine so that there would not be the harboring or infestation of parasitic conditions, or worms, or bacteria, or viral conditions. Chlorophyll is a primary benefit to the body. This can be obtained through the drinking of wheat grass juice, or the juice or puree of any dark, green, leafy vegetable. This, generally, will assist the body in removing derogatory influences from the same.

Flushing the intestine is a little more difficult, but any substance like a porridge (oatmeal), would act somewhat as a plunger going through the body. A large amount of the same - two large bowlfuls, so to speak - would be sufficient enough to remedy most any body of any residue, any parasitic condition, or any difficulty that would be considered a minor difficulty (if we can use that term) and this, too, would act as an expulsion influence in the body. It would help to reduce the effects of diarrhea; that is to say, the prolonged irritating, itchy, burning sensation that would be usually in the soft tissue in the anus or rectum.

The purpose is to remove whatever is the cause of the bile to be builded up (or the digestive fluids in the stomach to be builded up) and then to go through the body in somewhat of a large volume that it would burn the sensitive tissue. The corrosive influences of the stomach going through the intestine are sustained and are not painful, but when they are in contact with other tissues in the descending movement out of the body, or if there is regurgitation, these same fluids irritate the esophagus and even the throat (to understand how the body works). Diarrhea, therefore, can be given to the body as a blessing to remove obstructions and invading influences in the body.

Enemas or colonics can be given to the body to speed up the removal of viral or bacterial influences. This would be simply taking any antiseptic (Glycothymoline, Lavoris, or Listerine, for example), putting about a spoonful of the same in about eight to ten ounces of water, and then to give the body an enema, or to use the colonic or intestinal hydrotherapy to flush and remove the matter that is lingering or adhering itself to the large intestine (especially the ascending portion of the same). This would be the place to start to subtly remove those influences that are derogatory.

Taking the wheat grass juice or chlorophyll is helpful from the front portion (or moving through the stomach and small intestine). Taking the porridge (as we have given) would be most helpful pertaining to both intestines, small and large. Taking melons would be good to cleanse the same.

To the irritations in the small intestine, take water - let us say about a cupful (this would be about six ounces, or possibly one hundred milliliters or perhaps two hundred milliliters) - and put in a little sodium bicarbonate - a half a spoonful. The water should be warmed or room temperature, and then sipped slowly. This would begin to place alkalinity within the intestine. This would have a soothing or quieting effect in the body.

Herbals teas also are beneficial, and there are a variety of these. Stinging nettles, chamomile, burdock root, and other herbs that have either spikes or furry leaves; these would be the best to consume as a tea. The slippery elm tea, as well, would be good. This would be helpful in coating the intestine and making the intestine improved by what is being attacked or what is being affected in the intestine.

Coating the intestine with milk (goat's milk) would be preferred, but not cheeses or creams. This would be one way to soothe the stomach as well.

The inflammation and the irritation in the small intestine would take within twenty-four to forty-eight hours to reset or allow the body to balance. Therefore, do not force the body to eat solid foods, but rather, use vegetable juices to help keep the nourishment up; two to three ounces or one hundred milliliters or so of any vegetable juice would be good.

But understand, when there is diarrhea in the body, it is an invading force and the body is attempting to reject poisons or toxins that have been placed in the small and large intestine. Drink plenty of water or vegetable juices (or even fruit juices) to keep the body hydrated. Any drinks should not be cold, nor should they be hot. They may be cooler or warmer than room temperature. They should be sipped slowly. Broths made of the bones of fish, fowl, lamb or beef (but not of the pork) can be made. This would keep the nourishment and the strength of the body up. Broths made from meat stock - bones of the animal or lean meat that can be found - would be the best. This, too, would assist the body in assimilating without interrupting the digestive process.

Eat of the fruits that are grown in the vicinity or region in which the body resides. Do not sour the body, but do not over-sweeten it either. Eat the foods that are pleasant-tasting, but avoid all forms of sugar; although a little honey - a spoonful - mixed in a cup of warm water with a little ginger would be good. This would be energetic to the body. The honey itself would act as an antiseptic and, therefore, it may be taken, as we have just suggested, or a large spoonful of honey may be taken and ingested, a little at a time, like a lollipop or candy. Unpasteurized would be best, for this has the greater effect in reducing bacteria in the body. This would be seen as medicine for the body.

Now, there are other things that can be taken that would be made from nuts, and even the peels of fruit; orange peel in particular. But it is to remove the bacterial influences, and honey would seem to be the best.

Keep the body hydrated, and refrain from the body working very hard in the digestion of food, or the processes of digestion, you see, and the body should respond very quickly. Keeping the abdomen warm and increasing the blood flow through warmth would also be good. Place a hot water bottle on the area, or wrap the body with plastic or a blanket. But expelling that from the intestine is the quickest and surest way of removing what is derogatory to the body; that which would be a sediment, a toxin, or even a poison, you see.

Diarrhea in the body is a good thing, but is a re-balancing of the body's health by removing from itself those substances that need to be rejected expediently. For severe or chronic diarrhea that would be long-term, look for obstruction in the bowel. Look for an improper diet, or what would be a growth (like a polyp, a tumor, or some other appendage). Pay attention that parasitic conditions in the body may be undetected for long periods of time. Constipation or diarrhea is a very serious impairment of the body, but diarrhea is the natural reaction to constipation, and/or intrusion or invasion in the intestine.

In Western cultures, flatulence is considered embarrassing. Would you say that having gas is a normal function of the intestine, or is it a health condition that needs to be addressed?

It can be considered both, for as those foods that are taken into the body that do not completely digest (like beans, for instance) there is a fermentation in the body and, as such, there is a gaseous build-up or creation. If there is improper movement, slow or sluggish movement of physical congress, then methane gas is produced by the fecal matter that is not rejected from the body. If carbonated drinks are taken into the body, or if there is beer or alcohol that would have sufficient gaseous substance to start with, then there can be an increase in the gas build-up in the body. These are reactions to what is taken into the body.

If the body has poor eliminations, and if the body does not move the bowel (so to speak) on a regular basis (more than once a day would be appropriate), this is an indication of sluggish activity and congestion in the bowel. Look to a baby and you would see that bowel movements happen much more frequently than as one progresses in age. It seems to be the older one gets, the less frequent bowel movements occur. You might consider this the beginnings of what leads to the death; for some would say, death begins in the bowel. Largely this is due to the poisons, toxins, and digested matter not being secreted, and if it is not being secreted, then it is being reabsorbed into the body. If it is being reabsorbed into the body, then it is polluting the body.

The gaseous substances and the natural occurrence of the same are one thing, but when there is a chronic condition where the bowel is bent, or there is a restriction in the bowel (for remember, the bowel is like an accordion, stretching and moving as it assists in moving the physical matter through the bowel), naturally, if this is impeded, then the bowel may swell, or there may be some impediment. Indeed, this would soon begin the process of rotting residue in the body and the production of gas. Keep the bowel clean. Taking a bath on the inside of the body, periodically, is just as important as washing the body on the outside. Therefore, enemas or bowel cleansing, (including colonic irrigation) would be most beneficial in keeping the body's function at its highest level of function or normality, and it would reduce the gaseous build-up in the body, naturally. For if the body is functioning correctly, there cannot be a fermentation, there cannot be a rotting or build-up of gaseous substances that otherwise would have exited the body.

Peppermint is a good source to help reduce gaseous buildup, and charcoal tablets may be taken into the body as well, which act as a sponge to the gaseous substances. But understand the function of the bowel is to be such that there would not be a building up of the matter to allow the gaseous substances to prolong themselves in the body. Indeed, gulping of air or the interaction of different foods in the body naturally produce gaseous substances that are expelled in the body. This is found in nature; it is part of the digestion and eliminating practice. But if there is excess gas, or if there is excess substance taken into the body that produces gas, then one should look at, first, the diet. Is the amount of food (or types of food) being taken in warring in the body itself? And if they are warring, if they are not in harmony with the body, then they are being derogatory to the body, and eliminating these types of food from one's diet should be seriously considered.

Food types, or families of food, or groups of food should be considered also. Do not put things together that cause the body to war within itself, to be detrimental in the digestion, see? Melons should be eaten alone or left alone and not combined with other foods. The same also with families or groups of vegetables or fruits; eat the berries with the berries, the cherries with the cherries, the melons with the melons, the citrus with the citrus. Eat foods that would be of the same family with themselves. This would be in harmony and would help the body balance and not produce gaseous substances.

Also, to the sugars and candies and different foods that are given to the body, be wise and do not mix too many foods in the same meal. In this way, the body can properly secrete the enzymes and digestive fluids that would allow digestion to occur. Too many types of food taken into the body can produce a complicated series of digestive issues for a body. Be wise and eat foods that would be in natural combinations.

As this would be done, then the embarrassing situation of gas would be reduced greatly. Understand it as a natural occurrence in the body, but one which could be kept to a minimum if one would be a little wiser in simply selecting what types are taken in, and, indeed, the foods that are full of gas in the first place that could be avoided; for it is somewhat difficult for the body you see, but it is natural.

Please recommend a laxative that would be best for most people?

Olive oil.

Is it effective at this because of its ability to increase bile flow?

The cooked olive oil tends to produce an easier sensation and bile flow. The straight or uncooked olive oil tends to lubricate the intestine and also to cause the liver to secrete bile; yes.

Why does residue accumulate on the walls of the intestine?

Diet. Sugars and syrups, taken in abundance, carbonated drinks taken in abundance; in short, those that would be non-fibrous, sticky, gooey substances, mixed with bile and other discarded influences (or sediments) that the body would normally reject. These find their way through the depressions or the little cavities in the walls of the intestine. They then stick to, or become embedded in the intestine, in these little ringlet areas. For understand the intestine, in moving the stool through the same, is a pulsing, rhythmic movement, you see. And as such, this intestine movement squeezes on the lower end and releases on the upper end in a snake-like fashion. It pushes the matter (physical congress) through the intestine because of the muscle structure, tissue, and shape of the colon.

Now, in a healthy colon, this normally would not have any residue, but it would be (because of the diet given to even the child or the infant, and then prolonged through the body) that these chemicals, substances, food colorings, and so on are difficult for the body to eliminate. As such, they adhere to the wall of the intestine in the small nooks and crannies. They build up, they exaggerate the valleys or the cavities, polyps may occur, disease in the intestine may occur, and, as such, sluggish activity commences and then increases.

Of course, it should be looked upon that any particular food that comes out of a box or is pre-made (that is not really food grown or harvested in its natural form) would be considered adverse or derogatory to the body (to varying degrees). Rolled oats that come in a package or box are good, not bad. But taking oats that would be from a bin, harvested, and making them into rolled oats the natural way (although it would take longer) would be better; but both are good for the body.

But sticky or chewy candy, syrups, food additives, and all sorts of food that have been invented and sold in boxes (or even cans, for that matter) can be considered that which is adverse to the body, and difficult for the body to eliminate. Now, indeed, the food taken in would be of some nutritional value. We do not comment on this. But we answer the question as to what causes the colon to be coated with a residue, and the residue becoming more severe.

These items, or things, from our general point of view or presentation, lead one to understand that the place to start is with these items that have the attribute of being difficult to pass through the colon. Also, the lifestyle or lack of exercise is a factor. Humans do not work as hard as they used to in this society. They do not bend the stomach area. If they were to walk longer distances or physically tax the body, in physical labor or some sort of physical endurance, the colon would be massaged or assisted (as the lymphatic system would also). The lack of exercise, combined with a diet high in sugar, salt and fat, plus a lack of bile secretion, difficulty in the thyroid and pancreas secretions (or hormonal releases) and the fact that insufficient amounts of water are taken into a body to keep it hydrated (and thereby allow the intestine to function itself more cleanly) all contribute to poor digestion and elimination.

There is a condition of inflammation of the bowel, sometimes called irritable bowel syndrome or Crohn's disease. Generally speaking, what is the cause of this condition and what is the recommended treatment?

The condition in the body can be seen as the

body's drying up in the intestine (for lack of a better term). Bile secretions are suppressed, and poisons adhere to the wall of the intestine. They penetrate into the accordion-like areas in the bowel, and, as such, the passage of matter (physical congress) through the same is difficult.

Firstly, to the stomach and small intestine, there is a sluggish activity. The digestive influences are, indeed, functioning; but they are corrosive, and the slowing down of the matter moving through the small, and then the large, intestine occurs. The bowel (the colon or large intestine) becomes irritated when it is packed full of matter in the ascending portion of the same. Appendicitis is an indication of these irritations or poisons that are still within the body. The body is reacting, for the bowel is inflamed; naturally so.

The bowel does not normally reduce its function. When a child is born, there are no restrictions and obstructions in the bowel. What is taken into the body passes through the bowel very quickly, and the large amount of matter is excreted from the body. In a newborn or youngster, you can see the body functioning in a pristine state. Matter is moving through the body quickly. This is an example of how it should be.

This disease or irritable bowel syndrome is an indication that it is like unlubricated substances moving through the bowel; friction and irritation being cause of this painful passage, see? Constipation is a very serious ailment for the body, yet it is sometimes looked upon as being a simple inconvenience. It is not. Any restriction, any lessening of matter moving through the bowel should be considered of grave concern or an illness in the body. If it is overlooked, then Crohn's or other forms of intestinal disorders (inflammatory difficulties) are the result.

To increase the bile secretion is one of the solutions, the primary solution that can be addressed. Grapes, or grape juice, or even wine can be taken into the body, fifteen to twenty minutes before food is taken in. This will affect the thyroid, the pancreas, and, in turn, the bile to be secreted. This will affect the liver and the gallbladder, see? With this function enhanced or working properly, matter taken into the body passes through the body rather quickly. And understand this is important, for the assimilation process assimilates both the nutritious value, and then derogatory value, if there is still matter laying about or lethargically moving through the intestine. Moving through the intestine is better if it is done expediently or normally; any sluggish activity can be considered derogatory and dangerous to the body. Oils can be taken into the body, or foods that would be provocative in the body, which would make the body work in a normal or increased manner: sometimes prunes, sometimes pears, sometimes curry; whatever the body understands that makes the matter move through the body can be used to hasten the improvement.

But primarily, the irritable bowel is irritation. How to eliminate the irritation? Watermelon would be a good source, as it would move through the body, lubricating and cooling the bowel. Oils, like olive oil (as we have given) would be temporarily helpful, but not to be relied upon as a stimulant or a laxative to the body. However, using those foods, and enhancing the glands to secrete the bile is the remedy.

Sometimes, the osteopath or the chiropractor is necessary in aligning the bones in the spine, taking the pressures off the nervous systems which control the glands and the secretions of the same; and therefore the function naturally in the intestine.

Melons should be eaten alone or left

alone, but when there is irritation in the bowel, they should be eaten in excess to calm, cool, and allow the body to be flushed. Colonic irrigations would be very helpful in removing matter that has, for some time, adhered itself to the accordion-like crevices in the intestine, for it has affixed itself like an inner shell around the internal walls of the intestine. Once this occurs, the assimilative process deteriorates and the body continues to assimilate poisons and toxins through this matter that otherwise should have been eliminated from the body. This matter eventually forms a seal, and it is very difficult for the body to assimilate nutritionally. It only assimilates toxins or pollutants. This would require extensive bowel flushing or elimination stimulation (organically or mechanically).

Food or diet can be altered or changed to help the assimilative processes, but in this case, at this time (which would be late in the body's health), improving or removing sediments from the body would be the priority. Colonic irrigation is good, chelation therapy to remove sediments from the blood would be necessary. Ways and means to improve the circulation and the nerve flows would also be considered, and then the body would lose the cause of assimilation of poisons or toxins or sediments, and would function quickly or more readily.

However, for what has not been so severe, eating of the melons (especially the watermelon) would be most helpful to cool the bowel and allow the infection, or what is causing the irritation to subside. The sensitivity of the bowel being cooled and soothed would therefore also be lessened, and the bowel would not be irritated.

Think of the term "irritable bowel." Find out the cause that is irritating the bowel, and you will find the solution or remedy. But usually it is sluggish activity, retaining of toxins or physical congress in the body. Constipation is a very serious disease and should be looked upon the same, for it does poison the body; not the constipation itself, but what is happening due to constipation or very poor eliminations. Attempt to hold in the mind that eliminations are just as important as assimilation, and you have some revelation of how the body functions. A good balance between the two (assimilation and elimination) equals good health, always.

Colonic Therapy

Are enemas recommended for most people?

Would showers be recommended for each person? Indeed so, for as you would cleanse the body on the outside, then the body should be cleansed upon the inside.

Is there any danger from repeated enemas?

Is there any danger from repeated showers? Nay. The body would welcome the cleansing waters. For water itself is a healing effect, you know. There is an affinity to Man and water, for the larger percentage of Man is fluid.

What is the most expedient method to remove all accumulated waste from the intestine, restoring normal intestinal function?

There are a variety of activities, from the subtle to the extreme. Fasting is the basis, but one cannot simply stop ingesting food and expect the intestine to continue in its movement, or secretions, or moving forward that which is within, in the normal movement of the intestine. Therefore, water should be taken, to keep the body hydrated. Any source of food that would be helpful in cleansing out the colon could be taken; that is, foods that would give the self diarrhea, or food that would go right through the body.

The intention is to stimulate the colon benevolently. Castor oil packs on the abdomen, olive oil from the spoon, all would be helpful to lubricate the body from the top down, you see. From the bottom up, enemas or colonics can be given; not so much that they would cause irritation to the rectum, however, but castor oil (or any oil) may be placed upon the applicator. The intention is to move water through the colon, in and out. Massaging the abdomen over all areas of the colon (ascending, traverse, and descending) would be helpful, but care should be taken not to overdo it. The ascending portion of the colon is that collective part that would require the greatest cleansing.

We would suggest cleansing the colon over a week to ten days; enemas or colonics at the beginning of the time, then reduction to foods that would be more of the green, leafy variety put through a blender or made into a sauce or a soup. And then tuberous vegetables - the sweet potato, the onion, the turnip and the squash (the sweet potato would be best, but leave the white potato aside) - would be helpful in assisting the body, in moving through the body those conditions that would help scrape the sides of the colon and remove the residue that is in the pockets of the same.

Enemas and colonics, used when the body is fasting or taking into itself only fluids would be helpful during this time. A regimen can be sorted out and put on paper, beginning with the colonic and enemas through to the massage and the ingesting of oils. The intention is to make the colon as empty as possible.

Also in the stomach, there can be the cleansing of the stomach itself. We would not suggest swallowing a large scarf or cloth, as this has been done (especially in Eastern practices), but the intention is to coat the stomach with slippery elm, and this coating would prevent additional bile to be secreted into the body. The idea is not to keep the body hungry, but to keep the body satisfied, so that there is not secretion of bile in any excessive way.

Fasting for two or three days would be sufficient; this could be done at the latter portion of the week-to-ten-day program. However, it is a unique and different practice to do this, and the body and the chemistry in the body will change rather suddenly. There will be feelings of being provoked, or feelings of agitation. Meditation is, therefore, necessary, and placing pleasant surroundings is also necessary to keep the mind in accord, to keep the peace and calmness that the self seeks.

Is there any combination of substances a person could consume that would accomplish the same thing as colon hydrotherapy?

Understand the effect of intestinal hydrotherapy is, to some degree (in its simplest form), like bathing the body on the inside. For as it is advantageous to bathe the body on the outside, it is beneficial to bathe the body on the inside. However, the question goes to trying to assist the body in removing what has been built up over a period of time, and has adhered itself to the nooks and crannies of the colon itself. Enemas, therefore, would be good to bathe the body on the inside. The hydrotherapy has a tendency to agitate and remove what would be light material or sediments on the colon wall.

Primarily, attention should be given to the high colon or the ascending colon, on the right side of the body. A combination of difficulties are usually associated with this area, sometimes resulting in the removal of the appendix itself, because of the inflammation and irritation that is here, or the poisonous substances that can (and do) accumulate in this region of the body.

That said, understand that any constipation or congestion in the colon is considered unhealthy and should be avoided or remedied expeditiously. The most common ingredient would be olive oil, taken internally. The olive oil, depending on the condition of the person, can be ingested with the intention to remove that sediment or those concentrated forms (physical congress or matter) that has accumulated here. Taking a spoonful to two to four spoonfuls would be good; even as much as a cup of the oil, should there be boils and cysts present in the skin of the body (particularly the lower body).

Now understand there is mucous, as well as other items present. The intention of the mucous is to lubricate the colon itself, to some degree. However, when digestive juices seeping from the small to the large intestine occur, there is great disruption of the mucous and irritation of the membrane. Should this occur, then large amounts of water should be ingested, best in the morning, so that there would be a flushing (so to speak) of the stomach, the small intestine, and (to some degree) the colon as well.

Carbonated drinks should be avoided, for they are disruptive in the colon.

However grapes, grape seeds or grape seed extract can (and should) be taken on a regular basis to stimulate the pancreas and, in effect, the digestive system; but also to assist in the digestion and elimination coexistence or co-function, you see; for one produces bile in the natural way that allows an easement in evacuating the colon itself (or functioning with the colon).

Apples can be eaten alone as they, too, have a tendency to remove toxins or poisons from the blood, but can produce congestion or sluggish activity in the colon. Therefore, olive oil or some other oil should be taken with them. Flax seed oil is also good to ingest to repair the colon.

Melons (in particular watermelon) can be taken in large amounts to help to physically stimulate and cleanse the colon. Eat as much of the watermelon flesh as possible, but avoid the rind. This will effect a pushing through of any difficult matter here, in a gentle way, you see. The body can be eating the watermelon for a day, but best to eat as much as you possibly can at any one sitting or time, then let the body work.

Now in that which can also assist the body rather dramatically but effectively would be curry. “Hurry curry,” as its nickname implies, has an effect on the body to cause the colon to react, not in spasmic motion that would be harmful or painful, but in such a way that it would cause the contraction of the colon in its natural function to occur more in an accelerated or sped-up manner. This, too, will help reduce that which is on the wall of the same, and shed it from the body. Now if too much is taken, diarrhea will occur, but a thorough cleansing will occur. If there is irritation in the anus, then some cooling effect (let us call it that) of the olive or castor oil could be directly applied on the anus itself. Aloe vera, aloe vera gel or juice that could be tolerated or made palatable should be taken as well, after the curry treatment, but we would suggest this can be taken independently to aid or repair the colon. That which could be taken with the curry treatment would be yogurt. This would have a cooling or soothing effect on the tongue or palate, as well as the lower end of the body. The intention is to stimulate the body to bowel movement, and to clean out or cleanse the ascending portion of the colon (as well, of course, the descending or lower portions of the colon from this treatment).

As we have given, carbonated drinks should be avoided.

We would suggest that red meats, if the body is sedentary, should not be taken in large amounts. Pork should be avoided, unless the body does physically hard labor, bending and stretching the body. Best to eat soups or mushy vegetables prior to any attempt to cleanse the colon (or, shall we say, in preparation to do this).

That said, the colon would be stimulated or benefited by good bacteria. Yogurt is a good source of this; acidophilus is a good additive or tablet to take to stimulate and replace good bacteria. This can be done on a regular basis. And wheat grass juice may be taken as well. An ounce or two once a week would be helpful in keeping the gut in good condition and removing any bacteria that is unwanted or infestation of parasites and/or worms in the body, you see.

This would be a certain treatment that could be very effective at removing difficulties in the colon, but one has to work with the colon itself. The mental and emotional states, which are the constructive and destructive forces in any body, should be always positive, always flexible, always hopeful. For resentments can be the link between constipation and the attitude or the state of mind (the emotion that would result in the same, you see), as would the internal frustrations or anger held within.

However to the question: these would be methodologies that could be used in a regular way to aid the body in the effects of the colonic therapy or irrigation, although we would still recommend passive enemas on occasion, to simply wash the body topically in the colon, you see. Here, any bacteria would be also affected. Some diluting of peroxide, food grade, could be added to the enema. Antiseptic mouthwash (Listerine, or Glycothymoline) could be used - a capful or two in about eight or ten ounces of water - to help remove irritations here, or as a preventative for bacteria in the long part of the colon, you see.

Coriander

Why was coriander seed so highly regarded by ancient Egyptians?

Because it was rare. It had medicinal aspects to remedy the spleen or to keep bacteria out of the organs. It was used as a sort of anti-inflammatory, anti-bacterial medication or substance, you see. It was highly recommended by many. It was considered something of an offering to the gods as well; it was sometimes put in implements and incinerated. The smell would be somewhat acceptable to those in the vicinity. It was seen somewhat as a medicinal item that could cure through vapor or even through the vibration of itself.

Cough

What is the best way to eliminate a cough or lung irritation?

To begin with, the body should be thought of as a container, and the container simply with a little irritation here and there. The container has a small opening, the opening being the nasal and - let us say - oral openings in the head. Through this, to the lung, there are certain passageways and surfaces that attract or absorb those airborne sediments, preventing them from becoming trapped in the lower part of the body (the lungs). That is why there are glands and mucouses and other forces to prevent what would be the body becoming polluted or full of dust.

With this understanding then, know that conditions in the body (infections or other impediments in the respiratory system) can be eradicated beginning from the top down, or, if there is infection in the lungs, then from the lung or the bottom up. But to begin with, we would find that one can simply, with regular mouthwash, with any salt-water solution, on an irregular basis remove some of the difficulties that would be found in the mucouses of the palate and of the throat. For, on occasion, this can become very dry and it is a seat or an attachment location first.

We would suggest also the sinuses be flushed. This would be occasionally in the life, especially if there is a dryness in the house, or there is an infection or irritation in the sinuses, or at those times in which airborne irritants, allergies, or seeds, or bits of fluff that would be in the air can touch upon the sinuses or irritate the membranes. By taking an implement, like a teapot, a spouted container, placing into this container warm water and you may add a little antiseptic like a mouthwash (like Listerine or Lavoris or Glycothymoline, you see), or even a little hydrogen peroxide (small amounts, a few drops, you see). Then to hold the nostrils in a downward or head lower position, take this container with the spout and put it on one of the nostrils so that the water within the container comes out of the spout and floods into the nostril. It will fill up the nostril and the nasal passageways, and will exit out of the other nostril. The tongue should be at the back of the throat, closing off any possibility of this draining into the mouth. This will immediately remove sediments and irritations and may also be helpful in a remote possibility of aiding floaters in the eye (as it might be seen). This does not have direct connection, but to this, it would have a benefit.

However, this process would remove sediments and irritations that would be breathed in through the nasal passageways that would readily affect the soft tissues in the palate and nasal passageways. Attempting to clear out the surfaces within the bronchial and the lung, this would require the liberal use of pounding of the chest and the back, or massage. It would also require breathing into the self fumes that would be from the apple cider-brandy mixture. Take a container, filling it up with two inches or so of activated charcoal (available from the aquarium store). Pour into this enough brandy to cover the charcoal and let it sit for a day (or even two). Then, you may pour off the brandy and add instead apple cider. This would be regular apple cider, not vinegar, but unsweetened cider. Allow this to be in the now-closed or sealed container for another day or two, and the fumes would build up in this. Uncapping the container, and breathing the fumes into the nostrils, or even through the mouth would directly affect and remove any buildup of mucous or reduce the mucous itself in the throat and chest.

Now, it may require, with the pounding or massage, the body to spew out mucous from the mouth through the sputum. This particular inhaling of fumes will cause a shrinkage in the mucous itself and the massage would not be needed, or the clapping or tapping of the back and chest need not be engaged in, should there be the inhalation of these fumes. But prior to that, if there is a mucous buildup, then clapping, or banging, or pounding on the shoulder-blade area and the chest of the body with the head down will loosen up the phlegm and it will be spit out of the body. These two, although crude and simple processes of flushing the sinuses and inhaling the fumes, should remedy the condition in the mucous or the residue of the mucous, you see, as a housing or host for any viral or mucous condition.

The monolaurin taken will affect any bacteria or viral condition in a negative sense (as would acidophilus), which could be taken on a regular basis.

There are other concoctions or remedies that would be given to affect the viral or mucous conditions in the body, but this would be a simple place to affect a body in removing any irritations that would touch upon the palate, the throat, the bronchial, and then the lung, you see.

Curcumin (Turmeric)

Lately there has been a great deal of interest in the Indian herb known as curcumin, sometimes known as turmeric. The argument is made that it tends to inhibit the growth of fast-moving cells (for example, tumors and cancers) and, therefore, should be part of every diet. Please comment.

Taken occasionally, it would be helpful. It does seem to make the body sluggish, on occasion. Too much would tend to inhibit the reproduction of cells in the normal function (ordinary cells we speak of). It is best to take a little of everything, than hoarding or ingesting plenty of a single thing. The body is designed to take a little of everything. To the question: this is a positive effect, but no need to think of it as a medicine or to be self-medicating the body with this substance, you see. It does have some effect, but taken too much, it makes the body sluggish in its cell production, and it can also be detrimental in the long bones of the legs and the production of blood.

Deafness

What is the cause of deafness and what would you suggest as the best form of treatment?

There can be a variety of deafness here, and the motor controlling skills in the brain can have some damage or communication difficulty. Wax build-up can occur within the ear itself (the orifice or channel in the ear in which sound would travel the ear canal).

Then there can be simple fusing of the bone or recognition difficulty of the ear drum itself and the fluctuation of the ear to the inside part of the ear and the outside part of the ear, especially if there has been a perforated ear drum or some damage to the head, you see.

In an elementary way, keeping the ears clean, exercising the body, including diving underwater and coming up again to change the pressures, you see (for water does have a weight, and pressure would be increased easily and naturally in the ear itself, as pressure is exerted simultaneously and at the same rate). This minor or simple therapy would help to keep the equilibrium, keep the fluid within the inner ear, and keep the reverberating surfaces functioning correctly without too much skill or need to stimulate the ear itself.

Manipulations in the neck affecting the vertebrae (as well as the nervous system) can be given and hearing can be maintained to a higher degree, if this would be done. Head and neck rolls (or exercises with the head rolling around the shoulders) could also be given and this, too, would affect better hearing in the body and in the mechanical aspects of the eardrum itself, you see.

Keeping the ears clean is good, but the body needs to stimulate the lymphatic system in any form of simply jumping up and down, to a degree of full course workout would be sufficient. And, of course, the body, with increased blood supply, would be more able to allow more elasticity to occur within the membranes and the tissues and the bone in this region of the body. See?

Depression

Would you please recommend the best treatment for depression?

A good laugh! Here, each and every day, it should be the vocation of every living soul to laugh and to make others laugh, for through laughter, the soul becomes enlightened. Here, the physical state of the body alters. The chemical changes are for the betterment, and the body is rejuvenated through the laughter.

In relieving depression, it would be to watch the humorous shows, the humorous books, or the joke telling. Laughter secretes particles from the brain, and this affects the nervous systems, central and autonomic; and, as such, the body breathes health. Depression is a state of mind in conjunction with physical, chemical states. It can be altered, you see, through both the mental stimulae and the physical corresponding stimulus, which would be laughter.

In what way would diet affect depression?

Excesses cause continued depletion here. If any would understand how hard the body works when there is food taken in, then none would be the glutton who swells the body. But understand excesses in any form or manner (specifically the diet or the fluid taken in) would cause depression. For the food would be taken in to satisfy psychological needs, rather than the physical. As the physical form would puff itself up, furthering the discomfort or ill-at-ease appearance of self, then the body would become, in conjunction with the thinking, depressed.

You can take, however, a degree of stimulants. These would be seen as vitamins, specifically E and D (the groupings of these) or magnesium through the diet. The beet or the tuberous variety of beet greens would be helpful. Vitamin E, or wheat grass, or wheat germ can be taken also, for it is high in vitamin E. These would be stimulating; but, again, this is organically recommended.

Should there be conditions of inactive or overactive use of the thyroid, then there should be a degree of iodine taken in the system, either through the salt of the sea, or what would be kelp, or Lugol's iodine, which would be a good substitute for iodine here. These will all stimulate or quell the thyroid itself and, as such, alleviate artificially the depression.

But, depression is a chosen state of mind. Beware those who would be self-pitied, for above all creatures, they possess free will and choice, and if any possess their own choice and feel sorry for themselves, then pity them indeed. They deny themselves, they waste themselves, and waste is sin. Choose laughter, eat of the foods in moderation, for all things have some good to the body.

Then you would find, as there is a balanced state of mind and diet, the body would also be.

Detoxification

What substance is the best detoxifier of the human body?

Chlorophyll.

DHEA

For the hormone or timing agent known as DHEA, how would the average individual be able to determine if additional supplementation is required?

It would be primarily to test and record if the body is a little acidic for longer periods of time, and if there is a loss of physical strength. This can be measured as strength in the wrist primarily, and then from the wrist to the fingers; the color and texture of the blood flow in the body, too. If you press on the fleshy part and leave a white mark, then you would be a candidate for ingesting the same. If, however, you press on the part and see it recovering from white to red or pinkish rather quickly, then you would be one that is not lacking for DHEA, you see.

The effect of the compound is to allow the body to spread out or remove toxins and sedentary forces while, at the same time, allowing blood flow to be improved. Another test: take your thumbs, press them on the artery in the upper back or neck. If your arms go white, this will be an indication that you are a prime candidate for the DHEA treatment.

Diabetes

Please comment on the cause of diabetes and how it may be treated.

Diseases such as diabetes emanate from the pancreas and involve the timing or mis-timing of the thyroid gland. Understand that diabetes is a fear disease. Those who are fearful, sooner or later, will contract diabetes itself. The emotions are the constructive and the destructive forces in any body. Diabetes is an epidemic of fear (in addition, of course, to the intake of too much sugar in the diet). Consider this: most individuals are becoming predominantly knowledgeable about food that is being taken in. They read the label and there is fear that what they are taking is not good for them. This is subtle, but it is still fear. On a macro level, there is also fear of the effect of warfare, or terrorism, or fear of financial ruin. All stem from the same condition or emotion.

Can Jerusalem artichokes be utilized by a diabetic, in place of insulin injection?

Indeed so, and all who would inject themselves should eat of the Jerusalem artichoke. Eat upon a regular basis and there is the high probability that the injection would be done away with, for the body would assimilate and act on its own. Here it is to the state of fear that affects this organ.

How can an individual introduce this type of treatment?

By beginning to eat of the artichoke itself and reduce the insulin a little, and as they would continue to eat, then insulin would be reduced more and more, testing the urine to appraise the balance, as we see it. It would be an experimenting attempt. Here, a couple of artichokes would allow a reduction (as we see it) as the body becomes more accustomed to assimilating of the artichoke. Then the injection could be done away with. It would be a period in which injection would be necessary from time to time (every other day), then completely done away with, as we see it. It is done easily. The body will not tolerate any more or any less, for the balance between an artichoke or two taken would not cause an over-reaction; simply reduce the injection a little.

Would these be taken raw?

Indeed, eating as apples would be, yes. Best to be eaten raw, but they can be prepared; steamed or cooked.

Diets and Food

General, Blood Type, Paleo, Raw Foods, Vegetarian

Generally, what diet would you recommend for most people?

To become familiar with the dietary measures of the body, there are certain foods that must be taken into the system each and every day. Eighty percent to ninety percent of the diet should be more of the vegetable; the lowly vegetable is the key to the high success and health of the physical body. And yet, like most treasures found in nature, it is overlooked, for it is too easy to understand. Fresh fruit is essential in the body also, but only in season. Eat the vegetables and the fruit as they come in season, for the body has its seasons also. Everything grows in cycles, and when it is time for the squash and the turnip, eat of these plentily. When it is time for the pumpkin, the corn, and the sweet potato, eat of these also. When things are in season, it is the time that the body requires it.

Nature has its own biological clock, and any who study nature know that nature's clock is much more accurate than any that Mankind would attempt to set. Flow with the seasons. Eat the vegetable, exercise the body and spend a few moments each day appreciating self as a member of this wonderful Earth, this wonderful dimension. For the mind must be given compliment, good thought, and reassurance; but it is within the mind that thoughts are created, are directed to, and affect the emotional and physical states within the body. Simply speaking, plant the seeds of good thoughts and the harvest you will reap will be health and contentment, and peace in the mind.

Please discuss what foods should never be mixed in the same meal?

It would be better to keep melons together. Eat them alone or leave them alone.

You would find that dairy products tend to combat certain vegetables - lentils, beans, peas - as such, they should be eaten separately.

Certain types of meat, especially liver, should be kept away from any fried foods (onions or mushrooms), yet we see this is combined in current practice.

Onions should be eaten alone. This would be best as a model type of diet.

Fruit should be eaten alone, never mixed. We are referring to berries, peaches, pears, nectarines; these could be combined in that category, you see, and eaten as a meal. It would be best done in the morning.

Plums could be eaten by themselves, but they should be eaten only when the body is too much alkaline within, for they tend to produce acid within the system. Keep to a minimum here, you see. The citrus fruits can be combined and eaten together.

Generally speaking, all vegetables can be blended or mixed, one with the other, and it would be best to eat these half-raw where they are crunchy still and have not lost their vitamin content.

Meats can be taken with just about any vegetable, but fried meat can have a tendency to cause the body much stress. We would recommend more to the baking, broiling of meat, see?

White potatoes should be avoided. It would be better to eat the skin of the potato than to eat the content, for there is more benefit in the skin than the entire potato.

Nuts should be roasted, rather than fried, and these can be taken as snacks; combined with figs or dates, they would be helpful.

Dairy products, creams and even some salad dressings should be avoided here, for they tend to create gas or war within the system. Experimentation would give which should not be taken. Basically, this would be a rounded diet.

We would add simply: apples should be eaten only alone, and they should be only consumed during three days of cleansing or fasting in which the body would use the apple and a degree of olive oil (a teaspoon each morning for the first two days, and as much as can be taken upon the third day), to cleanse the body, for the apples would act as a cleansing agent for the kidneys.

There is currently a popular diet based on eat-

ing according to your blood type. Is there any validity to this?

This, of course, is valuable, for the blood type relates to the ancestral strengths and weaknesses in any body, see? Therefore, attempt to find what is homogenous or beneficial to the body. Look to the ancestral, native locations and you would find that those who were born in certain areas of the world where there is a lineage of ancestral influences (even to the present time) you would be able to find, by those who would live in the vicinity or region, foods that are acceptable or what should be rejected. This would be part and parcel of their upbringing. You will find that there are those moments in which the self may be tested, in which the self will find its ancestral heritage.

The body's assimilative ability, its strength and endurance comes from the blood and the organs within the same; usually the thyroid, which is the controlling center for the secretion of those timing devices you would call hormones, you see.

Look to the past to find the future, and the blood type will gladly lead the self towards the ability to ingest and digest the food and to extract what would be beneficial to the body, while rejecting what would be of little consequence. This is why it is better to eat of a large variety of things than to specialize in certain groupings or areas of food, where the body loses the body to assimilate them, and the body is therefore denied the influences of other objects, products, foods, see? Eating towards those foods that would be good for the blood means that the metabolism itself would work in harmony with them. There would not be a need to gorge the body, but a need to fulfill the body or eat without being overly expressive in this regard.

The blood type holds the vibration of the self and the soul. Eating in harmony with this vibration allows food to be ingested in the body much easier and assimilated more completely.

Could you please now examine a popular diet known as the Paleo diet, which its promoters say is the original diet dating back to Mankind's roots. Is this a good way of eating for the average person?

We have this as largely relating to raw food or meat and what would be high proteins or simple foods in mono meals; the Neanderthal or caveman mentality. For those who are coarse and more physically active, it could be considered in harmony with the self. For those who are of the higher vibration, and more of a sedentary lifestyle, then it might not be. See? The intestines need to be worked and, therefore, if there is bending and stresses or strength required to carry out the life or lifestyle, then these types of eating or assimilating can be considered doable or capable. However, if it is not so - when there is a more delicate constitution - then this would play a little more havoc in the ability for the stomach, intestines and the secretions therein to function. Again, one who is physically active, lifting, pushing, grunting, running, hopping, jumping, these types of individuals can use the more severe diet. Those who are finicky would require a greater reduction in their assimilation.

For the average person, is a raw food diet preferable to a diet of cooked food?

Depending on the habits of the self, one or the other is acceptable, but a combination of the two might be better. Raw foods prepared and eaten right after being gathered or harvested from the ground would be much more beneficial. The vitamin arrangement and absorption would be quite high. Therefore, eating raw foods (which is historically correct for any body) would be a good idea. However, depending on age, and the number of teeth in the mouth, there may be restrictions on this and, therefore, some foods that are heated up or cooked, either by steaming or broiling, would be best.

The so-called Hippocrates Diet, based on eating only sprouts and raw foods, has some extraordinary claims associated with it. Does it really restore health as claimed?

As was given, the body was designed to both assimilate and eliminate at the same time. However, in the modern condition, many in a state of poor health have lost the ability to do the same, and the toxins accumulate daily, making the problem more and more difficult to correct. It creates a downward spiral, see? This diet can be said to trick or fool the body into believing it is not eating at all; that it is in a condition of prolonged fast. The body, therefore, goes into a prolonged and steady state of elimination only, and it is because of this elimination that very large improvements can be seen within a short time.

The components of the diet have been altered or tweaked many times in the last thirty or forty years. Is there anything missing from the current program?

Oatmeal. A bowl a day would assist in clearing the poisons from the colon more quickly, as if a plumber were cleaning a pipe.

Is it prudent or wise to stay on the diet after a recovery has been affected?

The body has been designed to consume small quantities of many different things. No to the question.

For the average person, is a vegan or vegetarian diet preferable to a diet that includes meats?

Depending on the metabolism, for the average person, meat, meat products or protein from animals would be very healthy. For others, it is such that they do not require this type of protein, and it can be avoided. Better to eat of the fish, the fowl or the lamb, baked, broiled, or boiled, and what would be grown or caught in the vicinity or region in which the body resides.

But to the question: for those who have a feeling of offense towards the meat products, then they should be avoided. For those who have the philosophy that they do not require it because of the sacrifice of the animal, then so be it. For those who are attempting to balance their health, they may take it.

It is hard to say specifically. There is difficulty in making a generalization, because the peoples themselves are so diverse.

Given the choice between butter or margarine, which one is more beneficial to the body?

Butter itself would be better for the body. Margarine itself tends to be harder to digest, as it is not found in nature. It is a created food. With any prepared food (food that has been mechanically or otherwise prepared) there is a loss of nutritional value immediately and the body has difficulty in naturally assimilating the food that is given. Understand the food taken in is what builds up the physical self: mentally, physically, and emotionally. Understand that it is better to eat from a variety of foods, a wide range of foods, than to stick to a narrow grouping of foods, for the body learns to absorb or to rely on this narrow amount of food and it is denied the influences from the wide variety or the different foods that are at the disposal of itself; foods that build the body, see? Food to be taken in should be looked upon as a primary importance. Food that is all-natural (that is found in nature) cannot harm the body. That which has been adulterated in the cooking or preparation process, the food is lessened, the nutritional values are lowered, and the food itself then has a foreign connection or foreign function in the body. The body struggles and works very hard to digest what is taken in. Again, what is natural assimilates easily in a finite way. Anything else that is put in front of the self should be avoided.

Are farmed fish as good for the body as wild or "natural" fish?

The natural would be that which is fostered upon, much more beneficial, for it would be what would not be engineered, force-fed, or given those things that would be impure. It is always much more beneficial to consume what is from the wild itself. This would be the preferred way. That which is farmed is engineered, and engineers have profit on their minds! They attempt to produce a good product, but it is not as beneficial as that which would be found in the wild. It is acceptable, but if you are asking the difference, then that which is taken from the wild is much more beneficial.

What effect do fat substitutes have in a body?

This would be the different types of fat that would be put into the body. We would find that most fats that are sticky, that are tenuous in digestion tend to irritate the intestinal track, causing great difficulty in digestion and in the natural metabolism or the function of the intestine and the colon itself; sometimes remaining for long durations within the small tissue of the small and large intestine, thereby causing the exaggeration of compartments in the colon or the intestine, leading to irritations, polyps, ulcer, accumulation of bacteria or irritants, an exaggeration of the colon and, of course, disrupting the all-important function of elimination (physical congress, you see).

Other types have a tendency to function in the body as food and they build up the body, causing the metabolism to be stronger, to act more rigorously. These fats are those that would be absorbed into the body and are not manufactured, but would be more natural in their consistency, or as they would be ingested into the body in their form, you see. Of course we speak of a balanced amount, for understand any exaggeration or any - let us call this - imbalance, or greed, or hoarding of a certain type of food, limiting or restricting the amount of variety taken into the body, then this would be, of course, detrimental to the body. For any extreme in one direction is met by another extreme in the opposite direction, you see. Therefore, eating singular types of food to the extreme would, of course, be detrimental to the physical body itself.

However, to what would be taken in a modest amount (for each should attempt to put a limit on desires, you see) then, in this way, the fat substitutes or additions taken into the body would be seen as food and would be body building. They would act within the muscle and the cell as a fuel source. They would actually make a metabolism maintain a higher level of activity and they would tend to (as they would be somewhat of a grease, if you will) lubricate the body, causing certain forces within the body to secrete lubricating forces at the bone and joint level; but also into the cell level and the muscle itself (but more to the frictional regions of the skeletal than any other place). The cell does require some degree of lubrication, for it vibrates or moves individually and in groups. The waves in the body can be seen as longitudinal and horizontal (if you will).

DMSO

DMSO seems to offer health benefits to people. As you see it, what can this chemical be used for, in terms of health purposes or first aid?

It can be considered as something that would be organically a binder in the body. It would be a stimulant to the blood and would be therapeutic, allowing the body to be builded up as sort of a body-builder at the cell level, you see. This would allow the condition of a weak body to absorb or assimilate nutrients better and also to deliver them to the same need in the body. Similar to the affect of gelatin in the body, you see.

If the DMSO is not fully purified is there a risk?

It would be like eating a little saw dust or a little organic matter and cause some indigestion, so to speak, or some disruption. It would cause vomiting, or sickness, or diarrhea, if it is not refined to the fullest, you see. It would be like eating a little wood, you see.

DMSO is used topically by some people as an anti-inflammatory. For some (but not all) people, it can cause a general body itching and rash temporarily. Please examine this effect and comment on what is happening.

It is offensive to the nervous system and the nervous system recoils. It is toxic to some nervous systems and some blood types. If you look at the blood types, you would find there is some consistency in the type of blood and in the reaction. It makes the nerves shrink or shrivel. It is offensive to some nervous systems. It is toxic to some, and pleasing to others.

Down Syndrome

Down's Syndrome is not only a mental condition, but a physical one as well. Please explain the general cause and give a recommendation for treatment.

In examining the condition it is somewhat similar to certain body types, and can be considered that there is difficulty within the motor area or mechanisms in the brain; this would be to the rear, lower portion of the same. There is also some shrinkage to the thalamus or hypothalamus (what would be the primal or central brain). It usually dwarfs this part of the brain. During a pregnancy there is somewhat of a lapse of nutrition and at the very beginning of cell production, there is some misalignment.

As such, you would find that conditions in the body are both organic and somewhat difficult in the mechanical ability of the body to assimilate, especially certain types of minerals (or, for that matter, most minerals). It is like cutting some of the controlling nerve endings in the upper portion in the brain stem. There is an incomplete connection or association with the nerves, and, as such, you would find that this causes the mind to act in a simple way.

The appearance of the individual is caused by the poor assimilation of minerals, or the lack of minerals in the body itself. There is already some understanding of the dietary improvements (treating individuals like this as if they cannot digest and assimilate nutrition, and minerals). It would be sufficient for the development of the brain and the brain's activities, including the mental activity or the electrical activity in the brain itself. There is sufficient communication between the synapse and the brain, but there is a weakening effect in certain areas, relating to the developmental skills of speech, memory, and reasoning or logic.

This condition is a genetic weakness and, as such, it is a malformed or deformed part of the brain, where blood flow to the central brain and the motor skills of the brain has been diminished. There is difficulty in nerve flow through the brain stem; a disruption, a tear or a cessation (so to speak). The body can overcome this by increasing nerve passageways around the damaged areas or what would be the incomplete development or growth areas, see? Manipulation and stimulation in the neck, soon after birth, would maintain and improve blood flow into the brain itself.

However, the diet should be high in minerals; all types of minerals, that the body can assimilate, usually and naturally. As there is difficulty in the digestive and assimilative processes in the body, mother's milk may or may not be suitable and, in some cases, it may be producing phlegm or mucous in the body and the infant has difficulty in digesting mother's milk. Therefore there should be care given as to what is given to the infant, that there is no congestion, bowel obstruction or other difficulty in digestion, for this causes congestion in the intestines, and this allows toxins to form in the body rather quickly. Water should be given and enemas should be given if there is any obstruction or difficulty.

Plenty of protein should be given to the child as soon as possible, or as soon as the child can tolerate the same; not handfuls, of course, but small amounts, a spoonful or less. Omega oils may be given, and the body may be nourished through mother's milk or other milk substitutes. There are some already on the market that would replace mother's milk and they are somewhat suitable. Treat the body as being lactose-intolerant and understand that the body may eat and gain weight and become overweight. This does means the body is not absorbing the nutrition, and therefore care should be taken in personalizing the diet for each individual. Omit those foods that would be fried in oil, or deep-fried. Most breads would not be easy to digest, therefore omit breads. Milk and cheeses should be avoided. Sugar from the sugar bowl and foods that have high amounts of sugar within should be monitored closely, for these usually cause sugar level to be erratic in the body.

However, those minerals that would be common and easily digested should be given in abundance. The body should be given abundance of vitamins and minerals. Now, vegetable juices which would be freshly obtained would be much more potent, constructive and beneficial to this type of body, rather than the supplements that might be given (which may or may not be assimilated or digested). The juices seem to be easily assimilated. Minerals that would be helpful may be taken in small amounts and it should be the entire array of minerals. They might be better selected from the region or the vicinity in which the body resides. However, given the small amounts on a regular basis, in addition to the food that is taken in, the body should assimilate better or more completely. See it as a percentage of assimilation, rather than attempting to fix something. The body is incapacitated, or the assimilation process is diminished. Therefore, pay attention to the diet and the body's ability to assimilate; not to become fat, but to become balanced. There should be improvement in the mental skills, the eyes should be brighter, memory should be improved, and learning should be equal or above normal. The retention of the knowledge, and the reasoning and deductive skills, should also be above normal.

It might be laborious to prepare special diets, but those who have such children can learn from others who have had children and have found improvement in their way of eating. It should always be remembered that everyone builds themselves on what they eat or what they assimilate. What they assimilate is more important than what they eat! The body should not be stuffed or overweight. The body should be given a diet that is suitable and, in some cases, it might be simple and specific. However, the mental skills will improve both with what is given to the body to ingest and also with certain stimulations through the spinal column itself. Approximately between the shoulder-blades, those areas in the dorsal vertebrae should be stimulated with massage or with the thumbs more exactly. This will allow oxygen, through the respiration or breathing, to be higher in the body. This, too, will benefit the brain greatly.

For usually there are compressive forces in and about the middle part of the spine, between the second, third, fourth, fifth and sixth area. Combine with some compression in the cervical. On occasion, the cranium does not sit correctly on the top bones in the neck (the Atlas and Axis). These minor corrections (the manipulation between the shoulder blades), at a very early time in life, will allow more oxygen to be absorbed through the lungs. Manipulation of the cervical will allow more blood flow to the head. Convulsive disorders or other forms of uncontrolled reactions in the body can also be diminished or eliminated through the similar aspects of diet and spinal manipulation.

The form of acupuncture that would speed up the function of the kidneys can also be given, as this would be helpful in keeping poisons or toxins out of the body, for the kidney function usually is diminished as well. The acupuncture stimulates the life energy in the body, and the nerve flow to the kidney itself. Spinal manipulation or the use of acupuncture should keep the body balanced, and keep poisons or toxins leaving the body by stimulating the kidneys. These would be to the simplest ways to understand this condition in the body, and to give remedies that are simple or basic.

There can be more complex examination of the body's need for certain supplements or minerals, and analyzing clippings from the hair or fingernails can be specific in what is missing. Through regular analysis of the hair, it can be found what minerals are needed, what is overly-abundant already in the body, and what is depleted or diminishing in the body. Of course, the method is to increase what is diminishing and decrease any that are overwhelming in the body. However, with proper eliminations, good assimilation, good kidney function, and a good balanced intake of food, the body should respond quite well and would not be what would be lacking in brilliance, but rather would be what is closer to its personality, which would be called normal or balanced activity.

There is more that could be given, especially to the soft tissue organs like the liver. Increasing the blood flow through the liver helps to remove toxins from the body. This can be done by any form of heat pad or liniment that might be put on the body. The intention is to keep the liver functioning and not to allow the liver to build up with toxins, or for the toxins to remain in the body. It is very important that the body eliminates physical congress, and through the urination cycle as well, but also through the liver dump or discharge. Therefore, keep the body balanced. Grapes and grape juice may be taken as the body ages a little, see? However, as we have given, with monitoring the diet, manipulating the spine and massaging the body in the neck (and perhaps around the head as well) there should be positive response.

Dupuytren's Contracture

Please discuss the medical mystery known as Dupuytren's contracture. This disease of the tendons of the hand cripples the hand over time as the tissue hardens. Surgery is initially successful but the problem comes back, even after surgery.

No mystery! This is not a disease of the hand; rather of the brain. Signals to the brain become confused, and the brain believes the hand is being attacked, when in fact it is not. The brain, in error, instructs the hand to create new tendon for protection. Since the attack does not exist, the tendon forms needlessly and, over time, can diminish the utility of the hand to a large degree. Similarly for the attempt to do surgery to effect a repair, once the knife is inserted, the brain is more certain than ever than an attack exists. To compensate, it redoubles its efforts, creating new, but incorrect tissue, creating a cycle.

The cure would be found in any technique that temporarily breaks the connection from brain to hand, and resets the brain, the same way as turning a computer off, then on. When on again, the computer starts fresh. Once reset, the brain would recognize the error and stop the incorrect information. One method is acupuncture. Find one who is expert, and temporarily cease the nerve flow, hand to brain, such that the hand goes completely numb for a time, as might be the case in preparing for surgery; but, here, with different intent. The brain must be reset.

Electrical Towers

Do people living in close proximity to radio or electrical towers have a higher risk of illness?

They are exposed continually, whether they are awake or asleep, to extraordinary electrical-magnetical fields that are powerful and emanate from these devices or from the surge of electrical power that goes through these devices. It would be like standing beside a loud speaker that goes day in and day out, even though you may have earplugs in the ears and you cannot hear the speaker. The vibration of the speaker goes through the body and, indeed, headache and digestion difficulties, including insomnia, and other normal, peaceful activities would be considered disturbed or disrupted.

Silently, the penetration of frequency

through the body adversely affects the physical body, such as what is seen in these types of environments. Now the exposure to anything for too long is the difficulty here. Exposure to the same for short periods of time usually does not cause disruption to the body, but if the body resides in the general proximity of these, then, of course, the body is exposed to an extreme, and ill effects occur. The body is worn down by these powerful currents of magnetic influences.

Electromagnetic Frequencies

Many members of Western society use cell phones on a regular basis, despite warnings. How many years will it take of exposure before unwanted side effects appear?

Should there be a heavy use of the same, within one to two years. There would be seen effects that would be unwanted, or what would be the deterioration of mental function, physical control, emotional balance, hair loss, tumor, and hearing loss, you see. The effects bring on the influences or the symptoms of old age, and also can cause a certain whitening of hair in the general area in which the antenna would reside. It does not need to be too long, but, with constant use, everyday use, especially with high-powered devices, the effects would be within two years.

Many people have prolonged, daily exposure to electromagnetic frequencies from cell phones and other devices. If one must be in close range of EMF-producing devices, is there any way to block their harmful effects?

By pointing the top of the device away from the body and turning them off as much as possible; in other words, turn them on only to use them, and then turn them off. For it is their reporting cycle that is harmful, or it can be a transmission of frequency that is repeated and unknown, you see. Shutting the device off is one way of assuring there is no action and reaction to the calling or the sending of the device itself. Keeping the device away from the head, away from the heart, and putting it into a secondary packaging (like a purse or a bag) would be a good idea. These would help those who are sensitive.

Are there any ways to reverse EMF damage?

Attempting to affect the body's cells by putting the body in salt baths would be helpful. This would restore some of the (let us call it) fragmentation of the body's electrical-magnetical influences on itself. You may also take a bar magnet and go over the body, as if you would be taking a comb and brushing it through your hair. This will attempt to align the magnetic self, and the magnetic influences in the aura body itself. See?

Electroshock Therapy

Of what value are electroshock treatments?

Of little value, as it perpetuates the condition itself. In a small percentage, they do aid but, in most cases, they affect the central nervous system and the autonomic system, causing a degree of arrest to the lungs and heart, causing fatality, ultimately. They tend to be of benefit to a small percentage but, largely speaking, they do little in the way of good.

Epilepsy

Can you please comment on the cause of epilepsy and suggest a treatment?

Usually this is found within the brain and that there is a large deficiency of vitamins and minerals; an assimilation problem in the body. Manipulation of the vertebrae in the neck (especially the atlas and axis) or the manipulation of the bones of the skull can be directly beneficial mechanically and relieve the internal pressures of the brain itself and the fluids within the brain, including the blood. Manipulation of the atlas and axis or the skull would determine rather dramatic influences if this is the cause of epilepsy in the body.

However, blood supply and oxygen deficiency to the cells can be considered a condition and, as such, impairment between the outer brain (or thinking caps) and the internal brain (the thalamus and hypothalamus). Mechanical stimulation, traction, adjustment all would be helpful.

However, to the dietary influences: massive amounts of vitamins or minerals and the ability to assimilate the same need to be addressed. The assimilation can be done by increasing the body's ability to do so with the gelatin and with other combinations of foods that make the body easy to assimilate. In this situation, as well as in most, the body does not assimilate several different types of food at the same time easily or well. Therefore, eating foods that would be a monomeal - eating, for instance, a whole plate of squash for dinner or lunch - would be sufficient; or perhaps, boiled onions or sautéed onions for lunch or for a meal would be done.

The body's blood sugar level needs to be monitored as well and perhaps epileptics should eat four times a day, rather than three.

Sugar from the sugar bowl should be avoided, although sugar from nature would be acceptable; from the sugar bowl it is not, for it does cause the body to react rather quickly and adversely. However, honeys and even molasses (which is a derivative of sugar) may be given, but white sugar should be avoided.

With manipulation and with dietary assimilation enhanced or improved, perhaps even a cranial-sacral specialist could be utilized; especially in younger children after the birth trauma, if the skull can be reshaped by simple massage, these all should relieve the epileptic condition.

However, to a cause, it is largely poor blood supply in the membrane and the penting up of nerve flow in the controlling or mechanical end from the *modulus cerebellum*. There is an inability for the body to release this brain energy outwardly into the body. It is more of a mechanical release through the nervous systems and the deficiency of the vitamins within the body, not allowing the controlling center to monitor or control the body.

Now as the body would be pent-up with this energy, the body naturally goes into a convulsive state as the energy is drained off through the rapid movement of the body or the flailing of the limbs, causing great activity in the brain from the left and right hemisphere to be used up. Bleeding this off or draining this off can be done by the person being very athletic, very active indeed. But also having good posture, having manipulations to the back and neck (and even to the skull) to reduce the pressures so this can be passing and the self can overcome this impairment or impediment in the physical form.

Why do children with epilepsy respond so well

to high fat diets?

Primarily these individuals in this regard have difficulty in assimilating what they ingest into the body. Fats are very easily assimilated into the body more than carbohydrates, you see. As such, they tend to be absorbed in the body directly. They increase blood flow throughout the body and they do affect the areas in the brain, in the lower portion or back of the brain; the motor skills areas itself. These fats are used as fuel in the body in conjunction with oxygen.

Usually the oxygen levels in the body are quite low as well, and therefore these are considered (if you would pardon the comparison) like high-test fuel, as opposed to regular fuel being given to an engine. For here, the high-test causes the engine to perform better, cleaner and without much effort, whereas the regular or low-grade would have a tendency to be sufficient but not provide the extra power or performance. Carbohydrates cause the body to work in digestion. Fats do not cause the body to work as hard in digestion and assimilation.

The fatty tissue within the body allows for the conductivity of electrical and magnetical impulses to be much improved. They are building not only to the tissue of the body, but they are also affecting the central nervous systems and the other nervous systems within the body rather easily or like a conduction of the electrical-magnetical impulses, you see. Fats smooth in the gaps, increase the electrical-magnetical conductivity of nerve through energy or movement flow.

Epsom Salts

Cayce was a big proponent of Epsom salt baths for detoxification. How do they work?

The Epsom salt bath has the ability to extract toxins from the skin organ itself, opening the pores and removing toxins and poisons that otherwise would be shed through the skin as an organ of detoxification. It removes surface and below-the-surface toxins. It also draws poisons and toxins from the muscles themselves. It also improves the electromagnetic forces or currents that are above the body as well.

Consider this as a firming up of any difficulties in conductivity of the current or energy flows above the body. This, in turn, both indirectly and directly affects the chakra points and aura and glandular points that pulse, or give off different frequency readings. This bath would allow the chakra points to strengthen, if they would be weak. It also coordinates and allows the energy flows to pass through the chakras from the lower to the higher.

Indirectly, it affects clarity in the mind and allows more blood flow into the brain. As the muscles in the upper back and neck would relax, blood flow would naturally increase also. By directing the blood flow in and about the joints of the body, it repairs the joints and allows them to be all improved by muscle relaxation, and blood flow increases. It encourages an all-round lubrication or, more specifically, allows separation of the joints to be enhanced or improved so that they hinge better, lubricate more, and strengthen while releasing.

Remember well: it is the muscles that pull the body together, and the bones that hold the body apart! This type of bath allows the joints to expand.

Fasting

It has been recommended that each person should fast once a week, every week. How long should such a fast be maintained to continue good health?

There are varieties: a liquid fast or vegetable juices, you see, filled with vitamins, or water fasts, or what would be mono meal fasts (such as bananas or grapes, or cabbage). Should it be the desire to completely fast - no food, no water - then for forty-four hours this would be tolerable. At the end of this period, a little salt would best be taken, with a small amount of water to get the system back to par. If it is a weekly basis, once for a twenty-four hour period would be beneficial. If it is done on an irregular basis, then for five days, there should be the fasting.

We would recommend the apple diet, which would consist of eating apples for three days. A little black coffee or water would be tolerated also. Olive oil must be taken on the second and third day to alleviate or cleanse the colon. If this is to be done, once monthly or on an irregular basis as it is desired. But for the main stay of fasting for disciplining the mind as well as the body, twenty-four hours would be sufficient.

Are there benefits to a diet of maple syrup, lemon juice, cayenne pepper and hot water?

From time to time as a cleansing formula, yes; three to five days, some to seven days, for this would affect the urinary system. It would affect the bladder, the liver, and, to some degree, activate the gall. But it would primarily be utilized in the liver flush. Diets which would require a degree of fasting (and this would be one way) would allow the body to shrug off the toxins that are accumulated within the filter of the body. This would dislodge those entrapped within the liver and allow them to be discharged from the body. You would find the urine would become dark, orangey in color, indicating casting off of the toxins lodged within the area. All could benefit from these within the thirtieth year and older. We are speaking here primarily for the Western (the Canadian and the United States) type of diet, unless there is more of a vegetarian or vegetable enriched diet. Most would cause the liver to be plugged up, to some degree, by the age of thirty.

Could you please make any additional recommendations on proper fasting to be beneficial to the body?

Fasting, where there is absolutely nothing taken into the body, can be done for short periods of time, for those who prefer the same. However, taking into the body simple water, and not taking into the body any physical matter - foods of any sort - is a second way of fasting (and as much water as can be taken into the body would be good). In other words, eight to ten large tumblers of water. And, again, the water should be simple water (no flavor, no sugar, and it does not need to be carbonated). Simple water. Best to be taken at room temperature as well, for it does not need to shock the body as warm or cold water does. Room temperature is best.

To what would be sustained fasting for more than a week (perhaps up to a month), then broths, juices, teas, or water may be given. These forms of liquid intake will sustain the body's moisture, and as the body is hydrated, it functions without difficulty. It is impossible for a fast to go on without giving water to the body, and therefore fasting should be simply a denial of food or physical sustenance to the body, save for liquids like water. Those who would take into themselves milk during a fast, it is their preference. It is better to have liquids than no liquids at all.

The function during a fast is to give the body a rest from the digestive and assimilative processes of digesting food or allowing the body to go through the digestive processes of working to assimilate food. Enhancing the eliminations, cleansing the body during this time of fasting would be an excellent practice as well. For herein, the body would be heightened in its activity to excrete, urinate, or filter out poisons and toxins. To do so, much water should be taken in.

It is advisable that periodically the body would go through fasting, or that periodically the body would engage in long-term fasting, but it is a matter of choice. However, even eating one meal a day would be much healthier than eating three meals a day; but this, again, is a personal choice and is a matter for preparation. Likewise, the fasting of three days or even one day, periodically and regularly, would be healthy for the body. No machinery runs twenty-four hours a day, seven days a week, three hundred and sixty-five days a year. Rest periods for the body are most important to maintaining good health.

Fibromyalgia

What causes Fibromyalgia?

This would be cells that have been builded up (or have accumulated, let us say) cocooned parasites; viral conditions, inundating influences in the body. They become fibroid and build up as the body naturally attempts to corral, isolate, and then cocoon the invading influences in the body that are not otherwise eliminated from the body.

What would be best would be to drink plenty of water for all of the life, to make sure the kidneys and eliminations are functioning properly. Those who are susceptible to constipation, or burning urine sensations, or disruptions in urine eliminations, you see - blood in the urine as well, diarrhea or constipation digestive disorders - these are all susceptible, in a preliminary way, to this condition.

The body should engage in, from time to time, certain fasts in which there would be the removal of intestinal (let us say) resident parasitic conditions or bacteria within the intestine. This can be done quarterly or annually in which there would be eating of little else other than apples themselves. Olive oil, a large spoonful in the morning on the first and second day, and about an ounce of olive oil on the third day would be given. The entity may consume teas or black coffee, but little else. Seven to ten large tumblers of water each day. This would help the body, for the apples would act as a catalyst with the kidney here, eliminating, you see, toxins from the blood.

The kidneys should be pampered. The kidneys should be treated with massage, with heat, and with light. The spine should be manipulated or kept supple, so that there is good nerve flow to the kidneys, for the kidneys are the first line of defense of all disease in the body. As the kidneys go, so goes the body, you see. Yet the silent servants work tremendously hard to filter from the body all impurities. As the body becomes saturated with the same, the kidneys become overloaded; they become frail, weak, fatigued and fail. And, as such, the body, through this acidic, toxic condition increasing, the body begins to fail itself, you see.

There can be a removal of these forces, or if there can be instilled in the blood the assimilation of alkaline forces, then the viral or parasitic influence can be curtailed or eliminated. The tumor would, therefore, shut down or turn acidic and disintegrate itself. Or this can be done artificially from the outside, cutting off the blood supply in the tumor which already has the viral condition or the bacterial condition or the parasite within; and, as such, this would eliminate what is within, and the body would survive.

Flaxseed Oil

What benefit is there of borage or flaxseed oil in the average body as a supplement?

Flaxseed oil positively affects the brain, pituitary, thalamus and hypothalamus; it also affects the production of oil in the scalp. It affects the stomach and enhances elimination. It tends to improve the urinary function and also it can be used as a laxative in the body. It is best to crush the same rather than eat the seed whole. The oil from the seed is very beneficial to the liver.

Fluoride

Please examine the health aspects of fluoridation of water and comment.

In the beginning, the intention was that this chemical could be added to water to improve the conditions (for purification). It would be a low-tech, elementary way to improve water that would be taken from the ground that is not properly sanitized or (call it here) purified, you see. As such, there are effects.

However what is added to the water as a chemical is not what is readily found in large amounts in water, and the amount of fluoride in the water, of course, can cause (as any excess or extreme) difficulties in the opposite extreme. For, in many cases, there is a softening of the enamel of the teeth, there is (in some small percentage) an affect to nerves, causing nerve damage or feelings of nervousness, leading to paranoia in the extreme. To others, there is difficulty of the kidney and the stresses on the kidney and bladder. This does not cause infections on the body, but it can cause a numbing or a slowing down of the function of the filtering devices of the body. That is to say, a build up of the chemical over a longer period of time can weaken the kidney and weaken the liver itself and cause difficulty or susceptibility to irritations or infections (shall we say) to the bladder and the kidney itself, you see, as well as the liver. It does have adverse effects in a large percentage of the population. In others it has little effect, and, in some, it has no effect whatsoever.

Does fluoride build up in the pineal gland and cause calcification of the gland?

As we would examine the effects of this, we would find that it does have the tendency to make the hair thinner, the scalp flaky or sore and, as such, internally to the soft tissues it would be acidic and also causes the glands to be sluggish, you see. Yes, to the question. The answer would be there is some derogatory effect of what is added to water, as one extreme is always matched or balanced by another extreme.

It is best to have water that is filled with minerals, naturally filtered through and in the local vicinity in which the body resides. These minerals would be taken into the body. All too often, these filtration aspects remove elements from the water that would be positive or helpful to the physical body in the region in which the body would reside.

Fluoride is unnatural and, indeed, is in abundance (or too much). This causes dryness to the skin. A shriveling of the nervous system also occurs. We would find it does not allow the body to remove those rejected aspects that would be associated with the joints and, as such, this adulteration or this inability to remove sediments causes joint pain, you see. To the question: yes, there would be some derogatory effect at the pineal and the pituitary, and there is some sluggish activity or reduction of blood flow to these areas.

What is the best way to decalcify this gland?

Speed up the eliminations in the body, to improve all of the body, not specifically the gland itself. However, if you would use tuning forks and certain frequencies, they would cause a little bit of a headache, perhaps, but it would be stimulating the gland and internally there would be a pulsing or a throb, a squeezing of the gland almost (it would be described as). This would indicate some activity has been stimulated here. Coffee might be given and those fluids that would be good for digestion (like Swedish bitters) can be taken. This would help to remove sediments in the liver, the kidneys, the bladder, as well as the glands themselves, you see.

Do you see that fermented Skate Liver Oil or X-Factor Gold™ High Vitamin Butter Oil reverse pineal gland calcification?

They would assist and would benefit the gland itself. Yes, to the question. The intention is to have the gland itself pulse or vibrate (you might call it). These substances seem to help, especially that which would be trace elements of gold in the same you see.

Food Additives

MSG and High Fructose Corn Syrup

What are the long-term effects in the body of ingesting the food additive called monosodium glutamate (MSG)?

To some degree, it causes disruption in the small intestine. It can clog the Peyer's Patch, which affects the immune system itself, over a longer period of time. In short periods of time, it causes fluctuation in blood pressure and it does cause indigestion in some people (while in others it causes something similar to a laxative). The substance itself can retain in the body for some time, especially in the larger intestine or colon itself. It is difficult to eliminate in the body, as it adheres to certain tissues in the body; not that it starts a polyp, but that it could be similar to that, where it hides or adheres to crevices in the colon. It is difficult to assimilate into the body quickly or readily, you see, and, once assimilated, it is difficult to be eliminated.

As the body tends to increase in its weight, it is difficult for the body to eliminate more correctly, especially if the body ages and the same (or similar) amount of substance is put into the same. Best to understand that the body needs to eat from many sources of nutrition, or sources of food, so that it can keep the assimilation process functioning correctly. When the assimilation lessens, the nutritious aspects of the body lessen, and the body becomes susceptible to illness or dis-easement through the digestive systems in the body, causing elimination difficulties to extend around the body relatively easily. See?

High fructose corn syrup is added to many foods as a sweetener. If a body were to ingest this several times a week over decades, what are the effects in the body?

It seems to adhere to the body, first in the intestine, and then as plaque in the artery itself. The substance does not seem to be too easy removed from the body, unless, of course, the body is physically active. Then it tends to not be so invasive in the body or to cause disruption within the same. Otherwise it can cause a hardening of the arteries and also a certain degree of irritation in the assimilative process in the arterial and the venous systems in the body. Like crystal, or like sandpaper, or like sand, so to speak, these small, irregular-shaped particles can acquire a location or fixation and there jam up into a place, reducing the blood flow through the artery, or reducing the movement of a joint in the body such as knee or elbow.

Are there ways to counter the ill effects of MSG and high fructose corn syrup, aside from just ingesting less of them?

As we would examine these additives, or these that would be supplemented to certain combinations of food products, it would be to understand that one is a binder, the other appears to be a binder and a sweetener at the same time. As such, food that is prepared by others, and food that is put into containers - boxes or cans, you see - and is somehow handled or prepared by others, these would be suspect and would be, of course, the source of these conditions or these processes being enacted. See?

Therefore, for one who would wish to strictly avoid the same, one would need to prepare one's own meals, choose foods that are not prepared, and prepare the foods oneself. This would assure that these additives would not be put within the food, or in the processing of the food. This would be paramount for those who would have conditions of difficulty (or would be allergic, so to speak) to these items. Those who cannot escape the same and must use these foods in their own consumption (if they can tolerate the same) should simply drink plenty of water after there has been the consumption of these products (meaning within the next twenty-four hours), at least a liter or perhaps two could be consumed. This would help the body purge and flush from its system those aspects that would be the monosodium glutamate and the fructose corn syrup. See?

Also here, if the colon function is active or in good working condition, a bowel movement after a meal has been consumed would be good, and then sometime thereafter - four to six hours - another bowel movement. See? This would be normal functions in which food is put into the body or ingested; digestion takes place and then elimination naturally follows. However, in the normal cycle of things, in some individuals, this is only done once a day, making the body more susceptible to retaining the effects of these foods you see, in the body. Therefore to avoid the effects, have the body purge these processed foods as soon as possible, through the normal elimination systems. On occasion, it would be necessary for a steam bath to be given in which the body

would perspire rapidly, and thereby squeeze out of the skin those toxic substances that would accumulate in the skin; for understand the skin is an organ, as well as the others, and it does eliminate and remove from the body those things that are unwanted - toxins, poisons, and so on.

That which could be taken into the body would simply be those things that are alkaline in the body; those foods that produce alkalinity in the body. Certain leafy, green vegetables that would have plenty of chlorophyll within them, like the wheat grass juice, or the spinach leaf, or even the cabbage leaf itself would be helpful as well to help counter these effects in the body. The assimilative process, if it is good in the body, will more aptly assimilate these things than they would be, if there was a poor assimilative process, where these things would then be stored around the body.

In essence, the objective is to speedily remove the food through the digestive and elimination systems. If this could be achieved, this would be the best, for it would reduce the time of assimilation, and, therefore, foods that encourage elimination (physical congress) should be taken in combination or soon after foods that have been prepared with the MSG or the corn syrup should be taken. Often, the term "hurry curry" means that it encourages the body to eliminate quickly! There are other foods - fruits in particular, like pears - that would tend to offset the condition and hurry this through the body.

As we have given, it is a matter of moving these substances through the body and to reduce the time of assimilation. Also, a few granules of sea salt in a glass of water may help to purge or counter the effects in the body. Otherwise, the body will normally assimilate what is put inside it, and, as such, there is no real process to negate the effects of the binder and the sweetener; only to speed it up going through the body, or to attempt to reduce its assimilation into the body.

Grapes or grape juice, or a little red wine (an ounce or two), or a mixture of grape juice with water (two ounces of each) would be helpful. The intention is to speed up the digestion, by increasing the bile to be secreted into the system. This would most likely be the best process for most, generally speaking, for as the grapes, grape juice, or wine is taken in, it affects the thyroid and pancreas and, in turn, the bile to be secreted, and this would have the greater effect at speeding up the process and reducing the amount of assimilation of these particular additives. See?

The best, of course, is not to put them in the body in the first place. Do your own work. Prepare your own food, and then you are assured of what goes into your own body. See? Best baked, broiled or boiled. Avoid stir-fried or deep-fried foods or foods that would be cooked with oils or fats.

Frequency Healing

Rife Machine

If you were to try to compare the benefits of single frequency machines (like the Rife machine), where the body is bombarded in a particular area with a particular frequency to a device (such as the Tesla violet ray device) which bombards thousands of frequencies at a time, which, generally, would be more effective for the average person?

There would be a need for pathology, there would be a need for containment of the vibration and a need to point the vibration to be most effective. The single vibrational rate would affect only whatever would be affected by that vibration, and nothing else. The broadcast benefit (De La Warr's work, you see) affects all of the cells, but by exposure to lightning, or even to electric sparking, this can be accomplished as well.

The broadcast that is broad, like the violet ray, is beneficial to the body, for it affects a wide range of cells. Again, looking for the specific use, usually the broad band is for an uplifting or an enhancing of vibrational levels at the cell level - the retina in the cell - whereas that which is used as a single vibration is used for destructive purposes, attempting to eliminate or destroy certain cells. Therefore, it depends on your intention, does it not? However, we would suggest in either one or the other, it would be for the broad band broadcasting of vibration of frequency.

Even though there are many different people today claiming to develop and use Rife machines, they are experimenting without a grounding. It is not clear whether people have been successful in choosing frequencies which can generally enhance the body. Are Rife machines that broadcast specific frequencies, such as 528 Hz or 727 Hz doing anything of benefit for the body as a whole?

You have said the question correctly. Because there is not knowledge, there is experimentation. This can be considered arbitrary and, indeed, artful at best. As such, until there is the understanding of what is happening at the cell level, there should not be experimentation with accreditation given to what is taking place. There is insufficient pathology. There is incoordination between the effect, and the purpose. As such, on occasion, this can be quite harmful to the body. However, it depends on the duration and the intensity.

To the question, however: unless there is an understanding of what frequency does what in the body, it would be considered simply art and guesswork. From what you have given, we would concur that it is, at best, guesswork. The intention to be preventative and to keep the body healthy by stimulating the vibrational rate of the cells would be the correct way, rather than attempting to use this as a scalpel or as a death ray (so to speak) to viruses or cells. Again, in the hands of one who knows not what they do, it can be counter-productive.

The two most common frequencies, which, by experimentation, are supposed to be effective in helping the body are 528 and 727 Hz. Is there a particular frequency that you can identify that would be generally helpful?

The broad band broadcast, for those that are in the hands of individuals, would be sufficient.

Understand that different organs have different frequencies or vibrational rates. Somewhere between these two would be acceptable.

It is like throwing a bucket of water at the body, as opposed to using a garden hose and pointing it at the body. The bucket would broadcast and be playful to the body; the garden hose would be hurtful and even damaging because of the point of pressure. See the difference?

Let us be specific. The low vibration would cause bone to grow; the high vibration would cause the flesh to deteriorate. If the worker of such would be using these frequencies, they would cause their flesh to deteriorate and their bone to grow and they would be monstrous. See?

Gallbladder / Gallstones

Can you comment on the cause of gallbladder troubles and the best focus of treatment?

Any who would "be galled" or would be offended would find this emotion in the gall bladder as the condition here. Usually it is the blockage of the ductless gland itself that would cause the condition of gallstone or the irritant in the body. Care should be taken in those who have a family history of the same that they are monitoring their dietary influences that they do not take into themselves much in the way of dairy products or those foods that would produce the conditions of stone or calcium build up. They must be very active in their physical sense or being, should not pursue sedentary lives and, indeed, from time to time, would need to observe their indigestion, or their sensitivity in the stomach or digestion.

Swedish bitters or any fruit that is acidic - orange or lime - should be taken at meals to help promote digestion in the body while, at the same time, helping to prevent the build-up of the stone or the irritant in the gall itself.

When there is a spastic condition in the gall itself, usually there is some condition in the life that is stressful or irritating. Slippery elm as a herb or tea should be given, and there are a variety of other herbs that would be stimulating yet soothing to the stomach and the digestive disorder that is within the body itself. A gallbladder attack can be seen as a state of anxiety, or nervousness, or fear of the self being insulted, made fun of, or is under some sort of attack.

Watermelon can be eaten during the season in large amounts (and should be). This would help to reduce any impediment or stone; at the same time, it would allow the self to feel quite regulated and, indeed, in control or authority.

Is there an effective, non-surgical way to expel gallstones?

Depending on size, this would require changing the chemical balance within the body. Primarily this can be done with the use of orange peel scrapings (with a chemical oil found in the same). A few scrapings of the peel can contain enough of the oil or chemical to keep the body dissolving the stones, whether they be in the liver or gallbladder itself (or extending to the kidney, for that matter).

The diet would have to be altered so that there would be fewer items in the body that could form these substances.

There would have to be changes in the emotional states as well, for understand difficulties of this nature (stones forming within the glands) stem from thoughts that are harsh, bitter, fearful, or from the state of anger or anxiety (especially in the kidney with regards to anger). To the gallstones, it would be to the emotions that are resentment, and irritations or insistence (though insistence usually leads to cysts or boils in the body) with regards to what galls a person, what makes them frustrated or angry. To the liver, it would be the emotions of fear and (to some degree) held-back resentment.

However, these emotions are controllable through the mind itself; for who is the master: the belly or the mind? From our perspective, the mind is the builder, the mind is the way. The mind is the way that should be approached first. Any who wish to control the mind should engage in the exercises which are Eastern in nature - yoga and other types of these disciplines - for any who engage in this kind of exercise first challenge the mind, and as the mind is brought about in control, the body naturally follows (not the other way around).

As such, one should attempt to keep one's peace, throughout the daily activities, and through all the influences about the daily life. One must always remember that this is a time of extremes, a teaching time, or a testing time. And one can meet these extremes by putting limits on desires, trying to keep the peace within the self, and avoid being triggered by other experiences, activities or individuals. Then one can master the self, and no matter what comes toward the self, from any order, from any desire, from any activity, the self can remain true to the self or peaceful. For understand that emotions are either a constructive or destructive force in the body. As such, one should always look for constructive emotions and experience them, and to belittle or deny the destructive emotions, turning them through the will so that they would be of the constructive aspect.

However, to the physical body, the conditions described here could be altered or changed (as we have given) by scraping orange peel on the food from time to time, daily, and consuming salt from the sea (not table salt), as this would heighten the iodine levels within the cell. Also, remove from the system calcium, high levels of iron, and other forms which would give the ingredients to these congregations of sediments within the body. Blood cleansing teas, or vegetables, or fruits would change the chemistry and disallow the massing of these substances that otherwise should be eliminated from the body. Different types of salts, different types of stimulants for elimination would be best, including simply drinking plenty of water if one is susceptible to these substances.

Eat of the apple for three days and little

else, save for seven to ten large tumblers of water (although black coffee or tea could be given). We would recommend the bayberry leaf, the raspberry leaf and, indeed, burdock root and chamomile as well. The intention, here, is to stimulate and remove sediment from the blood. However, on the first and second day, a large spoonful of olive oil should be taken. On the third day, about an ounce of the same. Eat as much apple as possible (or wanted) in any form that you like, baked, boiled, diced, sliced, or made into mush. This would act as a catalyst, and, with the kidney, eliminate sedentary influences and toxins from the blood. This would directly remove the building blocks for these stones that would accumulate in the body. This should be done annually, if not quarterly.

Also, chelation therapy could be given to older bodies; these would be after the twenty-eighth year, and in particular after the fiftieth year of life. This would be intravenously given, and it would remove heavy levels of iron accumulation and plaque from the arteries (and other sedentary forces and toxins from the body). There are a myriad of herbs and herbal concoctions that would cleanse the blood.

This would be the place to start in the body; provided, of course, the body is eating a properly-balanced diet, ingesting plenty of water, and eliminations (both urinary and physical congress) are in good working order or proper balance. Watermelon can be taken in great amounts if there is difficulty in spastic bowel, or gallbladder stones in particular. This breaks down the stones, specifically in the gall, and helps to eliminate the same.

Garlic

Is garlic beneficial for most people?

For some, it is helpful to purify the blood (as are onions). But some cannot tolerate garlic or onions. Experimentation here. But, generally speaking, there should be more garlic in the diet.

Gelatin

Is gelatin beneficial to most people?

In small dosages or sprinkled upon food, it aids as a catalyst in assimilation of food. It makes the digestion cycle a little easier on the body. Yes, it would be of great benefit to those who have difficulty in assimilating; especially children who would be considered the bean-pole, skinny, or under-nourished, yet eat like grown men. Here, any who would be considered skinny should be accustomed to sprinkling the gelatin or Jello upon the food; for, again, it acts as a catalyst and allows the body to assimilate more proficiently.

Why does gelatin help food absorption?

It acts as a catalyst in the body (a conversion, so to speak). It speeds up the process in which the cells would be able to absorb. It acts like a medium or a conduit, you see, between the cells and the vitamins; and vitamins are more easily absorbed into the cells.

Genetically Modified Food

What is the effect on health from eating genet-

ically modified foods?

It depends on the food itself. Some food quality is lost for the intention to preserve food and to make it worthful, at the same time as reducing the effect of disease disruption or the spoilage of food, you see. It would be better for the natural way for the animal, vegetable, and mineral to be produced, as it is seen, but we cannot find all ill effects for what has been engineered. It is the assimilative and digestive quality; if this is not affected, then the foods that have been artificially tampered with, altered or improved (as it might be considered) would be digestible, assimilative and beneficial to the body. After all, it would be better to eat some food that would be modified by the will of Man, than to have no food available and the body starve. Somewhere between the two is the correct measure.

Improving foods that would not be susceptible to diseases, that would be able to be planted in difficult terrain or poor soil with poor growing conditions and still survive would be considered a good feat. But on the perspective of quality, when this is done, the food's ability to deliver benefits to the physical body is naturally affected or diminished. We do not find it as being poison to the body; simply modification of something given, something gained, something lost for some benefit, and it becomes a trade-off, you see.

Does the body recognize foods that have been genetically altered?

Of course it recognizes them and attempts to digest them. Sometimes it has difficulty in doing the same, but the assimilation of them is the real question. The assimilation does not happen as quickly, effectively, or efficiently as foods that would be naturally grown or found in nature, see? This form of manipulating nature does intend to feed the masses, but it is the generic version and the nutritional value is somewhat affected or lessened.

Germanium

What does germanium do in the body?

This mineral tends to attack, at the cell level, what would be irregular or would be adulterated by an attachment of a foreign substance, viral condition, or parasite. It tends to release what are called free radicals within the body and also causes an oxidization, in the positive sense, at the cell level to eradicate disease, especially in soft tissues like the lungs, liver, bladder and kidney; in a lesser way, pancreas and thyroid. The overall effect is to allow more oxygen to be absorbed at the cell level. It, in fact, allows the surface of the cell to absorb oxygen more readily; approximately ten times more readily. Therefore, it is somewhat of a cleansing agent on one hand; and an opening agent of oxygen at the cell level on the other. Understand that letting oxygen into the cell and having that kinetic or build-up of oxygen in the cell itself is the key to health and longevity.

Are there other substances in nature that act in a similar nature to germanium?

Of course. These would include any minerals or substances or vegetation that would be prickly in nature, from the cacti that would look like a man to the burdock root itself. You would also find that ginseng, ginger, avocado, and those desert flowers or blossoms would be similar in their effect at removing negative elements in the body and allowing the body to assimilate oxygen and strengthen the cell, or the hemoglobin outer layer. This would allow better penetration into the far reaches of the body without destruction of the blood cells themselves, and the oxygen delivery would be amplified or improved. You will find that sulfur is good at this as well.

Ginseng

Is ginseng good for most people?

It depends upon the potency here, as to structural nature. As the years would go by, it could be added to the diet to improve the activity in that which would be the sexual or biological functions. It would also be helpful to the regenerative or restorative mechanism to the thymus, see? Ginseng can be seen as that which is restorative to what is commonly considered energy flows within the body. It is somewhat of an aphrodisiac but also it heightens the metabolism in the body and restores blood in the smaller orifices or areas in the reproductive center of the body. Also, for some, it affects the heart in strengthening the same, and helps to repair heart damage, especially where there has been a denial of blood or where there is scar tissue.

This is an all-round stimulant. It can be likened to the lotus blossom, more so as an ancient remedy for - call it here - the stimulation of the libido through to the vitality or strength and endurance of the body. It allows more oxygen into different parts of the body and it stimulates the metabolism - the body's vibrational rate, you might say. Everything is speeded up. Ginseng can be used on a variety of deficiencies in the body, from sexual impotence through to respiratory difficulty, to a laborious heart, you see. It tends to stimulate that which has slowed down in the body.

Is there any difference in absorption rates, or benefit, in the roots of Western descent, as opposed to those of the Oriental descent?

One is considered hot and the other is considered cool. The North American is considered the superior to that which is grown in the Orient. That from the North Americas is considered the cooler or cold, while that from the East is considered the hot. Individuals from North America should eat what is largely grown in the vicinity or region in which the body resides, as these roots would be of the same frequency or electrical-magnetical rate, grown on the same water or water source in the same vicinity in which the human body resides. This method would be much more assimilative and harmonious for the North American body. Moreover, the Western root is of an overall superior quality and is recognized as such.

Glucosamine

A diet including glucosamine sulfate and chondroitin has been given in the mass media an "arthritis cure." As you see, what percentage of those already affected with arthritis would respond positively to this?

Over fifty per cent would immediately feel relief through the addition of supplements or foods that would enhance the lubricating forces in and around the joints, as well as the vertebrae itself. Couple this with peanut oil massages or other lubricating oils that would be massaged in and about the joints, and well over seventy-five per cent of the general public would feel immediate relief, long enduring relief of the nagging pains of arthritis.

If there would be radical changes to the diet and there would be hot and cold baths or water therapy (mineral baths, you see) as well added to this, then there would be an even higher improvement; especially in those bodies that would be seized or blocked up. For the body has the ability to mend itself, but it would take meditation as well as changes in the diet, for the more difficult individual conditions or cases to be remedied.

Glucosamine is currently touted as a "miracle cure" for arthritis. Could you please comment?

It tends to produce a liquefying force or a lubricating force at the end of the bone where the membrane has been somewhat damaged. It attracts fatty substances from the tissues to be formulated and directed towards the joint. It also tends to reduce liquid or excess water at joints and it tends to remove sedentary forces there as well. These would be like grist or like sand in the lubricant - the glucosamine isolates them and retracts them.

Now, if there is a lack of membrane, then the glucosamine tends to not work as well, for then you simply have bone rubbing on bone. But the body will attempt to repair this, even if there is no bone. This is very difficult for the body, for it needs some buffer, some membrane that can act as a bearing between the two points.

To some degree, it can repair or fill in the porous areas of bone as well, especially where the membrane has very little left or is missing. In this way, it acts as a patch or bandage, and allows the bones to slide back and forth, one on the other. But if the bone is greatly deteriorated, or in great disease, or porous to a great degree, this tends not to work as well.

Does glucosamine need to be ingested regularly, or is the effect cumulative?

If the body is somewhat sedentary and is not used or exercised, then the body tends to allow deterioration to take place. For instance, one way to keep strong bones is to constantly stomp the feet on the ground to send vibration through the long bones of the leg to cause the body to pay attention that the body's bones need to be repaired. Simply stomping the foot on the ground a couple of times each day aids the body's consciousness (if you will) in building, or directing strength of the body.

To some degree, the glucosamine may be necessary to take forever if the body is somewhat sedentary. If the body is un-exercised then sedentary conditions take hold. The body begins to deposit by-products of assimilation that are not able to be eliminated through the normal way of the urinary and bowel, or through the glands, or through the skin, or through the lymph system itself. The lymph can be considered the garbage sewer system in the body in which would be collected all the sedentary forces, and then these would be burnt up or consumed in the metabolism of the body. They also would be given out or eliminated in the mucous in the colon.

A body should remain active. If a body is active, or if a body is taxed in an aerobic way, and in a strength-challenging way, then the body will continue to grow. But if it is not, and the blood flow is reduced, as in most sedentary lifestyles, then this retraction of blood causes the reduction of building in the body and the glucosamine may be necessary to take forever.

Gold

What is the single best supplement that could be used by weightlifters or strength trainers to be able to maximize their workout potential? We are examining various aspects of the circulatory system, of the ability for the muscle to retain oxygen and for the muscle to thicken or grow in its size and in its capability for strength. Gold, or gold chloride, or gold in any form (although minute amounts) would be beneficial for the muscle, as this would speed up communications in the nervous systems, the nerve pathways and in the trunk lines, the nerve transitions, or the nerve system. It also affects or improves synapse function in the brain, and, therefore, the controlling center in the brain at the medulla, cerebellum and thalamus levels. It allows the muscles to be more regulated and stimulated.

But for the muscles themselves, the metal seems to allow the greater consciousness, or the muscles to be thickened while remaining flexible. The muscle being fatigued with lack of oxygen is the problem that can be overcome to maximize the potential. Germanium also can be taken to enhance the respiratory and oxygen equalization between assimilation and kinetic energy in the muscle.

Grape Juice

Cayce was adamant that taking grape juice with meals would assist in weight reduction. Could this be Nature's "fat burner," that many have been searching so long and hard for?

Grape juice stimulates the bile to be secreted into the intestine by affecting the pancreas, the thyroid and, in turn, the bile in the liver and gall. As bile would be secreted into the intestine, the digestive process would become more perfect and elimination would be unrestricted; the languishing of substances in the intestine is corrected. The movement through the intestine of fatty substances is speeded up and the assimilation of same is less effective. Because of this, obesity is reduced. More importantly, the thyroid production and the metabolism speeding up occurs simultaneously.

Graviola Leaf

There are a number of researchers who claim that the herb known as graviola leaf is excellent in combating cancer and other fast-growing cells. Do you see an advantage to this?

In some circumstances, yes. This would be for cysts, or fluids, or skin disruptions; not necessarily soft tissue metastasized cancers, but in lesser degrees.

Hair Dye

Could you please explain how the use of commercial or chemical hair dyes and bleaches may have a detrimental effect in the body?

They may affect the hair itself by weakening the same, but as the hair itself continues to grow, as long as there is a good blood supply to the root, then the hair itself - whether it has been dyed or affected in some other sort of stylish way - it will continue to grow and should not be adverse or derogatory in its development. But when there is a poisoning of the roots, or when there has been a chemical burn in the roots of the hair, or when there is any kind of absorption of the chemical into the scalp, then this affects the follicle and the root of the same, and there is a diminishing or a lessening in the absorption of the root in the hair itself. This diminishing of circulation naturally causes a weakening of the hair itself, and it may cause a thinning (and ultimately a balding) of the hair because there is no nutrient or blood supply given freely to the root itself. Take care that the chemicals taken do not burn the scalp or root. But as to changing the color, it seems to be quite capable of doing, without much danger to the scalp or polluting of the hair itself.

Hair Loss and Thinning

See also Male Pattern Baldness

Is there any treatment that can be taken to reverse the condition of loss of hair?

Indeed, when the minds of Men are calm, and there is no panic, no worry, no fear, or desperation, or indecision. When people come together in large groupings (tribes, or clans, as you would call it) and there would be more physical exercise, or movement, or way of making a living, then you would find that their hair would tend to blossom or grow. From the sweat of their brow let their living be earned, you see. Hats are, indeed, not healthy for the body and, therefore, if hats are worn, let them be abandoned, for this causes superheating in the hottest region of the body. This bakes the scalp, so to speak.

When people practice more of inverting themselves or standing on their shoulders (or head) this would invigorate circulation to the head and upper part of the body, naturally and easily. Then you will find that these forces of baldness will not exist in the body (or, more exactly, in the race or group mind itself). For when there is a tribe mentality, there is little fear. Very few find themselves alone, you see (or unloved, for that matter). Stresses are shared by all, therefore no one fears or lives in isolated panic or desperation. When difficulties come, reliance upon the rest of the clan can be taken for granted. These stresses immensely help the rest of the body physically or organically, and usually in such a setting food is plain (not rich, not fat, or spicy). And, indeed, if there would be migration to hotter climates, so there is much in the way of perspiration, then the body would also benefit by this. However, this is not to a migration of peoples, but more to living outdoors in the natural climate, breathing fresh air, drinking water from the creek beds that would be considered safe to drink, rather than what is water from the tap that has been removed of all minerals, nutrients that could be considered helpful. Then you would have the body able to be in balance, dealing with its natural occurrence, for hair upon the body is a demonstration of testosterone, physical strength and endurance, you see, in men and women.

However, as the cells would be stimulated by sound and light, along the lines of De La Warr's work, you would find that the vibrational rate of the cell would be able to be kept up. Static electricity would be seen as friendly and curative that it would knit the cells together and would stimulate the cells' vibrational rate so that, indeed, hair would be grown; no matter where it would be lessened, it could be stimulated and invigorated. Even other parts of the body would be stimulated, melded, or grown together, you see.

There are barometric chambers or tanks

where oxygen can be forced into the blood. Then there are light or steam rooms in which the body can be bathed in light, or steamed with water in which there is the migration of water through the cells; in the same time, there could be the stimulation of the root in the scalp. This is the place to start.

However those oils that would be taken from the skins of fruit would be seen as productive in this regard as well; and, of course, keeping the body greatly alkaline and removing the sedentary or toxic forces from the body.

This Source has recommended brewer's yeast for individuals suffering from thinning hair. Can you elaborate on how this works?

A little may be taken on a cracker or piece of bread, or disguised in some other piece of food. It has the effect of stimulating the hair and thickening the same. It adds to the preservative (if you will) of the hair and it affects primarily the stature in the hair by increasing the blood supply and the nutrients necessary in the follicle. It embellishes the root of the follicle and allows the root to soak up more blood.

Hair - Unwanted

What would you recommend as a method to remove unwanted hair from the body?

That which is grown in the body is natural to the body. By plucking the hairs out with tweezers or some other means, this causes the root to be reduced and, as such, the next generation of follicle has a reduced consistency and itself is muted in its reproduction. Removing the hair from the body in such a way is beneficial, but, here, removing from the diet those oils and fats that would be found in meat helps also to reduce the hair or the unwanted hair substance, by reducing the blood flow (indirectly) to the follicle or to the root of the hair.

Bright lights tend to reduce the hair growth as well, and therefore the brighter the light, the lesser the strength in the hair itself. Substances that would be taken into the body might be more iodine, and more protein; but not too much, for this tends to stimulate the hair growth as well. Testosterone levels, if they are high in the body, tend to produce plenty of hair stimulation, and, therefore, reducing the levels of testosterone in the body may be one way (however it may be difficult to accomplish). Exposing the hair to different temperatures would be good, and this would tend to dwarf or to affect the stamina by reducing the blood flow, you see, to the hair follicle itself.

Otherwise, there is no real reduction of that which is natural, save for the plucking of the hair and allowing it to dwarf, diminish, wane from the body. Eating mostly a vegetarian or a fruit-based diet would also affect hair reduction, or unwanted hair in the body, see?

Headache / Migraine

Could you please explain the cause of migraines and the best form of treatment?

Firstly, there are compressive forces in the neck and there is poor blood supply into the brain; hypertension, or anxiety, or the body being under states of anxiety would cause stress, secreting more adrenaline into the system, constantly causing the high blood pressure and the metabolism to be on guard. This can be considered a cause for this condition of internal pressure and poor blood supply. Simple relaxation of the muscles through any means are possible would allow for the neck (and the arteries that go through the neck) to sustain improved blood flow. Improved blood flow automatically means more oxygen in the brain, and more oxygen in the brain means no migraine headache.

Now the shrinkage or the reduction of the arteries in the brain itself due to low pressure may also be a cause, here. There are a variety of causes, from reduction of blood sugar level, to impeding the blood flow to the brain itself, through the neck, through the arteries, to a degree of restriction of the arteries (whether it be plaque, or growth, or a condition of difficulty). It does cause the arteries to collapse. This also can be on the venous side as well; however this is usually in the arterial that there is poor circulation in the brain, or that there is poor pressure from one hemisphere to the other. This causes the condition of headache or migraine to exist.

The condition of constipation or the difficulty of digestion and elimination on the other end of the body (the intestine) would cause severe difficulties or migraine itself. If, therefore, one can be regular and their eliminations be more correct, then there can be the reduction of the migraine or the headache. Protein-deficient diets need to be supplemented with high amounts of protein. This would affect both elimination and the blood supply into the brain itself. Therefore, if one is regular and capable, able to eliminate properly and efficiently, and the diet is of higher quality protein, this should eliminate the migraine. If there is a mechanical problem, the osteopath, or the chiropractor, or the masseur or masseuse and/or acupuncturist (or all combined) may be necessary to right the condition.

If there is a function of blood supply or improper pressure, then more serious examination may be necessary, and there could even be a necessity for surgery upon the body.

Check the stomach, check the intestinal tracks, check the blood supply and check the bone and vertebrae and how the head and cranium sit on the head itself. The top bones, the atlas and axis should be corrected or in line.

With a diet that would be bland, no sugar added, no color (no food color) no processing added - none - the body should be void of these conditions of migraine, you see. Check the foods that are also derogatory to the body, for some foods that are taken into the body are quite a poison and upset the body immediately. Notice what food is taken and, therefore, what reaction is given and there can be the dis-association of the foods that are pain-causing, you see, as a rule of thumb for this particular area of concern.

Do you agree that most migraine sufferers are sensitive to chocolate or caffeine?

A high percentage are affected by coffee, or caffeine, or chocolate, which has caffeine in it. There are many other reasons for migraine sufferers to suffer the migraine, from collapse of blood pressure in the body and, therefore, the collapse of the arterial, to low in protein or those who would have variance in their diet to the extreme, or those who would be constipated, or those who would have toxins or poisons in the bloodstream that would be at the higher levels. These would make up the greater percentage.

What treatment could be recommended for al-

leviation of migraine headache?

Generally speaking, it would be for the cleansing of the large intestine and some degree of alignment of the large intestine within the abdomen itself. For the colon itself, in the accumulation of fecal matter on the inside surface and the overstretching or lack of peristaltic movement causes a goodly amount of reabsorption of the poisons and toxins that were intended to be alleviated from the body through elimination. There is large blood supply at the colon. Any who would use suppositories would know that the colon is a good assimilator of drugs or suppositories and, as such, due to this large blood supply, it makes little wonder that when there is residue encapsulated or affixed to the colon (which it should not be) that the body continues to absorb what is in the intestine. When there are toxins and poisons there, then they will also be absorbed. Remember the blood that goes through the intestine, the stomach and the throat also goes through the brain. In the brain, there are finite arteries and when there are toxins or sediments within the blood system, they are trapped within the brain, causing the difficulty that is termed the migraine.

Hemorrhoids

Can you please comment on the cause of hemorrhoids and the best focus of treatment?

Commonly called "mad bumps" in the body (by those who would understand the same), this is a demonstration of anger that is either the person's anger itself, or the anger of others that is directed towards the person. It is an elongation of the internal pressures inside primarily the anus itself.

There are a variety of cures (or alleged cures); those that would be ointments that would be given to the body and from the nitroglycerin salve that would tend to shrink the same, to the popular creams that would be given. All have the same intentions: to bring relief, or a soothing aspect to the inflamed tissue.

However, the diet should immediately be a cold diet; green vegetables or foods that are cold. Ice, or lowering the temperature in the area of the hemorrhoid can be given and it would immediately reduce the swelling. Any cream that would cause coldness to occur in the general area would also reduce the swelling.

Then, as such, certain exercises that would build up and tighten the buttocks, thighs, lower abdomen should be given. This would tend to stop the inflammation or the ballooning up of the blood in the artery and, as such, would allow (call it here) a safeguard against the hemorrhoid itself.

However, in those that are expanded, and those that are elongated, surgery may be necessary. But, in a commencing, in the beginning stages, attempting to keep the attitude away from the anger, away from the inflammation of conflict, or battle, or war would be a good place to start.

However, what can be given to the body would be yellow eucalyptus oil combined with castor oil itself. If enemas are given or necessary to increase elimination, so be it. But the diet should be more of a soft diet, eating melons or squashes and plenty of broths or soups, you see (not to inflame or irritate the body).

If the condition persists and is difficult, then placing an insert into the body with a little castor oil (flannel would be good) may be helpful to bring soothing conditions (although it would be difficult to implant into the body, therefore care would be necessary or needed to be taken). This done, a little turpentine (a pinch of the same) in about four to six gallons of warm water, a little salt would be given, and, as such, this can be inserted into the body though an enema syringe or through an applicator with cotton or flannel wrapped around the applicator and inserted into the body, after being soaked in the solution. This would be helpful.

These mad bumps in the body are demonstrative of contained anger within the self. By venting the anger, it helps to vent the internal pressures.

But with the lowering of the temperature, the intention is to shrink the hemorrhoid itself and bring relief to the body. Direct application of ice cubes is the best remedy, even inserting the ice cube as best as can be done would be very helpful in remedying the condition. Castor oil may be smeared around the anus and internally, to help to remove inflammation from the hemorrhoidal tissue itself.

Hot Flashes

What is the cause of hot flashes and what may be done to eliminate them?

It is a chemical response; a stimulation (shall we call it) by a hormonal response. Understand the body goes through certain cycles, through the digestion and rest cycles. The liver also makes secretions, called a liver dump, and the other systems in the body have their routines. During this time, the body's heart rate increases. Restrictive forces in the arterial sometimes causes these hot flashes.

Celery juice would be helpful in reducing the pressures in the body, and helping to regulate these conditions or hormonal imbalance. More iron (liquid iron, perhaps) would be necessary also to regulate this imbalance. We find vitamin B6 and B12 as well as the vitamin D also to be taken would help to reduce the imbalance, and the heart rate would calm itself or not be so triggered into speeding up.

This condition is usually an imbalance of hormone, but sometimes a lack of selenium, and, on other occasions, a lack of zinc in the body. Usually it is a shortage of some mineral or vitamin in the body. Attempt to regulate the level of the blood in the body by avoiding those foods that rise up the circulation pressures or the heart rate, and taking onto the self those foods that would lower or maintain the heart rate.

Hypoglycemia

Can you please comment on the cause of hypoglycemia and the best focus of treatment?

Here it would be with the difficulty with the pancreas itself and what would be with the similar aspect of diabetes itself, as it is in effect with the pancreas and the thyroid. The condition within the body would be primarily the blood-sugar, glucose levels following or lowering themselves and maintaining this low area until it would be called upon in certain activities in the body (and, as such, this would provoke the need for additional food). The cause of this would be a lowering or shortage of iodine in the body itself, and this would affect the thyroid and the pancreas.

As this is such that the activities would require stimulation, either in additional food taken into the body or the conversion of sugar to affect the blood, the cause can be offset with stimulation through the glands themselves by osteopathic or chiropractic adjustment within the mid-portion of the spine to increase the activity of the nerve flow to the organs. The addition of the iodine, both atomic iodine (or Atomidine* as it is called) or it would be seen more in the natural way as the assimilation of kelp or sea salt (or other substances that would contain iodine within them); Lugol's iodine may be taken in droplet form or placed on the skin (the soles of the feet) for absorption.

However, iodine is one of the main building blocks for the body itself. Proper levels of iodine should be gauged or monitored, more or less. Usually the weight of the body is heavier and the metabolism is sluggish or slow. This particular condition affects former athletes as they have, indeed, engaged in what would be high metabolism rates, but have returned to some sort of sedentary lifestyle; and, as such, the body is less.

Those who would be considered nervous, or frightened, or have anxiety, or would be fretful, or fearful in nature, or those who would be sensitive (so to speak) or have their feelings easily hurt, these would be (as a rule of thumb) as categories or areas of people that would suffer from this and the accompanying state of mind or attitude itself.

With the affect of regulating the iodine content in the body and the proper alignment in the spine (or increased posture) and the reduction of weight, then the individuals would reduce their amount of intake (food itself), eat more of the vegetable, and refrain from the heavy meats (the rib meats, including of pork itself); more of the fish, the fowl and the lamb (and if they are sedentary, the dried fish, you see).

Does the condition of hypoglycemia often cause a person to have bouts of depression?

Indeed so, for you would find the blood sugar levels in the system would fluctuate, causing high periods or peaks. That, with the drastic drop, rather than a cushioned drop in sugar level within the system causes an artificial depletion; as such, this causes fatigue, and with the misunderstanding of the feelings physically of fatigue, the depression; yes.

Hypotension

Would you please explain the cause of hypotension (low blood pressure) and give the best form of treatment.

Firstly, there may be a heart that is strong and athletic which means that its normal beating is slower than usual. This would keep the blood pressure lower. For those who have such a heart, there is no remedy. It is natural that the heart is sluggish in beating and the pressure need not be raised in any sedentary or natural setting. However, when they become athletic, there is more to do; this allows the heart rate to go up, and as the heart rate goes up the circulation increases throughout the body. But it is not like hypertension. It is a matter of an athletic heart improving slightly its rhythm or beat. The advantage of this is to keep the body regulated and the respiration normal under duress, or work, or running (as you might call it).

Low blood pressure can be due specifically to the body's metabolism being tired, to arteries being exaggerated, to damage in the heart or to the chemistry in the body being sluggish. Usually blood sugar levels are hypoactive, the thyroid is hypoactive, and therefore the secretion of the hormones (the timing and balancing substances in the body) are off or low as well. For those who stay up too late at night, the body reacts as they are tired and oxygen levels are low in the body. Fatigue, therefore, can cause lower pressure of the blood.

However, assuming there is no impairment in the valves in the heart, that the circulation is going through the body relatively unobstructed, the lower blood pressure is caused primarily from the metabolism being quite low and the body being denied certain elements that would keep the body higher; usually natural sugars that would be found in fruits. Of course, increasing the sugar level in the body, increasing the protein level in the body, and, most importantly, increasing iodine levels in the body should affect the thyroid, pancreas, and, in turn, the heart to bring the blood pressure up to a normal level. When there is weakness, the body might want to examine the possibility of eating meat; this would bring more health to the body.

Infertility

For couples who are having trouble conceiving a child, what can they do naturally to increase their chances of becoming pregnant?

First, to the male, there should be the building up of the spermatozoa. This can be done by abstaining for four to six days or longer. Second, more protein should be taken into the male, and there can be massaging or heating up of the middle part of the body, to increase the circulation through the buttocks, the testicle and the reproductive centers. With increased blood flow, this would allow improvements in the lower end of the body. Then, eat of those supplements such as saw palmetto and others that would have a direct influence on the libido.

To the woman, there should be the washing of the body inside. There can be the primal position in which the body would be placed sort of kneeling on all fours; the insertion of the penis would be from behind and it would have, upon ejaculation, a downward direction for the sperm to flow.

Good diets, good exercise, and a loving attitude set up the act itself. Praying for a divine being to enter into the family in good health may also be given with some promise to take care of the child in a very special way. As we would find the prayer being given, and the diet having more protein, there can be more iron and other minerals in the diet increased. The hair sample or nails may be analyzed, and those minerals missing can be added or even those minerals and vitamins added, see.

Strength building exercises that are specific to the pelvis areas can be done by both genders. But the buildup of blood through the general area should suffice for one's strength for ejaculation and one's strength for the fertilization, when the two are brought together.

Inflammation

Inflammation is a condition in the body which, if allowed to continue, would create more serious problems. Therefore, by taking anti-inflammatory herbs on a daily basis, you can curtail this in advance. Is this a good strategy for those in Western society?

Not to get carried away, but yes to the question. Nothing should be given to the body in an extreme way. Better to be gentle and loving with the body and to take something of all things. However, to the question: yes. Removing inflammation from the body is most beneficial to the body. It does stop areas of difficulty in the brain, the erosion of the brain, and all disorders of the nervous system that are affected in the brain. Removing inflammation from the body and maintaining its absence would be a high priority to achieve. Then the thinking would be clear, the memory would be always excellent, and the eyesight and hearing would be at a high level of capability. Other body functions in the lower end of the body would also be maintained. Inflammation, irritation disrupts the body. Yes, to remove the same is most preferred. However, how it is done, there are a variety of ways.

Infrared Heat

There is a treatment which uses infrared or far-infrared heat over parts of the body to detect areas of sensitivity. When a practitioner determines there is a problem in an area, more heat is applied over the course of treatments until the problem goes away. Is this a logical or correct use of heat therapy?

The answer would be to the affirmative. It would be indicated that the sensor is reporting conditions of lack of blood, lack of blood flow, a lowered blood pressure region, while, at the same time, attempting to increase the blood and the blood flow to the localized region. This is not one hundred per cent accurate, for sometimes pain can be reflected in the body; felt in one area, but actually caused in another. Still, in most cases, this would have a tendency to be helpful or useful in the local or specific region or area of the body. It can be even directed to specific points, especially if there is broken tissue, broken bone, or difficulty in both the arterial and venous circulations, as well as the finer arteries that would radiate out about the muscle and to the skin itself, as well as those that would feed the marrow in the bone.

It can be considered an effective remedy, but one that is not fully reliable; again, essentially being more the artful approach rather than the specific. If the body becomes extremely hot, understand the dilated artery would collapse, and would work in reverse. Blood flow would not be abundant or increased, and then the body would feel pain, you see. No damage specifically to the artery, but there would be pain as the tissue would not have oxygen and/or there would be a lowering of the pressure. It would be somewhat awkward here, for the movement of blood with the higher temperatures.

Insomnia

Generally speaking, what is the cause of insomnia and what may be done to encourage better sleep?

Insomnia is felt when the body cannot relax and go through the natural sleep cycle. Usually the mind is working, worrying, attempting to solve some issue that would be fear-based. When there is anxiety, and uncertainty, indecision, and/or an injustice or lack of control, the mind is out of control. As such, it cannot separate the past occurrences that have caused the worry or concern from what would be the possible future occurrences which would result in some adversity or difficulty or loss to the self. When the mind is whirling around like a seagull circulating, looking for more garbage to put into its gullet, the mind becomes the same. And as the mind holds within it controversy, adversity, injustice, or worry, the mind simply cannot go to sleep. Insomnia may be considered the mind unable to relax and the mind working, swirling, wondering, fearing. These conditions, these emotional states are manifested during the attempt to go into states of sleep.

Controlling the mind is, therefore, imperative. Convince the self that what was happening in the past cannot be changed, but that in the future, the character of self will carry forth and the self will overcome. The future has yet to be. Putting those decisions off to some time in the future and not being too concerned about them is one way to control the mind or bring the mind back into the present moment. The mind swirls in time. The mind argues within itself. It argues with others to whom it gives some authority or position of superiority over the self. It does not take a strong mind to come to a balanced point of comfort; it takes only a mind that is in control.

Use those exercises that are Eastern in nature, as yoga, tai chi or other forms of stretching exercise first challenge the mind. As the mind is brought around in control, the body naturally follows. Insomnia, therefore, can be remedied as the mind is brought around in control. The mind, fixated on something, and worrying, fearing, and being concerned causes the mind to be stuck. It is like a sports car parked on the driveway, and the emotions are similar to the gas pedal. Someone is stepping on the accelerator or gas pedal and the engine is roaring away, yet the vehicle is not moving. Insomnia is the mind working while the body is stationary. The concerns in the life are stationary. Meditation is the way out of it, although there can be some herbal products that would help to relax or tranquilize the mind, and there are medications that would do the same. But as one would enter into states of sleep, by breathing slowly and comfortably, relaxing the body first, then the mind would be brought into the formula and the mind would relax. Then, the self would go forward, usually to a state of rest or a state of control.

There is no easy solution, but to understand to bring the mind into the present moment, not to worry about the past injustices or social circumstance, and not to fear the future (which may or may not be). Attempt to put off the decisions in time when they are supposed to be made; for instance, paying the bill at the end of the month, not worrying about it all month long. With this form of control, the self can tap into controlling the brain waves and controlling the consciousness of self. This is the way to bring control into the life. You may take those substances that tranquilize or relax the body, but it is control of the thinking that is important; to take the mind away from fear and worry and to put it into expectation and enthusiasm. With every solution, there, of course, has been a challenge.

Take the mind through the levels of Alpha, Theta, and into Delta, moving through the Beta ranges, all allow control of the mind, to exercise the brain waves selectively. Visualize the self going to sleep by relaxing or seeing the self going down a level or two, or see the self surrounded by pleasant images, or see the self assured by pictures of spiritual icons. These are all ways to focus the mind upon the possibility that a solution is coming and that hope will be given. This is necessary to set up the process of thinking, and from thinking to relaxing, and from relaxing to sleeping, and from sleeping to entering into the deeper levels of sleep.

Insomnia is, therefore, a mind out of control, a mind unable to relax, a mind unable to dissociate itself from those temporal, disruptive things in life that either have passed and there is little that can be done, or those uncertainties that are coming up that will be handled at a future time, not at the present moment in which the self is attempting to sleep. Those who have a nervous disorder should take medications or herbal influences that would allow the body-mind to relax. Stress in the life should be reduced and the body should be exercised or worked so that it is becoming tired before sleep. The room should be dark or black; no stimulation of television or radio or police scanners or other forms of electronic communication. Curtains should be put across the window to block out lights from the night. Clocks, phones or other stimulations should be subdued and not near the body. Put them in a drawer, for instance, or put them in a container of some sort. Keep the self pleasant as you go to sleep. If a night light is necessary; so be it. You may have pleasant music playing on a timer, to help the self enter states of sleep, but then shut it off so the self is in silence. Avoid stimulation from outside noise like sirens and horns. Keep the room sanctified or as a pleasant place to be. Even some fragrance like vanilla extract, roses, or whatever is pleasing to the self may be something that would, in a very light or moderate way, be given in the bedroom; not to overpower, but just to have a scent of pleasantness. See? Make the sleeping place pleasant. Have a good mattress and, in particular, a good pillow that would give cervical support. These are the basics that lead up to allowing the mind to go through the different stages of sleep.

Iodine

Edgar Cayce once said that iodine was one of the four major elements the body needed. Would you please comment on this?

Iodine is essential primarily to the nervous system, you see, in keeping the nerves communicating or the communication - call it - focuses within the nervous system functioning well. For whether it is known or not (whether it is accepted or not) there is a communication system or forces within the nerves themselves that communicate between the membrane, the muscle, the organ, and the brain, and from the brain back to the area in the body. The iodine can knit the nervous system together and prompt the channels of communication to be clearer, more timely, and indeed keep the acceleration pace up. For as bodies become older, the communication recognition, transmission, and judgment features that are affected with the nerve systems themselves tend to slow down. The proper amount of iodine in the body can delay this condition and, indeed, keep it optimum in its function, you see.

What percentage of the population of North America has an imbalance of the thyroid gland and therefore could benefit from regular intake of iodine?

To those who would eat the normal North American diet, the percentage would be very high indeed. This would be somewhere in the neighborhood of better than half, although it could be as low as a third. Therefore, from one third to one half, you see.

The painting of the sole of the foot with Lugol's iodine solution prior to sleep has been given in prior readings as a method of checking whether an individual is in need of iodine supplementation. If, after twenty-four hours, the stain has been absorbed, or disappears, this indicates a deficiency. Correct?

Indeed, for this can demonstrate the ability of the body to assimilate the iodine, and also to show if more iodine is needed; for if it is, the iodine stain will disappear by the next day. But if it is still evident the next day, then the body has reached saturation point of the iodine and the treatment no longer should be continued. Yes, to the question.

Iron (Excess)

What percentage of the North American population has excess iron in the blood, and why is this a concern?

As we would examine sources, it would appear to be quite high; somewhere in the sixty to eighty per cent range. The phenomenon of the body retaining the metal within the same largely is seen as lack of energy or lack of movement (what you call sedentary lifestyle), and the food being taken into the body being somewhat stored in the body as fatty substances, aggravated by obesity, and sugar consumption, and what you call processed food. Processed food tends to congest the blood and allow a high degree of sediments to remain in the blood.

More importantly (and a bigger concern) it allows higher levels of the iron to remain in the system. The danger is that the arteries themselves become (we would say) hard, but it would be more as if they would lose their flexibility. There would then be congestion or damming-up of certain small areas of the artery, preventing blood flow to radiate out through any narrow part, or restricted region, at a joint in a finger or a toe. This would lead to gout, to poor circulation, to lack of oxygen and deterioration of the skin and tissue in the general region in which the blood has been restricted. This will allow, also, the body to produce viral and bacterial conditions, for usually in such a body there is a highly acidic environment. That which is held on the acid side is more apt to produce disease, viral, and bacterial conditions in the body than one that is more alkaline.

First, there is impairment to the actual artery, breaking it down or blocking blood flow through the same. This, in turn, encourages the body's tendency to build up plaque on the wall of the artery and restricts blood flow through the same. This then adds to the body's inability to fight off viral and mucous conditions.

Juicing

With regard to juicing fruits and vegetables, which is better: consuming the juice and discarding the pulp, or blending the pulp and juice together and consuming both?

Firstly, understand that the quality of the fruit that is taken into the body should be of the freshest variety; that which is grown in the vicinity or region in which the body resides would be best.

To the question: either of these two manners would be good, but it depends upon the ability of the body to assimilate. In bodies that have fast assimilation, then strictly the juice would be sufficient. For older bodies that have a tendency to be sluggish in their assimilation, then pulp blending would be best. The juice assimilates in the body quickly, and passes through the intestine. However, with the pulp, or added fiber, or resistance (you might say), it tends to be held up or slowed down in the intestine and, therefore, becomes somewhat of a benefit to people who have difficulty in assimilation.

Now, either would seem to be acceptable. However, for those who are active, the juicing assimilation would be best. For those who are older and assimilation is a little more difficult, then the blending or the smoothie with the pulp would be considered advantageous to them, see? However, the fine line between the two is the condition of assimilation; that is the real question.

What are the best foods to blend to improve assimilation, elimination, and overall health as much as possible?

If fruit is to be blended or juiced, then let the fruit be of the same family. Attempt not to mix the different food groups or families too much; citrus with citrus, melons with melons, berries with berries, see? The fruit should be peeled prior to being blended, as the peel itself might act as a impediment to assimilation and, depending on how the fruit was treated, where it was raised or grown, and the exposure to chemicals or to sun or to other influences (insects and the like), the skin should be avoided as a precautionary aspect. This would add to the vitamins and the benefits of the fruits to the body.

If, however, the intention is to benefit eliminations in the body, then the juice should be of the green, leafy variety as the chlorophyll would give the greatest benefit. Wheat grass juice, spinach juice, beet greens, or any other dark, green broad-leafed vegetables would be best, you see. The chlorophyll or the leaves would improve elimination in the small and, later, the larger intestine. But here, primarily, it would be for the small intestine to reduce sluggishness and parasitic, or bacteria, or viral conditions that would occupy the intestine. Therefore, the type of food that is taken into the self, for the purpose intended, is to be considered priority.

You may mix some fruits and vegetables. Cabbage and carrot juice would be a good source of mega vitamins, but you may wish to add a little apple juice or apple to the mix for flavor. But generally, adulterating the families tends to lessen the impact. Therefore, attempt to be careful in how juices are blended or put together. Of course, all would be better than none at all.

Therefore, become familiar with the families and of the action and interaction in the assimilative processes. However, generally speaking, if you take one vegetable from below the ground and three from above, whether you eat them, or blend them, or juice them, the combination can be considered beneficial. It is primarily, however, the assimilative ability that is the question, and what we have suggested is simple, and would tend to work well if there is juice in the morning and a blending of green, leafy vegetables in the afternoon or evening.

Kerosene and Turpentine

There is an old home remedy of ingesting small amounts of kerosene, or using it topically for skin conditions. As you see it, what are the health benefits, if any, of kerosene?

Used topically, it has a tendency to be antiseptic.

It is petroleum-based, and has sulfur within. As such, this then removes bacteria and does seem to be, like any anti-bacterial substance, beneficial in this regard, especially if it is on sores, viral infections or skin diseases, you see, that are not open. Ingesting the same would be used to eliminate parasitic conditions or infestations in the intestine.

Another old remedy is turpentine, for anti-cancer and anti-fungal properties. Please examine turpentine and comment on what health benefits would there be to consuming small amounts of it?

One should be careful in assimilating any of these, and should do so with some knowledge or someone who has knowledge of the same. These would be used in old times; turpentine, especially for the infestation of parasitic conditions or what would be worms in the gut (tapeworms especially) as it would kill these on contact. It would have the ability to blend with the body's normal acidic fluids and, indeed, would affect those substances, parasites, tapeworms or abdominal worms (as we have given). It would tend to build up the acidic levels in the body, but in particular, be destructive to these organisms in the gut.

To be applied to the body, this would be seen as a topical substance that would remove bacteria in the same fashion. Used for impetigo, warts, blemishes, or itching, scaly surfaces to remove the itch and kill the bacteria. It has the ability to lubricate or to affect the cells, because it is an oil base, but has the ability to be primarily used as an antiseptic.

Laser Eye Surgery

Is the use of laser surgery, as currently practiced, a safe and effective approach to eye disorders and related vision problems?

In most cases, it tends to be a little too powerful to work upon the eye; it needs to be modified. There needs to be some containment so that there is not an accidental burning of tissue (or unwanted targeting and burning of good tissue), you see.

Therefore, to the question: depending on the application, depending upon the technician or surgeon, and depending on the use around the eye, this would be considered a question that would be to the affirmative. But again, there will be modification made in which the laser will be not as powerful as at present and, as such, this would enhance the safety factor, you see.

Lauricidin

What are the health benefits of Lauricidin?

To some degree, it stimulates the thyroid, can be associated with the prostate, and can be associated with stimulation of the thymus.

Leaky Gut Syndrome

If you would consider Western society (meaning mainly North America and Western Europe) as a "pie," how much of that pie currently suffers from leaky gut syndrome?

It is best not to include the European with the

Western, for the diets are greatly different. Toward the Western, you would find that it would be about sixty-six per cent, or two-thirds. To the European, you would find this would be about thirty-three per cent, or one-third. We are cross-examining here, and this should be considered only to certain age groupings; those who would be past puberty, even past the age of ascent (what would be towards the thirtieth to thirty-third year) or even in lesser cases. Depending on the amount of deep-fried foods that are taken in, and those foods that would be considered artificially colored, and the diet being primarily prepared or artificial food (not that which would be made from scratch or made from real food, but processed food) then the age would drop lower even until the second cycle of seven, or twelve to fourteen years. If this would be the case, then this would increase in the Western world.

However, it is not simple. In judging the various conditions - locations, climate, dietary habits, and types of preparation for food - those who would eat primarily fast food diets, or prepared foods, or those foods that would be processed before ingestion, these would be in the higher percentile. But, as a rule of thumb, two-thirds in the West (the Americas), one third, the European (and this, too, would only be in countries in which there is a lot of use of butter and deep fried foods, or oil to cook).

You have attributed leaky gut syndrome to poor diet, in particular fried foods and processed foods. Are there any other contributing factors to this condition?

The condition as you have directed us towards takes into consideration much more than the diet. Understand when sustenance is given to the body, the intention would be for what is taken in to be nutritious; that what the body would take unto itself would build up the body, would strengthen the body, and it would assist the body in reproducing those cells in the body that would replace the worn-out cells, and would strengthen the systems that function within the body, that would function normally, and in a healthful way.

The body has both assimilative and elimination capabilities. If the body was given simply a good diet, it would be sufficient for the body to maintain itself throughout its life. But other contributing factors to be considered or understood are that whatever is put into the body, the body must utilize, accommodate, handle, or find itself in a situation in which it may be disruptive or it may be strengthening to the body. There is no choice. Once what is taken into the body passes the lips and is ingested, the body therefore reacts to what it is being given. In the diet - good, bad or poor - whatever is put into the body, the body must handle. Unwittingly, poisons and toxins are taken into the body, or items that are not natural to the body: food coloring, processed ingredients in foods, or foods that themselves have been invented. These are not natural to the body or they are not natural in the world! But the body must, after being ingested, handle these substances. Indeed, chemicals taken into the body, known and unknown, taken in unwittingly perhaps, cause the body's systems to overact or to overwork. You have no idea how hard the body works when food or material is taken into the body!

However, depending on what is taken into the body, the body's functions should be considered. High amounts of acidic food are secreted in the stomach. Where does this go? Its primary function is to digest the food, which means to break down the food into such a substance that it can be assimilated through the small intestine, into the body. Carried by the blood, these nutrients go to places in the body. Have you ever thought about how the body knows where to take these nutrients or substances? Once they are delivered in the body, they are utilized, like raw material in a factory, to build up the body. Conversely, that which is taken into the body that is derogatory, or harmful, or unnatural to the body's function degrades the body (you might say, they pollute the body). Sediments, toxins, poisons are, therefore, stored in the body, for they have had to be accepted into the body, have they not? And now, what to do? These substances go to the nooks and crannies, to the soft tissues, to some low-priority storage area in the body. They do not build up the body. Instead, they pollute the body, infringe upon the body's function, and disease, stiffness, or other derogatory ailments prevail in the body. Think of it as a sewage or cesspool area stored in the body. Then you might understand what boils and cysts and pimples are all about.

However, the digestive fluids which are highly acidic (corrosive) migrate through the stomach (the valves in the stomach, the small intestine), and therein they begin to deteriorate the body's own tissue. Bile secretions are also acidic. They help to move the physical congress through the body. Both the liver and the gallbladder are responsible to assist the body in different functions, but of the same manner. The bile, the acidic digestive fluids, and other corrosive substances that have been given to the body (using a strong term here we understand) therefore begin to break down the body's tissues in the gut. Leaky gut syndrome is little more than perforations or holes in the intestine being the result of these corrosive substances not moving through the body as they should (and in fact, actually overworking in the gut, in the intestine). No wonder there would be a leakage of these substances, or these fluids, or partly digested food into the abdominal area outside of the intestine!

Beer guts or extended bellies are a result of the body taking into itself excess substances, liquids, and foods that congest the intestine or cause bloating and malfunction in the intestine. A poor diet can be considered the commencement of this disruptive influence in the body. Selecting foods that would be live foods, real foods, natural foods will not harm the body. But other foods that contain high amounts of fat, sugar, and salt, or other ingredients (like chemicals and food coloring), these foods that have been tampered with, these foods that are prepared foods or artificial foods, or something that has involved a manufacturing of real food into some sort of food (as you would call it), these are unnatural to the body and care should be taken about ingesting these secondary or lower-quality substances (that usually have nutrition removed in order to make the bulk that is taken into the body).

We are not talking about rolled oats or milled grain or ground-up meat. We are speaking of foods that are prepared, in which primarily preservatives have been added, and other substances (so to speak). Beer is not bad for the body (if it is all-natural), but beer that has been altered with chemicals is. Sometimes dozens or hundreds of chemicals are put into beer. The chemicals are not natural for the body, and they result in the body storing them. Unless the body is enriched with some degree of high-elimination practices, these substances are placed into the body, unfortunately stored for years, manifesting in cysts, or boils, or pimples and other irritations. Uric crystals are stored in the leg, and gout is the result. Once these substances are placed in the body, it is most difficult to remove them, but it is very easy to implant them! Care should be taken of what is ingested or put in the mouth (as it would be to guard all the gates of the body), for passing through the gate inward is easy; removing derogatory substances is not.

The function of the liver, the kidneys, the bladder, the gall, these are all important contributors to what would be imbalancing to the substances put through the intestine. The more acidic the diet (and usually in the Western hemisphere the diet is very acidic), the more corrosive the substances act in the body. Plugging up the perforations, the lesions, the lacerations, the thinning of the wall of the intestine, all should be considered ways and means to build up and to protect the intestine, and what is within the intestine (including the Peyer's Patch, the source for building up the immunity in the body or that which regulates the immune system).

Poor diet? Yes, this is perhaps a place to start. Disciplining the self as to what to put into the body, this should be considered even before what is selected to be better food. It is better to eat of a wide variety of all things, of items of food, than it is to specialize of any given amounts of food, for the body requires assimilation from all things. The assimilative process should be such that what is given to the body should be of the freshest variety and grown in the vicinity or region in which the body resides, for then it would be in harmony with the body. A poor diet is not the only issue here; it is how the body is treated and how the body is provoked to produce extra corrosive substances for digestion, and through the assimilative process, the sluggishness in the intestine, the blockages in the intestine, and the body's own function through the communicative systems of the nerves and circulatory system, so that there is a regulation or communication with the brain and those controlling centers in the brain. These, too, should be considered in addition to simply a poor diet. Why poison the self? Why give to the body those substances that are difficult to digest (or even derogatory to the body's own health)? It makes no sense.

But understand this: whatever is put into the body, the body is forced to handle. It will protect the heart and the brain at the expense of other organs and other parts of the body. Look to the peripherals and when you find stiffness in the hands and feet, or when you find circulatory difficulties in the extremities, then you would know the body has been, for some time, protecting the major organs in the body, and the body has been polluted and continues to be the same. Exercise is necessary for the body, so that the arteries expand and contract. This simple function protects the arteries from sediments. Likewise, the intestine should be contracted and exercised. On occasion, it should be rested as well. Fasting is a good function for one to three days, occasionally. Cleansing the bowel also; washing the body on the inside is as important as washing the body on the outside. This, too, helps to prevent this leaky bowel syndrome by removing sediments, toxins, and waste from the body.

Remember always, when food is taken into the body, there are two processes: one, the assimilation, or the strengthening of the body, and the other the rejecting or elimination of what is taken into the body which is unwanted and unnecessary in building up the body (the waste result of the digestive and assimilative processes). See? Keep up eliminations as best as possible, and the leaky gut syndrome would abate. Pollutants and sediments would be removed from the body, for the body would work in reverse; instead of storing these pollutants in the nooks and crannies, it would seek them out and eliminate them, for now the eliminations have been activated or are the priority in the body. This is what all elimination practices are about, from the body perspiring, to increasing good bowel movements, to high amounts of water taken in to flush the body. See? All have their result in preventing sluggish activity in the gut (or the corrosive results of what is sluggish in the gut) and which leaks into the body, poisoning the body.

Light

Full Spectrum Lighting, LEDs

Please discuss full spectrum lighting and its benefits for most people.

It is similar to the sun itself, for there are rays from the very long rays (the gamma rays) right over to the very small rays (microwaves and beyond). Full spectrum means full vibration. This is seen as a principal from that one who would be the inventor in which there was the multiple wave oscillator which used the same principle in a spark gap generator. There would be considered all aspects of vibration here. Affecting the physical body are all these rays and, as such, the body that needs a specific vibration takes it. Resting the body in the sun and tanning occasionally would prove to be just as helpful, for the ultraviolet would penetrate, and other aspects of the light would be beneficial. But the ultraviolet from this full spectrum is soothing and beneficial also. These would simulate, artificially, the rays of the sun and correspondingly would affect the physical body.

Currently there are light emitting diodes (LEDs) that appear to produce anti-aging effects on the skin (red and blue specifically). What do LED's do that benefit the skin?

They should not be seen specifically for the skin. Rather, it would be better or broader understood that there is an effect at the cell level. If you would understand tissue at the microscopic level, you would understand that there is a combination of cells that are bound or held together. The vibrational rate of the cell itself would be considered at the heart of this longevity question. If you would look at a cell as something like a balloon, then inside the balloon there would be a wire, or retina, or filament, like the inside of a normal light bulb. The filament would vibrate. The vibration and the reason it vibrates (life itself) would be perfect health. Cells vibrate at different frequencies, depending on their association in the body; bone at the lower frequencies, tissues at the higher frequencies. Understanding this in a preliminary way, one can understand that as the filament (or that aspect within the very cell itself) continues to vibrate at its optimum rate or its correct frequency, then optimum or perfect health is achieved. If, for any reason, it begins to slow down, then dis-ease is in the body, or aging is occurring. You might say aging is an elongated process of slowing down, ultimately stopping at the termination of life, or what you would call physical death.

Therefore, in understanding the stimulation of these frequencies, these are subtle, they do not bombard the body, they do not radiate the body, nor do they increase the vibration in the cell which, in itself, is an acceleration of this frequency, causing a burnout or an early or premature termination of the cell. Understanding the vibration is too high, it can be the destruction of cells (which in some diseases would be warranted), but in a normal body it would be best to avoid! However, there are evidences of the intense radiation or frequency increases that would be commonly known to cause disease in the body, or the breakdown and destruction of tissue in the body.

Light is, in itself, a frequency. For those who would not quite understand, it is a vibration that is radiating out from the light. Sound and light are the emission of frequency or vibration. See? The receptacle, the effect on the eyes or the ears would be the perception of these vibrational influences. To the question specifically: these different colors indicate different ranges of vibration, and, as such, they would affect different cells in different ways; attempting to tune up. If you would take two tuning forks, one would be stationary and the other would be struck and start to vibrate; if you put them in proximity to one another, the one that was stationary or non-active would in itself pick up the vibration that is emanated from the one that would be vibrating and itself would vibrate at the same frequency. This tuning between the two is what occurs between the light being applied, or radiating, or shining on the body with those cells that are a little sluggish or slow, or even diseased. See? The light tends to boost them to their proper vibrational rate (or at least a little higher than what they were), and the improvement is therapeutic.

Understand it is somewhat of a tuning of the body to a frequency that would match the blue or the red ranges of light and these low-level lights allow the vibration to be transmitted with the light source close to the body or in close proximity, as there is heat that is transferred. Heat and the transfer of vibration is adverse to the body, but vibration by vibration sources alone is more beneficial, you see. However, the technique, or the substances, or the units are not quite perfected in this regard. This is the beneficial effect on the body that causes the cells that are weakening or slowing down in their vibrational rate to correct their frequency vibration to what would be their normal frequency or vibration and, as such, a state of health occurs in the cell. Now, the light does not penetrate deep into the body as well, so the effect is more topical, or in the area, as we have given; physical touch or close proximity. This is the limitation of these low-level emanations of light or frequency when penetrating the body.

However, to the question: different frequencies affect different cells or different parts of the body. Usually red affects those areas of circulation and stimulation associated with heat and blood; green to digestive, and functions and secretions of the bladders themselves; orange affects the lungs and the heart; brown to the back and spine. Different colors applied to the body do affect the body; they affect the psychology and the thinking, the attitude and the emotional states, which are the constructive and destructive forces in any body. See?

What does blue light do?

It affects the thyroid, the throat, and the central portion of the brain - the thalamus and hypothalamus, usually reflected through the eyes.

Besides red and blue colored LED's, what other colors of LED's would be therapeutic?

The lighter colors of green or lime green, the colors purple and blue - the primary colors of the rainbow, you see. Yellow is good, but lime would be what is closer to combining the effects of both green and yellow. The red can stimulate, and the blue can suppress; the green can calm, and pink would cause a degree of detachment (and even depression, before it would create frustration). But depending on the gender, the colors which would be familiar to the genders would be associated or would have some psychological effect. See? Placing a person in a pink room would have a calming effect, while placing a person in a red room would have a tendency to increase their anxiety. These are known in psychology already. Similar colors would have similar effects on cells. But the primary colors - the purple, the blue, the red, and the green - would seemingly be similar colors combined with either green or yellow or lime.

What health effects would purple and green create?

The same as all the colors; they have certain frequency, and the frequency bones up, tunes up, increases the vibration of the cells that are slowing.

Liver Flush

The Edgar Cayce readings and this Source talk very often about giving the body an internal bath or colonic, but very little mention is made of cleaning the liver. Today, some people are attempting to clean the liver on a regular basis, using a combination of things like fasting, potatoes, olive oil, apple juice, apple cider, and so on. Will this, by itself, work to increase longevity over time?

Any internal cleansing would be beneficial. The

so-called liver dump occurs in the second to the fourth hour in the morning, when there is proper rest, or sleep, or deep sleep occurring; the liver dump through the tube that would lead from the liver itself to the top of the lymphatic system (or just under the neck, usually on the right side) and this dumping or secretion of toxins occurs in this fashion. When one attempts to control the organs in the body by the various liver cleansings, it is very beneficial to the body. But it would be better to have a normal diet; one that would be balanced for one's particular blood type or metabolism, and one that would allow the liver to function freely, normally. This would require exercising the body, stretching the body, hydrating the body with proper amounts of water, and eating what would be an acceptable diet, taking a little from all things.

To answer the question directly: if one knows what they are doing, they are provoking the body, and they are releasing the poisons, toxins, gallstones, liver stones into the blood system. This is provocative to the body. It is better that it is done than not done, of course; but the preferred way would be the natural function in the body.

However, the attention paid, at this point in time, to such improvements to the liver can be considered crudely acceptable. Paying attention also to the blood, to the kidneys, and the removal of toxins from the blood through the kidneys would, likewise, be a good thing to manage. Indeed, removing toxins or poisons from the body is an acceptable habit or practice.

The body is capable of doing the same on its own, however. Proper amount of water taken into the body is most important. Breathing is most important. And simple bending and stretching exercises - keeping the body flexible - is important, for doing so affects the internal organs themselves. Bending and flexing and stretching with simple isometric exercises massages the organs themselves, and the liver (being in the location it is) is massaged by simple exercises. The release of the diaphragm in the middle portion of the body allows the liver to function more correctly.

As such, it would be better that the body would function this way, naturally, in dumping the toxins or poisons from the same, which would be gradual, loving, and comfortable to the body than what would be a provocative forcing of the body to do anything, such as removing the poisons or toxins in one large dump, or extraction, or provocation. However, that said, better to do this than none; but there are risks when this is occurring; toxins and poisons are released into the blood system. They can make one feel delirious or imbalanced temporarily in their thinking, and so on.

Longevity

What supplement or therapy would be a rejuvenator of the human body, that would be the closest to a fountain of youth?

Lightning. As for a supplement, any that would affect the pituitary, and also putting off puberty. See? However, antioxidants, free radicals, gold and silver (assimilating or eating of the same) and any influence that would help to invigorate the nervous system itself.

How could someone be treated with lightning?

Lightning causes radio waves to occur, or vibration, or frequencies to commence. When there is a crack of lightning, there is an electronic discharge, and these electrons and particles of electricity crackle through the atmosphere, like a hand plunging into water. The waves radiate out like a pond, in all directions; so does this occur when there is the broad band spectrum created with the broadcasting of all frequencies at the same time, which is what lightning occurs or does. If you were to examine De La Warr's work, spark gap generators do the same; they broadcast a wide band of frequencies and the cell within the body (which has a retina, which has a vibrational thread in it) when it slows down, it becomes old or diseased; when it speeds up, it becomes overanxious and burns itself out (shall we say). At the proper frequency, the cell is healthy.

Lightning vibrates at the same frequency. The frequencies caused by lightning being created in a broad band spectrum influences the cells at the cell level individually. Because it is broadcast in a wide spectrum, all of the cells in the body receive an influence of these frequencies, so that the weaker cells are boosted, and those that are overactive are quelled or quieted. Like a battery in a car that is underpowered, when there is a boost of electricity, when there is another battery given, the weaker battery takes on the full charge and is behaving correctly, as if it would be healthy. Likewise the same for the cells in the body. See? When lightning occurs, there is a stimulation of those weaker cells.

There is an implement needed to control the same and there will be pathology and some degree of understanding of disease necessary to correlate the difference between the frequencies being generated by lightning, and the direction of the vibration into a weak body, a sick organ, or to a diseased area.

However, the point is that lightning generates a broad band of frequencies; all levels of the sound spectrum, you would call it, even light. See? This is necessary to excite seeds in the field or in nature to germinate; for the energy released by lightning carried through the air as frequency or vibration is constructive to the seed or the human cell, or the cell in any particular thing, you see; and it tends to excite it to the point of being healthy, or germinating, or growing, or vibrating at the proper frequency. It causes things to grow. In a body which is slowing or weakening, it enhances, and disease disappears, you see. It is not the lightning that causes this, but it is the corresponding frequencies that are caused by the lightning that affects the body.

Now, anyone who would stand close to lightning (perhaps beside a window where there is an open field and lightning is striking) can feel the resilience or the freshness of this vibration on their chest. This is what we are talking about; this particular sense of rejuvenation by having the frequencies go through the body. This is not unusual; this is done at music events, especially where there are different ranges or octaves of music. Orchestras have done this, and people who sit in the same can feel the resilience of the music generated without adulteration, through their bodies, and they feel enlivened. Other sources of frequency generation have the same effect. The low frequencies cause bone to grow, the high frequencies cause flesh to deteriorate. But through the broadcast of lightning or spark-gap generation, the amount of frequencies is considered positive and healthful to the body.

This Source has recommended gold to maintain a youthful body. How does ingesting gold achieve this?

his improves the communications in the body itself, as gold is an essential mineral (if you will) in the body. It allows the communication between the organs to be maintained and the vibrational rate in the body to be at a higher level as the body would age. Understand the body vibrates at the cell level; different vibrational rates in different organs. As such, overall, the body vibrates. As it ages, the vibrational rate begins to slow down. The body stiffens. Inflammation and disease come into the body and they are difficult to reject or to overcome. As such, the body then slows down in its vibrational rate even more. Ultimately the body reaches a point in which death occurs.

Seeing this as a vibrational improvement or keeping the vibrational level (if we can call it that) at the optimum or the highest point, then the body has invigorated itself. Blood goes through the body as it did when it was younger; the vitality of the blood and the vibration of the blood are what keeps the body vibrant, youthful, and healthy. In this way, the aging of the body is slowed or subdued to such a point that it seems to be forever youthful. The vibrations in the body or the vibrational rate is optimized, and the vibrations at the organs are at the highest level. Slowing them down causes the body to slip into dis-easement, but keeping them at their optimum level, the body is forced to be invigorated and to be improved. As the cells in the body change, the new cells replacing the old ones have remembered their youthful vibration or their youthful substance. And as such, the body does not subdue itself, but rather invigorates itself.

This is seen also when vibrations pass through the body; the body can be affected positively, or adversely, but it is the individual vibration of the cells at the cell level that indicate the health of the body, and indeed this goes from the middle or inside of the body outward, see?

Lutein

The supplement Lutein is currently used to protect the eyes in individuals past middle age. Could you please comment on this?

This has an effect to keep the moisture content in the eye and it also has an effect to replace the cells that would be generally replaced on a very rapid level - every four days or so - and also the effect that it has in removing the sedentary or clouding effects in the eye itself.

Magnetic Therapy

There are devices sold today which produce simple magnetic pulses. What would be the benefit of applying one to an affected, ill, or imbalanced part of the body?

Speaking specifically to the brain, it would tend to create intelligence; it would tend to specifically amplify that region for which the brain was designed. As one would examine this, they would find twenty-four points around the head, and, by stimulating these different places, it would be as if someone has programmed a new function within the brain of an individual who would be under such a pulse. This allows the body to have an increase in mental skills or ability; again, while you affect the area of the brain and the twenty-four sister points about the brain itself. You would find also the influence of healing or knitting together of bone and tissue. The pulse has an effect to penetrate deeply, rapidly, like a shockwave going through the body, both progressive and regressive (both bow and stern waves, you might say). And it therefore speeds up, corrects healing, allows skin and tissue to knit together. This would be the primary effect.

The marketers of these devices have said they have specific benefit for tumors. Do you see this as correct?

It affects tumors positively inasmuch as these devices would be somewhat disrupting of the captured viral, or bacterial, or parasite within the same. The tumor would be lessened and there would be no need for the thickening or growing of the tumor. For a tumor can be seen as a layer of skin - a prison of sorts - holding some derogatory prisoner within; and, as the prisoner grows and attempts to bust out of this cocoon or prison, the layer of tissue is increased, causing the tumor to grow, you see. If there can be a negating, or disruption, or death of what is capsulated inside, then the tumor will dissipate itself, for it would no longer be necessary to be in existence. Therefore, it would no longer be a jailor, you see.

Male Pattern Baldness

See also Hair Loss and Thinning

This Source has recommended crude oil as a treatment for male pattern baldness. Could you elaborate on how this works and suggest how it may be taken to help this condition?

The oil that is crude, taken directly from the soil, allows for the greater absorption of the minerals, for this type of substance is high in minerals, including sulfur. This stimulates the follicle and the blood supply to the hair itself, but it also places minerals into the area of the scalp. It helps the scalp to breathe, to increase the circulation, and to remove irritations from the same. But it primarily allows, through the use of heat and massage, blood supply to be enriched in and around the follicle, in and around the failing hair, and it awakens the follicle, you might say; it stimulates it. See?

Take a little of the crude oil, an ounce or less, and massage it vigorously into the scalp. Again, it is with the intention of awakening the follicle itself, which has gone to sleep due to lack of blood supply or of the blood being polluted with toxins and substances, or bad water (poisonous water, you might say), or water that has been high in other derogatory influences.

As such, these massages would be somewhat beneficial (although not excessively so) in increasing the blood supply to the area at the root or the follicle of the hair of the head. The stimulation of massage with the oils should be vigorous. It should be massaged in, so that the minerals, nutrients and stimulation of the massage would be worthwhile in stimulating the blood supply and, at the same time, absorbing these substances into the skin.

A heat lamp may be used to keep the head warm. Infrared light would also accomplish this in increasing the blood supply to the scalp. Any form of increasing blood supply is extremely beneficial, including inverting the body so that the head is lower than the feet, and the blood flushes to the head and to the scalp, and therefore aids the follicle by bringing nutrients through the blood. However, it is the minerals in the crude oil itself that have the benefit.

After there has been a massage, vigorously, the body kept warm (perhaps a heating bag or a plastic water bottle, filled with water and placed on or near the neck and head), there is a flushing of blood to the head and face, indicating an improvement of blood supply to the scalp. The oil itself may be rinsed off with any good soap and water, see? Not rubbed off, but washed off, and then the hair patted dry. However, it is primarily the minerals in the oil that are absorbed into the skin that benefits the hair itself. See?

Men's Sexual Health

See also Saw Palmetto.

Could you please comment on the practice of circumcision of the penis.

It is somewhat vanity to deform the body. The circumcision in the body is intended to affect the sexual desires in the body, by preventing the stimulation in the foreskin, and therefore this would be a willful attempt to affect the natural influence in the body, by surgically removing stimulating tissues at the end of the penis. However, there is an infection situation, there is pain to the body, and this can cause some psychological impairment in children. As such, for those who would participate in this, it is somewhat a painful and unnecessary procedure, although those who would have the same religious perspective it is their belief and their opinion that this is beneficial to keep a covenant, one to the other.

To the question: we would not recommend this, as it is an unnatural act. It does expose to the penis itself the possibility of increased bacterial influences, and there is a certain numbing effect to the natural nerve endings. This has the intention to desensitize the body's natural sexual function or drive and it has some impairments or difficulties for those who have had the procedure.

We would not recommend this, although no man can say this or that must be done. Each possess its own free will and free choice. The effect of circumcision is more to one of social and religious influences than it is for health matters, see? Why adulterate the body, that thy God has put together, see? Operations are always risky and this one seems to be a little unnecessary.

Generally speaking, what is the cause of erectile dysfunction, and how can this condition be treated?

Usually you would look to injury in the pelvis, specifically to the lower lumbars, where there are compressive forces, and there has been nerve flow activity diminished. You would also find that circulation within the reproductive centers can be considered the primary or secondary reason for this to occur. When you have plaque in the arteries, this, too, would lead to the inability for blood pressure to be built up into the penis, and you would also find degrees of impairment in the prostate itself. The enlarged prostate causes difficulties to blood supply into what would be lower or into the reproductive centers in the testicle and penis itself. These would be the primary reasons for this dysfunction.

If there is psychological nervousness or shame that is brought upon the body, this, too, would be a large factor in this dysfunction, see? Guilt feelings, resentments, and feelings of inadequacy can plague the entity in the inability to couple. See?

Organically there are reasons - physically there are difficulties - and also there is the mental attitude or opinion that would be considered difficult. However, look to the prostate as the organic difficulty. Improve the blood supply through this and into the gonads or penis and, of course, affecting the nerve centers or nerve endings in the reproductive center and in the back or lumbar. Altering this, the body should respond in a positive way.

It has been said that using an infrared heat lamp can help enlarge the penis. Can you suggest a more effective way?

There is a surgical procedure that can be used in which the tendons or those tissues that hold the penis within can be surgically clipped and the penis can be further extracted from the body. It is a common practice that helps for penis enlargement.

Otherwise, attempting to put more blood flow into the penis would be sufficient. But having manipulation of the spinal column (especially the lumbars) would also be helpful in that it would allow more nerve flow and, indeed, blood flow thereafter to be increased. One may use those yoga exercises that would be specific in keeping the lumbar and pelvis area flexible. As this is more flexible, again, more nerve flow and more blood flow would be to the testicle and the penis itself. As we would look upon the lumbar in the back, the spine at the fourth and fifth lumbar region, having this area flexible would help in the nerve systems.

Taking the saw palmetto would be most helpful in allowing more blood flow to the testicle, the prostate, and to the penis itself. The infrared light is beneficial, as any particular attempt to increase the blood flow to the genital areas, but it is more of a combination of improving the nerve flow to relax the tensions within the body, eating more protein and, indeed, utilizing those exercises that would build up the muscles in the genital area. This would allow, naturally, for the penis to enlarge itself, you see.

Taking saw palmetto, four to six capsules every day, perhaps twice a day, will help with the circulation in the body but, in particular, to the prostate. It would affect the reproductive centers in the body itself. Serraflazyme could be taken as well, to improve the arteries in their capability of conducting blood. This too, increasing the blood, affecting the nerve system, taking the saw palmetto to react on the bladder and other areas of circulation in the entire body (not only the genitalia, but also the brain, see) will have a positive effect here. Also taking horny goat weed, there should be an improvement rather quickly. A handful of vitamin E each day also should be taken, in addition to what we have suggested. The body will respond.

Walking briskly, doing knee-bending exercises, all help organically, preparing for the delivery of blood to the penis itself, to increase the spermatozoa in the testicle. Bathing the body in sunlight, or using an infrared light, or even a combination of infrared and ultraviolet in the general area of the reproductive center increases blood to the genitalia and also removes the bacteria that are preventing the expansion or the dilation of the arteries in the penis. Taking more of ginseng and ginger also would be helpful.

The key is to use the saw palmetto to remove sedentary deposits in the region or area of the penis, the testicle, the bladder, and the prostate. Masturbation can be also a benefit here, to encourage masturbation but not ejaculation. For longer periods, continue the masturbation without ejaculation and the blood supply would be encouraged to maintain itself within the penis and the general region of the genitalia. Not to ejaculate, but to keep the penis erected for long periods of time keeps the blood supply expanding or lengthening the genitalia.

Putting the oils that would penetrate around the penis to the low area of the abdomen also allows a relaxation to the muscles and the sheathe that surround and separate the organs, and this would allow somewhat of an extension to occur. Tension pulls back the sheathe that surrounds the central area concerned. Relaxing the muscles allows the sheathe to relax as well; this would be from the diaphragm downward. But also understand the abdominal cavity is surrounded with a sheathe that separates and suspends the organs itself. Tension in one part causes tension in all parts of the abdomen. See?

Increase the blood, affect the nerve system and the spine, and improve the blood through the arteries, for this will be beneficial to all other parts of the body (if there is plaque around the arterial, see), and there can be an increase that would be noticeable in the erection in size, thickness, and length (as well as a certain degree of firmness in the penis itself, see). Otherwise the surgical procedure would be successful as well.

Can you please comment on the cause of prostatitis and the best focus of treatment?

The initial irritation in the gland is seen as a resident virus itself. Keeping the body more alkaline and drinking plenty of water should function in eliminating the virus itself. The body would need to be consistently on the alkaline side of the acid-alkaline balance for a good length of time. Three weeks to three months would be sufficient. Usually this is a condition of impairment. There has been, perhaps, a stone through the same, or there has been an irritant in the body that has been resident as a string virus (so to speak), going from one organ to the other and it has taken up residence in the prostate itself, you see, in what would be the capillary or the irritant in the prostate. Usually the prostate is a little misshapen as well. Coca-cola syrup and water (a little of each) would be good. Willow would be good and hibiscus either as tea or supplements would be good in remedying these irritants, you see.

Melatonin

Melatonin is recommended as a sleep aid. Is this good to use in the body?

If sleep is hard to get, and digestion is difficult, try remedying with a little slice of orange or other acidic fruit, and see if there is improvement. If not, then we would find that melatonin can be taken, and there would be an instant sense or righting of the metabolism. Gaseous substances would not be highly produced in the intestine, digestive systems would be better. The body would not suffer migraine headache or stress headache, or dizziness. There would be a genuine increase in the rate of metabolism, and the energy levels; a more energetic self and a willingness to be physically active, you see.

This would be demonstrated also in the kidney. There would be darker color urine at first and then cloudy or flaky substances within the urine, indicating there has been changing, or that the metabolism has been removing sedentary forces from the body. In all cases, these results would be easily observable in anyone past their teenage years.

Microhydrin

What are the benefits from ingesting the hard-to-find supplement known as microhydrin, which is also known as silica hydride?

The effect would be for the cell itself to puff up, or absorb into itself nutrients, moistures, fluids that would be able to cause the vibration of the cell to be more harmonic with other cells itself, you see. As such, the body itself would be more in tune (if you will) with this supplement or these products. Also, it causes the ability in the body to sort out fluid (if you will) in the body, to speed up the function in the lymphatic system, to remove conditions of edema or fluid conditions in the body while retaining proper amounts of fluid in the body in a healthful way. In other words, it helps the body reduce excess fluid about the body that would be seen as storage or extra, and at the same time allow what would be utilized in the body's natural functions to be more properly delivered to the cell for which it would be intended. If you would compare it, the body would be able to perspire and remove toxins and poisons, while at the same time not dehydrating itself internally at the organs, you see.

Microwave Cooking

Could you please comment on the safety of using microwave ovens to heat or cook foods?

There is an effect to heat up the moisture within the food itself. This affects the structure at the cell level of the food. If the food is not readily eaten right after, or there is a cooling off period, or the vibrational influences on the food are allowed to settle, and then the food may be taken, it would seem to be acceptable to most bodies. If, on the other hand, the body is sensitive to these vibrational rates, there will be some difficulty in moving towards the acquisition or the engaging in ingestion. Allow a certain cooling off period (so to speak), a minute or two, for the vibrations in the liquid or water vapor content of the food to rest. Then it can be ingested in the body without any derogatory or upsetting effects in the body. See? The food structure does not seem to change; just the temperature and the moisture content. Yes, there is some loss of food value as well.

Miracle Mineral Supplement

Please examine the substance dubbed "Miracle Mineral Supplement," consisting of sodium chlorite mixed with a weak acid to form chlorine dioxide. When consumed, many users experience diarrhea, vomiting, or cold conditions when starting out, which later subsides. Why is this?

Like all things taken into the body, which are small but powerful, they have a tendency to tilt and imbalance the body (let us call it, shock the body), whether they be medications, vitamins, or substances like this. The first is a knee-jerk reaction. The body is shocked somewhat, upsetting the chemical nature of the body. Remember, small things on the inside make big things happen on the outside, and therefore what occurs (diarrhea or other conditions, vomiting, feeling queasy or even sickly) has the effect of two things. One, it causes the body to work internally. The body goes into a state of survival, and the secretions, through the digestive and elimination tract, are such that they are attempting to purge this substance that is foreign, unusual, or is shocking the system. Now as time goes on, the body compensates and, as such, there is need for greater volumes of the substance in order that the body would carry with it again an imbalance, or a desired result (referred to as our comment in shocking the body). The second is that it actually causes the body to remove the toxins and poisons that are within, and as they accumulate in the small and large intestine, they go past what is called the Peyer's Patch, especially if the body is younger; for as they are older, this part of the intestine tends to fade or reduce in itself, causing the body to be more susceptible to viral and bacterial conditions, or sickness, and aging processes are accelerated. But in the beginning (or in the younger individual), it tends to cause a purging or a surging of what would be toxic substances, and there is a high inclination, a high level of accumulation or purging going on in the body.

Now when you accumulate many conditions that are - let us say - responsible for sickness in the body, and they are put through the body, the body becomes sick. Understand the liver as something that would be a collector, and a storage place. Poisons and toxins are isolated or compartmentalized within the liver. When such a substance (or substances, or medicines, or remedies) are involved, they release these substances or poisons back into the body. This causes great chaos to take place within the softer tissues of the body, from the brain, through to the heart, though to the reproductive centers. And, because this causes chemical changes with the release of poisons in the body, the hormonal structure changes. The glands begin to react somewhat (overacting or underacting, depending upon their methodology or purpose) and, as such, this would cause these reactions within the body. The more poison is extracted from the liver or other soft tissues and put into the system to be exited from the body, naturally, the body causes itself to be sickly and attempts to expel, in any way it can, these harsh and harmful substances (including vomit, fever, sweats, or perspiration, excretion through the ears as ear wax material, under the fingernails and toenails, through to the other more daily practices of excretions and voiding of the body in the elimination system).

Now, usually these substances are taken without any preparation to the body. This compounds the results or reaction. If one were to begin the cleansing process by using these rather powerful stimulants (or imbalances, might be a better term) then the body should be already on a program of elimination; not fasting so much, but drinking plenty of water, taking those foods that would help cleanse the bowel, or produce an increased activity naturally through the elimination cycle (physical congress). Steam bathing the body to cleanse the pores allows the body to react less, so that there is not such a violent or sickly reaction as the question describes.

Depending on how eager these individuals are, and we caution patience, that these substances be given in smaller amounts for the first three to seven days. As we have given, the body naturally adjusts and uses them not in a provocative or reactionary way, not even in a rebellious way, but in harmony.

Which would produce the best results for most users: a sustained, small, four-drop dose of chlorine dioxide, taken twice a day over several months (or longer), or a fifteen-drop dose taken two to three times a day?

The former, rather than the latter would be much more in harmony with the body. But we would say that a middle ground between these two extremes could be built up or worked up to. Depending on the physical stature, the amount of physical labor or athletic activity (or sedentary activity, for that matter), a rule of thumb would be that if the body is more active, then more drops could be builded up and taken sooner. If the body is sedentary, then we would suggest it becomes more active and ingests lesser amounts.

Consumed orally, is the chlorine dioxide capable of extricating from the body that which has adhered to the intestinal walls over time?

It does seem to be peeling, as we observe the action here, the rubbery, black substance. Yes, it does seem to be wedging itself between this substance and the intestine, without causing any perforation, or inflammation, or bleeding. Yes to the question.

Long-term, what effect would it have on the body's pH balance?

It depends on the medium that it is taken within. We would have it somewhat balanced, but slightly more to the acidic state.

Is there any additional information you can five about oral chlorine dioxide?

As we examine some things here, we would find this would be helpful for parasites and other intestinal infestations. Also it causes a removal of the good bacteria in the intestine, and, therefore, replacing good bacteria in the intestine after some prolonged use would be necessary. This could be done in a traditional sense with yogurt or acidophilus, and this would also place, as any supplement here, good bacteria or culture within the intestine. For the intestine must have good bacterial activity to assist in the digestive processes, you see; whether it would be kelp or wheat grass juice, these would be helpful in restoring the - let us say - desired bacterial activity. Yogurt is good. You may also take sardines or the juice from the sardine can. Watermelon would be good to assist the colon, the intestine, and also to relieve any spasms that may take place, should there be a zealous use of this material and the intestine cramps, or goes into spasm.

Mold

Problems with toxic mold in buildings appear to be a new development. Why has this problem arisen only in the last few years?

It was not too long ago that certain physicians in the Sarnia (Canada) and Port Huron (Michigan) area were bringing forth the assertion that mold, mildew, and fossil fuel chemicals were airborne, causing huge allergy problems. They were chastised or they were dismissed as unsubstantiated claims. The answer to this question is: in the last few years, there has been some research or the ability to acknowledge the airborne molecule causing the allergic reaction or the affect at irritating the cell at the cell level (as well as irritating the nerves themselves, you see). For here, the allergic reaction is largely repulsion; a contraction within the cells or groups of cells in sensitive areas of the body, including the nerve systems (central, sympathetic and parasympathetic). The detection, determination and acknowledgment have been the reason this has come to light in the last few years.

Also buildings that have aged have been builded with different materials than more ancient buildings, which would have more air flow through the same - the plaster and the building lathe. Modes and procedures were not modular but were considered craft or made on the spot. This allowed for a porous type of product, and the building materials were not as heavily-laden with chemicals as now. Therefore, the natural breathing of a building would allow for the escape of mold and mildew-causing forces, primarily moisture as well as pent-up gasses or methane. In the present buildings, again, the chemical consistency is different.

There is more determination to prevent drafts, or air flow from without to within (and vice versa). The heating utensils or products and equipment are basically different and, again, there is not a high and low fluctuation of temperature, thereby providing an environment for moisture to be maintained (trapped if you will) in vapor barriers and thereby providing an environment that would be conducive to the production of mold and mildew.

What is the effect on the body to these molds?

To the cell level, it disrupts the normal function of the cell. Like sandpaper, it grits the cells, you see. It does affect the nerves themselves. Pain is incurred, pustules in the area of irritation are formed, and circulation is difficult in the general regions. In short, it is a very dull poisoning of the body. It is an invasion into the body of a foreign product or irritant and the body responds in pain and in kind, attempting to combat and reject what has been smeared upon itself (usually in the moist, tender, soft tissues that are, of course, designed to trap sediments and foreign invasions of bacterial or virus conditions).

It is an irritant that can, left unchecked, spread in the body as well, where fungus or growth of bacteria may occur. The mold or mildew may be transferred to the body itself, usually on the areas of the toes, and folds of the body, as well as in the skin of the body. Left unchecked, it can cause conditions of eczema, psoriasis, and other diseases of the skin.

Monolaurin

Of what benefit is monolaurin in the human body?

This has the effect of removing bacteria or germs from the digestive tract, or removing bacteria and virus from the blood, without affecting the host body. This would be seen as a tonic or benefit that works in the subtle worlds; it removes the conditions of impairment. As such, it has a tendency to affect the bacteria by simply disrupting it or destroying the bacteria. There is no cohesive force; it surrounds and separates the bacteria in small globules and, as such, with the bacteria attached or attracted, it cannot form strings or lines of reproduction. In short, the bacteria is confined and ultimately destroyed.

Moringa Oleifera

There is a plant known as *moringa oleifera*, whose leaf powder is made into a green drink. Please describe the health benefits of consuming this daily?

It does seem to have a high effect like sulfur coming into the body; it is quite acidic, as we see it, and has somewhat of a chlorophyll effect, although it can make one nauseous, as it tends to disturb the digestive fluid in the body and even cause it to congeal a little or make it into a slimy paste. This change occurs and allows the cleansing through the stomach and the small intestine. As a cleansing agent itself, it tends to remove some toxic substances like uric crystals. They are dissolved and then they are carried away by this substance itself. Seems to be quite aggravating to the stomach and small intestine as it does tend to bubble or cause a reaction within the intestinal tract itself.

What are its actions in the human body that bring about these benefits?

This removal of the residue on the intestinal tract does tend to act as a scrub brush of some sort in the intestine. It removes from the intestine fecal matter, excess digestive fluids, partly-digested substances, parasitic influences, viral and bacterial influences. It acts somewhat as a scrub brush, you see. However, it is quite abrasive in the stomach and the small intestine. Not corrosive, but certainly along that area, like putting sodium bicarbonate in water; it tends to bubble.

MSM (Methylsulfonylmethane)

Could you please comment on the supplement MSM and its effect in the body?

This is primarily to affect improved assimilation in the body while at the same time helping elimination in the body. It affects the soft tissues throughout the body itself but is primarily seen as an effect upon the stomach and the digestive systems (or manners in which the body assimilates, you see). It can be used for a variety of benefits in the body from improving nerve damage or nerve communication through to the restoration or acceleration of cell production, especially in soft tissues like the mouth and the eye, as well as the nerve and artery tissues. It does seem to affect the arteries in keeping them more flexible as well. It can be seen as working well on the small or the minute artery in the body, and in both aiding and opening the orifice, allowing blood flow to be enhanced through these areas or regions. It does affect the liver too, as we see it. It can especially aid or help inactive bodies; those that are sedentary, handicapped, or do not move, or are considered not ambulatory, you see.

Multiple Sclerosis

Please examine the condition known as multiple sclerosis, commenting on the causes of the same and suggesting the best form of treatment?

We would find that usually it is of several different causes. However, amongst those would be a thickening around the nerve trunk that would be from the spine radiating out to various parts of the body. This would be similar to Parkinson's itself, only what would be higher into the brain or the brain stem. Here, in this particular occurrence, you would find that the loss of nerve control in the body is caused by thickening of the sheathe that surrounds and separates the nerve itself. This is caused by hormonal imbalance in the body; also pollutants, sediments and toxins that have been absorbed through the skin or have been breathed into the body. Dust, mold, petroleum product residue, mildly affects the body in an allergenic way, see?

In this instance, as in some others, the body needs to be sedated. Here, in the localized area, in the lower extremities or the legs, or in the spine itself, using bee venom can be most suitable in stopping the thickening of the nerves or the squeezing tightness of this sheathe that surrounds and separates them. In this regard, this would be locally affecting various parts of the body, but primarily in the area of the spine. This would assist the body in allowing nerve flow to radiate out to the lower extremities in the body and it would cause the sheathe to shrink or any thickening of the nerve material or cells to shrink as well. This would be carried about the nerve endings by blood and absorption through tissue or muscle especially the soft tissue itself.

Strong concentrated white light (laser) and, to some degree, ultrasound can be used upon the body to likewise improve the condition, or at least to delay the onslaught of restricting the nerve flow in the body. These are in cases in which there has been some paralysis or some disruption in the nerves affecting a loss of sensation, feeling or controlled movements in the muscles. The venom would be helpful. The bright white laser light shone upon the body, the Rife machine light or ultrasound would stimulate and improve both blood circulation and, at the same time, reduce the tension in the muscles, thereby reducing tension in the sinew and tendon.

Also to remedy the condition would be to open up the arteries and allow increased blood flow. This can be done with any particular substance that would help to remove plaque from the arteries throughout the body, but in particular in the base of the neck; the arteries leading into the controlling centers of the brain (medulla and cerebellum). By removing fatty tissue or plaque in these areas, in the neck and the base of the brain, this would relieve the condition somewhat remarkably quickly, and would allow the blood flow to be enhanced through the body. In particular it would allow the nerve flow to be advanced into the brain. There is already some use of this (although it is controversial) for more than half, as a remedy for this particular restriction or difficulty in the body. Think of this as a strangulation of the nerve function or nerve flow in the nerves themselves, like pinching a hose that is running water through it. The more the pinch, the less water that flows through the hose itself. Likewise, is the nerve flow being restricted.

This form of procedure is simply to open up the artery and allow improved circulation to the body; a stretching of the arterial, so to speak. This can be done with hot and cold baths which would cause the muscles to contract, and then expand. Place the body in very cool or cold water, then very hot water (as hot as the body can stand) and then return it to the cold water (as cold as the body can stand). Repeating this three to six times, until the body is fatigued, would be like a massage of the arteries inside the body and it would be helpful, restorative and curative to the body at the cell level.

Now, in what would be given to the body through acupuncture, would be helpful in redirecting the chi energy through the body, to those centers in the body that would be helpful; not to circumvent, but to improve the nerve flow. Then, at specific times of the day, this would allow the nerves that are weakened or restricted to be energized or to be increased in the nerve flow energy. This would have a tingling effect in the body, but it would allow the nerves themselves to be excited or to increase in their communication. Those who would be skilled in the thing would understand the process as if turning off valves here and there and turning on other valves, in order to circulate the energy around any restriction; but, at the same time, reverse the flow through the nerve to open it up, to allow it to function more as it ought to. In this particular situation, it would be rare, but it would allow the nerves themselves to energize and revitalize themselves, that their frequencies would be raised to the point of wellness. See?

However, the acupuncturist can be used to redirect the flow through the nerves themselves. This would be as a reconstruction or a curative measure, especially using this in the lower body. The condition, therefore, is firstly, a restriction of nerve flow through the nerves and the nerve tissue itself. Second, it is a condition of blood flow being restricted in the base of the brain, affecting the nerves themselves and the nerve flow not being direct and the blood supply being light, causing the nerves to diminish or wither. Thirdly it is for the nerve flow itself to be redirected through acupuncture, through alternative communication lines in the body. These would be called meridians, which would redirect the energy, improving the condition in the body, but also helping to alleviate and remove any restriction in the muscle at certain points where there is restriction to the nerve itself.

This would be a basic understanding. Those who would be the specialists would further understand that the flow through the nerve is first being disrupted by pressure (a squeezing or a thickening of the wall of the same). The venom would be helpful in reducing this.

Negative Ions

How important are negative ion supplements for most people?

These occur from time to time, just after there has been a heavy rainfall. There is a bombardment of negative ion supplements. These can be artificially induced and would tend to harmonize the body and make it feel at ease and give it a charge or a build-up of energy. Those that are opposite (the positive ions) tend to disrupt, scatter and discharge the body's electrical-magnetical energy; negative tends to bring it together. Important? We find it would be soothing and harmonious and thereby would add years to one who would practice, on a regular basis, the use of the negative ion generator. Taking a shower also produces the same effect. Metal houses, or roofs, or air conditioning tend to ground out the negative ions, and that is why there are irritations in offices during the summer months (those that are air conditioned). They tend to bombard those in the office with disruptive positive ions.

Night Sweats

What causes night sweats, and what can be done to remedy this condition?

Primarily this is a function of the blood pressure rising in the body. Here, taking a diet of cooler vegetables, the dark green, leafy variety, would be a basic way to start. Taking a tranquilizing effect (but not a tranquilizer) would be helpful here. This can be either the slippery elm tea (as a calming drink during the day and prior to sleep) or a small amount of warm milk. The intention is to reduce the activity or the sensitivity in the stomach, allowing the body organically not to become excited or impaired.

Reduce the stress, or worry, or frustrations that are going on in the mind. Understand, the mind is the builder. What is held in the mind is manifested in the body. When there is fear, worry, concern, anxiety, frustration or other forms of threat during sleep, the body (which the mind is still connected to) tends to go organically through the states of mind that are carried on during sleep. If the mind can be calmed or soothed prior to sleep, and this can be maintained during sleep, the body's normal temperature would be maintained, for there would not be increased heart rate due to the anxiety that is carried on during sleep. Evidence of the type of anxiety during sleep can be seen in grinding on the teeth during the sleep as well.

There are also conditions in which the first and second dorsal vertebrae in the back can be manipulated or adjusted, and this would regulate the heartbeat. Taking celery or celery juice during the daytime for those who would have higher blood pressure, or those who would be on medication also would have the same effect in organizing or keeping the blood pressure lower.

All these blood pressure-related conditions stem from worry, fear, or anxiety that is held over during sleep. This causes the body to work hard, to gobble up the oxygen in the blood stream that is tentative or static (taken in during the day). The body, in using up the oxygen in the blood during the early parts of sleep (because of the raising heart beat) tends to speed up the heart rate even more so that there can be more delivery of oxygen to the brain. Enormous amounts of oxygen can be used up during this type of worried sleep (aggravated sleep, you might call it).

Oil of Oregano

Is there an advantage to taking oil of oregano in small amounts with water into the body? This does seem to affect the small arteries and veins in the extremes of the body, in the hands and wrists, and also into the toes and ankles, you see, opening up the orifice, allowing more blood flow; but primarily affecting sedentary forces in the removal of the same here. It does affect, specifically, the valves in the stomach and the small intestine as well.

Olive Oil

Edgar Cayce and this Source have recommended olive oil above all other oils. Why?

Olive oil is a non-saturated fat. It can be considered a food to the intestine, and it can also be considered a lubricant to the intestine, or to the body; and, in a general way, is easily assimilated. It would be considered less sluggish or difficult to digest because of the heritage, or long-time use of this from antiquity. It does harmonize well with the body, and does not digest overly so, or affect the body, or impair the body in its natural movements of digestive and elimination systems or processes, you see.

Is there value to ozonated olive oil? Its promoters say it is a "miracle salve."

Concerning ozonated olive oil, the effect is to speed up the oxidization and the healing process locally. If it were to be placed in open wounds, it may cause some irritation in some; in others, it would cause a softening and coagulation of blood and tissue, a reduction in pain. But most of all, it would enhance the knitting together of the tissues, by bringing oxygen to bear in the area of the injury or sore, or to the disruption at the cell level. It does not seem to affect the circulation (the heart); but more the tissue and the blood, in the bringing of oxygen, which normally would be assimilated and transported through the hemoglobin.

Orgone Therapy

According to proponents of orgone therapy, a vest (for example) made of alternating layers of organic and inorganic material would attract to the wearer, orgone (sometimes called chi) and be a beneficial therapy. Do you agree or disagree with this?

It would be best to have certain degrees of exposure of the bare skin to the elements: sun, water, wind, and even the Earth. This type of element or armor tends to isolate the body (as all clothing does). Placing metal around the body for short periods of time may or may not be beneficial. This particular vest would be a crude way, like Eeman screens, to affect the body's electrical-magnetical fields, and we would suggest that this, in some conditions, would be positive. But it should not be relied upon to be an authoritative improvement to the body.

Osteoporosis

Could you please describe what may be done to treat osteoporosis?

In general you would understand the disease as a weakening of the bones and a weakening of the body itself. Understand the body is the end result of what is held in the mind, what is taken into the body (or assimilated) and what is left from the body (or eliminated). It is also the end result of the treatment of the body.

Understand that the body goes through a complex development from conception to casting off the clay (if you will). The transitions in life are based on the activities and the use of the body. Of course, the mental attitudes and the emotional states must always be considered, for the mind is the builder; the mind is always the way. The emotional states are the constructive and destructive forces in any body.

With this as a parameter, we assume the question is more about the organic aspects of the body itself. Weakness of the bones comes from poor assimilation, poor use of the body, and from a weakening or a rusting of the body (if you will). If you look at children, you will see them running endlessly; they are full of energy and they seem to have endless energy, constantly bouncing, crawling, running, and jumping. This indicates that the body is being builded up through these activities. In later years, you will find those who are weak of body have little in the way of exercise programs, little in the way of activities that would test or strengthen the body, or (more exactly) call on the body to engage in feats of strength.

Flexibility and strength in the body are the keys to maintain throughout the lifetime to avoid this disease and many others. Usually as one progresses through life in the Western culture, there is more of a sedentary lifestyle. For those who choose the same, or who become sedentary, it is the same dilemma. However, the body itself needs to be tested, needs to be strengthened, and needs to be used. It should not be a surprise to anyone

when they do not use their body as they did when they were children, that the body loses its strength and loses its ability to assimilate. This allows the pollutants in the body to build up because the eliminations of the body are also slack or improper. An active body is a healthy body. Without manipulation, without movement, without stretching the body and using it fully, the body basically allocates resources to those parts of the body which are active, and it diminishes or retards those parts of the body that are not active.

A rule of thumb, therefore, to prevent conditions of weakness in the bones and the muscle (and the rest of the body) is to use it, to exercise it, to keep the machine lubricated, full of fuel, and active. Breathing is a most important exercise. Understand that the arteries, as well as the bones, are affected by the circulation. When one stresses or exercises one's body, blood pressure is increased. The blood is forced into all the nooks and crannies of the body. The arteries and the veins expand and contract, as the blood pressure goes up and down, due to the activities or rest periods, naturally. During these times of exertion, the body builds up the muscles or the bones to strengthen the body, for it knows it is being called upon, and that the body itself must endure what is being called upon to do. It is as simple as that.

Therefore, when the condition is that the body has weak bones, circulation difficulties, impairments in elimination, or building up of toxins, deposits, calcium, crystalline forces, pollutants in the body, or plaque in the arteries, it is largely due to the result of poor movement in the body, poor exercise, poor exertion of the body. The reverse is true. When weakness in the bones is found, then slowly, and in increments that are in harmony with the body, the body needs to be builded up. For instance, if weakness is found in the long bones of the legs, stamping the feet on the floor every day, or bouncing up and down on the floor, or using a rebounder or other form of exercise, will make the body call upon its legs and all the circumstances surrounding the stamping of the feet or the bouncing of the feet (including the balance). When the body stamps its foot on the floor, shock waves go up through the limb from the sole of the feet all the way up to the top of the head, but mostly it is felt in the bone. If you can see this, and understand that by stamping the foot, even a dozen times each day (taking turns to stamp both feet, of course), then the body, in a subconscious way, in those motor skill regions or the consciousness within, knows that the bone must be builded up, and resources are sent to build up the bone.

This form of exercise is simple. One need not try to put one's foot through the floor, but by simply stamping the foot, creating the circumstances in which the leg itself is called upon to work, the body naturally strengthens what is needed. Now, it would take several days and it should be practiced life-long; that is to say, calling upon different parts of the body. Lifting the body off the ground, as if you would be swinging on the branch of a tree can be mimicked by having some device over the doorframe of a door, in which one can lift oneself up by a device or apparatus. By putting a rope on a tree and swinging on it back and forth, one can improve the body immediately in the upper arms, shoulder-blades, neck and those parts of the body in the lower extremities that leave the ground and return to the same. Simple childhood play movements or exercises that would take place in the park address the issues of strengthening the body; from the monkey bars to the slide, from the swing set to the teeter-totter.

Look at the different combinations of bones and muscles that are used, and the activities that call upon. Ever remember that the muscles hold the body together; the bones hold the body apart. The blood goes through the tissues of the body as well as the bone. The bone secretes and is surrounded by lubricating forces. The movements of the joints of the bones are important. As they increase the lubrication, they call upon the bones to function differently and they strengthen, as the body is used.

For instance, when lifting things, if you simply rotate the wrist while you are lifting a weight, you cause at least thirty to fifty per cent more benefit to the muscles and to the bone than you do by simply holding the wrist and lifting the weight up and down. The same with the feet.

The body is made to rotate, and the range of motion is important to maintain throughout the lifetime. This causes the muscles to stretch, the joints to open up, and the bones to strengthen. Paying attention to this simple lifelong form of making the bones work as they ought to, by strength-building or calling upon the body to do things — simple things that children do — then the body will be strengthened, and there will be no fear of weakness in the bones, or hardening of the arteries (as it is called) or a diminishing of the body, even to the last day.

Breathing is an important element in keeping the body youthful, as well as keeping the body full of oxygen and the blood delivering the oxygen to the brain (and other places in the body). This keeps the body youthful. The healing, restorative and replenishing forces in the body through the blood build up the bone and the muscle. Now, iodine, protein, iron (especially liquid iron) and an array of vitamins are necessary, including several minerals. Taking a sample of the hair, or a clipping of the fingernails and having them analyzed to show what is diminishing and what is in abundance, should be something that can be done annually. This would give the person an analysis of minerals that are needing to be replaced, or elements that the body requires.

The best is to keep the body active. "In the morning, work awhile. After lunch, rest awhile,. After supper, walk a mile." A very old saying that is very true! For, as the body exercises, the internal organs are exercised as well. The organs of the body are designed to extract from what is taken into the body and build up the body, replenishing the cells, strengthening the bones, improving all areas of the body as it naturally goes through its life. In the life cycle, every cell in the body is replaced about once in every seven years. Repeat: every cell in the body is replaced in every seven years. As the body is maintained in good form, the replacement cells builds up the body and keeps it youthful, flexible, and strong.

Walking is a good exercise that should be maintained rain or shine, every day. Breathing outside fresh air is extremely beneficial. Open the windows up and refresh the household. Do not live in a box excluded from the elements and from fresh air. Sunshine is most important to the body. Having a good suntan and maintaining it in the seasons that are best suited to have suntan allows great amounts of vitamin D to be absorbed into the body and into the bone. This is a natural process, and it means that one must be outside to do this or to have this tan. When one is outside, one is usually not sedentary but rather moving, walking, exercising, working. In other words, the body is active.

To keep the self inside your dwelling with the windows closed, in very poor direct sunlight, and stuffy air, is to weaken the body and to speed up the weakening of the bones and the muscle. Therefore, part of the cure is to go outside! If you lay on the ground, this is good for the body; no padding (perhaps a sheet or blanket). To simply lay the body on the ground is refreshing and brings back ancestral memories. The body adjusts to the ground; this should be done periodically as a therapeutic exercise for the body. It need not be done every day, but do lay on the ground and energy from the very ground itself will emanate up and be restorative to the body. It is also essential that one walk on the ground with bare feet. This is restorative to the bones in the feet and causes the bones of the feet — the toes, the ankles — to function differently than when wearing hard shoes (or any kind of shoe, for that matter, that separates the foot from the ground). Therefore, walking on a sandy beach or walking on a grassy area, on a regular basis, is very therapeutic to the bones in the feet and also to the rest of the body (even balance in the body).

The elements of fresh air, being exposed to sunlight, tanning the body, moving or exercising the body, and taking into the body plenty of fresh water are the elements that will build up and maintain the body throughout the lifetime. However, when one comes to that point of need, strengthening the body (as we have already given) by stamping the feet, slapping the hands on the table, jumping up and down, using a rebounder or simply a hard surface (like a floor or the ground itself) are all beneficial. Going through a routine of stretching the body, like tai chi, qi gong, or yoga, is one way to bring the body back; not to extremes, but simply to go through range of motions. Strength-building, by lifting weights, is also beneficial; but, again, you need not go to extremes. By building up the body through already-known strength-building exercises, the body will respond.

Taking into the body more protein, more minerals and more elements to build up the body would be necessary. Omega oils or fish oil (or more fish) taken into the body is beneficial to the joints and the bones. Massaging the body using peanut oil in particular, (although castor oil, lanolin, and camphor and mineral oils are all beneficial) will keep the body lubricated, and help to build up the bones, by increasing the circulation through the arteries (which, in turn, build up the bones).

Calcium should be taken with two other elements (copper lactate and magnesium, for instance). Taking it all by itself, the body rejects it. It needs a combination to assimilate into the body. The best time to take vitamins into the body is in the early morning; however the best concentrated form would be the juices of vegetables. This would allow the greater assimilation of the vitamins. Remember, it is not what types of vitamins and how many you take, it is the assimilation of the same. Therefore, learn what the body assimilates and take plenty of the vitamins, especially as the body ages past the fortieth or fiftieth year, or more in the sixtieth and seventieth year.

Keep the body active at all times. Specifically for the bones: protein, iron, calcium, manganese, magnesium, a little copper, silver and gold elements or influences are needed. Most bodies are deficient in iodine, as they lack the diet that would be more from the sea (which, historically, would be correct). Eating oils from the fishes and from other sources (seed oils, in particular) will also affect the intestine and the bones in particular.

Therefore, keep the body strong by watching what is taken into the body and eating a little more past the balance point of those foods that are alkaline-producing, but are necessary for the body. Each body is different, and therefore one must have a diet that is correct for oneself, but also have a diet that is specifically to build up the bones in the body. Make no mistake; a good circulation and a good form of stretching or testing the strength of the body will, indeed, build up the bones to the point where they will not be fragile, brittle, or easily broken or fractured. Eat more minerals. Find out what is needed in the body and then consume it. It is not difficult; it is only necessary to know what the body is lacking and then to ingest more of it. A good rule of thumb would be: eat a little of all things. This will benefit the body in all different ways, see?

Specifically, however, taking into the body the minerals, and beginning to use exercises or techniques to build up the strength of the body, within the third to the sixth month, there will be noticeable strength in the body. Now, for those who are having difficulty, it is the assimilation of the minerals and vitamins, and the strength in the body that is missing. Consume broths and soups made from the bones of fish, fowl, lamb or beef, to build up the strength in the body.

Breathe, exercise, eat well, and (most importantly) eliminate well, and the body will be youthful and strong. The joints will be flexible, and life would be much more comfortable. Avoid the sedentary lifestyle. Swim in the water, walk on the land, jump up and down. Look at the children in the park and wonder what happened to the self, and know that you can return to this vitality, if you want to. Otherwise, the body will continue to function in its mechanical way of allocating its resources to other parts of the body that are used — the buttocks, the hands, the legs — those surfaces that are used for sitting, see.

You have before you light and life, or death and darkness. Choose what you will choose, but, as for ourselves, we would choose light and life. These are simple rules. Make sure the body is eliminating, and if it is not, take steps to improve eliminations in the body. Place the body in water — seawater is good — at least once a year. Increase the endurance of the body, by taxing it somehow, making it work or exercise; whether you are swimming, walking, running, or doing some form of stretching or isometric exercise, or other form of exercise. Keep it up, rain or shine, and you need not have any fear of the bones breaking, shattering or splintering because the body cannot support itself.

Think of it this way: with pollutants and sediments in the body, the body is rotting on the inside-out. Therefore, clean the body from the inside-out. Increase the circulation by moving the body, which allows the blood and organs that filter the blood to extract the toxins, poisons, and pollutants, and eliminate them. The most important first step would be to drink plenty of water, and to make sure the bowels work each day. If they do not work, then take steps to improve this; even laxatives, if necessary. But modify the diet and the body should respond quickly. A large spoonful of olive oil may be all that it takes to keep the body regular each and every day. It is most important that you pay attention to eliminations, otherwise, these toxins and poisons are sent to the nooks and crannies of the body — the joints and bones — and, of course, the body rots.

It is a personal choice, but it is one that, if you wish to have youth in your old age, then it is a life-long process to be maintained. Fix the body where there is injury, give to the body those things that are necessary to build it up, then (like any machine) keep it lubricated with massage oils or activities, and the body will respond in kind. What is held in the mind is manifested in the body. Choose to keep the body youthful, and be active. There is no mystery!

Oxygen Depletion

Looking at the oxygen content of the blood of insects fossilized from thousands of years ago, it is clear that our oxygen content on Earth is depleting. Is Mankind adjusting to this, or is this causing health effects?

The oxygen content is not being replenished at the same rate it is being consumed. This is true. The oxygen content is being replaced with toxic or non-breathable gases; this is true. Now the Earth is prepared to adjust (and has, in the past, adjusted) to these types of gases from volcanic action, from forest fires, grassland fires burning or consuming, you see.

However, the planet itself has been given derogatory influences in its atmosphere, from pollutants to radio-active effects. Air quality in the northern hemisphere in particular is greatly diminished. The weight of the atmosphere has changed as well. Those who are sensitive tend to be irritated and made ill by the poor quality of air. Those who are a little stronger tend to be able to ward off the adverse effects. Those who are susceptible to viral and mucous conditions or diseases tend to become sick very easily through the assimilation of poor air. Yes, the air quality has diminished greatly. The production and relying upon fossil fuels, in particular for airplanes, machinery and manufacturing production, all have contributed to this condition. When there is a change to power that is more ancient and simple, and lessening of the reliance on causing combustions or explosions to occur within mechanical devices to produce power, the better off the planet will be, you see.

PanaSeeda

There is a new product called PanaSeeda, which contains different seed oils at their full potency: sunflower seed oil, pumpkin seed oil, black sesame seed oil, golden flax seed oil, and coriander seed oil. What is the long-term health benefit to consumption of these oils?

Like all things given to the body, there is a benefit and there is a waste product (so to speak). You would find that the long-term benefits would be to enliven the nervous system, the glandular systems in the body, and to invigorate the Peyer's Patch in the small intestine. This, of course, would be beneficial directly to the immune system and it would also affect the pituitary (and, to a lesser degree, the pineal) gland in the body. All ductless glands or soft tissue glands would be benefited by these oils in the long-term, for they are the essence of the seeds, and, therefore, the vitality. What is beneficial to the body would be of its greatest value.

As for the use of the same, they can cause some congestion in the kidneys and bladder of the body; they can affect the gallbladder adversely. They can affect the liver adversely. And therefore, like all things given to the body, there should be a rest time, that the body would not be given these substances for a period of time, and then they can be resumed. Otherwise they would tend to congest the soft tissue organs. Like an allergy that is both stimulative to the person and derogatory to the person (depending on the threshold reached) these oils would be the same.

Any particular concentration given to the body should be done with a degree of common sense; otherwise, understand the body is prepared to assimilate some seeds that have been crushed by the teeth or otherwise mechanically crushed, during the process of assimilation or ingestion, you might say. However, in the concentrated form, they tend to have a boost to the body and are beneficial primarily to the soft tissues. As to the organs from the thyroid, the pancreas, the heart and lungs, through to the liver, spleen, bladders in the body and even to the gonads, they have stimulating and invigorating effects.

Parkinson's Disease

What causes Parkinson's Disease?

This would be a deteriorating in the electrical-magnetical forces or the nerve communications in the body. Usually the brain tissue, like the lungs (the soft tissue, you see, in the body) is susceptible to trapping or holding onto diseases within the body, or to the sedentary influences of physical matter that are taken into the body. You would find that blood supply in the brain has been changed or altered somehow first. Whether it is the absorption or penetration of toxic substances or metals (such as mercury from teeth) leaking into the blood system, and then resident in the brain, or whether it is from injury that has been sustained in the younger years and there is bruising, or there is the effect that is commonly referred to as concussion within the brain (which is, in fact, brain damage, you see), or whether there is some other influence (disease) within the body that affects the brain tissue, understand that Parkinson's disease usually deals with tunnel-like disruptions within the brain. In this particular disease, there is a sort of on/off switch that is stuck on, or stuck off, and the brain itself cannot function in a totality. Instead, one segment of the brain will attempt to boost, assist, or aid another part of the brain. There becomes a miscommunication or jamming up of the signal. This results in involuntary movement of the body. It is like a light switch left on and the connector is sparking or is not quite connected. This causes the rapid and consistent shorting out or jumping of the signal through the nerve center, nerve ending, or the nerve line itself - the line of communication, the trunk itself, the plexus point, you see.

As such, this particular disease can be caused by disruption in the brain in which there is some deterioration of the brain tissue where there is some lodging of poison, or toxin, or heavy metal, or metal influence (including mercury) that has leached from the body. It can also be thought of as the assimilation of - call it here - chemical or metal toxicity through the lungs that is taken into the lung and circulated through the blood, for it is taken through the nasal passageways and directly deposited in the upper part of the forehead, directly affecting the brain. It is like pollution in the brain, you see.

Plastic

Plastics have been in common use in society for almost half a century. Have there been unintended health consequences?

Plastic itself has a consistency or a longevity that can cause the containment of bacteria (and the pacification of the same) and the longevity. Like capsules, garbage bags or garbage containers can breed enormous amounts of bacteria that are detrimental. These are released into the ground, or thorough the dumps, or other containers or placements and they can cause, in a down-wind direction, very real disaster or bacterial-laden conditions in the air or wind stream that can be absorbed into the body by a variety of means. They also become cesspools for disease and for insects that would carry the disease forward into the normal living regions or conditions of humans.

Also look to plastics absorbed into the body, and because of the inability to break down, they can lodge within the body in minute areas and disrupt the body as sediment would (or as rust might in an automobile), seizing up joints, stopping the function of the cells as they would change or interact, and even causing irritants, blockages in the body (if there would be significant amounts). We speak both of the airborne molecule as well as the - call it here - patch, particle, or slice of plastic.

Plastic does have very good characteristics and, if properly directed, can be used for the hygiene and welfare of the human itself (speaking of sewer conduits and other packaging, so to speak). If there is a transfer of the plastic through the touch, or through the nostril, or through the mouth, then there can be some detrimental effects inadvertently here. In particular, where there is some heat on plastic, or where there is some friction on plastic, or where there is some touching (so to speak), the weather conditions or temperature conditions, in consideration of the same, can cause these to affect allergies, to affect irritations in breathing in the nostrils and extending up to the pineal gland itself, you see (as well as the pituitary).

The effects are primarily more to absorption and a sedentary situation in the body that can inadvertently affect those who can be sensitive to the same, especially those who are sensitive to petroleum products, you see, to cause great upset or difficulty. They can disrupt the nerve system and affect the nerve flow in those who are sensitive, lodging themselves in the small arteries in the nasal, sinuses passage ways and, thereby, making their way to the brain itself, you see.

Does water stored in plastic acquire some of the chemicals from the plastic?

If the fluid is acidic, it may activate in the beginning, but as we would see it over time, the amount would be less and less to the very minute amounts. We speak of certain types of plastics. Those that are harder or formed with heat would tend to seal themselves, and this effect would be minute. Therefore, if there are kegs or plastic that would be made such as there would be ABS-type pipe plastic, then the answer would be yes, it would be more of a concern. There would be a leeching (if you will) of the chemicals into the fluid. If it is more of what is commonly used for carbonated drinks, then this would be negative; or very small, if any, effect would be seen here.

Post Traumatic Stress Disorder

What would you recommend as a course of action to treat people who are suffering from post-traumatic stress disorder?

Like any unusual and frightening or terrifying experience, it is engrained in the mind. Understand that memory is associated with emotion, and that a memory can trigger an emotion. In the combination of this, the mind reverts back to that moment in which it has suffered the experience that would be called traumatic. In order to overcome this disorder, attempt to understand that the mind is stuck. Just below the surface, the memory, the fear is resident. It is almost impossible to separate the memory or the thinking part of the mind from the emotion that is experienced or felt.

Understand that the way memory works, in some regard, is that the stronger the emotion, the more vivid the memory is engrained in the memory cells in the mind. The key is, attempt to divorce the experience and the emotion. Over time, this usually takes place, and those traumatic memories of childhood, for the most part, are buried deep in the mind itself; not erased, but masked or covered up. These memories never fade, but controlling the same (or, more exactly, averting attention away from these traumatic times or memories) can be accomplished. In time, and with distraction or getting on with life in different regards, these events fade into the past, usually. However, when there is associated feelings of guilt, feelings of injustice, feelings of pain or torture or regret, then they are not so apt to be forgotten. They are relived every day, and, when recalled, the memory plus the emotion is brought to the surface and the experience of that moment occurs again.

Now, understanding how the mind works, you would see that people look up when they attempt to see or remember something, and they look down when they attempt to cover something up. They look off to the side when they are attempting to conclude something different than the fact. The eye movements themselves are key in understanding that they move in correlation to the function of the mind. One simple way to attempt to reduce the connection between the memory and the emotion is to change the movement of the eyes while recounting the memory. Let us say a woman has seen a child drown in a swimming pool; she froze solid and was unable to move, in order to save the child. She remembers this moment. She feels guilty that she did not do something about it, and she feels horrified that a child died because she believes it was her fault (even though it might not have been, but she assumes it is). By remembering this in the mind's eye, there can be the vivid picture of what happened. Usually, there is a reliving of that moment. The heart begins to accelerate, respiration is increased, the fear, the emotion of pain or anguish rises up. Just prior to the commencement of any of this, while remembering the event, the movement of the eyes can be helpful in erasing the bridge between the memory and the emotional response.

The person who is in pain can look at an object that would move back and forth in front of its face and its eyes would follow the object, about sixty beats a minute. If a ball was put on a stick, move the ball back and forth, causing the eyes to follow all the way to the right, then all the way to the left. Shorter movements can be done, so that the eyes are moving back and forth quickly, about the same speed as we have given. But it may be thirty movements to the minute to start with, and then to accelerate so that the eyes are comfortably moving back and forth. The subject would relax the eyes and the body would begin to feel drowsy. This is not hypnosis, but it is attempting to disconnect the memory and the emotion from the event, which is engrained in the person's mind. This simple technique will help to separate and then isolate those rather horrific or traumatic emotions from the event itself, so that, in the future, there can be the remembrance of the event, but there will not be the triggering of the emotion of the event. This is one way to do it, you see. Mechanically have the eyes going back and forth, and while this is done, the connection or bridge between the memory and the emotion is dissipated.

Of course, forgiving oneself earnestly is a beneficial aspect as well. Realize that sometimes when witnessing events, one cannot do anything about it. Then convince the self of this truth or reality, and one can begin to let go. There is also a visualization technique of seeing an older self and a younger self. See the younger self asking for forgiveness from the older self. This is another way of communicating from the Low Self to the High Self and this, too, is a purging of feelings of guilt, and this would be beneficial to any. It takes one to move or swing an object on a string, or a ball on a stick, and this back-and-forth would take ten minutes (or perhaps a little more or less) but, at the end of this — perhaps only a single session — there should be a relief. There should be a break in the combination of the mind being triggered and emotions being brought forth from a traumatic event that has happened somewhat in the past. This would be, generally speaking, suitable and quick for those who have engaged in difficult circumstances, see?

Premenstrual Syndrome

What may be done to alleviate the symptoms of premenstrual syndrome?

To some degree, there is agitation and leakage of menstrual blood into the surrounding tissues. There are chemical changes that are affecting the body's chemistry. This is a complicated circumstance in the body, but as each body would be slightly more alkaline than acidic in its balance (for bodies vacillate between acid and alkaline), this helps to reduce the acidic influences leading up to the menstrual cycle. We would suggest also molasses can be taken or honey may be taken, a spoonful or two each day prior to the cycle commencing. It is important that the spinal column is in good movement or alignment, especially into the lumbars three, four, and five. Osteopathic or chiropractic manipulation may be necessary (and usually is) to align these lumbar in the lower portion and in the pelvis also, to address the tilting or misalignment here.

We would find that eating only the meringue from a lemon meringue pie would help to reduce irritations in the bladder and, to a lesser degree, the chemical imbalance in the uterus itself (although this is not extensive). Occasionally this is in combination with difficulties in the elimination centers (of physical congress). Mucous or candida can exist in the body and, as such, this, too, leads to this painful effect. Reducing this condition in the body can be done by three enemas, one right after the other, helping to remove the condition in the ascending portion of the colon. Of course the colonic therapy can be given to the body and might be considered from time to time; for washing the body on the inside is just as important as washing the body on the outside. Affecting or removing congestion in the large intestine assists the reproductive centers.

The body also may be cleansed on occasion with douching the body, with any simple solution, from salt in the water to more sophisticated additives, herbs, or substances. Apple cider vinegar (one quarter teaspoon) in an amount of about eight to ten ounces of purified water can then be administered to the feminine aspects, and this would be a cleansing. After there has been a cycle, there can be a cleansing again, and the body may engage in baths or a series of douching once a week leading up to the cycle commencing again.

Castor oil packs may be applied in the low abdomen area, helping to reduce inflammation or irritation in the abdomen, from the intestines to the reproductive centers themselves.

With the manipulation in the spine and the reduction of irritation, the ovaries would function more correctly and there would not be such a surge of movement through the ovary. Eating melons and fruits like avocado or Jerusalem artichoke (or any kind of artichoke, for that matter) would be helpful, in a subtle way, towards balancing the menstrual cycle. Usually, however, it is a high acidic level that causes the premenstrual pain or bloating to occur.

On other occasions, there are difficulties in the small intestine; what is now called leaky gut syndrome. The slippery elm would be good to coat the small intestine in this regard.

On other occasions, there has been injury or compression in the spine, as we have given. This may be mechanically corrected. Eating of those foods that are of the cool variety would lead to relaxing or soothing of this condition. This includes melons and salads that would be of dark, green vegetables or leafy vegetables. The melon should be eaten alone or left alone. Encourage, as much as possible, chlorophyll in the intestine.

What we have given is very general and has been given for the widest variety of conditions. This would be beneficial for those who have engaged in these types of difficulty or pains. Usually the more severe pain is evidence of menstrual secretions outside of the womb, and there is irritation in the abdominal cavity. This is not a surgical problem (although it could be corrected by surgery). It is similar to a hernia. The castor oil would be helpful in this regard, as might be other massage oils.

Probiotics

Is any benefit to using probiotics which aim to restore healthy bacteria?

Probiotics replace what would be destroyed in the intestine through excessive digestive juices, and also through chemical medicines that would be ingested that have the effect of removing bacterial influences from all sources or levels in the body. They are beneficial to the body in breaking down food and in removing parasites. This good bacteria keeps the intestine working right, keeps it cleansed and moving. It discourages a build-up of toxic forces at any particular point in the body. It can dislodge residues in the intestine; those that have attached themselves to the inside of the intestine, small and large, and created pockets.

It also works well in removing some degree of polyp in the body which tend to arise from the body holding onto some penetration or irritant, whether it is dirt, metal, or toxin. The body encapsulates the same, and it is held in a pocket in the intestine. Like stones that have been worn away through the passage of water over time, and a pocket carved out, so can the intestine be affected by adverse food that is not digested correctly; or is over-digested, or where too much digested fluid or juices penetrate and irritate the skin or tissue of the intestine. Having these proactive (if you will) bacteria aids the body, and restores the body from these harsh effects.

Psychic Surgery

Would you please discuss psychic surgery?

The concept here (as we see it) is the advent of one to place their flesh (their hand, you would call it) within the flesh of another without the advent of knife or tool, causing the removal of substance or alteration of organs; as such, healing instantly that particular complaint, and not leave a scar or an opening within the outer flesh. Yes, there are those who can attune their flesh to mix with, enter into, and alter the flesh of others. It is simply done, for the vibration of flesh can be attuned by one who is trained in this manner. With a degree of energy current through the hand, the touch can be called surgery, for it would remove the cell that would cause the complaint or discomfort. This would be done by any who would possess considerable control to attune their flesh with the vibratory rate of the patient. It exists, yes.

Radiation

Please briefly describe any ways to undo the effects of harmful radiation exposure that are not already known.

It would be to stop the radiation going through the body, taking precautions to stay away from devices that produce radiation (like computers and cell phones), or surrounding the self in a room with copper mesh in the walls, like a cage. The copper mesh will negate any penetration of even strong microwaves. If this is unavailable, then it would be simply to place the self in an environment in which there would be isolation from at least the short waves, or the longer waves, for these are affecting the bones and the muscles. Placing creams on the body to soften the tissue are good for the softening effect, but they also act as a small barrier to weed out the cell phone waves, you see.

What is the effect on human health of eating irradiated foods?

It depends on how soon after the food has been irradiated, you see. To some, it would be a benefit in which there would be the reduction of bacteria and negative influences of the food. To others, it would be a lessening of the food quality. But it is not seen to affect the physical body adversely.

The amount of radioactive waste in our environment grows year to year. What affect is this having on the population at large?

It is primarily forcing evolution to occur; adaptation at the cell level and stresses or irritations in the organic-physical level. The bombardment of these rays is causing the onslaught of what would be older age or wearing out of the physical body. Mankind usually does the right thing for the wrong reason, you see. As such, this will have an invigorating effect, a change, and an adaptation that will allow the ability to weather high frequencies, to build up the body. The radiation being felt upon the same will not deteriorate the cell, but rather would invigorate it, strengthen it. Like a bone that is weak, if it is taxed or stressed, the bone becomes stronger. The body has always been adaptive; lazy on one hand, aggressive on the other. Lazy inasmuch as if the body is not worked in a certain way, it will lose the ability that it had, aggressive inasmuch as the body continuously replenishes itself within every seven years. It is willing to heal, be it the broken bone, or the wound of the flesh with great speed, accuracy, consistency and at the various levels of sustenance or (call it here) support.

There is a device now being sold to be worn around the neck, usually in the form of a small coil or oscillating circuit. Its supporters claim that this bracelet protects the average person from certain negative or harmful waves and other forms of radiation. Do you see this as having any basis in truth?

The effects are minute. It would be better to put circles around the joints of the body made from metal, and affect the body that way, than to have a trinket like this. Any metal or organic matter worn about the body about the wrist, the elbow, the shoulders, the chest, the abdomen, the thighs, the knees, the ankles, the neck and including the top of the head (like a headband) all have tendencies to corral the energy and affect the electrical-magnetical forces within the body that spin and are radiating from the body itself. To some degree, they are like doors in a dam. They stop the flow of energy of the body like the dam gate would close; it would stop or hold back energy for a time. Then, as the water levels continue to build, they would then reach the top plank or the top of the door, then spill over. Likewise would be the wearing of any copper, any gold, any silver, any metal object and precious stone or gem. They all have effects on the physical body.

The intention, of course, is to build up the body to its optimum amount of containment of this - call it - creative energy. For then they will, of course, spill over the top and radiate out. Wearing an amulet or device (copper band) tends to counteract the negative aspect or thoughts upon the mind-body and, as such, mechanically sure up the energy flows out of the body. Wearing the metal, here, is a benefit to the body, but it should not be worn all the time, nor should it be worn in the same place all the time. At the wrist, and behind the knees, and at the ankles, and at the base of the neck, these are the most vulnerable places from which energy escapes, and if you examine historically from ancient times through more recent history (and even to the present day) you will find that these points are always adorned with jewellery in a circular fashion or form: ankles wrists, waist, neck and headbands (in the way of material, or hat, or even a sweatband). The reason is to contain the energies that radiate out and are wasted (shall we say) from the body.

There is a theory that radiation therapy works on tumors because radioactive material contains high frequencies which destroy tissue. Please comment.

This would be correct. The higher the frequency, the more disruption to the soft tissue. But it depends on focus, for broad band broadcasting is not as harmful as restricted or focused broadcasting of the high frequency. Yes, to the question.

Is it correct that the Japanese nuclear disaster at Fukushima has already changed our ecosystem for many generations to come in a derogatory way?

This would be affirmative. You would find that throughout the oceans themselves, the sea creatures are fleeing their basins, in part due to these toxins or poisons. Mutations are taking place and large areas of the oceans themselves, especially radiating out to the East, North, and South, have already demonstrated effects that would be adverse or difficult (and there is more to be determined here). Yes, there would be effects here for a long time, as we see it. This is affecting the fishes of the sea, which are diminishing in their populations.

What can people do to minimize the negative effects of this?

Remember, the body is ever resilient. Taking into the body some charcoal tablet, on occasion, would be helpful. Take more drops of iodine, especially what would be Atomidine*. Flush the liver occasionally and remember that when there is chemical exposure then the body's filtering systems need to be assisted. Having plenty of liquid or water in the body is good. Taking those substances that would act as a trap or container would prevent the body from filling up (the liver, especially). Drinking plenty of vegetable juices, especially the carrot and the celery, aids the body in eliminating these substances that might inadvertently be absorbed through the skin, breathed in through the nostrils, or consumed on food that would be taken into the body. Therefore, washing the food thoroughly would be a good place to start, and washing the body on the inside would also be a good thing to do periodically, especially if the body is exposed to such things. Simple things, but positive things. See?

You have given in past readings and books that the Earth's magnetic field is already in the process of changing (and scientific research has confirmed this). What effect is this having on the immune systems of the population at large?

It is having somewhat of a very difficult effect on the body. It is weakening the very essence of the body. Bones are rattled. Emotions are triggered, and fluctuate greatly. The hormonal system in the body can be considered imbalanced. There are feelings and senses of vertigo and indigestion. An overall state of anxiety or depression may result from long-term exposure to this severe condition of the body being bombarded from influences from space itself, see?

At these points in time, keeping the body's alkaline imbalance high is good. Keeping a high amount of iodine in the body is good. Keeping fresh air and oxygen in the body is good as well. Attempt to avoid spirits and alcohol (although a little red wine for the digestion at mealtime is acceptable). This is a time in which the emotions fluctuate. It does not seem to matter how old the self would be. Keeping this balance would allow the self to overcome any effects of radiation from space. Of course, it would help to know when there is going to be a bombardment upon the Earth in relation to the location when the self resides. For if the self is behind or away from the sun, and this occurs, pushing the magnetic fields around the planet in a flame-like configuration, then those who are on the away side would be benefited, and those who are on the forefront side would be tortured (so to speak). Staying indoors helps. Isolating the self with steel mesh would be better than not. You may hide in the ground, or you may use oils that would be somewhat protective. However, what bombards the Earth goes through the human body like invisible bullets, see? Shielding the self with metal in the walls or a metal cage of some sort in the house would be helpful for these short periods of time in which the body is exposed to influences from space without really comprehending what they are.

Take more iodine in the body to affect the thyroid, which is the master secretor or timing device in the body. Attempt to stay away from meats that are difficult to digest (pork and beef). Eat rather light meals; the fish, the fowl, and the lamb. Keeping the diet light will keep the blood supply higher and the oxygen in the body more readily available. Plenty of iron should be taken as well and protein should be taken in any form or way (even protein shakes). Mineral water may be taken and sodium bicarbonate may be taken every other day, one quarter spoonful in a cup of water.

Protect the body with some sort of coat that would act like a grounding or shield in the body. There is a jacket or coat made with a mesh or copper lining. It need not be heavy, but if there is some desire, make a room and put copper mesh in the walls. This will help to stop any radiation, plasma or material that has come from the sun through sunspot exposure, explosion or activity. Otherwise, magnets can be strewn around the house and the magnets would tend to act as a benefit also.

Radio and Satellite Waves

What effect do radio and satellite waves have on the human body?

Understand our planet is being daily bombarded with ultra-high frequency signals far beyond simple radio signals, including what you call microwaves and other short, intense, and highly destructive frequencies; frequencies harmful to the human organism. These are being beamed indiscriminately upon populated areas. This is having an adverse effect, for it is causing states of anxiety, states of irritation, and other uncomfortable states of mind. This is also having an adverse effect upon the vibrational rate of the cells in the human body. The human body is not designed, at this point, to take in such electrical-magnetical frequencies in such large volumes. These are adversely effecting the human body; in particular, the glandular systems, pancreas, and thyroid. They are disruptive even to the human soul itself, making the human race much more agitated and expectant of violence, and those who would perform the violence to be enraged, more violent and more aggressive. Those who have a propensity towards violence are agitated to take violence.

Radionics

Would you please discuss radionics, or the science of tuning into each cell of the body?

You would find that the healing of vibration and the detecting of vibration of cells as to their - you would call this - disruption of vibration will be detected and radionics itself will prove to be the basis for vibration effect that will cause limbs to regenerate and grow anew, and cells that are not wanted (cancerous cells) to be destroyed or eliminated, for it would awaken the body to conditions within.

The understanding of vibration within the body will lead to those who will deal with tools that will utilize electrical and magnetical forces that will emanate vibration through sound that will affect the physical form, for the welfare or the disruption (depending upon the application of the vibration). For vibrations or frequencies will be critical; they will need to be isolated.

But this underlying healing program, radionics, will be widely used. For if you would understand chemicals, you know that the pill you would be taking into the gullet would consist of its own vibration, and it would stimulate those centers within the body, once it has travelled throughout the entire body through the bloodstream. When it comes to that area that is needed for the vibration that the medicine would consist of, it would distribute it to that area. Now, this would be the long way around. The short way would be to get the frequency directly to the ailing portion of the body. Much simpler, is it not?

You would find also the detection of disrupted cells within the body can be diagnosed with a degree of ninety eight to one hundred per cent accuracy, rather than the ten to twenty per cent of accuracy that is now currently the rate for those of the healing profession.

Salt

Is sea salt better than table salt?

It is more enriched than all minerals here; for the sea, you see, possesses all elements. Sea salt possesses high quantities of gold and silver and other minerals that are not necessarily within table salt itself. In this regard, yes, sea salt, salt from the sea, is much better.

Would pink Himalayan crystal salt be a suitable substitute, or would sea salt be better?

We often suggest the sea salt for it is not combined with aluminum chloride, or other chemicals that cause it to be free-running. This is the purpose, you see. Any salt that has its original crystalline force or that cakes together is demonstrating that it has not been adulterated or infiltrated with aluminum or other metallic derivative, you see.

Sassafras Oil

What is the benefit of sassafras oil, often recommended in massage mixtures?

This affects the nervous systems themselves and can be considered a soother, a tranquilizer to the nerve systems in and about the injured area. It thins out the massage oil and allows the oil to penetrate deeper into the affected area. In muscles that are knotted, it tends to allow them to release and relax; at the same time, to increase the blood supply going through them, and, at the same time affect the nervous connections (the electrical-magnetical impulses) in a positive way.

Sauna

The readings have, time after time, recommended the wet sauna over the dry sauna, and we are in a period of time when the most popular consumer product is the so-called infrared sauna which is a dry sauna. What are the advantages of the wet sauna to the body?

There is not intense heat, and the air, atmosphere inside the sauna that is breathed is soothing to the lungs, as opposed to what would dehydrate or irritate the fine tissues in the lungs, causing perhaps even destruction (or irritation at the very least) to the lung. The hydration does affect the cells, or the pores in the skin in the same manner. That which is wet is soothing and beneficial; that which is dry is irritating. It is like rubbing a moist cloth, a lubricant across the face, or sandpaper across the face.

To the question, however: it is primarily to the direction of what is breathed, or what is taken into the lungs. This is the reference or the difference, primarily, of the two methods, you see.

Saw Palmetto

Why does saw palmetto berry work to help prevent prostate problems in men?

Primarily, it affects the prostate itself, and it allows the substance, the core ingredient (which is basically the fermentation of the vitamin-enriched pepper) to be isolated, or to be driven directly to the prostate gland, you see; isolated for the use of the same. It does tend to allow certain hormone secretions to occur; and there is a beneficial oily substance that would appear on the prostate itself that would not allow it to be thickened, or the outer skin there toughened, you see. This softness would allow the flexibility to be maintained, and would not cause the organ to become puffed, or stretched, or elongated. It does affect the cell level by keeping the surface skin or surface levels breathable and flexible.

For men approaching or past middle-age, should this be taken preventatively, or prophylactically, or should they wait until there are signs of distress or congestion and then begin treatment with saw palmetto?

We would suggest this be used as a mainstay of the diet. This would help to keep the body slightly more alkaline; eating this substance would allow the prostate to be less embroiled in disease and less susceptible to infections and viral conditions; and, therefore, less in the way of swelling or mass.

Schizophrenia

Would you please explain the cause of schizophrenia and explain the best form of treatment?

Schizophrenia is a simple disease in which the brain itself is not receiving sufficient amounts of blood supply. There is usually tension in the body throughout, and this comes from early development stages of fear in which the child has suffered abuse, there has been trauma to the brain, there has been injury to the body, or there has been some form of accident like whiplash in which the brain has bounced around inside the skull. These are organic injuries to the body. The emotions are usually to the extremes of great fear; fear of death, fear of the Almighty banishing the self to Hell, fear of being incorrect from a teacher's overbearing bullying, fear from bullying or excessive criticism,belittling and derogatory remarks, causing one to lose one's will, causing one to lose one's identity.

These extreme emotional bruisings or injury leads to the brain itself malfunctioning. Usually there is some difficulty in the spine or neck as well. There are compressive forces affecting the central nervous system. You would find that difficulties in the teeth, causing irritation in the nerves that go from the jaw or teeth to the brain are causing imbalances, fantasies or provocation of derogatory thoughts or imaginative thoughts - monstrous thoughts. Upset stomach and irritations in the stomach also cause these emotional responses or expectations.

Fear is the basis of this, and it has gripped the entity and has changed the personality from what would be a sensitive, lively, and balanced mind, to one that is filled with fear (imagined or real), in which the self has retreated into its own world, for safety, or to be simply withdrawn from the circumstance in which it finds itself, see? We would find deficiencies in the vitamins and ability to assimilate vitamins in the body and long periods of time where there would be lack of protein - not starvation but similar to it. The body would need to be builded up. There would need to be improvements to the blood supply in the brain through osteopathic, chiropractic or massage therapy. There would need to be relief and trust builded up but, most importantly, there would be an education on how to feel, to experience emotion without being suddenly, inexplicably punished or dehumanized by a teacher, a parent, a relative, a friend, a neighbor or someone associated closely with the family. Losing this fear, learning how to trust, but most importantly learning how to feel the emotions is the remedy here.

You might say the schizophrenic mind is incapable of feeling affection, or relating to other people, but not consistently or consecutively, but in fact, it has difficulty in feeling anything. Now, they do go through the full range of emotions from anger and jealous, murderous thoughts, to loving, fanciful, perfection thoughts, as most do. But they have a tendency to view it as real, and when they are upset or when there has been a perception of an attack against them, they respond very aggressively, inexplicably, spontaneously, and they revert to the animalistic side of themselves. These individuals are attempting to overcome the animalistic influences of action and reaction or occurrence and reaction, like an animal in pain. As they learn to trust, and are assured that they are not in jeopardy of being treated like an animal, then they can ascend from this level.

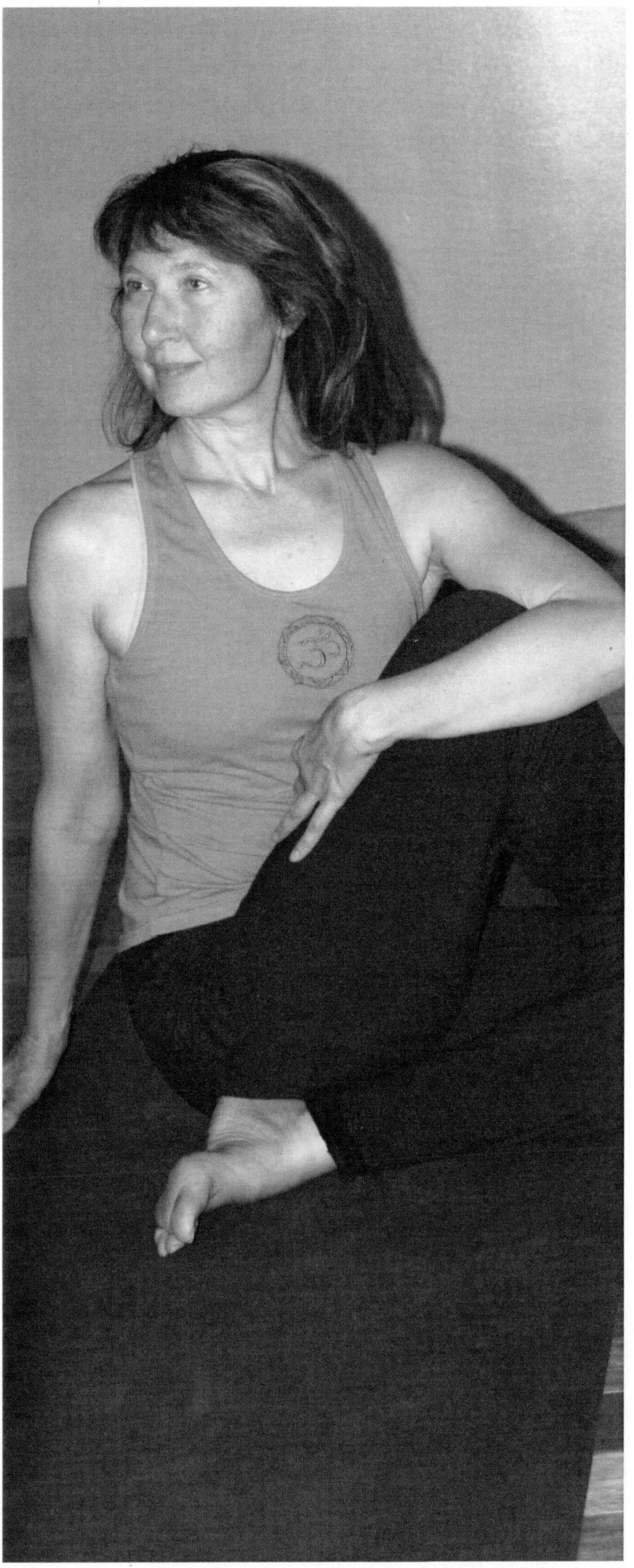

Sciatica

Can you please comment on the problem of sciatica and the best focus of treatment?

In what would be a normal problem in this area of the body, which is the pelvis or tail-end of the body, it is simply that poor posture, heavy work loads, difficult life all have a tendency to affect the body in which would be considered old age as a cause. This would be the wearing out of the bone or the fusing together of the bone as the body natural ages. It would also be an indication of injury in the body, understanding that the pelvis is the pivotal point or foundation block for the body so that the body would stand upright.

Therefore the cause of sciatica, or what would be pressure on the sciatic nerve, the coccyx, and extending into the lower end or limbs themselves would be pressure on the nerves themselves, causing muscles to go into spasm in accord with (or similar to) the wearing out of the bone and, therefore, causing the angle or the stacking of the vertebrae in a less than perfect alignment (sometimes even rotation of the bone, one upon the other, directly placing pressures on the nervous systems and extending indirectly into the sciatic nerve).

Treatment is, of course, realignment of the vertebrae, affecting and enacting good posture at all times, and selecting proper seating that would align the weight of the body or the body's natural position in sitting or reclining in such a way as to keep everything in line - the leg, the pelvis and the spine. Traction, massage, heat can be applied by ultra violet, infrared light sources or moving water (whirlpool or therapeutic bath) or as heat transfer devices (such as hot water bottles, hot rocks, heating pads or hot sand, you see). For anything that would be held next to the body and allow the heat to penetrate would, therefore, allow the muscles to relax or become fatigued and blood supply to increase greatly through the general region or area, thereby releasing the pull or tug-of-war between the muscle groupings in the body itself. For remember, the bones hold the body apart. The muscles hold the body together, and is their natural function to pull against the bone.

As there would be a release, there would be a proper realignment, and without impacting the body (meaning there is not injury or bone deterioration, either natural or by wear and tear on the body) where there is not part cartilage missing, there would be a realignment, recirculation established, nerve flow functions more correctly and, most importantly, muscle groupings would be such that they would be in balance or harmony; not one pulling more than the other (in other words, one in spasm and the other fatigued). This would relieve the condition. Of course, massage oils and other therapeutic adjustments such as osteopath, chiropractor or one that would be skilled in the thing would accommodate the remedy here.

Seasonal Affective Disorder

Can you please comment on seasonal affective disorder and the best focus of treatment?

Indeed. Humans (as you know humans) have evolved to a point in the modern society in which they live indoors consistently, instead of living in the environment in the region or vicinity in which they have taken up residence. No longer do they walk upon the ground all the time (speaking here more of urban than rural individuals). As such, they are losing contact with the natural cycle, the natural environment, and the natural environment that they reside in. If anyone would monitor their whereabouts, they would find that from the early morning when they rise out of their bed, they reside in their house until they go to some place of employment. They may leave their house briefly, get into an automobile and drive to the place of business or work. They then reside all day in this place, this building. At the end of the day, they leave this place, get into the automobile and go home again. Very little time in the workday has been spent in the out-of-doors, a purpose for which humans are primarily designed.

As they would then, in the evening perhaps go out to visit, or for some form of entertainment, again, they go from one place to another, and they maintain their presence inside a structure or a building. This adds to the ongoing deterioration of an individual, for they are inside all the time. They are now artificially stimulated by light from lamps. These lighting sources can wear and tear down the body, for some of the lighting sources are not healthful to the body; given that the winter months come and that there is continued residence inside, and they are deprived of the natural light outside, even further. They are not strengthened by the changes in the environment. They are not strengthened by the exposure to the elements and, as such, like anything that is not used, it rusts.

The immune system becomes somewhat

dampened or less, the body's vitality becomes less, for the weakened state of the metabolism is very affected or very susceptible to the seasons as they change. One who would work outside all day would be healthier than those who work inside or stay inside all day. One who would walk upon the ground with their bare feet would immerse themselves with the life-giving energizing forces from the ground into their feet. For even those that would immerse their fingers into the soil would be receiving somewhat of a healing, you see.

Therefore, it is obvious that those who are not in the elements, but are in an artificial capsule place are not exposed to fresh air, to the challenges of the elements, and to the vibrational, gravitational, electrical-magnetical vibrations of the Earth itself; and, as such, it wears them down. However, light deprivation is an indication that is most readily accepted. This fatigue, irritability, listlessness are demonstrations of this, the body weakening and becoming less; for as one would be exposed to the elements, one would enjoy themselves in the out-of-doors for longer periods of time. Then the seasonal adjustment would be more acceptable, and there would not be the seasonal complaints, you see. For when one goes from the summer weather to the winter weather, the moisture in their household is changed dramatically (as is the climate), as is the effect. See?

In thinking of this, many parallels can be seen for many extremes from inside to outside. However, the adjustment is primarily that the individual does not gradually go through the change of the elements as would the residents in the out-of-doors; if their house would not be on concrete, but on the ground itself, you see. This, along with the changes of water, the food sources, the climate-controlled dwellings all attempt to keep the body in one particular state, as opposed to the on-going changes through the different seasons, and this is the difficulty. One extreme is met by another extreme, you see.

Serraflazyme / Serrapeptase

Could you please discuss the silkworm enzyme serraflazyme, also marketed under the names serrapeptase and cardiopeptase.

This surrounds certain elements within the blood. It cocoons them and allows them to be eliminated, especially those that would be metals; iron especially; non-organic, you might call them. As such, this compound has an ability to not only remove that which is fluid-bound or suspended in the blood, but it does have, taken over a period of time, the ability to bore away at that which would be encased or encrusted in the liver and the brain itself, you see, especially where there have been deposits of aluminum, iron, or other metals (or substances, for that matter). These would otherwise be detrimental to the electrical-magnetical pulses of the brain and the liver and, to some degree, the heart as well.

It has a cocooning effect upon these substances that are foreign and allows them to pass out of the body. It accumulates, separates and finally encapsulates and allows that which has been collected to be eliminated in a rather easy form. It coats sharp and odd-shaped metal particles and makes them smooth, that they might pass through the arteries easier, rather than hooking onto the shelves or orifices in the arteries, as well as the veins.

To some degree, it improves the blood flow or content of oxygen in the blood. It keeps the level high, you see. It somewhat can be considered a vacuum cleaner of the blood. It does work with the pancreas, kidney, spleen, and bladder. It is quite compatible, you see.

It strengthens certain muscles in the heart as well, and also improves vision, specifically the smaller muscles in the eye and the eye's ability to react to light. It causes the vision to be less cloudy as, again, it would remove sediment here. Think of a dust cloth that attracts dust through static electricity. It has the same magnetic ability, you might say.

Once it is, however, in contact with foreign particles or sediments, it tends to incorporate them into itself like a cocoon and then eliminate them out of the body.

Governments in the West are trying to restrict access to serrapeptase, claiming that in larger doses or higher strengths, it is dangerous. Do you agree or disagree?

If it is taken in moderation, it cannot be harmful. If it is taken slowly and consistently, like anything taken into the body, it would be balancing the body itself. "Higher dosages" is an arbitrary figure. But, to the question, generally speaking, nothing should be taken to extremes in the body. All things should be taken in moderation, and therefore if you refer to high doses over long periods of time, we could find it may be detrimental, for it provokes the body, weakens the body, and, with anything taken over a long period of time, the body loses the ability to assimilate or to function in its own way or right.

To the question: generally speaking, it would be not so. But the body can sustain benefit from this element, especially if there is congestion in the arteries; especially if there is disease in the soft tissues; especially if there are irritants in the gut (the intestine, you see).

Silica

The health supplement silica is good for hair, skin, nails, and blood vessels. Are there any benefits from silica supplementation that remain undiscovered at this time?

It has a tendency to rejuvenate the cell level, this is true. It affects those growth cells or speeds up growth cells or T-cells. It has the ability to affect bone to grow, and tissue to knit together in an accelerated way. Yes, it has a growth hormone similarity, but primarily it can be used to speed up recovery of broken bones, or when surgery has taken place in the body, or wounding has happened (either through stabbing, or gunshot, or explosion, or even burning). The body seems to respond to this in a benevolent, yet accelerated way, to heal the body (especially bones to knit together). It could be used in legs where the bones have been diagonally broken which is usually a very difficult mending or healing. This has a tendency to speed up the production or the bone knitting together; in a subtle way, not in a forceful way, it speeds up the healing, see?

Skin Conditions

Rashes, Cysts, Boils, Pimples, Eczema, Seborrhea, Psoriasis, Freckles, Moles, Warts, Scars, and Stretch Marks.

Is it correct that pimples, acne, and skin rashes are caused by problems in the digestive system?

This would be correct. The poison that is not

taken out of the body has to go somewhere, and so the body, in its wisdom, naturally takes these pus-laden substances through the lymph and through the blood, and deposits them in little chambers or storage places in the body. Notice that the same pimple or boil will occur in the same place in the body more often than not. This is largely due to the body system removing the poisons and toxins and putting them in the same place. When the boil is lanced, or the pimple popped, or the pimple is expelled through the pores of the skin, the body is dumping these poisons or toxins out of the body. The movement or friction across the skin of water, clothing, or other substances (for instance, going through bushes, there would be the striking of leaves and branches) these all are indications of how the body can move the poison out of the body, in what would be a natural and expedient way; through the pores, see, through perspiration.

These are natural eliminating substances, and if a sample of the perspiration would be taken, there would be seen that for one who is secreting poisons and toxins, this would be quite potent toxin indeed. The skin is a great organ and great eliminator of poisons and toxins through the natural process of perspiration. When there is congestion, the pimple or the boil occurs. When there is lack of movement or exercise in the body, the lymphatic system becomes sluggish and poisons or toxins may be stored in boils, pimples, cysts, and other pockets which the body chooses to hold the poison, keeping it away from the essential organs. Remember, a cyst, or a pimple, or a boil builds up in the body. It is an indication that the body itself is not eliminating correctly or properly, both internally and externally. A body that moves, exercises and perspires uses one of the main methods of eliminating (and that would be through the perspiration).

Would you please comment briefly on the cause of cysts, boils or pimples and the best focus of treatment?

First, to the emotional realms: these would be on someone insisting all the time that their will be done, or that their will is right, or that they are right. Here, they should take a little bit of insisting and be a little more accommodating (or not insist at all). For this, therefore, would allow these little pockets of poison to dissipate from the body itself.

These would be little collection points, whether they are cysts, or whether they are boils, or whether they are pimples that are large. The intention is that the body, again, has had part of the lymphatic system blocked, or that there has been a poor secretion of the toxin or poison into the lymph system, or the elimination through the body has been impaired (and, therefore, cysts or boils are collection points). If they are above the surface of the skin, they are exit points to get rid of this toxic substance within the body.

Understand the poisons in the body are quite immense at any given time. The body manages these and does channel these to elimination points, as it should. However, on occasion, there is an impairment, or the movement is impeded, and a ballooning out of a lymph node, or pocket, or weak point in the lymph system occurs; and, as such, a cyst is formed in the soft tissue.

The apple diet would be useful. Use enemas to the body itself (or colonic hydrotherapy, if you will). This would stimulate and remove from the colon the irritants that may be impacted, for usually poisons that are bubbling up in the body are a result of what has been backed up in the body. By improving the way out of the body (the elimination), then the cyst, or pocket of poisons, or balloon (if you will) of collective points can be readily addressed and stimulated, and elimination improve; so would the cyst dissipate.

Touching the same with healing and curative oils would also get the poison moving through the body, and it would not rupture or break the skin, or rupture the tissue in any way, you see.

However, olive oil from a large spoonful on the first or second day (not as part of the diet but simply as a maintenance for elimination) would, indeed, attempt to make the body more regular, and normal elimination would occur.

We would strongly advise cleansing the body internally with the enema: two or three enemas, one after the other. However, the colonic therapist can be used (as we have given). This, too, would be of great advantage to removing cysts, boils, and pimples.

The body should be washed or scrubbed and encouraged to sweat or perspire, as the skin would be a good source of elimination as well, and in addition to what we have given. This would be sufficient in a general way (as we see it) in the body.

Can you please comment briefly on the cause of eczema, seborrhea, and psoriasis and the best focus of treatment?

This is usually an indication of irritation in the small intestine, in which there would be an excess amount of digestive fluids given and the bile, you see, is not readily functioned or digested; as such, causing the body to sour or eliminations to be poor, and the reabsorption of these substances or toxins through the intestine back through the blood system and deposited into the surface of the skin itself. There can be, indeed, the attack of some viral or material influences on the body - mold, or mildew or some other form of invasion at the level of the skin.

The furious combination of removing the dirt, the irritant, or the viral condition with a good soap, or with the combination of tincture of iodine or tincture of turpentine with a normal amount of water or simply mouthwash that would be antiseptic in nature, or food grade hydrogen peroxide diluted in water, topically this would remove any virus or bacterial condition that is attacking the body from the outside.

From the inside, however, it is evident that there is poor blood supply to the affected area or region and that there is insufficient oil in the diet and oil in the cell level to warrant perfect skin or perfect condition of the skin, you see. Thereby, replenishing oils in the diet, replenishing oils topically may also be helpful; but, in any case, there needs to be an increase of blood supply to the area or region. This can be done with infrared light source, or it can be done by simple calisthenics or exercise that would heighten the blood pressure, thereby pumping more blood from the artery in the center of the limb outward here, to the surface of the limb, or to the area of the body affected. Then, with the topical application to remove the virus or bacterial condition, and new blood supply emanating or circulating in or about the area, the body's natural healing forces would have a greater chance to bring about restorative conditions and removal of these diseases, you see.

But again, vitamin E, aloe vera, or any other of the antiseptics can all be used, including the combination of oils that would tend to remove the same. Vitamins, massive amounts can be taken and assimilated into the body. Two ounces of carrot juice mixed with two ounces of cabbage juice, add to this a little gelatin, and this would act as an assimilative influence for the vitamins, you see, and they would be directed at the cell level to the affected area in the body.

The diet should be one that is high in alkalinity (high in vegetable) and yet there can be those foods that can be taken into the body to lubricate the joints, which would also affect the skin. But rose water, rosehip water may be taken and touched upon this and it would help to purify the region.

There would also be a condition of nervousness, or some degree of impairment in the spine which the osteopath or chiropractor could address to improve nerve communication, and this would thereby allow the body to heal or remedy itself. This is a very general examination we have given here. Usually the body does not have the ability to assimilate great amounts of vitamins, and the catalyst (or the gelatin) would be helpful. To strengthen the body, give the body broths made from the bones of the fowl, lamb, and even the beef, you see. This would be a place to start. The vitamin absorption could be increased or enhanced with the gelatin and, as such, the body should recover from this condition, which can (and should) be considered both topical and yet initiating or commencing from the small intestine. Yogurt, chlorophyll to be ingested to affect the small intestine would also be helpful.

Is there a way to remove freckles?

Certain lotions can be applied to the body that would even out the secretion of pigment in the skin. These would be a combination of beeswax (as a base cream) with aloe vera within the same, and, to some degree, shark cartilage ground into a powder. Some berry juice (like raspberry or blackberry concentrate) can be added. The blackberry would seem to be better. Into this, add a little camphor oil - a few drops - to help the absorption, and a little gelatin powder as well - a pinch or two.

Ground into a paste and then placed on the skin, it would seem to have a little - let us say - shielding effect, and prevent the strong rays from penetrating into the skin at specific points. It would diffuse the light and, therefore, would have an easier tanning effect; the pigment in the skin would be spread out more evenly, you see, rather than in spots or freckles, as would be seen.

The body should also be cleansed regularly; no grit or grime in the pores. Steam baths would be good to increase circulation in and around the muscles and the skin itself, thereby allowing, again, a diluting effect of the pigment in the skin. This would seem to work most of the time, as we see it.

Can you comment on the causes of moles and warts and the best focus of treatment?

These are simply cellular disruptions, you see. Moles and warts come from the skin or surface being ruptured or affected with some form of injury, you see. They can also be seen as certain disruptions of the skin level as mild states of irregular cells growing into the wart or the mole itself, you see. These are associated with disruptive cells that would be similar to cancer in nature.

The process would be to streamline the mole or wart with oils or lubricants that would allow the old cells to be discarded and the new cells or underlining cells to replace the old ones, but not take on the same vibration or shape, you see.

Mechanically, moles can be tightened with a noose and the blood supply to them cut off and they would simply deteriorate and fall off, leaving a mild scar underneath. The blood supply severed, they no longer function or grow.

Warts would be seen as a viral infection in the body and, here, they can be treated as a virus, covering the same with some form of sealant (such as nail polish or what is used for ringworm too, you see), blocking off the air supply and causing, therefore, the virus to eliminate, or cease, or desist.

Remember the earlier comments on cancer: that the body builds a cocoon on any invading force or any attempt in it. The mole or the wart can be seen as the body doing this on the surface of the skin, you see.

You can also use any astringent or antiseptic (including peroxide diluted in water) and touch this upon the wart or the mole itself (for the wart that would be infected with the virus, you see). This should eliminate the virus, should eliminate the body's need to build up a cocoon around it of skin, you see. Again, they may be removed from the body, but with the viruses dead, the tissue would turn acidic and disintegrate, you see.

As to moles or age spots, we would suggest that a little baking soda and olive oil be smeared upon these. It would have the effect of diminishing or reducing the size of the moles and, with some consistency and persistency, the effect would be to remove the mole completely. Moles are very difficult and are quite odd, for they are cells that are normal, save for slight discoloration and mis-shapement, but they function with hair growth and other means correctly. They are also excitable to rapid growth rate; therefore care should be taken not to apply the knife to the same (although the laser maybe given to remove the same). However, once the virus is out of the wart (or if there is one in the mole as well) they should reduce in size. However, the castor oil and the soda bicarbonate combined, perhaps with a little beeswax and royal jelly, they would tend to dissipate and eliminate.

What would you suggest to reduce or remove scars or scar tissue from the body?

Depending on the amount of scar, castor oil can be simply smeared upon the same and allowed to sink or soak into the body. Lanolin may also be used, and peanut oil as well. All three can be combined, or they may be used independently on the body. You may simply smear the oil on, or you may put a heating pad on, or put the area of the body under a bandage, or under a glove. Keeping it warm, the pores absorb the oil. The castor oil has the ability to penetrate greatly into scar tissue and to soften the same, and also to hasten the healing or knitting together of the skin or the tissue, see? The peanut oil is more of a lubricant and has a tendency to keep the skin lively and flexible, see? Good movement with the oil.

Arnica cream may be used as a remedy to pain or bruising (as castor oil might be used as well); lanolin to soften the skin, and camphor to heat up the area to allow the increase of circulation. Absorbine Jr. or wintergreen oil may be used to heat up and increase the circulation temporarily in some areas. This can be used around the injured area or the scar, but it is primarily for the scar tissue to be used, to receive the oil and to be flexible, softened, and the scar tissue, therefore, becomes pliable or relaxed.

What would you recommend to improve or

eliminate stretch marks on the skin?

Indeed, these would be caused by pressures from the inside of the body outward, where the expansion of pressure is disrupting the cells, causing a tearing apart of the surface structure in the upper portions of the skin. Now, what would be beneficial to prevent this would be, of course, in advance, when there are tiny fissures, cracks or fractures occurring in the skin, that there would be immediately applied to the skin lotions or potions that would ease, at the cell level, this disruption of the cells. Lanolin would be good; a combination of one ounce lanolin, one ounce rose hip water, one-quarter ounce of mineral oil, and one-quarter ounce of peanut oil (perhaps adding a little castor oil in, one-quarter ounce as well). This would be soothing and beneficial to the skin itself; that is to say, it would prepare the skin that is under stress. In pregnancies, the abdominal area can be coated and the oil can be absorbed into the body. Stretch marks do not occur on all abdominal areas; only those that have low fat surface (or the reverse: those that have too much fat) and, as such, the skin is ruptured at the upper levels of the same.

Castor oil itself can be applied directly on the marks or the rupture or irritation points, and this will help to shrink the tissue and to almost eliminate the scarring on the body itself. The point is that the skin is being pulled apart at the uppermost level or tissue. What is deep or underneath (the dermis cell level) is being intact and we do not find disruption even deeper where there would be irritation to the cells or to the circulatory system. In preparation for pregnancy, the abdominal area can be prepared to stretch or to expand, as it would be seen. Other cases in which the body's skin will be stretched to the point of rupture or ripping would be cases in which there is too much fatty tissue under the skin, and the weight or the density of this is causing the skin itself to rip apart. The best would be to reduce the mass of the body, by utilizing a proper diet and proper movements or exercises. Isometric or stretching exercises would be good. Bouncing or jogging the body tends not to be helpful when the very movement, through gravitational influences, will cause the skin to rip or strip itself apart, see?

Plenty of sun is beneficial to the body to keep the integrity; therefore, what would be helpful would be to either tan the body artificially or in sunlight, but do not dry the tissue out. You may take a good astringent like witch hazel to remove bacteria and clean the skin, and then, with some heat or in the sunlight, the oils can be penetrated into the body. It would be beneficial upon any application of oils. Basically, any combination of most moisturizing oils would be suitable or helpful, but let the body be heated up or the pores opened. This can be done by placing the body in a warm place, like a sauna or steam room or wrapping the body with a piece of plastic. Make it like a tent, so to speak, with the head exposed or outside of this tent, of course, and the body would heat up and begin to perspire. Poisons or toxins may be stroked or stripped from this by taking any metal implement or any available implement and basically wash the sweat or perspiration away by scraping it like a squeegee on a window. The poisons or toxins that have come to the surface would be swiped away. Then, the potions, lotions or oils can be applied.

What we have given is a basic formula for most skins, however some might be irritated by the lanolin and some might be irritated by the mineral oil. What we have given would be generally acceptable and, as such, this can be applied to the body. Now, there are other stretching creams that are usually used for facial purposes and these, too, may be placed on the body. There are many expensive and moderately expensive creams that would be used, but the formula seems to be basically the same.

Keeping the skin moist and in preparation for expansion or stretching of the abdominal area, then the marks would be noticeably less (and possibly avoided from appearing on the body altogether). When they do appear, act right away. Use the castor oil and/or the combination of oils, as we have given, to help remove the scarring circumstances. Lanolin would be good. Increasing the blood flow through the area also would be good, by exercising or by placing some heating device near the area (a hot water bottle or heating pad). Let the oils soak into the body with the pores open, after the body has been heated up, and this would prove to be the best to elimination of the scars. There are a combination of oils that could be used, but what we have given would be accessible and useful. Olive oil itself may be smeared on the skin as well. Coconut oil as well. Flax seed oil as well. Do not put lard or fat on the skin, thinking this will moisturize and be beneficial. If it is put on, fat or lard tends to go rancid and would be detrimental to the skin. See?

Slippery Elm

Of what benefit is slippery elm to the human body?

It has a tendency to cool and calm the intestine and therefore to cool and calm the mind, for there is a direct association between the stomach and the mind. As such, what is given coats the intestine, protecting it from leaking and protecting the intestine from diseases that want to get in under the skin. This allows the body to be nourished. It also has the effect of calming and soothing the body prior to sleep, and it has a certain calming effect on those who are irritable or have difficulties in sleeping or approaching sleep. See?

Take the plant - the leaves or the root (the root might be best). You may cut it, or slice it, or you may use it whole. Allow it to be put into a pot of boiling water, and cover it with a plate or top. Allow it to sit exactly two minutes, then remove the plate or covering. Allow it to sit for another minute, then it should be consumed. The process is simply as if you would brew any other cup of tea.

Smoking

Is smoking detrimental?

Eight to ten cigarettes a day would not hurt. However, if there is a degree of congestion within the breathing, then we would suggest that this be refrained from. It is not detrimental in some, for they need the nicotine to get moving. It is a stimulant. Others could do away with the smoking completely. But when there is affliction within the breathing, the sinus, the esophagus, the bronchial tubes or lungs, smoking should be avoided, yes; it is common sense. But generally speaking, a little taken does not hurt. Moderation.

One of the big criticisms of the Cayce material on tobacco is that there were never warnings of the dangers. Is this a valid criticism?

From the time of about seventy years ago until

present, you would find that there have been great changes in the chemical composition of the tobacco used now for smoking compared to then; the difference being that the tobacco then was more of a natural substance. It was not given a bath of chemicals for flavor, durability, moisturizing, burn quality, and so on. Instead, it would be seen as a simple plant taken and, with little adulteration, made into tobacco that would be used for the consumption of smoking. There were great differences even with what would be put into the soil as chemicals then; there would be very little in the way of chemical fertilizer, compared to the present saturation of the soil with chemicals in the more modern times, you see. Understand what is found next to the root is absorbed by the root of the plant and, therefore, becomes part of the plant, as food would become part of the body of one who would ingest food into their body. So, the chemicals given to the plant become part of the plant, and then, again, part of the processing would also, by necessity, penetrate chemicals into the tobacco leaf. These chemicals and their residue are toxic to the body and can be directly related to the body's inability to ingest, to filter out, therefore causing cysts, tumors, and other erratical diseases within the body, you see.

Space Syrup

Someone in Los Angeles came up with a formulation of garlic, olive oil, honey, apple cider vinegar, cayenne pepper, green tea and a Middle Eastern spice known as asafoetida. Please comment on this concoction (known as Space Syrup) and its effects on the human body.

Understand all things that are put into the body have an effect, chemically, in the body. The combination here of these spices would, indeed, effect some influences, mostly to the colon itself, some to the stomach, and some to certain blood cleansers, you see. This is a combination of those things that could be taken independently, is it not? Therefore their influence would be felt more directly for what they would be suited. The dilution of these and the cooking of these seems to have made a certain elixir that is a combination of the influences. While we cannot see extensive healing benefits as this would be touted as some sort of "wonder syrup," we would see it as having some effect to reduce the excess amounts of bile, and yet to stimulate the small intestine; not as a cleansing agent to the intestine - small and large - but as that which would accelerate the movement and assimilation in the intestine, here.

We are looking for and attempting to find specific benefits. We see the benefit being minor or small in the body. The honey is good; it affects the assimilation. The tea is good; it affects the chlorophyll in the small intestine. The spice itself also is good; it has somewhat of a calming affect in the body, affecting the central nervous system itself.

Sugar and Honey

Please explain what negative effects sugar and glucose may have on the physical body?

Firstly, there are fluctuations within the blood sugar levels within the body. These are done rapidly and extreme heights (we would call it) in the energy level or sugar content - glucose - also within the bloodstream itself. As sharply as this level rises, it falls.

Now the body, being a rather moderate machine, and not (you would say) shockproof, it has a tendency to respond to the influx of the sugar level within the blood, causing the anxiety levels or the energy level within the body to increase most dramatically. This places stresses upon the heart and the respiratory system itself. It causes the blood to rush through the veins at an increased rate. As the blood would, and the blood sugar level rises (as we have given) it drops drastically. As the body is gearing up to balance the physiological increases, it then is depressed. It goes down below from where it originally was, and, as such, this craving, this need for more of the substance of sugar (which would be burned as energy in the body) is great. This causes a reverse shock effect and this coil and recoil within the body affects the heart vessels itself, the very function of the valve action, as well as the pressure at the heart, in the heart, and then in the arteries and veins, with the fluctuation in extremes (as you would know extremes). Here, the muscles and the fibers begin to break down.

As we have given, the body is resilient, yes; but it is not shockproof. These sugars tend to shock the body. Also here, the residue from the sugar tends to lodge itself in and around the cardiovascular system, particularly the coronary system itself, causing a restriction of the arteries. It places stresses into the oxygen lines (you would call this), the heart feeding itself with blood and oxygen; it causes restriction here. Those who would suffer a by-pass operation would be chronic users here, in large doses of sugar; and, again, they would suffer the consequences. But the body cannot suffer shock after shock.

Sugar from the sugar bowl should not be tolerated in the body. A little would not hurt, but not much. Brown sugar and molasses would be much better in the system for the body, but honey as the natural sweetener would be best. For these would not tend to clog the arteries, pressurize the heart, disrupt the action of the thyroid in relationship to the pancreas and, as such, affect the stomach, ingestion, and digestion. They would be more harmonious. For white sugar is bleached, you know. It is better to have the molasses that is left than the white sugar that is taken; much more healthy, as we see it. Again, white sugar, sugar from the sugar bowl should not be consumed in large amounts. Baking with it is alright, and is helpful. But, again, the body is not able to handle the residue once the sugar has been ingested and transferred into the agents in the blood, and the circulating system becomes overloaded. The pipes that carry the life-giving blood become clogged.

Is honey good for the average person?

We have touched upon this, yes. We find honey is good for the cell pattern, mixed or blended. We are speaking of small amounts, not gobs and gobs. In warm water or apple cider, in lemon, stir it and take it. This would be helpful for the purification for the lymphatic system. Here also in the respiratory, it would affect the capillaries of the lungs in cleansing the grit that is taken into the lung. Yes, honey for the average person could be considered helpful. But again, anything in moderation. Gobs and gobs are not better and better, for it would be overloading and taxing to the liver and could affect the fluctuation of the heart beat. Moderation. No need to be fanatical.

Suntanning

Of what benefit is a suntan?

It causes a variety of activities to take place in the body. By increasing the pigment in the body, it regulates the secretion of pigment of cells so that they might be reproduced and regenerated and replaced in the same pigment or pattern. Also, it allows the vitamin D absorption into the body in a more regular and intense way. Indeed there would be seen certain benefits throughout the body, but it causes a deep penetration of heat and light into the body. The heat, of course, dilates the artery and allows the blood supply to flood the chambers in which the body is being tanned by the light or the sun. As this absorption of vitamin D continues, the processes in the body are amplified and they, too, benefit from this suntan or the time in which the body is exposed to the sun. Vision is somewhat affected, some positively, some adversely, but it is affected. As the blood supply floods out through the body, the heat relieves and reduces the tension and, indeed, the tendons relax and, from the rib cage to the hips, there is a resurgence of lubricating influences around the joints because of the heat, and because of the dilation of the artery. Everything in the body moves at a more comfortable rate, see? Inflammation is suppressed and the body's joints, through the expansion of heat, move freely. If there is some impairment of drugs, sand, sediments, arthritic condition, grit, the body can heat up and allow the dilation to occur and for the particles of blood to carry away the disease or the disruptive influences, including the toxins. See? The blood is the carrier of good and bad. The suntanning allows the cells to fill up with blood, to be invigorated and rejuvenated, and a youthful appearance will occur.

Are commercially-available sunscreen ointments safe to use?

Those that are more of the natural oils or those that would be filtering to the body would be best. Coconut oil is an excellent sun inhibitor, but those that are made from more chemicals that can be aligned with preservatives, those that have a tendency to embed themselves in the pores of the skin, these can cause irritations and these can cause disruption in the cell (blister or cell disruption, the misshape of the cell or even a slight tumor, you see). However, those that would be found in nature would be natural; the jojoba bean, the vitamin B oil, aloe vera and a variety of others (including bear fat or animal fat from other beasts you see, as has been proven by aboriginal peoples). There are also plants that can accommodate the same.

The intention here is that the complex construction of plants does not absorb into the body and simply sits onto the layer of the skin as the skin would naturally transform itself (the pigment becoming browner or darker). Instead, the oils would be assimilated into the body in a beneficiary way of building up the body. Therefore, the sunscreen can be seen as food or benefit to the body, if those who use the same are not simply putting this on the surface of the skin, but it is being absorbed into the skin as a shield or as a reflector of certain types of light or frequencies of light.

But in fact, after the oil is, to a degree or percentage, absorbed directly into the body, and is carried by the body's blood forces to other parts of the body (if it is not absorbed into other parts or regions) then it is eliminated in the natural way. All things put on the skin are, in such way, absorbed through the layers of the skin and are absorbed into the bloodstream; if excess, they are carried out of the body through the natural filtering means. Therefore, what is put on the arm may go through the entire body and be eliminated in the colon, you see, or the urinary tract. One should be more careful of what is put on, you see.

Do sunscreen ointments actually filter out the harmful portion of the sun's rays?

They simply diffuse this a little, you see.

What would you recommend as a good treatment for sunburn?

When there is sunburn on the body, there is irritation at the cell level. What would be especially effective to reduce the pain and soothe the cells would be aloe vera gel. This would immediately stop the stinging and begin the repair process to the burn area. Thereafter, castor oil or other oils with a softening effect may be used, such as lanolin.

However, as the body responds, as the body adjusts and heals the skin, moisturizing the skin with any oil - from mineral oil, to castor oil, to peanut oil, to creams and potions - the aloe vera gel would be the best. Sunscreen can be used to affect, improve, or prevent sunburning, but one has to be careful.

Supplement and Drug Cycling

The Cayce readings and those given by this Source talk about taking drugs or treatments in an on-again, off-again cycle. Yet, it is very common for individuals to be given prescriptions to take every single day. What is the result of ignoring the suggestions about cycling?
Primarily, it is that the body becomes dependent on the drug, and this dependency is created by the artificial stimulation provided by the drug, which tends to be, again, like driving in a tack with a sledge-hammer. This is overdoing it, you see. Therefore, the body, which is very agile and accommodating and accepting, tends to allow the drug to be utilized first and, therefore, shuts down all its own peripheral activities as well. The body becomes a little lazy; it capitulates, and finally allows the drug to do all its work for it. The drug becomes an artificial intelligence within the body and simply carries out what it is designed to do, circumventing the innate intelligence - the desire to heal - within each body.

Tapping Therapy

Advocates of tapping therapy claim that it can be used to relieve a variety of disorders. Is there truth to these claims?

We would see they would excite the nervous systems, and the nervous systems would themselves balance the body or bring into play certain consistencies or communication with other parts of the body. We do not find it as a curative, but more as a communicative skill, you see.

Like all things, there is a vibration that sets up in the body through the cranium, skull, or blood itself. Vibrational rates are signals or physical changes that can be meted out or cured. The effect is to align the nerve energy or chi energy that moves through the body, and embellish it or to have it amplify itself, and, in the beginning stages, to keep it moving in the body itself. There are meridians or lines around the body in which the energy follows or circulates, like blood circulating around in the arterial and venous systems of the body. The amplification of this energy, which is natural in nature, is somewhat of the creative force. It can build up the chi energy within the body and allow strength to occur, especially in a body that has been deprived of sleep.

Pathology would show that certain vibrations in the body can be influenced and, when they are, the low vibrations cause bone to grow, and the high vibrations cause tissue to erode. As such, the body, when it is in the middle, keeps the form rather healthy, see?

The health of the body, therefore, is at the cell level, where there is exciting of the retina or the vibrational rate in the cell itself. Exciting it keeps the cell healthy. Deactivating it causes death to come to the cell. See? The tapping, therefore, is to amplify or energize the cells or speed them up when they are sluggish or slowing down. The health and improvements may come about in the body. It is truly the body staying youthful.

Tattoos and Body Piercing

Could you please address the phenomenon known as tattooing and body piercing which have become quite popular, and comment on whether there are any unknown risks to these practices beyond the obvious possibility of infection through breaking the skin?

Take care that the piercing of the body should not be in those areas that are sensitive to metal or to wounding of the body. One who would be skilled in ascertaining the nerve ending points or those that would be the meridians upon the body itself (especially those that would be crucial meridian points, acupuncture or acupressure points, which should be avoided) should be actively pursued, for sometimes the piercing acts as a stimulant to the area, and on other occasions, it acts as a deterrent or a lessening of the area. Therefore, knowing where the piercing is going to occur and to wisely avoid those sensitive points on the body can keep the body energetic or enthusiastic.

In what would be given as tattooing of the body, then the substance that is soaked into the skin and the depth of this soaking in of the substance should be considered (if it is at all), and the types of dye used, for some are toxic to the body, and they weaken the skin and the muscle. Care should be taken not to affect any of the arterial or the venous areas in the body, for these substances, these paints, dyes, oils that are placed upon the body are, for the most part, reabsorbed and the body must handle these toxic substances that are put into the same. To some degree, they remain in the surface of the skin, and as long as the skin can breathe, or the pores can open, then there is some sort of tolerance for these intrusions (as these colors and dyes would be seen as penetrating into the body itself). These can affect the nerves (weakening the same); they can affect the muscle tone, and they can act as poisons or pollutants in the body. If they are topical and the depth of penetration is not too severe, then the body, seemingly, can adjust or accept what has been given to it, without exception or protest. See? The use of tattoos, depending on the location on the body, can mean that the body is put under duress, depending on the type of dye or chemical used, see? Notice how the cells of the body continue to accept the dye and conform to the same color or the same pattern.

The needle holes in the body, from the insertion of the dye, usually are accepted, but, on occasion, they remain permanent, allowing the body to remain susceptible to invasion of surface bacteria that would come across the skin.

Tea (Herbal)

What herbal teas are best for most people?
It would depend on the specific uses. The chamomile, rosehip and mullein would be but a few that would be beneficial. They would soothe and deal with the circulation system and the nerve system.

Tea Tree Oil

Could you offer a recommendation for the use of tea tree oil?

Tea tree oil can be used on the skin, and it can be used in wounds. It can also be used in lacerations or internal bleeding as well. It has the ability to act as a binder and it fills in (so to speak) between the two opposing walls or opposite sides of the laceration itself. By bridging the wound and then filling it in, it draws the wound together; it does not allow a crustation or a divider to embed in the wound itself. This is of great benefit, for it does remove and reduce scar tissue, you see, at this level. It causes the skin to knit together a little faster or more naturally. It is somewhat of an adhesive to the two walls of the wound, but does not get in the way (so to speak). It does not allow oxidization and crustation to occur or scab (as might be seen) to form too quickly on fresh wounds. This allows the oxygen-enriched blood to be delivered to the surrounding wound walls of the same. At the same time, it does improve some conductivity between the two sides, electrically. We speak here of primarily skin wounds, but this can be used also for conditions in the bowel, and also in the stomach itself. It can even be used on the scalp as well.

Is tea tree oil useful as a toothpaste as well?

It works by tightening up the gums on the tooth and removing the foreign bodies from the same, without allowing bleeding to occur. Yes, to the question.

Teeth and Gums

For dental health, there is a practice known as 'oil pulling', where one takes about one to two tablespoons of coconut oil in the mouth and swishes it around, keeping it in the mouth for twenty to thirty minutes before spitting it out. Could you please examine this practice and comment on what benefits, if any, this has to teeth and gums.

This seems to have the benefit of keeping the enamel strengthened and the teeth whiter. We would find it also has the effect of seeping into the gums and adhering to the enamel, going down the side of the teeth, under the gums, and helping to remove plaque or sediments that are affixed to the teeth themselves. This also has some anti-bacterial effects in removing bacteria associated with halitosis that have accumulated in the mouth. Yes, this has an effect, as it moisturizes or it softens the tissues in the mouth. It strengthens them and improves the circulation in them. It directly affects the teeth by affecting the enamel, and increasing the thickness of the enamel (if you would see it as that) over time.
Are there any natural ways to repair cavities, aside from the current dental procedures of

drilling, filling, and crowns etc.?

Of course, the original and best would be to remove the substances that cause decay to happen; usually sugars and other food particles that rot between the teeth, turn acidic, and break down the enamel. Having good assimilation and vitamins in the body affects the enamel, and the teeth themselves. We would find that the more the teeth are used in which particles of food are deposited between them, the more one should floss or pick the teeth, so that there are no particles left between the teeth. Eating fish bones that are crunchy like the spinal bones of salmon or other fish bones that would be digestible or consumable would be helpful, as there would be a buildup of the element of the bone, itself that would directly affect the teeth.

Ipsab or the prickly ash bark could be used to strengthen the gums and indeed, as the gums adhere to the teeth, then the forcing of food particles down the side of the tooth is somewhat diminished and the teeth themselves are maintained.

Having good teeth is simply having a good dental program and watching what is taken into the body. Avoid those foods that are poor for the body — carbonated drinks, soda pop, drinks high in acid and sugar levels or syrup and chemicals (preservatives especially) — as these tend to erode the enamel, weaken the gums and cause decay to occur much more quickly. Pay attention to the diet. Keep the teeth clean, and avoid those substances that are left on the teeth that actually wear down the enamel. As such, there will not be cavities or weakness in the surface of the enamel. This is the place to start, for understand the enamel is supposed to prevent the teeth from decay.

That said, as we have given, the bones usually found in tins of salmon can be eaten, as they would be crunchy and assimilated in the body much more readily than calcium in concentrated form. Using the prickly ash bark, using antiseptics like Glycothymoline, Lavoris or Listerine (which are antiseptic mouthwashes), these strengthen by removing the bacterial influences in the mouth. As to what can be directly taken, any tincture of gold or silver (gold especially, what would be confectionary gold) can strengthen the body and, in particular, the teeth.

However, once there has been a breakdown of the enamel, we find that restoration of the enamel is very difficult, but possible, with an increase in calcium and magnesium. You might also take monolaurin, which is an antiseptic, antibacterial substance, see? Eat from the strength of the meat, and have more protein, and this would seem to benefit and repair cavities. But not allowing them to be exasperated is the first step, and to allow the ability of the body to repatriate or to heal small intrusions into the enamel can be done by taking minerals and the gold (like gold chloride, see).

But also we find the vibration or frequencies of light can be used on the body and upon the teeth themselves, and there already appear to be some use of this in which there would be frequencies put in the mouth to deaden the nerves, while medical or dental procedures are exacted on the body. These white lasers can be used to strengthen the body, and the fullness of vibration can restore the teeth. There seem to be a set of frequencies already used to build up bone in the body. We have it as a square patch. Replacement of little bits of sand and the vibration can be used on the body. It is usually used to deaden the pain, to have resonance with the nerve. But this technique can be used to restore and strengthen the teeth also. Some application is already being made. White laser also shined upon the teeth will help to remove bacteria and then the body can recover or build up the normal coating on the teeth, see?

Tinnitus

Would you please explain the cause of tinnitus, a loud ringing and/or clanging in the ear?

Basically, this is in conjunction with the lymphatic system. There is little attention paid to this process, this system, the lymph system, in conjunction with the anodes and lymph nodes. However, it must be understood that this, too, is an important elimination system within the body. For those who are unfamiliar, it would be tubes made of tissue in which mucous and toxins pass. Ultimately, they would empty into the intestinal tract and be eliminated from the body itself. The nodes or collection points (as you might call it) would be those places in which there is a degree of accumulation. Then, through the pulsation of these, with the natural bending and stretching of the body, these push the fluid downward into the intestine, again for elimination. Often, there is a lump in the mammary, or in the chest, or under the arm, and this is lanced. Here, the pus or mucous is alleviated from this point. However, as the body is in a more acidic state, and there are more toxins within the surface of the skin, this elimination system collects these toxins and eliminates them.

In the uppermost portions, in what is connected to the sinus and the inner ear, there is a degree of movement of fluid. Now, if you would take water and strike a tube in the water, while having an apparatus in the water for placing the head (if the water container was large enough within the water), specifically the ear, there would be heard much clearer the tone or the vibration through the water. For, you see, vibration travels through the water much better than it does air. As such, within the inner ear is fluid, as connections to the lymphatic. A blockage anywhere within the system - be it in the chest, or the throat, or upwards to the inner ear -the fluid tends to grind in the lymph nodes and anodes. This grinding could be heard within the inner ear, which is the sensitive portion of the ear itself.

Now, if there is congestion here within the ear, or at the base of the brain, then this, again, is amplified and the fluid moving or attempting to move through the system causes a ringing. For it is the perpetual vibration through friction means that causes this ringing, or clapping, or the sound of oceans, or the bell, or the hum within the ear. Massage of the lymphatic system or adjustment of the upper vertebrae in the neck tends to alleviate this. A combination of both, occasionally, is needed. But here, if the body would be cleansed through a cleansing of the large intestine, it would help, see. Yea, it would prevent the body from becoming over-toxified. But understand, if there are conditions in the lymphatics that are taxed, then surely the liver and the kidneys are taxed, see.

Travel Illnesses

Lately, large cruise ships have reported massive outbreaks of mystery diseases affecting almost all passengers, to the point that choosing a vacation on a cruise line is now laden with

risk. What is the mystery disease?

There is no mystery here. As these vessels or containers get larger and larger, as more and more of the population develop weakened immune systems, the design of the air systems here (internal air exchange, instead of bringing in fresh air) effectively means that the illness, or virus, or bacteria is now shared by all. If people spent weeks on an airplane, instead of hours, you would see the same result.

There has been anecdotal evidence that airplane travel is unhealthy for the human body either because of the electrical effect, or because of the poor air quality, or because of the proximity to radiation from space (or for reasons unknown). Please comment.

We will first assume you mean jet plane travel rather than slower plane or single prop engine plane travel, which is different, you see. For the higher altitudes obtained in jet flight, indeed, there are a variety of reasons for a concern here; but only for those who are frequent travelers, you see. Those who would be occasionally traveling in these devices would do so with some (let us say) stresses, but it would not be enduring.

First, it is and primarily the pressurization of the cabin of the plane that causes the effects that would be on the body. All other influences would be secondary. The recycled air within the cabin is, first of all, depleting of oxygen, if it is not supplemented, and this causes the traveler's oxygen in the blood to become depleted. This then allows acidic conditions in the body to increase and allows gases and substances to develop in the blood. It impairs the nervous system and, indeed, the voluntary and involuntary functions of the glands in the body itself.

However, it is primarily the stresses that are put on the body; increased pressurization of the atmosphere in the cabin. The movement through the air itself at five hundred miles an hour is also stressful, for this creates affects to the electrical-magnetical influences, or (as you would call it) the life force and aura about the body, for they stream out behind you as the plane would move through the atmosphere (or though the levels of resistance you might encounter, such as the magnetic fields of the Earth and other barriers).

The proximity to radiation from outer space (or the space that is above the cushioning or blanketing effect that the atmosphere provides) also can be of some concern. If there is sun spot activity, or if there are other gravitational disturbances or meteor showers, this can cause disruption, indeed, that the body would be influenced by. However, it is the altitude, the changes in breathing, and the air or gas that is given (the atmosphere, you see), that are the greatest hazards to the traveler.

Ultrasound

Is ultrasound a beneficial treatment for stiff joints and tendons?

Temporarily, it is, yes. Ultimately, if it would be maintained, it would prove to be detrimental. It causes a degree of activity in the circulation of blood within the joints and tendons.

When an ultrasound is done on a pregnant mother, does it cause any harm to the fetus?

It is shocking to the fetus. We find that the vibration, amplified by the liquid contents of the womb itself, causes some disturbing effects. It is like a bell being clanged up close to the ear. As to the physical effects, we do not find this being derogatory or dangerous, unless this would be repeated quickly. We do not find difficulty or damage to the fetus, although it can cause some shock or trauma, like any loud and suddenly-unexpected noise or sound. In some cases, there is difficulty in the eyes and in the ears, if there is direct application over these areas, causing some shrinkage of the membrane. However, generally speaking, there does not seem to be a derogatory effect, causing life to be threatened or diminished.

Vaccinations

In the period of the 1950s and 1960s, governments introduced into the population mass inoculations, initially against polio and, in later years, for many other things. Critics of these programs say that these vaccines contain unwelcome elements. Have these vaccination programs done any significant harm?

Humans (as you know humans) usually do the right thing, but for the wrong reasons. Why poison the body to start with? The body has its own mechanisms or capabilities for defense, and has (for all intents and purposes) the capabilities to ward off any and all diseases. When there is disharmony, when there is an invading force, or when there is an exposure to some disease, and the body is weakened, for whatever reason (which is a different question) then the body takes on the disease. The gateways to the body should be guarded always against the invasion of bacteria or virus. However, in a weakened state, the body becomes ill.

That which is injected directly into the bloodstream can be considered dangerous for several reasons.

One weakened disease, put into the body at any given time, can be addressed by the body. The notion that the body itself would prepare for a greater invasion or a stronger strain of the same disease does hold.

The question is that several diseases are implanted, or injected, or inoculated into the body at the same time. More horrifically, they are given to younger and younger individuals, even to infants whose nervous systems are not yet fully developed. No matter how weak the diseases might be, the combinations are rather extreme, and the body cannot handle the same! Disease hides out in the body, you know, in different soft tissues, building a nest.

To this end, we would find that, indeed, the manufacture of these diseases, if it is taken from an animal host, carries with it the vibration, the inferior aspects of the animal and this, indeed, inoculated or injected into a body can be considered quite disruptive to the entire immune system or to cells in the body. Why take from the animal kingdom that which would be crude and inject it into the human body, which would be refined? It can be, considered in its present form, disruptive.

Now, for those bodies that are healthy, that are strong, and the nervous systems are fully developed, this can be tolerated, and is often done so to great benefit (especially when one takes oneself into disease-infested areas, communities, or regions in the world) and therefore, there is merit.

Asking us to agree or disagree depends on the circumstance and the situation. But here (as we have given) generally speaking, the body is fully capable of preventing any invasion of disease through bacteria or viral conditions. Keeping the body strong, keeping the body slightly more alkaline than acidic usually is a good preventative. Now, understand when one moves from one region to a foreign region, then this would be a different condition in which the body might benefit by inoculation. But, generally speaking, that which has been given over time does not seem to have been perfected to work with the body.

But, indeed, through impatience, there seems to be several strains of bacteria or viruses given to the body - disease, if you will - that are supposed to strengthen the body. Why poison the body? Why put disease in the bloodstream? There is no conclusive expectation or prediction how these diseases function in any body, taking into consideration that some bodies are in different stages of development or in different levels of strength to ward off disease in the first place. ~~But~~ definitely, when disease is placed in the body, the body is altered, almost permanently (and it is weakened a great deal).

Varicose Veins

What could you recommend to remove varicose veins?

These tired veins themselves can be strengthened. This requires some exercising or some improvement in the veins themselves. You may take grapes (the concord variety) and put them in a fairly large plastic bag. Put the leg in the plastic bag as well, from the ankle to the knee. You may tape the bag at the ankle so that it will not leak. Then mush the grapes, seeds, skins and all into a pulp and allow this to be smeared onto (or surrounding) the leg. You would have a mixture of crushed grapes and liquid, that you would lay the leg into, front or back. Allow this to soak into the body for about fifteen to twenty minutes, and then you may do the other leg; although both may be done at the same time, if you prefer. It is a little messy, however the grape juice will affect the veins in the leg and cause them to shrink. This would be improving the circulation through the vein. Serrapeptase may be given which would likewise, subtly and with some patience, cause the remedy to occur in the shrinkage of the sediments and the varicose veins themselves would dissipate. Massaging the calf of the leg would help the veins to be strengthened as the muscle is strengthened. Try these alternatives and keep the circulation much more proficient.

Vertigo

Generally speaking, what is the cause of vertigo and what may be done to correct it?

There are various types of vertigo.The condition is a sense of imbalance or a sense of disorientation in the mind. It is an uncomfortable situation; it can be readily understood for many who experience the same. Those who become seasick for instance, are suffering motion vertigo. Those who fly in airplanes and have reduced oxygen have some form of oxygen deprivation vertigo. Those who are under the sea have pressures that can cause a disorientation which would be similar to vertigo.

As there is compression in the neck, especially in the atlas and axis vertebrae (or cervical vertebrae), this can restrict blood flow into the brain and this, too, would have the sensation of imbalance or vertigo. Conditions in the inner ear may also affect this. If there are infections, if there is a buildup of fluid, or if the lymphatic system is not draining properly in this region where balance is acquired or referenced, then there is a sense of disorientation and vertigo.

Understand that the brain itself requires blood, and when there is compression and the circulation in the neck is depressed, this causes a depletion or a restriction of blood flow into the brain, especially the areas of the controlling centers: the medulla and cerebellum. But also, it affects the registry or the nerve masses feeding the brain, in conjunction with the inner ear balance; as such, vertigo is exacted.

Therefore, in attempting to understand the condition, attempt to understand the variety of effects that produce the imbalance or sense of disorientation. Those who have a heart injury or suffer surgery feel or sense the room is spinning, yet they are motionless in bed. These sensations are caused by blood flow interruption, by nerve misinterpretation, by fluid imbalances caused by injury or disease (infection), temperature fluctuations or other forms of illness in the body. When there is improved blood flow, when there is reduction of congestion in the lymphatic system, or when there is a range of motion increased in turning the head left or right, up and down, these conditions can disappear.

Vertigo or dizziness starts slowly and then builds in the body. As the body ages, sediments and crystalline influences affix themselves to the vertebrae. As this occurs, then you can see restrictions in the body's function also must occur and, as such, the restriction in registration of balance, or the movement of fluids inside the head can cause this artificial disorientation. It is primarily a mechanical problem in the body, save for when there is infection in the lymphatic system, in the sinuses, in the ears, or even in the inner ear. This infection can be considered a disease causing the problem, which is simply causing the fluid not to move, to thicken, and therefore to be out of balance, out of equilibrium.

Remedying the body by removing disease allows the fluids to return to their normal balance or their normal movement in the body. Circulation and lymph circulation are similar. Nerve flow between the nerve endings is different. However, by increasing the liquid movements (fluid movements might be a better term), then the body balances itself. This can be done with medications or with other applications of herbs or inhalants to affect the reduction of the thickening of mucous in the lymphatic system and to speed up the circulation.

The circulation of blood in the body is another matter. One who would be skilled in the thing that could apply traction to the neck - massage techniques to the neck and shoulders - or that one who would use some range of movements to increase mobility in the head and neck, this, too, would improve, mechanically, the circulation and, therefore, the nerve activity (and, therefore, more oxygen being distributed in the brain). The body naturally resumes its balance point. When circulation is decreased, oxygen levels are lowered in the brain and this brings about a sense of dizziness and then vertigo and even unconsciousness or collapse takes place. These are the conditions of vertigo.

When it is not a disease in the body, it is usually a misalignment of the cervical or the cranium sitting upon the atlas and axis, a stretching of the brain stem. This creates a blood flow problem to the controlling centers in the brain, or pressures upon the arteries (more than the venous) that feed blood into the brain or into the cranium itself. These delicate arteries and circulating points within the brain, when there is depletion of circulation or oxygen, suffer the sensation of imbalance or vertigo.

Remedies for this, of course, vary from medical intervention through medicines, herbal extracts or vaporizers with medication (as we have given) to the mechanical manipulation of the cervical vertebrae, the muscles and, indirectly, the arteries. Special massage techniques with degrees of traction, rotation of the head left or right, up and down, affecting or moving the fascia under the skin or around the muscle, relaxing the muscles and tendons so that there is more of a perfect alignment and the brain stem or spine is not stretched (or at least there is a reduction of tension), all would prove to be along the way of correcting the body.

To the diet, foods that would be high in vitamins should be consumed, or vitamins that are obtained from the food through juicing. The higher the blood pressure, the more difficult and risky the circulation is in the brain. Celery juice taken in abundance would help to reduce the pressures of the blood in the head as well as the rest of the body. Any form of herb that would be a relaxant (like kava kava or slippery elm) would help to reduce the pressures in the body by reducing the stresses in the body.

Remember always: the mind is the builder, the mind is the way. When stress is brought into the life and maintained, then usually some form of vertigo will take place. Where there is a disorientation or dizziness, or where there is a complete imbalance to the point where one cannot stand up, sit up nor become ambulatory, it is the same. Vertigo, therefore, is a sense of imbalance and a loss of control of the balance and mobility of the body. On a lesser degree, it is a disorientation in which there is a physical sensation of movement even when there is none, and indeed there is a lack of coordination between the body and the mind. The body needs intervention, even to feel comfortable and to reduce the swimming or swirling sensation of the mind, in the body.

What we have given is temporal and preliminary; we have not examined other conditions that would be affected; for instance, growth, tumor, aneurysm, or other such physical ailments affecting the circulation in the brain, and the cramming of the space in the cavity where the brain resides. Nor have we examined injury to the head, which may also affect the nervous systems even to the central point of the corpus colossum. Brain injury, trauma, and buildup of fluid are exceptional to this preliminary discussion of vertigo. Influences of stress are much more severe and are the cause for many types of vertigo than we have described, you see. Meditation is most important, along with a better diet and a higher intake of vitamins, along with mechanical movement of the head in clockwise circles and anti-clockwise circles or even stretching the head away from the body by elongating the neck in a very simple traction movement.

Violet Ray Device

Could you comment on the violet ray device, which was recommended by Edgar Cayce and this Source in a number of readings?

The violet light has a tendency to remove influences that are adverse (or bacterial-building). It tends to eradicate upsetting bacteria or forces that would be derogatory to the cell level. It cleanses, so to speak. On one hand, it improves the atmosphere and the environment in which the injured or sick body would be found; and on the other, it tends to invigorate the body's life force directly at the cell level, thereby improving the vitality, improving the strengthening of the cell, improving the health of the body, you see. It does tend to affect the filament within the cell and bring it up to its more proper vibrating rate or level.

Now understand: this is a certain segment of the light spectrum. Lightning would be a much better source, or any spark gap generator, but still this is a good frequency range to affect cells, either by direct contact, or to be nearly rubbed over or passed over the cells. Those cells that are too high in their vibration are calmed down; those that are sluggish or low in the vibration are speeded up. Perfect vibrational rate equals perfect health at the cell level.

Again, this was mainly used as an antiseptic almost removing irritants, conditions of disease and impairment and disharmony; and, on the other, it was used as a direct boost or stimulation to the cell to bring it in line properly in its vibrational rate.

Viral, Bacterial and Fungal Conditions

AIDS, Herpes, SARS and related questions.

What substance is the best natural or plant-based ant-ifungal, anti-bacterial, and anti-parasitic?

Hydrogen peroxide.

What causes AIDS, and what is the best treatment?

Concerning the immune disorder itself, it is exactly that there is an effect on the immune system in which the body becomes weaker, and weaker, and weaker to what would be its own natural defense mechanisms to ward off those things that are taken into the body, whether it is food ingested into the body, whether it is water or liquids taken into the body, whether it is air or atmosphere that is taken into the body, or what would be the excretions of the body, or the exchange of body fluids left in cavities of the body; all the effects are the same, that there is a degree of waste or rejected material that the body does not need, and this is not completely removed from the body. The body, therefore, re-assimilates these waste materials that usually are on the subatomic, or the viral and bacterial levels. As the effect is seen in the body itself, the normal mechanisms within the body to ward off invading influences in the body are diminished to such a point that the body becomes defenseless. As the body is defenseless, any invading influence in the body takes over the physical body to a point at which the body can no longer function, and it is so taxed with inflammation and disease that the body capitulates or becomes so taxed that it cannot fight the battle again and it expires. This would be along the line of preliminary understanding of cause.

It comes from the combination of diseases mixed forming a hybrid disease which affects and has strength (if you will) over the immune system of bodies themselves, so much so that there is no antibody, no natural defense mechanism currently in most cases of what you would call AIDS itself. However the body is prepared. There are changes within the physical form and, through evolution, there will be a natural resistance builded up. Not all are affected by the viral activity itself. Some blood groups are more susceptible than others, you see.

As to the cure, putting more oxygen in the blood is good. This can be done by immersing the body in an atmospheric chamber in which there would be three or four atmospheric pressures imposed upon the body. This forces oxygen into the blood as the oxygen is pressurized by three or four atmospheric levels and is, therefore, forced while assimilated into the blood through the natural breathing mechanism, you see (and also through the body itself). This reinforces the body and allows the blood to begin to remove the sedentary forces, the derogatory forces, the diseasements or toxins in the body. The body itself should immediately be put on a detoxification diet. That is to say, all foods and herbs that would be known or geared toward blood cleansing, reduction of sedentary forces, reduction of toxic production in the blood. The body should be moved towards alkalinity (slightly more alkaline than acid, you see). For whether it is understood or not, each body swings between the acidic levels being higher back to the alkalinity levels being higher. If the body can be slightly more alkaline in its balance than acid, then it tends to improve the body's health. For no viral or mucous condition can exist in a body that is consistently slightly more alkaline than acidic.

The body should be given plenty of water and given plenty of foods that would stimulate the eliminations in the body; both the urinary tract as well as the physical congress. These would be the steps or the actions to take to help remove the onslaught of this (or any other) viral effect or attack in the body, from the common cold through to any disease that would attack or invade the body.

SARS, which almost shut down one of the largest cities in the world, is said to have migrated from animal to Man. Is this view correct?

This is not a natural evolution. This is a manmade virus, made in a lab, with the specific property of destroying lung tissue on contact.

Conventional understanding is that when a person is infected with the herpes virus, he or she can never eliminate it and is subject to outbreaks for the rest of the life. Can anything be done to relieve the symptoms or eliminate this virus from an infected body?

Indeed. Herpes and hepatitis would be of the same; different strains. However, combined, they are difficult in the body. Yes, indeed, they have outbreaks in the body. Because the body has initially the strength in the immune system to diminish any viral or infectious disease given to the body, provided the body is slightly more alkaline than acidic, no virus or bacteria influence can exist in the body. And therefore, firstly, with any diagnosis or understanding that this is in the body, the body should be maintained slightly more to the alkaline side of the balance. Litmus paper can determine if the body is slipping more to the acidic or maintaining more towards the alkaline. This is the first place to start. Keeping the body always on the alkaline side of the balance between the two, the body should be able to eradicate any viral condition in the host body.

That which is known as monolaurin may also be taken, for this affects bacterial and viral influences in the body without affecting the host body itself. This would be a spoonful of the crystalline substance, every other day, for a long period of time. Of course, one who would be skilled in the thing could be consulted to monitor and determine the dosage and the method of ingestion and the time it should be maintained.

Injectable vitamin C may be given to the body, or ascorbic acid may be taken, and ingested or drank as a fluid in the body. However, the injectable vitamin C would be tolerated by most (not all), and would immediately eradicate herpes or hepatitis virus in the body. It is largely used now to affect other diseases in the body as well, including those that are parasitic. However, maintaining the body strictly by diet, and diet alone, to keep it on the alkaline side should usually and consistently keep the body free from any disease of herpes or other viral or other bacterial influences. This is the place to start.

Acupuncture may be given to the body to stimulate the kidneys and to allow the kidneys to remove the poisons and toxins from the body more perfectly. Fasting is helpful as well, and the fasting would consist of plenty of water and plenty of vegetable juices. Therefore, it is not actually fasting by abstaining from food, but it is fasting by abstaining from solid food. The juices from the vegetables are much more potent and nutritious for the body than eating the vegetable in any other way (except, perhaps, raw). Lightly steamed is good. Boiled is good. But the juices would be the best of all. There cannot be any adulteration in the diet. It has to be strictly followed as primarily a vegetarian diet. However, fish, fowl or lamb may be taken, baked, boiled, or broiled. Avoid animal fat. If chicken is to be taken, then remove the skin. Just eat the meat in small amounts. The breast meats sliced in small, thin slices would be good.

Absolutely no carbonated drinks. If alcohol is to be taken into the body, then watch the alkaline-acidic balance very closely. A little red wine would be much healthier than a mixed drink with spirits and soda pop, see? This should remedy the body in a basic way. More use of those exercise vehicles like treadmills or bicycles can be used, but it would be beneficial not only to exercise the body inside, but most importantly, outside. Plenty of sun and fresh air, and give the body a good suntan. This helps with the vitamin D being absorbed into the body to affect the liver soft tissues (in removing the poisons from the same). The body should be washed occasionally, either through an enema program or colonic irrigation, on the inside, removing toxins and mucous conditions that tend to keep the body slightly towards the acidic side permanently.

The Peyer's Patch, that organ in the small intestine, should be stimulated by taking several oils that would be edible, and these would be beneficial to the body. Take many of the oils that are available, a spoonful or half a spoonful at a time. By taking these oils, a few drops under the tongue, or a spoonful during a meal, the body should be able to strengthen the immune system, by strengthening the Peyer's Patch.

Now, also electrical stimulation of static electricity is beneficial indirectly to the body, or the use of what would be the Violet Ray machine. Its glass tube would be filled with a gas that can be excited like argon or ozone, and then this applied to the body, over the area of the liver would be stimulating to the cells themselves. This, too, would strengthen the immune system.

Acupuncture being given to the body to stimulate the kidneys, the liver, and the large intestine or colon would also be a method that can be periodically given, once a week or once a month, that would help to maintain and improve the body to a point where it will recover from the viral or bacterial material.

Understand as the process now occurs, the body's immune system manages almost to eradicate the virus, but it hides out in the body. It has its own consciousness, and it hides in faraway places, nooks and crannies in the body. As the body become more acidic, this remnant strengthens itself in a new environment of acidic activity, and then it breaks out again. It is best to avoid the cycle by keeping the body alkaline, tanning the body, and not allowing those acidic influences, even slightly. It is crucial that the body stay on the alkaline side of the alkaline and acidic balance, see.

Of course, plenty of water and vitamins through vegetable juices can be given, but take care that the eliminations are always correct and improved. Sweat baths or fever baths may be given as well, and these would work well to eradicate the virus in the places, nooks and crannies in the body. Fever is good for the body. It is its own mechanism in getting rid of viral and bacterial disease in the body, see?

It has been discovered that certain bacteria and fungi produce a protective substance researchers have called biofilm that protects the invading organism somewhat like a turtle's shell. This is why fungal infections are extremely difficult to eliminate. How can fungal biofilm be dissolved or eliminated?

In essence, it would be with the herbal products or the vegetable juices. A body that is slightly more alkaline breaks down this sheltering effect, and no virus or bacteria can exist in a body that is slightly more alkaline than acidic. The acidic influences in the body bolster the disease in the body, and the protective environment in which it finds itself. Yes, you would call it a turtle's shell, or a cocoon, but the idea is that this is like any additional clothing put on a body; it insulates on the inside, and it resists penetration on the outside. The key here is to keep the body slightly more alkaline. As this is done, then the other influences in the body can eliminate the residence of the bacteria or virus itself.

Fungi in the body are, indeed, invading influences, like parasitic influences in the body. They can be eliminated at once if they, too, are surrounded so that they cannot expand their influence or to be tenacious in hooking into the body itself. The best at removing these from the body are vitamins and antioxidants. Light also affects these conditions. Like mushrooms growing in the darkness, when there is bright light or different kinds of light, this readily affects the fungi or the hooks (if you will) that allow them to tenaciously exist in the body. With light, it sort of dissolves or disintegrates their ability to hook into place. Understand that they hook themselves in certain places or environments, and without this stabilizing, hooking or attaching, they become free. Without support, they move through the body and are eliminated in the natural ways. This is the way to affect or remove fungi; not to allow them to attach in the body. See?

Antiseptics, or any form of unpasteurized honey, or any derivative of peroxide would be suitable for those fungi found topically. If there is difficulty on the skin, warts can be smeared over with fingernail polish, which would isolate them and cause the bacteria to suffocate. In the same way, honey (topically) causes fungi, or skin disease, or irritants in the skin to suffocate. The idea is not to allow the fungus to attach to the body; but if it does, to isolate it, and, topically, these things can be given. Internally, the vegetable juices would be the best at keeping the body more alkaline (as we have given).

Chitin forms a protective covering that protects certain organisms (such as fungi) from being eradicated by the body. What supplements or foods could a body consume to dissolve or inhibit the chitin?

We would suggest lentils and green vegetables such as cooked spinach or asparagus, and those nuts like the almond and other roasted nuts, rather than acidic fluids, which tend to amplify the condition or aid in the enduring of the protection. In addition, figs and dates could be taken to help the body in this regard.

Dr. Hulda Clark first developed and promulgated low-voltage products that send a current into the body, ostensibly to destroy parasites. It is known as a Zapper. Does it work?

Yes, these, even at low voltage, disrupt the life cycle of many parasites; not all parasites, not all areas of the body, but useful nonetheless.

Vitamins

Are vitamin supplements a good idea?

For those who do not have a proper diet, what would be the balanced diet, yes, they can be assimilated; but we would recommend a period or cycle: fourteen days utilizing the vitamins, the supplements, then leave off for three weeks. Then return and take for two weeks and then leave off again for three weeks. Let this cycle continue, for if you do not leave off, ultimately the body loses the ability to extract the vitamins to assimilate. Itself it would become wholly dependent upon the concentrated vitamin.

Of what value is vitamin C?

It affects, to some degree, the texture of the skin and also, to a degree, it reinforces the body as a preventative to mucous or virus conditions. It allows the body to be prevented from these states, for it causes some degree of alkaline conditions within the body (specifically speaking of the upper torso of the body, in the large organs, lungs and heart). This could be its benefits here.

Sometimes this source has recommended vitamin C, instead of a combination of baking soda and castor oil or olive oil. Vitamin C and baking soda are considered by some people to be opposites. Why is vitamin C just as effective in these combinations?

You assume it is for the same purpose, yet this is not correct, for the different uses are for different purposes. Both are an attempt to modify or affect the bacteria, or to alter, or change at the cell level. The sodium bicarbonate and castor oil mixture shrinks moles and cells by affecting the vibration and the filament in the cell that is already disruptive (the mole or the growth in the body). The vitamin C used is, in effect, to be corrosive to the cell, like dropping acid on the same. It is a different inference and it tends to affect the bacteria.

Vitamin C is now injected into bloodstreams, and it is effective in reducing bacteria; again, in a very harsh way, but it is very successful with herpes and hepatitis viruses; not so to other parts of the body. It does not corrode the arteries, or the veins, or the soft tissue organs in the body.

Again, different applications, for different reasons.

For those living in cold climates, up to what levels of vitamin D would be appropriate?

It depends on size and body weight, of course. But, for example, if there would be a unit that would be officially recommended as ten now, then that recommendation should be at least multiplied by five or six times to fifty or sixty.
[Note — the current U.S. RDA for Vitamin D is 600 IU. Dr Douglas seems to be saying that, if you live in a wintry climate, 3000 or 4000 IU is more correct. After reviewing papers on Vitamin D dating back to the 1960s suggesting that, when taken for short periods, daily doses up to 10,000 IU produced many benefits with no side effects.]

Is it correct to say that vitamin D acts more like a hormone or timing mechanism?

This would be somewhat correct. It does affect the nerve system directly in repairing the nerve sheath or "skin of the nerve" as you would call it, and it does improve the electrical-magnetical impulses, or ability to transmit along the lines of the nerve communications. And, on occasion, it can be used to repair severed or damaged nerves, you see, along with vitamin E.

You have suggested that vitamin D supplements (in pill or oil form) by themselves are not effective unless there is also exposure to sunlight. Could you please clarify?

Let us add that it is not as effective as what would be given from the sun. It is, to some degree, effective, but it is not derogatory to the body. Therefore, that which is taken in, in tablet form, is like a featherweight; it is inconsequential to the body. See?

Liposomal vitamin C is a product where ascorbic acid is blended with soy lecithin in an ultrasonic cleaner. Of what benefit is this?

The combination is assimilated into the body without causing certain stresses or distress to the assimilative tissue in the lining of the stomach, nor any disruption in the bloodstream as it is assimilated. See? This particular vitamin combination allows it to be assimilated rather rapidly. This would be the main benefit. Secondarily, the taste seems to be pleasing and not offensive. And finally there is the complete digestion of the combination of items. See?

Water

It is suggested that the tap water in many areas is actually better for the body than bottled water, because bottled water sits without protection, exposed to sunlight for long periods of time. Is tap water, in fact, better than bottled water?

It depends upon the area in the world you are speaking of (the tap water being delivered). If water is moving through the natural filtration of the Earth (that which is found in fountains, for instance) then this type of tap water is usually pure or easy to assimilate; it is called "soft water" or easy to assimilate. Water from the tap in some regions in the world has fluoride and other things added, especially if it has gone through a filtration plant, where it has been reclaimed from sewage and recycled back into the system as drinking water. This might be considered "hard water."

Water all over the world is different. It is important that when one moves into a region or vicinity, as soon as possible they start to assimilate the water of the region or the area they have now resided in. This is beneficial to the body, and it acclimates the cells in the body to the region or area. This should be considered in the question.

However, bottled water is stagnant water. It does not have the movement, the filtration, or what would be the oxygen content, and, indeed, as it is exposed to light and other elements, those systems within (those microbes or small life forms) can develop and be unpleasant. If one would take a bottle of water that has been sealed and put it on a shelf and leave it for some time, over time, there would be seen some derogatory effect, or the water would be called stale. Understand oxygen is most important to be high in water, even though it is made from, in part, oxygen itself.

It depends upon the region you speak of, for tap water in Italy is different than Germany, Germany is different from Argentina, Argentina is different from Canada, or America. Bottled water, if it is fresh, if it is bottled and consumed shortly after, then it would pose no threat. But usually bottled water can be considered not as good as water from a fountain. Water from the tap, if it has been given fluoride or other treatments, can be considered less than the fountain, and less than the bottled. It is a complicated perspective you have given us to examine.

If you are looking for a rule of thumb: bottled water, if it is taken and fresh, then it seems to be a good substitute. If it sits on shelves and it is taken from long distances away, then it tends to diminish in its value. However, water is better to be taken this way than none at all. See? For water hydrates the body and allows the function of the body to occur.

It is believed by some that long-term drinking of pure, steam-distilled water, since it is devoid of minerals, will leach minerals out of the body. Is there truth to this?

We do not see this as a reverse-osmosis (so to speak). We see it as long-term drinking of water that is void of minerals is not supplying the body with new minerals, or the new vibration that the body would attain from the water. For understand, water is a multi-influential thing; it is a liquid, yes, but it carries certain frequencies, vibrations, substances (like minerals) into the body. It also performs, in a transfer of building up the body, the ability to remove things as it absorbs, or is given those things that need to be removed from the body, through urinary function. See? Therefore, it goes through some changes in the body already.

What is the best method for the average person to make sea water drinkable?

Simple evaporation techniques. Let the water evaporate, and then reclaim the water by cooling through a tube. The sun's energy can be used to heat up the water or to cause it to move into vapor, then the vapor into a condensing tube, then into a retainer again. It does not seem to be the best method, but a simple one, you see.

Could you please comment on a device known as the Wellness Filter and the claims that it can purify water?

The device itself does affect the water. The intention of moving water through various substances does indeed affect the water itself. Like a babbling brook, it would cause the water to run over many levels of stones. As it would descend from one height to another, the water is cleansed. The cleansing of the water is simply the separation of unwanted elements and the intention to be pure or closer to the element that would make up the liquid itself (hydrogen and oxygen, you see).

As such, the condition in the particular device is not only to remove certain elements and change the structure from removing, perhaps, imperfect water elements; then it would be to attempt to add to the structure those elements that would be reabsorbed and then, of course, taken into the human body. The device is complex. There is some benefit to the extraction of dirty particles (if you will) and the adaptation of some particles that would be mineralized into the water itself.

Hunzaland (near India) is one of a few areas in the world where people enjoy great longevity. The inventor of the Wellness Filter attempted to have this device mimic the water from Hunzaland. As you see it, did he succeed?

As we have already given, there is a certain effect of water moving downhill over various elements that causes the water itself to change. The water in this particular region has been influenced by the geographical location in which it is located (as would food and vegetables, you see). Mimicking this, in some small way, the answer is affirmative. Mimicking it exactly, the answer is not at all.

One cannot take geographical locations and transport them in small containers and expect to have the same geophysical effects, gravitational effects, air and water pressure, the movement through various salts, minerals, earth, and so on. For water travels great distances under the ground before it is brought to the surface and, as such, has many things affect it. However this would be, to a small degree, attempting to compare a forest fire and a match.

Kangen water is an alkaline, iodized, antioxidant water produced by a device made by Enagic Inc, of Japan. If one were to drink this regularly, would it help with colon regularity issues?

It is not necessary. It is always better to consume food and water that is of the vicinity in which the body resides. This might be of some value, occasionally - once a year - for it is better to consume a little of everything than to pay attention to a few (or a limited amount of) things.

Can you recommend a source of alkaline water or a device which would make regular drinking water alkaline?

It is best to use those substances that are found in nature. Sodium bicarbonate would be effective. Add this to water, mix and then assimilate. This would be the fastest way for the body to acquire a higher level of alkalinity. However, by taking vegetables or vegetable juices - those that are the freshest variety and grown in the vicinity in which the body resides - this would allow a steady and dynamic incline towards high alkalinity in the body itself. Mineral water found in natural sources would be effective also.

There are very few converters of water to alkalinity; however, there are some that would remove the acidic levels in the body. This would be through osmosis (even reverse osmosis, you see) or other forms of removing sediments and chemicals from the water itself. This would lead to the preferred neutrality of the water. This would revert the water back to its original state, away from the acidic levels. Any acidic level being neutralized or reverted would make the end result better or preferred. In attempting to remove acidic conditions in the body, it is basically attempting to counteract the acidic with a base itself.

However, we find that water that would be tumbling down a small waterfall - it could be an artificial one with a tray of rocks, and the water would enter from the top and bubble down to the bottom - this would appear to change the structure of the water and allow it to be more acid-depleted and the alkalinity levels would be higher. Otherwise, it is necessary to put something in the water, to change the consistency.

If the water is from certain areas that have a reputation for alkalinity, or there are high minerals or sea salt deposits nearby, this would work or function correctly. Otherwise, there is very little that can change the water structure or content.

Wheat

Please comment on whether wheat is something that is beneficial to the average person, or should be avoided.

As it would be unadulterated wheat, not made into a hybrid, wheat in itself can be tolerated by many who ingest the same. The problem occurs when there is manufacturing or adulteration of the wheat, either in the style and manner of the wheat as a seed, or the wheat being adulterated with preservatives and other chemical treatments, see? You might call it processing. As such, generally speaking, wheat in itself is digestible. It is acceptable to some in various forms (usually in powder). For the general public, depending on the constitution, the work activity (whether one is sedentary or active), this should be somewhat considered and evaluated before it is taken into the body arbitrarily.

Therefore, in answering the question, wheat can be avoided by those who have difficult assimilations and digestive processes in the body, or those who have a sedentary function or job in their life or daily career. Otherwise, it is active [in the] stomach, can be taken and maintained.

Wheat Grass Juice

What is the benefit for the average body of taking in wheat grass juice?

It depends if it is dried or fresh. If it is dried, it can be less beneficial. If it is made from fast-frozen or fresh wheat grass, then there is no mold or mildew on the same, and it has the benefit of improving the stomach. It can be seen as a food to the intestine, and the chlorophyll has a tendency to be given in large amounts in this manner or way. It tends to allow the body to open up its ability for more oxygen assimilation through the intestine, through the bloodline itself. What is put in the intestine is assimilated into the blood. This also has the benefit to migrate through the intestine and remove sedentary forces in a beneficial way, you see. That which is in the intestine can be considered as progressive and favorable to growing good bacteria within the intestine itself.

However, the primary benefit or purpose would be seen to remove irritants and to fight off bacterial and viral influences in the intestine, while at the same time allowing the body to be more vitalized.

Wine

Is red wine better than white wine?

Red wine is good for the blood and tends to enrich the blood and aid it to be builded. In this regard, yes, it is better than white. It depends on the body, for all are not the same. Some tolerate red wine and it would be as food to the body. It is a matter of histamines in the wine itself. The effect usually is to act as a suppressant, or tonic, or tranquilizer and, indeed, envelope the systems of digestion and elimination by increasing the production of bile in the system. For the wine in the red affects the pancreas, thyroid and, in turn, the bile to be secreted.

White wine would act similarly in the body of others, or what would tolerate the same; this would be in a lesser group than those in the red. Again it depends also on the carbonation introduced in the wine, if it would be more sugary or less sugary, or sour, for these would have an affect upon the pancreas as well.

Therefore what would be - let us say - base red wine would be seen as invigorating to the body and act as a blood builder, or would influence the blood to reproduce itself. It would thin the blood a little, ease the movement of blood through the body, and affect the production of cells in the long bones of the body. For an optimum, it should be sipped and be room temperature for this form of ingestion or intent in the body.

White wine, on occasion, is somewhat devoid of the production or influences of bile production in the body and, therefore, it can be seen as a little more acidic to the body; but it can, in some bodies, affect the physical metabolism the same as red. However, for part of the understanding, it is the lack of, or change of histamines in the body of the liquid itself and, to some degree, the positive or constructive influences, since nutrients in the white wine have been removed that would be body-building (or blood-building more exactly) as the red wine would be, you see.

Wrinkles

Can wrinkles on the skin be lessened?

Yes. Good blood supply to the surface or skin is essential. Keep the body moving or exercising, keep the blood pressure up and then allow it to lower. When doing exercise, or when there is physical stress to the body (work or exercise is the same, you see) then the body is resilient. The tissues do not lose their elasticity, and the blood goes through the body, flushing through even to the smallest arteries that would be located in the surfaces of the skin. This renewed and invigorating blood supply to these areas invigorates and enlivens the skin and the body not only has good elasticity in the skin tissues, in the muscles themselves, and in the underlying areas of tissue, it has good blood supply (as the arteries themselves expand and contract) and this flexibility is the basis for all good health and for all good circulation. See?

Yes, the systems in the body can be provoked, but it is largely due to keeping the body flexible, keeping the body's heat rising and falling, and keeping the blood supply to the smallest capillary or artery possible in the body; by increasing the internal pressures through exercise, or work, or some other form of movement, it forces the blood through this. This keeps the skin clean, the blood supply balanced through the body, and, as such, there is not a condition of difficulty or impairment; but rather there is a harmony. See?

Many people in our society are using diluted botulism toxin for cosmetic reasons to reduce the look of wrinkles. What percentage of the overall population is likely to react negatively to this?

The body immediately sets out to remove the botulism or the toxic substance and, depending on the vitality of the body, it can be slower or longer in its removal of the same. However, the body is immediately under stress, and this causes stresses to occur in the soft tissue muscles of the body, including the heart as well as the kidney, the spleen and the liver, you see. If it is builded up in the body then, of course, over a period of time, it would be like any poison taken into the body, slowly causing the body to deteriorate, lose its vitality and then its resistance to fight off other diseases in the body or (more exactly) invading forces; viruses, as well as bacteria, you see. If it is a little in the body, the body may accept it. If it is constantly done for longer periods of time, it can cause the body to lose the ability to fight off bronchial and mucous conditions, you see.

X-rays

Do the scanning or X-ray units which are now used at airports pose significant risk to health?

Of course! They add to the radiation to the body. The risk is not significant, in that the body will be deteriorating (where the body is traumatized, you might say). But depending on the amount of X-ray exposure, the body becomes impaired - specifically, the endocrine system itself, or the ductless glands and (to some degree) the nervous systems (central as well as sympathetic and parasympathetic), in the respiratory areas, and the reproductive centers, depending upon the frequency (or use of the same).

In other words, if one flies annually, it is not so affective. But if one flies several times, and is exposed to this invasive trauma to the body, then, of course, it would be more. It depends on the dosage of the investigative intensity of the ray, and the amount of exposure, you see. Then it might be considered significant. But even once would be invasive or intrusive in the body.

**Note: Atomidine is a registered trademark relating to a retail iodine product allegedly based on a specific electro-chemical preparation method given by Edgar Cayce in a number of readings. Several years ago, a controversy arose. An A.R.E. member took it upon himself to replicate and utilize the equipment suggested by Cayce, and found that the end-product did not look or taste like the retail products bearing said trademark. The individual in question then proceeded to offer his own version of "detoxified iodine," made in small batches, and strictly following the original formulation. Generally, all mentions in this book of "Atomidine" are references to the original Cayce formulation, as confirmed in a reading by Douglas James Cottrell. - R.A.*

CONCLUSION
LOOKING FORWARD: A PREDICTION OF HEALTH IN THE FUTURE

In the year 2112, will the people of the future still struggle with illness and disease as today?

We would find there would still be some disruption in the physical form, if this is the question. As there would be the frailty of the human body, there will constantly be those things that would plague the body.

However, to understand it, there would be different procedures. There would be more use of light and light therapy. There would be the use of concentrated light and concentrated water, that these might be used like a scalpel to remove tissues like skin tags, or warts, or things like that. Temperature therapy will be used as well; high fever baths will be used to remove bacteria in the body, and cold packs or rooms will be used to repair damage to internal organs. There will be the use of vibration contained in metallurgy or items in which the organs will be affected to their proper vibrational rate. This will be shared with others who practice the same technique. See? The use of these forms of therapy will be temperature, light, and the understanding of frequency.

There will be various understandings that the cells in the body vibrate at a certain rate or frequency, and there will be, again, knowledge on how to affect the vibrational rate at the cell level. Therefore, their techniques in dealing with the body will be somewhat different, as they will attempt to understand the body at the cell level, including the certain primary systems: breathing, ingesting food, and elimination. And in particular, there will be great care in the preparation of food and the assimilation of the same. Therefore, what will be done is that small amounts of food, rather than larger amounts of food, will be taken into the body as a course, to keep the body happy, successful, or healthy. Instead of three meals, perhaps one, or a combination of smaller meals, four to five a day, meaning eating only a little, and allowing this amount to be sufficient for a shorter period of time. There will be more of a hunter-gatherer diet, rather than prepared foods now, and foods would be prepared in communities - one big pot for everyone, so to speak.

There will be a difference in living together that would allow the health of the body to be more sustained, as the implements would be such that the organs of the body would be made strong, and, if surgery is needed, it would be accomplished or done in such a way to repair the body and to speed up the healing process, by understanding the frequencies of the cells affected, in regeneration of skin, or muscle, and even bone. The very low vibrations, you see, would cause bone to grow, and the very high vibrations would cause tissue to deteriorate. There will be a good understanding of this!

There will be much more use of vitamins and the understanding of the benefits of each. New vitamins will be found. They will be assigned numbers rather than letters. Food intake will be seen as medicine or body-building. There will be less in the way of food eaten for enjoyment or pleasure.

Water will be of a major concern indeed. The lack of it and the quality of it, you see, will be the focus of the concern.

There will be a great conquering of the small worlds, the micro-worlds, and the influence of those disruptive viral and mucous conditions. There will be found on the subatomic level the key to what is actually beneficial and body-building. Life spans will increase.

The future lies in understanding frequencies and how they affect the physical body, both adversely and constructively. Ultimately, when aging cells slow down, they will be boosted or amplified, and the body will be able to maintain a youthful ideal or appearance. The understanding of the body as a complex, multi-leveled being will also be more readily understood. Nurturing of the spiritual, mental, physical, and emotional (even financial) levels will be of consideration here.

Doctors would not be as you would now understand them. They would rather be advisors, although there will still be surgeons and those who would repair broken bodies that are ill and/or injured. However, the use of the same would be done in accordance with a new understanding of how cells multiply; how frequency or light upon the body can bring cells back to a normal state or health; and how other aspects of light can affect the body to remove unwanted parts like warts or body hair.

The genetic makeup would be such that there would be a lot of pre-selection of the conditions of the physical body. This would be maintained during the gestation period and after the birth as well.

Light will be seen, as will music, as great healing tools. The scalpel will be made of different metals but will be still seen as a scalpel, yet acting via light that would be considered both magnetic and anti-magnetic. That is, the body would be opened with one frequency, and sealed by the opposite or reverse frequency. There will not be needle and thread, like is presently seen, or the use of metal clips or staples. The body would be able to heal and repatriate itself rather quickly.

When science can finally understand the subatomic world, Man will be able to understand how two physical masses can seemingly occupy the same physical space at the same time. They will understand why the coffee cup sits on top of the table, instead of migrating and passing through the table; for both are, indeed, not solid at the subatomic levels. Understanding how they stay apart and not merge with one another will be the great invention, the great discovery.

What lies ahead in the field of healing?

Whereas most research today is directed towards the tiny world, and there is some understanding of gravity; and some understanding of frequency; and some understanding of the shorter waves; presently there is a notion that they are destructive; but, to the contrary, there will be discovered these waves which - originally considered capable of causing only death - will, in fact, be able to generate life. It is the intensity, and the duration, and the vehicle by which they are directed to locations within the human body that ultimately brings about the positive result. The investigation will be into the effect of the subatomic modalities, triggered largely because of military interest but, in the end, the very same research will be used for humanitarian interests, as we see it.

How will diets of the future differ from today?

They will eat foods specifically for themselves, relating to their type of body, their blood type, and what is beneficial to them, in such a way that they will eat highly nutritious food to build up the body and to maintain the body. They will not eat food for recreational reasons or purposes, although they would certainly have social activities in which food would be prominent or present. The diets would be more natural (shall we call it) eating the foods that would be grown in the regions or vicinity in which the body resides. However, it would be the combinations that would be acceptable.

How effective will the medical technology be in bringing about what at this time would be called a miracle; for example re-growing lost hair, replacing lost or damaged teeth, or curing conditions suffered since birth?

They will understand how to make the vibration of the cell speed up or slow down. This will be the basic premise or understanding in how to accomplish these major improvements in the physical body.

This Source has predicted that, in the future, the use of poisons to attack cancer (such as chemotherapy) will be completely abandoned in favor of a new mode of treatment. What will that new mode likely be?

It would be to treat the body with oxygen, with light, with frequency, and the understanding of how the body handles parasites within the same and, therefore, how to void the body through proper eliminations in all systems of elimination; physical congress, the urinary tract, perspiration of the skin, the exhalation of the breath, and through the proper mechanisms of meditation. For whether it is understood or not (or whether it is believed or not) the mind is the builder. The mind is the way. The emotions are both the constructive and destructive forces in the body.

As Mankind starts to understand the power of its own mind, then there can be the

teaching of how to use the mind to overcome disease (or, more exactly, how not to allow disease to become part of the body) as well as the attitude, as well as the emotional and mental states. For you will find great sickness, great plagues, principally and historically appear after great political, economic, and social distresses, you see. When the mind is happy or content, the body is reinforced, and its susceptibility to virus and mucous conditions is lowered. When anger, hatred, worry, stress come into the body, the body naturally is under duress and is susceptible to disease within.

The single-most important medicine of the future will be in how to have the mind so that the mood of the body will be constructive; and by that we mean how the mind will be in control, and how the mind will be taught to be in control so the mental natures and the emotional states would become constructive. Stress must be counteracted with play.

In the future, one will seek employment through vocations that are like play; something one truly loves to do. Contentment will come from the simple things of life, and there will be a return to the simple aspects of agricultural-type life. But there will be the assurances of information delivered to the household without restriction. There will be sources of power that will heat and cool the house without great expenses, and the production of food would, indeed, be more prominent, for the planet itself is quite able to feed all the people on it (and more so, each and every day). Understand that the planet produces all that everyone on the planet could possibly want.

APPENDIX
THE MIND'S EYE VIEW: SAMPLE D.T.M. HEALTH READINGS

The following are transcripts of Deep Trance Meditation (D.T.M.) health readings given by Douglas James Cottrell for a actual clients. We offer this selection of transcripts for their informational value only and they should be used in a reasonable and practical manner. They should not be relied upon as a medical authority. In order to protect client privacy, names and other personal information has been removed from the transcripts. Transcripts have been edited for length and ease of reading.

SAMPLE ONE

Deep Trance Meditation Health Reading
Date: August 20, 2008
Subject: "Michael"

Please go over his physical form, examining it thoroughly and identifying any disease conditions that you find, giving causes and recommendations for treatment.

As we would examine the physical form, we are aware also of the mental and emotional states within this entity. We would find that the mind is quite intelligent, and the entity has degrees of ability. We would also find that there is an impairment within the physical form that would be the cause of the physical and mental conditions within the body, that would stem from the glandular functions within the body itself. Understand that physical conditions in the body are the end result of those things that are held in the mind; what the mind constantly dwells upon, the body ultimately takes the shape, or becomes what was held in the mind. Understand the emotional states are both the constructive and destructive forces in this (or any) body.

With this understanding then, it would be to organically look at the body and indicate some imperfections or difficulties, but always to bear in mind that the attitude, the realm of concentration or contemplation held in the mind is the key to relieving what, in a chain reaction, occurs in the organic or physical form as that end result.

Now, it is such that the body has some impairments within the spinal column, in the lower end, or the lumbar and sacrum areas (low portion of the spine). There is some compression and deterioration taking place here; some sediment or crystalline forces building up, and some bone loss or (as you would call it) wear and tear taking place in this lower end of the body. The posture and inactivity of the body, or the weakening of the body is the cause. The body is rusting a little, if we can use that term, as is the mind. The entity would find conditions of impairment starting or commencing in this, the spinal compression or subluxation, so to speak, in the vertebrae, affecting the nervous systems that would radiate inward and outward or upward to the body itself. This would be the central nervous system, and also what would relate higher in the body (the parasympathetic and sympathetic systems).

Here, there is real difficulty in the lower end of the body, and it is affecting the nerve systems that would control and assist the reproductive areas of the body and also the elimination systems in the body. As this is impaired, and these systems are not functioning correctly, it allows certain degrees of toxins and poisons to remain within the body, where they should otherwise have been eliminated, and these substances circulate within the body, debilitating the physical form or making it susceptible to disease to form in the body. As such, this causes the body to lose its strength and there is a depletion of oxygen in the blood, bringing about a certain fatigue in the body and listlessness.

Now, as the toxins build up in the body, it affects the thinking; it clouds the thinking. Headaches or disturbances in the head can be found emanating or commencing from here, the small and large intestine regions of the body. Combined with poor elimination and, as such, poor kidney function, these toxins are allowed to maintain some presence in the physical form.

Now, there are other conditions in the spine, in what would be between the shoulder-blades in the fourth, fifth and seventh dorsal, and what would be slightly higher: the upper back and base of the neck. We find some rather severe compression in the third cervical, and some difficulty in the atlas and axis (the upper part as of the neck). A degree of traction, or manipulation, or massage, or even head and neck rolls - rotating the head in large circles around the shoulders and chest, clockwise six times, anti-clockwise another six times, and repeating this a time or two, or even three times (as a cycle in the day) - would be most helpful in improving specifically circulation into the brain. This would allow more oxygen to be circulated into the brain, and when accompanied with any exertion or even breathing exercises, more blood with more oxygen in the blood would be transferred into the upper part of the body (the brain) and extending to the tissues and glands in the head itself - pineal, pituitary, affecting the thalamus and hypothalamus, and also the motor skill regions of the body, the medulla and cerebellum. Blood flow increase between the two hemispheres, in the corpus colossum, would be most helpful in that this would bring some balance between these two rational and creative aspects of the brain, or the intellectual thinking and even to the spiritual or intuitive thinking.

Now, the entity is somewhat susceptible to the mental and emotional states of others; he can absorb the same, or become aware of the same, and mistakenly identify those mental and emotional conditions of others as part of himself, when, in fact, he is simply being telepathic, or sympathetic, or clairsentient towards these emanations (emissions from others, you see). As such, to be aware of this, then the entity can understand that, on occasion, some of the influences upon himself may not come from within, but may simply be what he is getting in touch with intuitively, and they may come from far away, or very close-at-hand influences.

That said, manipulation of the spine by the osteopath, or chiropractor, or one who would be skilled in shiatsu, or rolfing, or other forms of deep massage would be most helpful in restoring, firstly, communication that radiates around the body to the organs themselves, or systems, and what would be the upper part (the brain itself). As we have given, the body's posture and, indeed, physical exertion need to be improved. Now, with manipulation of the spine, this would be very helpful as it would pinpoint the affected or weak areas of the body. Building them up would be a little more strenuous than a quick trip to a masseuse, or chiropractor, or osteopath, or one who would perform specialized massage, like shiatsu or other forms of relief in this regard. Acupuncture would be of considerable help to the body. Within the first three visits, we would find the greatest improvement to take place; thereafter it would be more like maintenance. But with any form of this therapy or improvement to the nervous system, the spine, and the energy lines upon the body, the entity would respond quite quickly.

But thereafter, the entity would need to maintain a form of exercise or exertion. This would be affecting the body organically or at the physical level, and the influences would be transferred up-line or they would go the mental and emotional states, and this is where the greater healing would occur. But the body must engage at this, the lower level, first. The idea is to increase the oxygen in the blood, and to improve eliminations in the physical form. These two factors will alter the entity's condition dramatically and quickly. But it will take some tenacity and some discipline to maintain a routine to accomplish this. It can be done, and the entity's life will be greatly improved.

To start with, any form of exercise that the entity would engage in would be helpful; even walking around the block, or walking and trotting a little, or moving the body in any way that it can would be helpful. Now, there might be some debilitation, or some lack of movement, or being uncomfortable, but the entity can, in any way, improve its condition by movement.

In the beginning, there was the Word, and the Word went out throughout all the Universe. This vibration caused movement to occur in all things of physical matter. This movement can be termed life in the physical form or in the physical world (as you would know it), and therefore, the kinship with any condition, any form, any improvement to any organic being is to move. Lack of movement, and decay sets in. Increase movement, and health is provoked. Therefore, any exercise that the entity can accomplish would be of great benefit. As they say in flying airplanes, "little moves on the inside make big moves on the outside." So it is within the physical form or body.

Movement, walking or increasing the heart rate in any way that the self can accomplish this would be of great benefit and would be a blessing to the physical self. Understand all things start with the self, all things are a result of what the self does or does not. Understand there is both the sin of commission, and the sin of omission, and the sin means simply being off the mark or out of harmony with the self and the life. By asking the questions, the entity is attempting to regain that center point, to regain that health within the physical form, and therefore, the entity is not lost, nor would he continue to be lost, even though it might seem to be a sea of despair. He is reaching out for that life buoy, that life jacket, and is willing to do so (as we see it) to improve the self, commencing with saving the self. For when one is in the sea, the first person they must save is themselves, in order that they might save others, so that a greater thing than themselves may occur. The entity has the wherewithal to improve the self, but it begins right now, this moment, this day. By choosing to do so, the self has already began to recover from what has led it astray.

Understand that engaging in exercise or movement of the body is the place to start and it will cause many systems in the body to improve, to increase their function and organically strengthen the physical form. This, in turn, will bring some degree of enthusiasm back into the physical, mental, emotional states that will pull the self up by the bootstraps, so to speak, and allow the self to walk tall, to have a good sense of esteem, and to keep the self out of those shady realms in which the mind would be fogged with all sorts of influences. In other words, the self will find its way out of the forest, and into the valley of plenty; from darkness, to beauty. But it begins with this moment and this time, and with a degree of discipline or self-determination; not knowing what the end might be, but at least moving towards some profitability, or some change that would lead to profitability or newness. Now, simply put, isometric exercises, pushing the hands together, would be a place to start. Then, attempt to, with the hands at the side, reach up to the ceiling and attempt to stretch the body all the way up to the ceiling while holding the feet firmly on the floor. Then, push the feet as if trying to push them through the floor. Then, using isometric exercises, the self will feel the heart rate increase, and then walking around the room very slowly, slowly indeed will also assist in bringing the heart rate up and the body's temperature will increase. This will then provide exercise or stimulation from the inside-out. The body's natural functions to eliminate would be increased as well.

Now, in order to facilitate this, more water should be taken into the body; about four quarts a day. This would be the amount of liquid total; of this, teas can be made, juices may be made, and, as such, the volume would remain about four quarts, but it would be varied throughout the day. This would be most helpful, as it would hydrate the body and allow the carrier (the water or liquid in the body) to remove the poisons and toxins that are within the body, and would necessarily be required to leave the body by this therapy or practice. Early in the morning, drink as much water as can be taken. If a quart can be consumed, so be it. If not a whole quart, then as much as possible. Green tea or teas that would be flavored, or teas that would be herbal, that the entity would prefer would be suitable. Burdock root, bayberry leaf, raspberry tea, cherry teas, green leaf teas, spearmint teas, all would be good. Chamomile, sassafras tea, all would be good. The best would be those herbs that would have spikes or would appear to be a little furry on their leaves or stems. That would be good. Even dandelion tea would be helpful here. These would have a tendency to provoke the body in removing the toxins and sediments from within the blood and within the kidneys and bladder. It would also help to remove the edema or fluid condition in the lungs.

The physical movement, exercise, or manipulation of the spine by one who would be skilled in the thing, and the body, within three weeks, would be greatly different than it is now. The entity should consider those exercises that are Eastern in nature, for any who engage in this form of exercise would first challenge the mind, and as the mind is brought around in control, the body naturally follows. Now, this form of exercise can be in increments; the self can see improvements that the body would be accomplishing each and every day. Do not overdo it, or be in a hurry, but go through the process of these stretching exercises and see how the body responds.

Then, the body should be outside at least a good portion of the day, to tan the body; not to avoid the sun, nor to fear it, but welcome its healing forces. For it is good for the body to have a good tan. Avoid the direct sunlight between the eleventh hour in the a.m. and the second hour in the afternoon, but before that or after that time, do welcome the sun upon the body. Use coconut oil or cream as a sunscreen, but try to tan the body as quickly as possible. This will, with huge amounts of vitamin D being produced in the body, lift up the spirit of the self from within and there would be less and less of these depressive thoughts, or these victimized thoughts, or these thoughts of self-condemnation.

Drink of the teas, and tan the body, as well as increase the breathing and the physical movement in the body, even if it starts with a slight routine. But keep it up each and every day, and the body will become stronger and stronger, each and every day noticeably, you see. Ultimately there will be a shift or change in the physical appearance of the self that would be for the better.

As for foods to be taken in, let it be of the fish, fowl, or lamb, baked, boiled, or broiled. Of the vegetables, let it be two of the green, leafy variety, and one of the bean or the pod, and one that would be from below the ground. They should be of the freshest variety and grown in the vicinity or region in which the body resides. Eat of these four vegetables each and every day. The dark, green leafy vegetables are very helpful for the self with iron that would stimulate the blood. Eat mostly of the colored vegetables; what would be orange, green, yellow, purple. Avoid what would be white vegetables (although the cauliflower would be good).

We would suggest at least once in a while that the apples would be eaten for three days. Only the apples. You may eat them any way you wish: sliced, diced, or made into mush, or eaten from the core, but eat as much of the apple as you would care to. On the first day, take a large spoonful of the olive oil, and the same on the second, but on the third day, perhaps an ounce, or two to three spoonfuls would be good. Drink plenty of fresh water, or water that is alkaline, for alkaline water is very healthful to this body (and, indeed, others). The apples will act as a catalyst with the kidney and aid to remove sediment from the blood. The urine will be cloudy, indicating that sediment is leaving the body (as this would be evidence to the body, you see).

As the body would remove from itself alcohol, caffeine, and sugars (or sugar from the sugar bowl), the body's metabolism will balance, or come to a more balanced position, and not feel a weight or a burden that would be upon itself. The metabolism will actually speed up. Now, you may add into this grape seed extract to be taken before a meal, or at least once a day, and two ounces of grape juice mixed with two ounces of water, sipped slowly before food is taken in.

Avoiding greasy foods and deep-fried foods, eating more of the steamed foods, or baked, broiled, or boiled foods, the entity would do well. Avoid shellfish and those that would be considered fish that would crawl on the bottom of the ocean. Eat of the fishes that would have gills, scales, and fins; this would be true fish, and the others are not true fish. As such, the seafood would be helpful and restorative.

Avoid table salt, but take into the self salt from the sea; what is cakey salt, as it might be considered; salt that cakes and does not run free.

This would be the place to start, taking into the self sufficient liquid to flush out the system, keeping the body regular. If there is any constipation present in the body, then take a spoonful of olive oil, or those foods that may cause the self to void the body more correctly (as pears or watermelon might). We would suggest that the entity consider eating foods of the same family, per meal. If you eat melons, have a whole meal of them, but do not mix melons with other foods. If you would eat salad, then have a whole meal of salads; oil and vinegar would be good toppings.

Eat of the watermelon, as much as possible; as a whole meal would be, you see. his would be helpful in cooling the bowel and preventing any spastic activity here, but also aiding in flushing it out.

Citrus with citrus, berries with berries, grapes as a snack.

Now, the entity would require more zinc in the diet, and we would find that the almond would be a good source here, if not supplements.

When the mind begins to worry and become agitated, take of the slippery elm as a tea or a supplement. This would coat the stomach, reducing the amount of digestive fluid secretions in the stomach, and thereby not to affect what would be in the small intestine (the bile production) to increase.

There are impairments within the thyroid and pancreas. The sea salt, or more iodine in the diet (kelp would be a good source of this) can be taken. The iodine would affect the conditions in the body and make the body more active and enthusiastic.

Now, kava kava may be taken also as a source, as a tea or supplement, to bring the body more in line with feeling positive or enthusiastic. Do not take foods that suppress or depress the body, but take those foods that are uplifting and beneficial. Always pray before food is taken into the body, for this has a subtle and profound effect upon the self from the inside-out.

Chickpeas, okra, peas and green beans are good. Avoid the brown beans if possible. Have a favorite soup and enjoy a bowl of soup at least once a week, if not every day. Avoid the breads, save for what might come as a round, dark rye bread in a paper bag. All other breads in plastic should be avoided (especially the white variety, you see).

Of the seeds, let it be of the sesame seed, the poppy seed, the turnip seed and watermelon seeds may be taken as a snack or as what would improve the body. This would be the place to start.

The self might engage in an enema program to improve eliminations. Take three enemas, one after the other, massaging the left side of the abdomen the first time, the middle-upper abdomen the second enema, and the right and lower-right side of the abdomen the third enema, one right after the other. This would help to remove what is sluggish in the colon, and, as such, this would be a refreshing feeling, you see. As it would be wise to wash the body on the outside, it is imperative that the body should be washed occasionally on the inside. If this would be done occasionally, this would be quite exhilarating and advantageous to the physical health, you see.

There is more that could be given as the body would progress. We would suggest serraflazyme to help remove the plaque and/or sediment in the blood, you see; a sort of chemical chelation. Intravenous or chelation through an IV drip could also be given to the body and would be very helpful, especially in removing sediment in the brain, as well as other parts of the body, reducing extra or heavy metal saturation in the tissues.

We would suggest the supplement nitrogen oxide, or systems that would have such; these are supplements available, as we see. This would help to remove congestion and improve neuropathway communication in the body, also aiding in removing some of the plaque conditions in the brain and elsewhere in the body, you see.

With this, the body should be in good condition organically. But what would be most helpful would be to engage in those things that would bring some enthusiasm into the life. Now, at first, one would need to take a phone book, go to the pages that would have all the activities that one could engage in - fitness clubs, scuba-diving schools, tennis schools, archery classes, baseball or soccer schools - and look around to see in what age bracket they would provide, or have for the self. Then, do one of these that you would find (and there are quite a variety, as we would see) from fishing, to rowing, or motor-boat activity, sailing activity, through to investigations of animals, and observations of birds, through to motor sport, racetrack, dogs and horses, dancing classes, exercise classes, sports classes and clubs; there are many to choose from. Try one that would appeal to the self. Even considering flying lessons, or at least a free lesson to see if the self would like it! This would take some motivation, some determination, but it starts with the selection process. Observe the many opportunities of the many things that are taking place, and then do something. And when you find something you are enthusiastic about, know that this enthusiasm is the weather vane, is the compass needle point, is your direction finder (so to speak). And herein, the self may engage in these forms of activities that will build up the enthusiasm.

Now, small accomplishments are necessary for the self to feel purpose or to feel accomplishment, to feel good about the self. But in order to feel good about the self, something has to be done, and what we are proposing here is a way to initiate this process. It is not the end of the road; it is simply the beginning, and when one begins anything, there is always a little unsuredness, a little indecision, a little informality, and the self is uninformed or unfamiliar. Give the self the expectation of having no solid expectations to start. Simply, take a class in something, learn about something, or do something that is fun or is exciting (or at least entertaining). This, then, leads to the next step; not to judge the self and not to simply dismiss things. If you listen, people will offer, and you should take them up and accept their offer. If someone says, "Would you like to go for a boat ride?" then go for a boat ride. Do not say, "No I've done that before. It's not too exciting." If someone says, "Let's go for a drink. There's a favorite tea or juice bar nearby," then do not dismiss it. Go and have a drink, a tea, an ice cream, a treat for the self, you see. The world is filled with activity.

The mind, when it is focused on a single concern, problem, challenge, difficulty, or regret (or even self-condemnation or self-admonishment) it is like putting dark glasses over the eyes, and trying to see the beautiful vista in front of the self. It makes it difficult, does it not? Take off the glasses, see the world on its own terms. You will feel quite satisfied when you overcome the difficulties and challenges that the self may come into. If you wish to be a strong person physically, you must work the body and build up the body by lifting heavy weights, and doing ever-increasing, more difficult exercises. The idea is the more difficult the exercise, the more challenging lifting of the weights might be, the stronger the body gets. Therefore, it is part and parcel of life. The challenges, decisions, and difficulties are put in front of the self to make the self stronger. When a problem or challenge is put in front of the self, handling it right away (after some prudent consideration as to what to do) makes the self stronger and stronger. The idea that the judgment of the self is the key that delineates just how important or how great the self is (or, more exactly, how capable the self might achieve some form of accomplishment or greatness), it allows the self to have a good pride for the self that is justly earned.

For it is decisions and judgment that are always faced in life, with the alternative of prosperity or non-prosperity. As one learns from decisions that are erroneous or mistakes (and any who refuse to make mistakes are indicating they are refusing to learn, you see), the self, by being willing to make mistakes, is willing to learn. And by doing so, every time a mistake is made, and the self says to the self, "That's one more lesson we have gained towards our ultimate success." But sooner or later, if you make all the mistakes in the book, then you will know the true way, the only way for success; and by repeating that only way, you cannot help but be successful.

However, finding this way of being successful in anything you choose takes a little time. And for the self, learning to be patient is, indeed, one of the spiritual lessons that will bring the self to a point of greatness; of self-esteem, yes, but of understanding just who and what the self is; for this, after all, is the reason the self is in the present predicament that it finds itself.

As the mind changes, as the thinking, attitude, and routine changes each day, the life is certain to change. It starts with the will, and the self, by asking these questions, has already started. Most importantly, it takes a degree of activity to bring about the ultimate reward. Some might say to the fireplace, "Give me heat, and then I'll give you wood." Of course, they will never get heat by saying or doing this. But if they say to the fireplace, "I now have the proper equipment to get what I ultimately desire (which would be heat), then it is up to me to fetch the wood, prepare the fireplace, and light the match, and, therefore, light the fireplace fuel or wood, and I will automatically receive my reward, which would be heat and comfort." Such is life.

Prepare to take a trip on an airplane for a vacation. What are the steps that the self must take? First, decide where the self is going to go. Then, what airplane is going to take it. Then, what hotel is going to provide accommodation. Then, what luggage container will be used. Then, what clothing and personal items will be put into the luggage (always bearing in mind what will be needed at that point on vacation, or that destination point, and then, providing a few extra things just in case). Then, the ticket must be purchased (if not already). Then, transportation to the airport must occur. Then, going through the airport with all its confusion, and its uncertainty, and the struggle to go from the front door or the parking lot to the door of the airplane. It can be trying or stressful. But, indeed, all the steps taken must be taken in their sequence and order, for one cannot do something out of order and expect to have a good vacation. One cannot send their luggage ahead, or ask that their luggage be sent later. They must take their luggage with them, and, therefore, they must tote the luggage themselves. They must take every step singularly themselves.

Such is life. All things in life must be taken one step at a time, and the self must take those steps, in the right order and without fail and it must be always to the completed end. Then, the self will arrive at where the self wishes to be. Begin right now, at this moment, deciding where the self would wish to be next week, next month, next year, and then do everything in your power to make those things come true. Continue to take the steps every day.

What we have given would be beneficial organically. What we have also given is to prepare the mind and the spiritual aspects of the self to have the wherewithal to engage in the proper order; those steps that will lead the life to being changed for the better, and the self to be, indeed, a contributing light in the world itself. But begin by finding something that increases the enthusiasm within the self. Begin by understanding that loving the self is most important. For if you do not love the self, then others will not love the self either. For they would simply answer the prayer of self; for what you think about is, indeed, what you pray about, for prayer and thinking are but the same thing - contemplation of some future inevitability. Therefore, change the thinking. Think of the self as having good things, and contemplate the good things within the self. What is it that the self has above all things that is good? Do not concentrate on the imperfections of the self, but concentrate on the inevitable genius, or blessing, or ability of the self.

Usually humans (as you know humans) discount the genius, the greatness, the beneficial aspects of themselves and tend to concentrate on some minor flaw in themselves. Learning how to reverse this line of thinking takes some effort, but in doing so, it allows the self to tolerate the imperfections of the self while amplifying the strengths and the capabilities of the self, which is how everything else in nature seems to work. This will then open the door to the spiritual aspects of the self, and you will become determined and self-sufficient, and you will indeed be on the path again to becoming a true human being; not to pity the self, but to praise the self, and then you would be willing to engage life on its own terms, for you will have found some respect for the self; you will be able to understand (as all great men have) that they have imperfections and weaknesses, but so does everything and everyone else have such. It is the human condition. But they also have, with some minor flaws or imperfections, some perfection within the self. And concentrating on that, and that alone, will change how the self feels about the self this minute, this hour, this day, this week, this year. For if you study anyone who is great, who has achieved much in the world, you will find they have this one unerring quality: they accept themselves with all their limitations, as they are. But they also have one thing that they do extremely well, and that one thing is the source of their sustaining life, their essence for life; indeed, that which allows them to enjoy their life.

When a mind is powerful and has creative tendencies, it can go in several directions, but no one can take a trip, go on a vacation, and go to several destinations at the same time. One can only go in one direction, and have one destination, and must do everything in their power to get to that destination, before they might move on to another destination, or a third or fourth one. Order of events. One step at a time.

The self can overcome the inadequacies or weaknesses in the self by amplifying the strengths that are abundantly evident within the self, but it starts with determination that the self is going to do this. And then it does not stop there; the self takes the action and does what is needed to be done. One step at a time, even if it is baby steps to start, the self has now veered off from the inevitable result of falling into a pit of despair. Instead, self, by taking a tiny variance and improving itself, even in the smallest degree, will, in time, be miles and miles away from what might have been. Now, the self is in the light, and has greatly improved its life, even by taking a small step. For if you understand a compass, if you take one step to the left or the right of the path that is in front of you, in a short time, by that a few degrees of change, the self will be greatly advanced from where it was. Such is this time in the life. Such is this, the aspects of having plenty at the fingertips of self.

All that is needed is to do something, and it starts by saying, "You know, we have a few problems, but we also have a few advantages." Take stock of the self. Talk to the self in such a way to always amplify the goodness, the benefits, the strengths, and those things that come easy to the self. Take advantage of them. Be willing always to love the self and to forgive the self, for when you make a mistake, say simply, "We must be getting one step closer to success! God bless us." And then forgive the self for making the mistake. But understand, it is the human way. Trial and error at life is the only way to live the life. Do the things that bring enjoyment to the life. Avoid the things that are vexatious or derogatory in the life, and you will find you will be amplifying your free will and free choice, and you will find yourself closer and closer to those things that bring all aspects of God into the life: health, wealth, and peace of mind.

SAMPLE TWO

Deep Trance Meditation Health Reading
Date: May 9, 2005
Subject: "Jackie"

What is the most important thing I need to know about my health, right now?

There are some points within the physical body that could use attention. To the spinal column, we would find some compressive forces within the lumbar. These would be expressing some difficulty through the nerve activity, but they are minor here. They are affecting the bladder. They are affecting blood supply through the reproductive centers (shall we call it) and there is some degree of difficulty (although minor) within the lower leg. Blood supply to the limbs could be improved here. There is some difficulty in the neck, which relates to some sluggish activity in the lymphatic system and the drainage through the cheek, jaw and throat. Manipulation of the spine, here, or the neck - more specifically in the third and last cervical - would be helpful in improving lymphatic secretions or movement here.

The heart is good. There is tension held across the chest or diaphragm itself, and a mild degree of stiffness or difficulty in the smaller joints of the body. In what would be helpful in, indeed, improving the systems within the body would be to effect some manipulation of the spine by the osteopath or the chiropractor, and, indeed, to engage in some form of massage that would stimulate blood flow through the spinal region, especially in the lower portion or girdle of the back, and extending into the legs and even to the feet themselves. The oils would be a combination of castor oil, peanut oil, and camphor oil. The castor and peanut would be one part each; the camphor would be one-quarter part to one-third part. This would heat up the areas, as the oils would be massaged into the same, but it would be primarily to remove and lubricate; removing degrees of sediment and irritation, or even inflammation, you see; and, indeed, to the lower part, or the peanut oil and the spine itself in the lower end, to enhance the lubricating forces here. As this would be done, the nerve flows to those centers would be improved. Blood supply to the bone also would be improved, and while there appear to be some weakness or thinness to the bone in the body, these particular forces - increasing the blood flow and the nerve activity - would enhance the body indirectly.

The grape fruit seed extract can be taken to help to remove degrees of mucous in the body (or infections, for that matter). The bayberry leaf tea may be used as a tonic throughout the entirety of the body. As the bones would strengthen, they would need to be, first of all, challenged or some degree of strength-building (so to speak), especially with the legs. There could be simple weights put on the feet (or weighted shoes) and some support behind the knee, or in a sitting position, the lower legs lifted. There could be also stamping or bouncing on the legs as well. This may, if done to excess, be somewhat irritating to the hip. Therefore, the bouncing or stepping should not be too severe, but rather slow and rhythmical. This would send vibrational aspects or frequency through the bone, which would cause the bone to strengthen or grow; but, in particular, the movement up and down would affect the circulation in the lower part or the trunk of the body, which improves those organs within the body, including the kidneys, bladder and liver, you see.

In what would be also taken to affect or improve some activity in the liver (to remove any irritation), a little Coca-Cola syrup, one-quarter spoonful to one-half spoonful, may be added to warm water and taken - not too warm, not too cool. This would, as a preventative, remove irritation in this, the urinary tract itself. As there would be examination, here, we find some difficulty in digestive juices as well that would be somewhat irritating to the lower stomach or duodenum. This is inconsistent in the body, and, as such, what would be helpful would be flushing the intestine, occasionally, with chlorophyll, or wheat grass juice. Best ingested from the frozen, rather than the dried, you see. This would repair and restore degrees of bacteria in the small intestine, but more exactly, it would dilute and remove the irritations from increased amounts of secretion here. The slippery elm herb can be taken as a tea, and this, too, would help the body rest or enter states of sleep.

The body is in very good condition. There are some weaknesses in the bone (as we see it), and there is sluggish activity in the lymphatic system. Therefore, entire body massage would be helpful, here, from the head to the toe. One who would be skilled in lymph drainage techniques could be utilized, specifically. However others who would be simply skilled in the same could do the massaging. Use mineral oil or Johnson's baby oil, you see. This should be given after the body has been in a steam room, warm shower, or bath, so that the pores are open. The oil will penetrate into the body and, indeed, more oil if the body is heated, as we have suggested; and, as such, the oil will affect, directly, the arteries in the body itself, making them elastic or flexible.

There is some plaque or some residue on the heart, in the upper portion of the same, and the artery that would be ascending towards the neck the same. The serraflazyme may be taken to remove these sediments, or plaque, that would be found in the smaller arteries, you see, especially in the coronary aspects of the heart.

The heart is in good condition; the beating is somewhat regular; a little skip here and there. The pressures in the first dorsal (or top of the back) are causing this mild condition of arrhythmia. Any manipulation or correction here, in the upper back (movement of the spine, you see) would relieve the pressures on this, the central nervous system and the sympathetic and parasympathetic systems as well. These would affect the lungs and heart and would be beneficial.

As to the teeth and the jaw, there can be the use of the prickly ash bark or Ipsab that would be put on the gum itself. This would help to remove inflammation and, indeed tighten, or strengthen the jaw and gum itself, you see. If there are irritations in the mouth, then a simple solution of hydrogen peroxide (food grade, three to four per cent) can be utilized, either directly, or it can be diluted fifty percent (or one part peroxide and one part water). Then, take a brush, and this would be scrubbed or brushed on the gum itself. This would remove bacteria in the mouth and, indeed, would strengthen the area of the gum itself. This would be done periodically, but as it would be done, the entirety of the mouth would be improved; but not to do this too much; once in a while would be sufficient.

I am presently having problems with the bone marrow and plasma. Is this a life-threatening situation?

Not at this time. There is some concern. What we have given would be an affect to cleanse the blood or to remove the sedentary forces. In attempting to address this as life-threatening, while there is concern, here, that this may get out of hand, we do not see this developing. Instead, the degrees of anxiety, or to the mental and emotional states - and understand the emotions are both the constructive and destructive forces in the body - the emotional aspects taken towards hopefulness and the reduction of fear that is surrounding the mind would directly relate to this condition being lessened.

We would find that oxygen in the body, oxygen in the blood, the increase of oxygen in the corpuscle, would tend to settle the body down. What we have given so far would be a cleansing of the blood itself. As we specifically look towards the marrow and the attempt to strengthen the bone, as given by these bone-strengthening exercises, this would indirectly have an effect upon the bone itself, especially in the leg, that would be positive and remove any threat.

The kava kava, as an herb or tea, may be given, and the apricot seed or apricot extract from the seed can be given, and this should quell the condition in the body. We do not see it as life-threatening; we see the self being a very sensitive soul indeed; and, indeed, one that is intellectually, as well as emotionally advanced, tending to absorb these anxieties or fears that surround the mind and absorb them into the body. In this, the almond, the avocado, and the apricot taken - especially the apricot - would be very helpful in reducing the rapid or (shall we say) expanding growth of the cells.

T-cell production is good. Recognition of irritation in the body is taking place. Also here, this would be attempting to keep the body slightly more alkaline, in eating those foods that are alkaline-producing. Any chart that would show the difference between acidic and alkaline foods could be found. Eat mostly, if not all, from the alkaline side.

Indeed, two other treatments may be given; you may put the self in what would be a barometric pressure chamber - one that is used by scuba divers, you see - and they would increase the atmospheric pressure one or two times. This would flush the body and increase the amount of oxygen in the blood, and it would be seen as a blessing, here. These radicals within the blood would be suppressed or eliminated. We would also find that the body should be heated, and, indeed, if the condition persists in the body, hyperthermia as a treatment could be given to the entire body. This would raise the temperature to about forty-six degrees Celsius inside the body. This should remedy and remove any viral effect; for this particular condition can be viewed as a virus, you see. Otherwise, the body may be put temporarily in steam cabinets and, indeed, the body may be heated up to fever level: one hundred and five to one hundred and eight degrees Fahrenheit. This would not cause the body any harm; it would not cook the brain or affect any of the soft tissue. What it would do, however, is increase the blood flow through the dilation of the artery, and it would inhibit any further growth of any viral or disease in the body.

SAMPLE THREE

Deep Trance Meditation Health Reading
Date: April 1, 2008
Subject: "Jason"

Please examine the physical form and indicate any problematic conditions in the digestive, respiratory, and elimination systems.

As we would examine the body, we would find that there are some conditions that would be evident in the skeletal system that are affecting the glandular system and the area of the elimination systems or glands, as has been directed. You will find that within the body itself there are degrees of impairment that could be altered or corrected that would improve elimination; and as the body itself would remove the toxins or irritants in the blood, the entire benefit would be seen in the body.

As such, there should be sought the osteopath or the chiropractor, for we find difficulties in the low spine, predominantly in the lumbar region, fourth to sixth. These are compressive forces and the bones themselves are somewhat rotated or out of alignment here. There is also some fusing taking place here, or what would be stiffness in the lumbar, which we see also has extended naturally into the sacrum. The coccyx itself is somewhat off to the side or slightly out of true alignment to the vertical line of the spine itself (or plumb, you might say). This is indicating some irritation, but not extensively, to the reproductive centers themselves.

The manipulation of the coccyx could take place with the internal adjustment, but we would find there should be the manipulation of the lumbar, and exercises and massage or what would be a certain degree of attempt to free up the movement in the lumbar with heating pads, bottles or infrared light. The osteopath or chiropractor would manipulate the bones, but prior to that, we would suggest the castor oil pack to the body; taking castor oil, warming it, putting it into a cloth (flannel or cotton would be good), and then in a strip or a line, from along the spine or pelvis to the curvature or - you might call this - the saddle or small of the back. Place the castor oil pack and allow the oil to soak into the body. Now, a piece of plastic or towel may be placed under the body, as the body would lay on its front while the oil and pack would be applied to the upper or top of the body on the back or spine region. On top of this, a piece of plastic may be put and the body can be kept warm with a blanket, or flannel sheet, or terry cloth towel, you see. On top of this, a heating pad may be applied or hot water bottle, and the heat would allow the oil to penetrate deeper into the body, and this would affect the spine in this general region.

This would help to remove any inflammatory condition in the bone or around the vertebrae, and, to some degree, it would assist in removing the uric crystalline forces that are somewhat evident in the area, although they would be seen more in the lower portion or the legs themselves. Sometimes sciatic pain or twinge in the body can be caused by the misalignment of the coccyx, but it can be also the pelvis being tilted. As there would be more perfect alignment in the lumbar, there would be more perfect alignment in the pelvis, and any twinge or nerve contraction resulting in contraction in the leg would be eased with this simple process of the oil penetrating into the body; the heat allowing the muscles and the surrounding tissues, sheath, sinews to expand or relax (or align more directly) in their normal state. Any mechanical manipulation with massage or adjustment to the lumbar would be enhancing or speeding up the process of perfect alignment.

Now this would then allow nerve flow through the sympathetic and parasympathetic nerve systems and into the central nervous system as well. For we find there is also some condition of impairment between the shoulder-blades, at the fourth, fifth, sixth, and twelfth dorsal and higher in the neck as well, at the third cervical and at the fifth. Manipulation in these areas should also be attempted or accomplished. In any event, manipulation to the lower area of the body or spine would be the place to start. This would allow improvement to nerve flows and nerve controllability to the organs.

Taken into the body grape juice two ounces, mixed with two ounces of water, sipped slowly before food is ingested would assist the process; first the thyroid, and then the pancreas, and then the bile to be secreted into the intestinal tract. With improved nerve flow or function, and with bile secretion being enhanced or improved, elimination (physical congress) should be accomplished much easier and naturally in the body. However, should there be constipation present in the body, or only partial elimination, and the body is not completely eliminating the full amount, take a little olive oil from the spoon; one half a spoon to one spoonful would be sufficient, prior to retiring for the evening. This would also affect a softening condition in the stool of the intestine or the stool, and it would allow the improvement, as elimination, in a natural way.

Now in the blood we would find some toxic substances, and the body should avoid polluting the blood, or taking into itself those substances that would be adverse to the body. Carbonated drinks should be avoided. Sugar from the sugar bowl should be avoided. Any icing sugar on donuts, cakes, other pastry should be avoided. Although food has sugar within it, attempt to eat food that is low in sugar, and also those foods that are low in preservatives, for preservatives that have been added to bread, cakes and other forms of food are somewhat difficult for this body to digest, and they do adhere to the cells in the body, causing certain degrees of difficulty in the mass of the cell or the body, you see. Therefore, eliminating these would be directly helpful, first to the cell, then to the elimination systems, then to the health of the body in general.

Eat rather of the vegetable juices and of the vegetable for this would help the body gain strength and improve the health and longevity of the body. There are fatty tissues at the heart and fatty tissues in the small intestine. We would encourage the entity not to combine too many vegetables, but attempt to have vegetables of the same family; although there can be added the carrot and cabbage juices - two ounces each - and this would give massive amounts of vitamins to the body.

Other foods: gelatin may be added or given, and this would act as a catalyst or an improvement to absorption of the vitamins, or assimilation of vitamins, you see. We would find that this would be most helpful for the body.

Although fatty substances are digested correctly, attempt to avoid too much of the product from the cow. Cheeses, ice creams and milks from the cow should be kept to a minimum or very small amounts, otherwise they tend to produce mucous in the body.

Attempt to speed up the elimination process. The body should be hydrated or given plenty of water. Amount that would be normal for this body would be about a liter of water per day. If the entity can consume almost a liter of water in the morning, as best as can be done (for it would be difficult to engage in this, but as much as can be taken in the morning), prior to taking anything else into the body, this would help to flush the esophagus, stomach, and help to eliminate food sluggishness in the digestive process. It would cleanse, as well as give a medium acting with the kidneys, you see, to remove the sediments and toxins from the blood.

Caffeine is acceptable, but we would suggest it be kept to a minimum. Again, soda drinks or carbonated drinks, pop or other sodas, should be avoided. Alcohol should be kept to a minimum in the body. Beer that is commercially available should be avoided, or at least kept to a minimum. It would be better to drink of the wine itself; a little red wine would not hurt, taken with some dark rye bread here. This would actually add as a blood-building food to the body, but avoid the chemically-laden beers. If there is beer that is more natural, or without too many chemical additives, then it might be tolerable in the body, you see. But all other aspects in moderation here.

However, as to the meats, they should be of the fish, the fowl and the lamb, baked, boiled, or broiled. Leave off from the hog, for all aspects of the hog would be detrimental, save for a little crisp bacon from time to time. Kelp and sea salt should be taken in the body, but table salt that is largely commercially available should be avoided. Better to eat of the salt that cakes up, than what runs freely, you see.

We would find that the exercises in the body should be body-specific, looking towards the middle part of the body, especially what would be twisting the body like a corkscrew, side-to-side, and bending and flexing the middle part of the body. With the body standing, attempt to touch the head to the knee, so to speak. With the body on its back, bring the knees up to the chest, rock back and forth on the spine as if the spine would be a rocking chair, you see. These simple exercises will manipulate the spine, will affect the spinal nerve conditions, and will also affect mechanically the intestinal organs and the elimination systems in the body.

We would suggest this entity consume the raw apple for three days, taking plenty of water - eight to ten large cups - each day, and a little olive oil on the first and second day (about a spoonful), and on the third day, a large amount (an ounce) of the olive oil itself. The apples will act as a cleansing agent and a catalyst here, in assisting with the kidneys in removing toxins from the blood. This should be done periodically, at least annually; but two to three times or four times a year (quarterly, you see) would be an abundance of this. But whenever the self would engage in this would be sufficient.

To cleanse the system of the skin itself, which is an organ that detoxifies or eliminates, it would be best to place the body in a steam bath; wet heat, rather than dry heat. Saunas should be avoided, but, if necessary, utilized; but the steam bath would be best. The body should be scraped with an implement, a good scrubbing brush with soft bristles, or a metal implement that would be like a hoop. Once the body is thoroughly heated and the body is perspiring, only then should there be some scraping or brushing of the body. Then the body should be rinsed or perspiration washed from the body; for in doing this, great amounts of toxins will be exited from the body. The body has some susceptibility to irritations, or viruses, or bacteria, fungus, you see. As such, scraping the body in such a way from head to toe or scrubbing it while it is still warm and perspiring would be most soothing and beneficial.

Here, upon the spine, and also extending to the arteries in the body, mineral oil should be liberally massaged upon the body; that is to say, massaged into the body, wiped upon the body, so to speak, and then attempt to be smeared throughout the general areas so that the oil will soak into the pores and into the body, and have an effect upon the arteries in a stretching or resilient way upon the arteries itself.

Now, as the body would improve eliminations by taking into itself large amounts of water, as it would take into itself the grape juice (which would assist in the production of bile in the intestine), and as eliminations are generally improved throughout, the body will greatly improve in its health. You will find it will not be so tired, or shortness of breath would be reduced; for the oxygen content in the blood would be increased or heightened, you see.

Vitamins in the B category - B12 especially, but all of the B vitamins - should be taken into the body in a supplement form, or those foods should be ingested that would be high in production of vitamins that would include the B vitamin. For this one, okra, chick peas (even what would be made into hummus or ground peas) and dates or figs can be taken and would be helpful to the body in building it, or allowing eliminations to improve, at the same time assisting the body.

Thereafter the body might engage in experimenting with different types of food by engaging in mono meals; taking a single food like sweet potatoes and eating them as a meal; on other occasions, a meal of onions, so to speak, cooked, sautéed, or whatever the entity would wish to engage in as the preparation method. Not that this would be as a way or style, but it would be for the entity to eat those foods, and then there would be a determination made as to which foods would be strengthening or body-building, and which foods would be seen as tiring or - let us say - debilitating. We suggest this, for the entity should eat lettuces, especially the dark green variety, and they may be made into puree or chopped, diced, or made into salads; whatever he would wish or prefer. But in such a way by eating foods in a mono or singular way, the entity can right away determine what is enthusiastically desired or taken in, and what should be avoided or refrained in the diet.

What we have given so far is simple, but important. The drinking of water that would be slightly more alkaline than other types of water would be the better type, and would assist the body. Give the body the medium of water to remove the irritations that are in the system at present. Flush the body with either enemas or the colonic. Cleansing the body on the inside, you see, is just as important as washing the body on the outside. If enema therapy is given, then it should be done three enemas, one after the other. This would affect the lower, middle, and upper colon, and this would be beneficial to be done at least once a year, or periodically, as the self would determine.

The benefits of massage, especially to the feet and lower limbs would be readily seen. Use the combination of peanut and castor oil (one ounce each), a little lanolin (about one-quarter ounce), witch hazel or Absorbine Jr. (one for the astringent, and one for the heating effects; these may be added individually or combined, about one-eighth ounce each, you see). If camphor oil is available, add a little of this, about one-eighth of an ounce as well. If it is not, the wintergreen or Absorbine Jr. would suffice. Give the body a good, brisk massage so that the skin would be a little reddened in color, or the blood would be circulating to the surface; this would be a frictional massage. But the oil should be massaged into the joints, especially the folds of the legs or the hips.

This should remedy the body, per the direction we have been given: to examine the middle part of the body that would be in our examination, to the intestinal tract, the organs or glands of the body, touching upon the bladder, the liver, the intestine and, to some degree, the reproductive centers (although not extensively). Manipulation of the spine by the osteopath or chiropractor would heighten the body, improve the desire in the body, as well as eliminations and posture of the body. The entity should have good shoes with good arch support; this would help from the heels right up to the neck itself. Traction or manipulation in the neck - that is to say, some simple stretching of the neck by pulling the head away from the shoulders gently - and gentle massage of the shoulders and neck would be very soothing to the entity. But keeping the body's posture as correct as possible would be most important, and there would be reduction of headaches or difficulties. These come from the posture, but also from the congestion and poor eliminations in the body. Again, so go the eliminations of the body being regular and complete, so goes the health of the body. For what is taken in, the pollutants and toxins, are readily rejected (the waste material), and the body is invigorated. Any form of isometric or stretching and bending exercise - yoga and tai chi - would be most helpful, and it should be done at least once a day, every day.

There is more here that could be given, but we would find this would be sufficient. The eyesight would improve and nasal congestion would also be improved from what we have given or touched upon.

SAMPLE FOUR

Deep Trance Meditation Health Reading
Date: May 8, 2005
Subject: "Patricia"

With respect to my current physical body, are there health issues that need attention?

There are some concerns within the form itself. In the upper portion, paying attention to the spinal column, there would be a degree of difficulty located here, in the middle portion, the third to fifth dorsal. These are placing pressures upon the sympathetic and parasympathetic nervous systems, readily affecting the right side of the body: the neck, shoulder and shoulder-blade, but also what would be the soft tissue, extending into the artery and to the lung areas itself. There is mild degree of difficulty or what would be nerve flow difficulty, into and affecting the respiration. The diaphragm itself is mildly affected here. We would find that, indeed, there is some inflammation, and irritation into the shoulder and into the neck. This would extend further, higher up into the base of the skull itself.

There would appear to be sediment in the joints or nooks and crannies of the body as well, in these areas, but also extending further out into the body itself. Indeed, there could be improvement to eliminations, and this would be beneficial to the body itself. There is congestion within the ascending portion of the colon; not that it is severe, you see, but that if the elimination systems would be improved, all the body would receive some benefit from the same.

There are compressive forces into the third to fifth lumbar that are affecting this particular condition in the body. The lymphatic system in the body is sluggish as well. If this were improved, or if there would be mechanical stimulation of the same, this would aid the body in removing the sediments that would affect the upper part of the body, but also throughout the same.

Therefore, in beginning to improve the body, to remove conditions of rigidity or inflammation in the body, you should first pay attention to corrective measures in the spine. The osteopath or chiropractor would be helpful, but also degrees of massage and, indeed, stimulation to the liver, the bladder, and to the lymphatic system from the throat and sinuses down through the upper part of the body as well. This would allow the body to have greater energy, more oxygen in the blood, through increased activity or breathing in the lung itself; and, as such, this would perk up the entirety of the body.

There is some difficulty in the heart, on the right side, upper portion. There is some sediment in the blood itself. What must be done to the body, therefore, is to improve the same, in the simple or the lower ends of the body, to improve the conditions - you would call this - of impairment, and then allow the body to send the healing forces to those various aspects, but removing the conditions, as we have just given.

To begin with, after there has been some degree of corrective measure, or during the same time in which the spine would be aligned, there would be need also for manipulation of the shoulder-blade. For here, the weakness in the shoulder (and there is some thinning in the smaller bones, collarbone, and degrees of difficulty held here in the trapezium, lateral or to the back of the body, you see, towards the neck) there could be the use of the acupuncturist here to, indeed, increase the chi or flow of energy through to the shoulder and hand itself, you see.

However, as there would be some mechanical manipulation here, this would dislodge or would cause movement in the body that would be beneficial, both to the lymph and to the artery, as well. Serraflazyme may be taken as a blood cleanser. There could be chelation therapy given to the body, for there is some degree of heavy metals in the blood, but these would be light or not consistent in the body. The serraflazyme would be a supplement manner or chemical cleansing to the artery and the blood itself.

That which would be given directly throughout the upper part of the body (but could be done to the entirety of the body) would be massaging the body with the mineral oil (Johnson's baby oil would be good, or some similar mineral oil). The body should be heated or warmed first, and the oil applied. This would have a tendency to soften the arteries by allowing them to be more elastic in their fluctuation. This would carry the blood forward throughout the body easier and the restrictive points (plaque upon the same) would be not as severe. There would not be felt the burning sensation, or heating up in the arm or leg, you see. However, the serraflazyme should also cleanse the internal parts of this.

This would be, therefore, removing from the blood those sediments, those irritants that have long been attached to the body. Plenty of water should be taken into the body to assist in this cleansing process. Olive oil from the spoon should be given as well. This will help in the removal of the deposit of matter (physical congress) in the body and, indeed, the body would be refreshed or invigorated.

There can be given to the body protein powder, as a drink. Also the goat weed may be taken, or either stimulants that would be good; the prickly ash bark may be taken, and burdock root, as well (as teas, you see). There can be the bayberry leaf, spearmint, and raspberry leaves taken also. These would be anti-inflammatory, and would be helpful not only to the blood, but also to the muscles (as we have given).

However, blending castor oil one part, peanut oil one part, olive oil one quarter part, and camphor one quarter part, these oils can be applied to the body in specifically the joints and to the spinal column itself. This would bring relief, as it would allow range of movement to be increased, and also it would affect the inflammatory

juices secreted. For this is a good mind and a sensitive soul, and, indeed, there tends to be - not a nervousness - but a degree of secretion of adrenalin through the adrenals, if you will. The digestive fluid is triggered by this, and some tension is held in the diaphragm.

To the mammary and to the lymph, the stimulation may be done manually by one who would be skilled in lymph drainage. The oils can be applied to the body. The serraflazyme may aid the blood, but this would need to be a thumb-like walking through the body.

The apricot seed or pit, either extract or the pit itself roasted, can be taken. This would effect to remove any lumps, or congestion, or irritations (cells) in the body. It would help to break down the congestion points or congregation points - not tumors, but coagulation of fluid, you might say - in the lymph, as also a degree of tissue that has blended (fibroid, you see). It would have a tendency to break this down, as would the serraflazyme, as would the massage of the lymph, you see.

The almonds may be taken regularly, and zinc also may be added to the body to affect these centers. As eliminations are improved, the body's natural healing forces should bring about a degree of improvement to this body, you see.

There is more that could be given to the circulation in the legs, and to the bones in the hips and knees; but following through with the same oils, the same massage techniques would be beneficial. As there would be improvement in the middle part of the body, there would be improvement throughout the body.

But understand the emotions are both the constructive and destructive forces in the body. That which the self would enter into - the states of meditation - would bring about the healing forces, and the relief of those traumas, tensions, worries and fears, you see. For these are affecting the body as if the body would be stuck with pins. These are real and do affect the body, especially as pressures at the heart, internal pressures of the blood, and the natural eliminating forces, as we have touched upon.

You may consume ten to twelve large tumblers of water a day. Attempt to drink most of the water after rising or in the morning. You may take grape fruit seed extract also, as a removal of mucous or toxic conditions that would affect the reproductive centers, as well as other soft tissues (removing phlegm or mucous from the body, as well as catarrh, or yeast infection, you see). However, the bayberry leaf as an anti-inflammatory should be a tonic for the entire body.

Glycothymoline may be taken also, and a little may be actually swallowed in the body, but this would be a good rinse for the mouth, especially in the morning, but it may be taken in the evening, as well, for there is some irritation in the throat or palate that would extend into the esophagus. There is a coating or layer of mucous here, also, that should be relieved. This will assist in removing the germs or bacterial influences in the mouth, and the upper portion of the throat.

What might be taken also would be a little vinegar, one-quarter spoonful, in about an ounce of warm water, and a little honey may be added to make it palatable. Rinse the mouth and swallow this first thing in the morning; room temperature water would be good. This would help to remove the coating in the back of the throat, and the esophagus itself, beginning the cleansing or flushing process. This may be done regularly, but we would suggest periodically, as it is a little cumbersome to do, you see.

Avoid carbonated or caffeinated drinks. Avoid those foods that would contain preservatives within the same; and, indeed, the cookware should be copper or stainless steel. Copper would tend to be good, for this would absorb some of the copper into the body and this would be helpful. You may take a little gold leaf also (what would be decorative for pastries) and, indeed, ingest this; for here, the body is a little low in gold. Taking the carrot or the carrot juices and the cabbage juice - but the carrots in particular - would add gold into the body, as a good source of the same. However, he two juices would add amounts of vitamins in the body that would, indeed, perk up the health in the body itself, and, indeed, this should be done regularly. Add a little gelatin powder, or gelatin itself, into the food, and this would help the assimilation process, to take the vitamins to the lower levels.

Any headache or difficulty in the head would be seen as restrictiveness or conditions of impairment in the neck and in the artery. The massaging oil can be applied to the neck, but also a little traction can be given. This would relieve greatly the pressures behind the ear, and allow more blood into and around the brain itself, you see. This would be beneficial for all of the glands in the system. The oils would be helpful, especially throughout the lymph system. The physical touch, and the soothing nature, and the self attempting to enter into states of meditation (in which the body would be relaxed) would be very good for this condition in this body, for there is wear and tear upon the body.

The self tends to absorb the fears, urgencies and conditions of others, due to the clairsentient ability or the intuitive abilities of self. Learning to shed these from the self would be good. This can be done by placing the body in warm water or a normal bath, or a shower; but also even wiping the forehead, as we see. But in this, it should be taking time to allow the body to rest and, indeed, through the states of meditation, enter the holiest of holies; attempt to take the self into an inner sanctum, a sanctuary where there can be little affecting the self in which there would be peace profound, and in this state of peace you would feel the warming light. As this warming light would come upon the self, it would melt away crust or scabs, or unwanted tissue from the body, from the skin, from the very mind of self. See them as that: being disposed of, you see. And as such, beauty would come to the body, would come to the mind, would come to the heart. There would be enthusiasm returning into the self, and periods of suppression or even depression would be eliminated. Understand, you tend to be a sponge, picking up this and that, from here and there.

As this would be a regular process or practice, you may also enter into states of bending and stretching exercises, as those that would be Eastern in nature; for any who engage in this form of exercise first challenge the mind, and as the mind is brought around in control, the body naturally follows. As this would be done, including the breathing exercises, the body would, indeed, be in better physical condition. The mental and emotional states would be uplifted, and there would be an intrigue as your ability to see, introspectively, the conditions of your own body, but also the conditions of those who are meaningful to you, you see. This can be done easily; you need simply to be consistent, but not to be inactive mentally. Understand the mind becomes very active in this state of relaxation. You may focus upon the body (as we have given) in dislodging or removing those unwanted tissues, or unwanted scabs, or appendages, you see. It would work very well for the self.

However, what we have given should increase the activity or the purification of the blood itself, removing of the toxins, and it would, therefore, allow room for more oxygen to be adhered to the corpuscle itself, thereby bringing the healing agents throughout the body.

But hope must be given to the body. Light must be increased in the mental and emotional aspects of the self, so that, indeed, there is an enlightenment and enthusiasm that would blossom within. For there is much to see and much to learn, you know. As this would be done, there would be an invigorating force within the self; a desire for movement. Walking is good; bending and stretching the body is better; and working the mind out is even better still. Allow the mind to be built. Allow the discipline that is already established to further the inquiry to the higher realms, to the Greater Consciousness itself. Then the body will be brought around in control.

There are other minerals and amino acids that may be added to the body as well; amino acids that would be replaced that the body does not produce. These can be tested for, through the hair or fingernail, to determine, clinically, what would be needed at any time. Additional information may be gathered from another source, book or computer.

This would be a broad improvement in the body. Otherwise, eat plenty of vegetables; as a rule of thumb: one from below the ground and three from above the ground. Of the three, two should be of the leafy variety, and the other of the bean or the pod. They should be of the freshest variety and grown in the region in which the body resides. That which is grown in a ball (head lettuce) is largely useless for this one (and, indeed most). Of the meats, the fish, fowl or lamb, baked, boiled, or broiled. Juices from the meat, especially broths made from the bones that have been cracked or cut, would be very helpful to enliven the body as well.

However, immersing the body in salt water would be a return to its ancestral influences and this should be done as often as possible. Otherwise, allow the body to be put in the whirlpool bath and allow the favorite fragrance to be included. Inhale it deeply. This would affect the pituitary, and, indeed, the pineal itself, for this is an intuitive mind and body we have here; it needs to absorb pleasantness, not fear or anxiety, you see, for this is the normal nature of this entity.

We have gone over the body, addressing some of the systems in a general way, paying attention primarily to the blood, skeletal and lymphatic systems.

SAMPLE FIVE

Deep Trance Meditation Health Reading
Date: May 8, 2005
Subject: "Bob"

Please address any physical issues of my body that need attention.

We would find some difficulties in the neck, in the jaw, the palate, and would extend, here, also into the middle portion of the spine, or the back itself. There are some pressures at the heart, and there is difficulty (although minor) of the heart receiving blood to itself, you see. The pressures in the body, especially to the area of the heart, fluctuate; perhaps arrhythmia here.

We would also find a degree of mild difficulty in the abdominal areas; this appear to be an old hernia, or some stretch or tears in the sheathe beneath the skin. We find also mild difficulty of blood flow through the gonads. This is causing mild impairment and some mild irritation in the bladder. Circulation to the lower portion of the body is good, but it could be improved, and there is some rigidity taking place here in the larger joints of the body. There is mild condition of fluid or edema in the lower lung.

To begin with, there can be manipulation by the osteopath or chiropractor, but gently done in the middle part of the back; third to fifth dorsal, also the first dorsal, in particular. This would increase the nerve flows through the nervous system that would increase the activities or influence to the heart and lungs. To the lower portion in the lungs, there should be practiced breathing that would be in the lower lung; fill the lungs up from the lower part up towards the top of the lung, rather than the other way around.

Indeed, the body is slightly acidic at this point and is susceptible to viral and mucous conditions. Refraining from any products from the cow would be good; milk and cheeses, creams, and so on, you see. Pastries should be kept to a minimum or should be avoided, especially those that are made with lard, you see. Sugar from the sugar bowl should be avoided, and pastries or breads that have preservatives in them should be either avoided, or kept to a minimum.

The entity's ability to assimilate is diminishing. It can be accelerated or improved by putting or sprinkling a little gelatin powder on all food that is taken into the body. Broths, juices from the meat, soups, these would be good for the body to aid in the assimilation of the strength of the meat itself. However, pork should be avoided. Although a little crisp bacon would not hurt, all other aspects of pork should be avoided.

As there would be increased breathing activity, what would be helpful would be certain stretching or bending of the abdominal area. This can be done by sitting on the floor, then kneeling on the floor, and then arching the back up and then concaving or becoming sway-back or saddle-back, pushing the abdomen down. Lift the head up and forward, as this would be done, and a sort of stretch or tension will be felt in the chest. Then, repeat. Arch the back, and then concave the back again. This can be done for two to three sessions. If the body could be slightly inverted with the legs higher and perhaps putting the legs on a bed or couch, this would rest the legs, but it would, indeed, aid blood flow into the upper portion (the head or brain).

Indeed, some massaging, specifically to the neck would be beneficial. There is some rigidity or sediment taking place here; calcium build-ups between the vertebrae. Therefore, the traction or massage would be very helpful in stimulating this area. But it would be to improve the memory, and the functions in the brain, or the motor skill areas of the brain by slightly inverting the body; for here, the pressures would be increased into the head. This may be a little painful or disorienting at first but, done repetitiously, the blood flow would refresh and enliven the activity into the brain itself. The visionary skills would be benefited by this, as would the hearing and memory activity, you see.

Zinc may be added to the diet, as a supplement, and the prickly ash bark or the burdock root, goldenseal and willow root all can be blended as a tea and taken periodically. These would be cleansing to the blood and to the small arteries into the brain itself. Indeed, this entity would benefit by the serraflazyme as well, especially into the smaller ends of the artery and venous, you see; and for this, a tablet or two per day for the first week or two would be beneficial (and then there could be, every third day, a tablet taken). This would keep the movement from the smaller arteries and venous subtle and progressively beneficial.

There can be the castor oil packs across the abdominal area; this would be to take a large piece of flannel or cotton, soak it into the oil itself, and then, as it would be warmed (room temperature or slightly better) place it across the abdominal area. This would soak into the body and would be beneficial to the intestine, to the wall of the abdominal area, to the liver, and, mildly, to the stomach itself. This can be done once a week or periodically, as would be desired. There would never be too much of this. However, it is a little clumsy as well. Place a piece of plastic under the body. The body may be bathed or it may not be.Keeping the body warm is important. Then, place the oil on the abdomen. You may smear it on or massage it on, and, in addition to being absorbed in the cloth, this would help the process of assimilation. Then, place the castor oil pack on the body and allow it to remain for some thirty to forty-five minutes. This would be invigorating and, slowly, there would be improvement to the wall of the same. Although it would not knead together the tears in the membrane, it would prevent further tears in the sheathe or membrane below the skin. This would be beneficial to the prostate region or area, as well.

Nutmeg may be taken, either in granule form, or what would be a supplement. If it is available in a tablet, then it would be a tablet or two taken once a week until there have been three to four weeks. Then every other month or every once in a month could be done. This would be specifically for the testicle, for the bladder, and for the areas leading to the urethra through the body itself. Coca-Cola syrup - a spoonful in about an ounce or two of water - could be taken when there is irritation or burning sensation in the urine itself. This would be an indication of bladder infection, and this would be soothing to the self.

Kava kava may also be taken, to relax the area in the upper chest, the throat, and act somewhat as a relaxant, in a general tonic way, throughout the body. Should there be difficulty in sleeping, or irritation in the stomach, slippery elm (as a tea) may be taken; a cup would be sufficient, you see. These would allow the body not to be suppressed, but it would be relaxing to the body.

In what may be taken specifically to affect the thirst or the throat would be dill, and this could be taken as a spoonful of the liquid from a dill pickle jar, you see, or the herb, the dill itself, may be put in some vinegar and water - about a spoonful of vinegar in about four to six ounces of water - and it would be allowed to not dissolve, but at least sit there for a few days or so. Then, it can be taken, a spoonful or so at a time. It would be a little harsher to the taste, but a spoonful of the pickle juice would be most helpful, especially when there is difficulty in quenching the thirst.

For this entity, the citrus fruits may be taken, but they should not be combined with other fruits. Limes, lemons, grapefruit, oranges, you see, can be taken, and can be mixed with each other. But, indeed, no other fruit should be blended with them. Indeed, fruit may be taken, but it should be eaten in families. Eat the berries with the berries, the melons with the melons, the citrus with the citrus and, indeed, to help the digestive system, grapes may be taken. Eat them all, pulp, skin and seeds. Flax seed may be taken also, and a little flax seed may be sprinkled on food independently of taking the spoonful of flax oil from time to time (at least weekly, you see).

However, before food is taken in, two ounces of grape juice mixed with two ounces of water can be sipped slowly. This would affect the thyroid, pancreas, and, in turn, the bile to be secreted. Olive oil from the spoon can be taken when there is congestion in the body as well. And, on occasion, grape seed oil may be taken as well. This would be food for the liver, and for the intestine; a spoonful every other week if there would be a regime or regimentation, you see.

Icing sugar or donuts should be avoided. They tend to put the entity to sleep, you see, for it does affect the thyroid and pancreas adversely. There is borderline insulin distribution difficulty here. The Jerusalem artichoke may be taken or substituted to produce insulin in the body.

As such, this would be the place to overcome the weaknesses, or the body's sluggish activity, paying attention primarily to the endocrine system or glandular system in the body; also paying attention to digestive and elimination systems in the body. The castor oil pack would be very soothing, as well as beneficial, for the workings of all the vital organs themselves.

We have gone over the body, not paying too much attention to the vision, but more to the conditions in the throat, in the chest and in the reproductive centers.

SAMPLE SIX

Deep Trance Meditation Health Reading
Date: May 7, 2005
Subject: "Cathy"

I have an aneurysm in the splenic artery. Could you please describe a course of action to remedy this issue?

Indeed, as we would examine the body itself, we would first pay attention to the skeletal system in the body. There is difficulty in the upper portion (the neck itself). The cranium does not sit properly on the neck; minor degree of adjustment here to the Atlas and Axis, the top two bones in the neck. Also what would be in the lower neck, or the last cervical itself. We would find degrees of compression in the third, fifth, seventh, eleventh and twelfth dorsal, and degrees of compression in the second, fourth and fifth lumbar, or the lower part of the spine. This would extend slightly into the pelvis, into the sacrum and the coccyx.

If there would be alignment in what would be higher, the upper part of the back, and manipulation or adjustment in the lower part, the pelvis itself would realign. There would be improvement in the bones in the hips and knees. Fatigue would not come so easily into the lower part of the body. Circulation into the feet would be much improved; but, more exactly, the nerve flows through the sympathetic and parasympathetic nerve systems would be enhanced. Also there would be enhancement of the nerves in the reproductive centers in the body and digestion; the nerves that would control these organs or systems in the body.

There is not great difficulty here but, indeed, it could continue as the bones would further the inflammation that is already evident modestly in the lower end, but also what would be to the upper part across the shoulders and into the neck. This would be the place to start, aligning the structure; for understand the bones hold the body apart; the muscles pull the body together.

However, in what would be across the shoulders and through the neck, there can be massage; this would be also a degree of depth of massage that would not be too severe in the upper part (the neck), but it would be rather a good depth of massage through the upper and mid-back. The shoulder-blades also could utilize some relaxation or manipulation. The combination of oils to be used upon the body would be one part castor oil to help reduce the inflammation, one part peanut oil (this would be for penetration and lubrication of the vertebrae and to allow the bone to be slightly more flexible), lanolin one-quarter part, camphor oil one-third part. You may add also a little witch hazel, about one-quarter part or less, to allow the oils to be more lubricating or thin. You may also add to this a little rose hip, if it is available in oil, or, if not, in water; a few drops you see. This can be then mixed and liberally applied across the back, and it would be soothing to the back itself, as to the touch. This would affect the spinal condition, the nerves, and the lymphatic system that would parallel the spine; and, indeed, all systems would be improved. There would be improvement also to the heart, to the lungs, to the esophagus and to the blood flows into the base of the brain, and also what would be to the drainage of the sinuses. Headaches or fatigue would dissipate.

We would add to the diet the protein powder (the weight-lifter's powder, you see); about an ounce of this in any medium that would be preferred (warm water, juice, milk - rice or soya). This would be given to the body on a regular basis and this would strengthen the form.

In what would be to the blood circulation in the body, we would suggest there be taken the serraflazyme. This would affect the removal of particles and blood particles, as well as sediment or plaque that would align itself on the inside of the arteries itself.

This would be as an improvement to the

entire body, but it would particularly improve the small ends, or the small artery and venous in the hands and feet, and also into the brain itself. In what would be specifically given to affect the arteries in the body from head to toe, including the attempt to shrink the same, as to any expansion in the artery (as we have been directed) - this does not appear to be a thinness in the wall of the artery, but it appears to be a ballooning or an injury to the artery - therefore, the wall, although perhaps expanded, is not thin, fickle, or to be considered vulnerable. Mineral oil may be placed upon the body and this would be given externally. Best to have the body immersed in hot water; whirlpool bath would be good, but any normal water that would be as hot as the body could stand would be good. Thereafter, allow the oil to be placed on the body, especially in the upper back of the head, extending right to the scalp or hairline itself: about the ears, paralleling the neck either side, through the chest, across the shoulders and to the back itself. The oil will absorb into and will affect directly the artery itself, allowing all of the artery to be more elastic or pliable. This will indirectly and directly soothe and aid or heal any of the arteries that would be injured.

There are three other points in the body that would appear to be pinched or injured. While we do not find scar tissue, extensively, we can find some disruption to the corpuscle as blood would pass through these points. The serraflazyme would be helpful in maintaining or reducing, internally, the conditions of sediment in the blood. But the oil itself will affect directly the artery and will be carried forth, you see, to other points that would be soothing or allow elasticity to be maintained. This massage should be done at least weekly, if not twice weekly; however, the more, the better, shall we say, but at least weekly here.

Then, there can be eaten the almonds themselves. The figs and dates would be helpful, but almonds would be specifically beneficial to the artery. There can be taken the kava kava as a tea or as a drop on the tongue. This would be helpful directly to the soothing or calmness, again, in the throat, paying attention to the gag reflex and the areas within the bronchial and the upper portion of the lung. There should be maintained a degree of breathing or regimen of breathing in which deep breaths would be taken, from the low lung upward, you see. This would affect the diaphragm and would be an internal massage, you might say, inasmuch as the diaphragm flexing, as it would be during normal deep breathing, would affect and push the organs and allow the lungs to expand naturally and this would improve. There is tension held here, in the diaphragm, and this, the sheathe, you see, naturally, is pulled to one side, as each body is slightly stronger more on one side than the other.

There is considerable stress and strain in the muscles through the middle part of the body and this simple technique would help the internal aspects of the body, but it would also affect the rib cage and the girdle muscles in the back or small part of the back of the body itself. Infrared light may be put upon the body to aid the circulation to these areas, the sides and ribs and under the arms, shall we say, but more to the larger muscle masses, across the abdomen, across the low back and including the buttocks itself. Then to the top of the legs also, there is some degree for massage or stretching of the tendon here. One who would be considered knowledgeable in pressure points, or Shiatsu, or any form of massage that would release these tendons and muscle groupings, specifically into the back of the leg and the inside of the thigh as well, should be consulted. Again, the oils that were used for massage may be applied, or simply the pressure points excited. It would be uncomfortable to a little, or even painful, but it would release the larger muscles and here, the back of the knee and the lower leg would be benefited. The legs are not quite in alignment, and this would allow them to reset or be more perfect vertically.

There is inflammation in the knee and hip. The oil, especially the castor oil, can be applied to the back of the knee, inside the thighs, to the hips and to the small of the back. This would help to remove any resident inflammation, you see. The liver's function is good; not as good as it could be, however, it functions (it has been slightly injured). Grape juice - two ounces - mixed with two ounces of water, sipped slowly before food is taken into the body would affect the thyroid, the pancreas, and, in turn, the bile to be secreted from the liver, you see. This would be very beneficial to the colon itself.

Castor oil may be placed on the abdomen, massaged on the same before sleep, and then left to soak into the body (if you would see it as that) overnight. Otherwise, olive oil from the spoon may be necessary to take when there is some disruption or difficulty in elimination (physical congress).

For the self, grape fruit seed extract may be taken to remove some degree of buildup of mucous or irritations that may crop up in the reproductive or feminine aspects here. This would be seen as anti-inflammatory but, more exactly, in reducing mucous in the body, it would also aid, indirectly, the lymphatic system. As the body would adjust to the various positions or injuries, these muscles can be given a very deep massage itself; not Rolfing, but a sort of similar, deep massage, at certain adjoining points; these would be where the muscles come together that would be opposing groups (one side stretching while the other side expands). Those connecting points may be either pressurized or massaged. They would release the hurt in the muscle and the muscle would relax. One who would understand Trager work, where the muscle would be gently vibrated, could be consulted or utilized. This would release the internal tension that is maintained in some of the strands of muscles in the various parts of the body (the legs and arms, so to speak).

However, into the diet, eat more of the vegetables and the vegetable juices. Attempt to keep the body slightly more alkaline. Refrain from milk from the cow or other forms of products of the same (cheeses, *et cetera*). Sugar from the sugar bowl should be avoided, for there is some mild disruption in the glands (the thyroid and pancreas). Any icing, or chocolate, or other forms of sugar would tend to cause the body to become a little sleepy, you see.

With manipulation in the middle of the shoulder-blades to the spine, the third and fifth dorsal, there would be corrective measures, here, that would allow, through the nervous system - sympathetic and parasympathetic - energy flows to the pancreas that would be acceptable or corrective. In the meantime, eat of the Jerusalem artichoke, a time or two. Make it an additive to the diet on a weekly basis, and this should be sufficient to stimulate the pancreas itself sufficiently.

We have gone over the body, paying attention to the arterial aspects, the skeletal portions of the body and, to some degree, the muscle groupings here. We have not paid in-depth attention to other systems in the body, but as the protein would be ingested, and as there would be gentle traction in the neck, and, indeed, the neck would be heated or gently massaged with the oils that would be restorative and remove any inflammation to the bone and the muscle, blood flows to the brain would be enhanced and this, throughout the glandular and endocrine system, it would benefit the entirety of the body. Those aches and pains should be paid attention to and seen not as inconveniences, but rather as signs of the body needing some release of a certain tension, specifically in the diaphragm itself.

Iodine from the salt of the sea could be sufficient, if taken regularly to correct this. Table salt should be avoided. The trace elements of aluminum within the same are detrimental to this body, and even to the brain itself.

Zinc supplements should be taken, you see. Flax oil and flax seeds themselves should be taken - the spoonful of oil periodically, and flax seeds may be sprinkled on the food. This would also be beneficial to the brain.

SAMPLE SEVEN

Deep Trance Meditation Health Reading
Date: May 5, 2005
Subject: "Randy"

I have some problems in my feet, knees, and chest. Could you please offer some recommendations to improve my health?

As we would examine the body, we would find, indeed, some difficulty that would originate from the lower back, or what would be in the lower section. The pelvis is slightly pushed forward in the lower portion; this is causing some degree of alignment difficulty in the vertebrae, or what would be the bone. This is placing pressures upon the nervous system, the central nervous system itself, extending into the lower extremities through the sacrum; and although the coccyx is not out of alignment vertically, it is slightly, horizontally, in the lower end. This is placing pressures or stresses to the blood flow through the reproductive centers; also placing, to a sluggish degree, you see, pressures in the limbs, extending to the feet, and the lower leg on the left side is slightly out of alignment with the upper leg itself. There are pressures in the arches, and there is some compressive force (or shrinkage, more exactly) taking place, again, from the hip, from the back itself, to the large tendon that radiates down the side of the leg.

Here, the manipulation through massage of the leg, especially into the hip, or through the groin, and through the knee, and then into the ankle, and then to the toes could be accomplished, by one who would be skilled in the thing. There could be given to the side of the leg from the hip to the ankle the combination of oils that would penetrate into the same. While the castor oil and peanut oil would prove to be helpful, we would suggest there be the Johnson's baby oil (or any mineral oil). This would penetrate into the skin and affect the tendon itself. This would allow the pressures into the limbs themselves, into the segments of the limb to release. For understand the bones hold the body apart; the muscles squeeze the body together.

There is some irritation or inflammation in these joints, and extending to the lower portion, the ankle and feet. Massaging the body here, and with infrared light on the side of the leg, there would be some relaxation or some release in the tendon. The muscle groupings in the thigh and the calf of the leg would correspond or release as well.

Manipulation by the osteopath or chiropractor in the lower back would also be accommodating to what would be in the lower portion, the leg itself. However, in what would be the circulation or increasing the blood flow into the feet, we would suggest that not only there be given the massage of the feet and the ankles with these, the penetrating oils (one part castor oil, one part peanut oil, or even it could be a little more peanut oil to one-and-one-half parts to one part castor oil; there could be a little witch hazel added to this, about one quarter part), this would penetrate into and around the muscles, but also the feet, and, indeed, it would enhance the circulation, you see.

That which would be helpful to increase blood flow throughout the body, helping to increase circulation to the extremities, but also into the chest and into the larger arteries feeding the heart, and what would be vertically through the body would be serraflazyme. This could be taken periodically, for this difficulty in the body does not appear to be excessive. This would help to remove any condition of impairment, or restriction in the larger arteries, and also the small ones, you see. This would be two tablets of this taken daily, for as many as ten to fifteen days, then leave off for a week or two, then commence again. As this would be done, the blood flow to the extremities, especially to the feet and to the chest would be helpful; also to the brain itself. The massaging effect of the oils, the traction or tension into the leg itself, and the corrective force to the posture in the pelvis should relieve any wear or tear into the compressive forces in the body. But to the bone, the oils, too, will help or assist in the reduction of inflammation, you see.

In that which can be given to the body specifically would be the bayberry leaf as a tea, or perhaps as a supplement. Kava kava may be taken as well, to help the respiration and relaxation to occur through the upper chest throughout, in which there would be improved breathing or restriction lessened in the throat. These two would aid in the amount of reduction of inflammation in the body. It is the oils that will act as lubricating forces; like any machinery, requiring some lubricant. These would be directly topically put upon the same.

You may seek the services of the acupuncturist, and there would be the placement of one needle or one pin in the buttock, to the side, you see. It would be excited by striking the same. This would cause what would be a surge of energy from the hip to the foot and from the foot back again. Not a shock, but a certain degree of surge of the body's electrical impulses. This would be sufficient to affect the limb as well as the back itself, you see, and causing lengthening to take place to the legs.

Now, the feet, especially the arches, can be massaged directly by one who would be skilled in the thing (a reflexologist) and this would be into the center point or just behind the pad of the foot. It would be painful to the touch, but there are certain sedentary forces here; you would call these crystalline forces (calcified elements). The massaging of this, specifically this part and portion of the foot, would be beneficial to all parts of the body, but in these two areas, the sole of the foot and the corresponding area of the chest itself, the rib cage would feel slightly constricted, but with this massage it would feel as if it would expand much easier; or, as you would call it, the flexibility of the muscle between the rib or the bone itself would be indirectly influenced, but in a positive way. It would be touchy, or a little painful or uncomfortable, but within the second or the third application or treatment, the feet will feel more supple. There would be less contraction or bone against bone in the ankle, you see, and blood supply would be enhanced throughout.This would be sufficient in remedying the conditions of the inflammation or the compressive forces of the bone itself.

Chondroitin may be taken in the body, or glucosamine with the same, but larger amounts should be done. As we would also indicate to the diet itself, there can be added those supplements, those foods that would be helpful to strengthen this condition; these would be primarily dates or figs. They will indirectly affect the intestine first, then what would be lower in the extremities itself. However, the serraflazyme should work within a very short period of time. Pressure in the legs or limbs would balance, or would be slightly different one to the other, as we see it.

Again, to the abdominal area, as there would be the acupuncture, perhaps the single treatment would be sufficient, energy flows would be enhanced or increased throughout the gonads, and extending here upward into the small intestine itself. Secretions throughout the area would be improved.

Digestive juices tend to be a little extreme or excessive, and they could be irritating the small intestine, from time to time. And while yogurt may be taken to assist or to replace the bacterial in this, the intestine, what could be taken would be the slippery elm as a tea. This would coat the stomach, and would reduce the excessive amounts of bile or digestive fluids in the small intestine. There should be an increased activity or enthusiasm here, as the blood flow would be increased throughout the body.

The goat weed as a supplement or tea could be taken, and this would allow an energetic influence through the chest and to the entirety of the being. Grape seed extract could be taken to affect the pancreas. This could be taken periodically for this one, and, as such, this would help the fluctuation of the pancreas, and the Jerusalem artichoke should be taken as well. This indirectly would affect the blood as well as the gland, and would be a balancing between the thyroid and pancreas, as we see it.

As we would examine the lower and mid-back, there are compressive forces between the shoulder-blades here - this would be in the third and fourth dorsal - not severe, but rather seen as "room for improvement" to allow the lungs to function energetically or more consistently. There is, again, small degrees of inflammation throughout the body, and here, the increased volume of air taken into the lungs would benefit those conditions of irritation in the body itself.

There is mild compressive force in the first bone of the back. This is mildly affecting, through the nervous system, the beating or pressures of the heart in a way that is not consistent, you see. This is very minor indeed. Into the neck and the brain, we find with some degree of traction or slight adjustment here. Blood flow into the brain would be enhanced or improved. Again, the serraflazyme would be beneficial to the small arteries and veins in the body itself.

Would you please offer some suggestions for my wife, "Kathleen" to remedy the condition of cancer and nerve pain.

As we would examine the body, we would find that throughout the body there is difficulty; there is fatigue, and extending to the lymphatic system, there are irritations here. There is some difficulty in the bone and also the lymph throughout the body itself. There is some difficulty in the soft tissue in the back of the brain. The body would be in difficulty, and what would be given to the body would be combinations primarily to have nutritional values in the body increased (although there is some nausea or difficulty here); plenty of water, increasing the assimilation process of the vitamins, and of the strength of the meats itself. Also fresh air and, indeed, some inspirational reading or the use of scripture or books to advance the entity's enthusiastic and optimistic aspects within the same.

Therefore, in what would be given, if it can be available, the entity should engage in a combination of vegetable juices or vegetables, or vitamins that can be taken; yea, by the handfuls almost. Allow these to be taken into the body and, indeed, there would be a building up at least at the cell level, to affect the immune system itself. The ingestion of these vitamins, especially the D and B or B1 (and extending to the B12), can be absorbed into the body by juices, or they can be given by supplements. But there should be gelatin powder added to help this assimilation take place, and direct these to the cell level.

Infrared light can be given upon the body to help the condition of difficulties and heighten the circulation. In what would be directly added (or, if it would be available, attained) would be the treatment of hyperthermia. This would be the process of surrounding the tumor with what would appear to be wires and, as such, heating the body up to forty-six degrees Celsius, at least around the affected area. The entire blood supply may be heightened or heated up, but we do not find it affecting the brain itself. This would cause the tumors to shrink, and the improvement in the lymph and the blood to be such that the misshapen cells themselves would dissipate or turn acidic and dissolve in the body. Speak to one who would be skilled in the thing, as that one who would be a pioneer; this would be the Valley Cancer Clinic in Pasadena, or Panorama City here; one or the other. *[Note: Bicher Cancer Institute (formerly Valley Cancer Institute) is one of the largest hyperthermia research and clinical treatment centers in the Western hemisphere.]*

As this would be done, this body could begin to right itself or rid itself of this. But primarily, eliminations would need to be improved as well. This would require colonics or enema therapies to be given to the body. The body could respond positively. Plenty of water would need to be taken as well to help the filtering and removal of these sedentary forces.

To the pain or suffering of the intensity (or what would be the painful mechanisms of the body), what would be given would be simply those aspects, those ingredients that would tend to put more oxygen into the blood or heighten or exaggerate the amount of oxygen in the blood. What would be given also would be a little alcohol; this would not hurt the body. And we would find also what would be in nature, any of the plants that would be from the nightshade family - these would be derivatives of the eggplant and the tomato - and would be ingested into the body itself would cause some easement of the entity's pain. Of course he oils that are anti-inflammatory - the castor oil - can be smeared upon the body itself, from the throat to the abdomen would be good, paying attention to the throat itself. And here, the key aspect of this would be the blood in the body being affected. Chelation therapy may be given intravenously, and this would be helpful as well, and it would help both the circulation and the reduction of toxins that are affecting the cancerous areas in the body.

This would be sufficient if the hyperthermia could be obtained, to alter the body. But here again, the rule of thumb would be plenty of water to be taken throughout the day; vitamins by the handfuls that would be easy to absorb in the body, with the added effect of the gelatin, you see; and indeed, breathing great amounts of air out-of-doors would be better than indoors; and, as such, what can be given intravenously would be chelation fluid, or, if it is also available, some injection of vitamin C, you see. This would tend to boost the metabolism itself, and the oils that would be anti-inflammatory would seem to soothe.

However, the condition in the body is stagnant. We do not see it as increasing its growth. The lymphatic system can be stimulated by one who would be skilled in the same who would understand the lymphatic drainage and, as such, could enhance or stimulate the lymph. This may be a little painful, but it would be beneficial to the body.

We have gone over the form here, paying attention to this. Understand that the mental and emotional states are, indeed, directly related to the benefit of the body. As the body itself would adhere towards the constructive emotions, the enthusiastic aspects, the body would be able to activate those healing forces, those curative systems in the body. Currently, our comment would be that the body is not at rest, but we do not find rapid and outrageous growth of cells at this point in time. There are other applications that will be brought about the body to affect the T-cells in the same. As the body would be in this dormant state, then there can be activities brought upon the form that would bring about advantageous recovery. If the body is wounded, or if there is surgery, then the body would continue to move towards a rapid effect, as growth hormone would kick into the body's system and develop a speeding up of cell development, you see. Our comment is such that the body is, again, not dormant, but in a state of rest at this point in time, you see.

SAMPLE EIGHT

Deep Trance Meditation Health Reading
Date: May 7, 2005
Subject: "Mary"

I was diagnosed with polycystic ovarian disease. Please examine my body for any health issues, giving causes and recommendations for treatment.

Indeed, as we would examine the body, we would first be directed towards the glandular system in the body. Beginning in the brain itself, we would find there is some degree of activity. This is the nerve function or transference of thought, nerve activity, across the bridge, corpus callosum, you see; what would be from the left to right hemisphere seems not to be as good as it could be. Blood flow is somewhat sluggish here. As we would examine the neck, we would find difficulty in the third cervical and a little in the Axis and Atlas; compressive forces here, and a slight bend in the neck. These could be corrected quite easily by the osteopath or the chiropractor. This would immediately enhance the blood flow into the brain, and it would affect the balance between one hemisphere and the other. There will be felt some slight irritation as the blood flow would enhance, even some dizziness or some disorientation, but not severe. This would require more than one adjustment, and, as such, the blood flow enhancing here would affect the other portions of the brain, the thalamus and hypothalamus, and the pineal itself. Motor skill regions in the medulla and cerebellum would also be enhanced, but this would be along the lines of what is already the present activity.

There is difficulty in the third, fourth, and fifth dorsal; this are minor compressive forces here. These are directly affecting the thyroid and the pancreas. There is some difficulty lower in the spine; pelvis is slightly rotated, you see.

There are some difficulties in the lymphatic system here and also what would be the kidneys and liver. As we would examine the cells in the body, we would find also some depletion here, and some susceptibility to influences of preservatives, you see. As we would examine the pancreas, we would find some inactivity here, but it does not seem to be constant; appears to be less and more. Thyroid also seems to have some shift or altering, you see; and there is some residue of irritation in the liver, in the tissue of the body (viral or bacterial conditions). These are all minor and lead up to a degree of impairment here. With manipulation into the spinal column itself, in particular the neck, but also what would be between the shoulder-blades and lower, into the back and pelvis, rather quickly, the body would adjust or allow itself increased nerve flow.

To enhance the body, we would suggest a whirlpool bath, taken with one cup of apple cider vinegar in the water. This would excite or allow a degree of growth to take place to the nervous systems, improving the communication flows. To what would be helpful for the pancreas, we would suggest grape seed extract. This would be three to four capsules in the morning. This would affect the pancreas specifically, and, as such, the metabolism will enhance itself.

To the diet, eat of the vegetable. Good rule of thumb would be: one vegetable from below the ground and three from above, and of the three from above, two would be of the leafy variety and the other of the bean or the pod. But indeed, to the vegetable, what is grown in a ball as head lettuce should largely be avoided. Of the meats, let it be of the fish, the fowl, and the lamb, baked, broiled, or boiled. Leave off from all aspects of the hog. Broths, stews and soups would be body-building, especially if there are soups made from the bones themselves in which the bones of the fowl or the lamb would be broken open and boiled, you see. This would add strength to the body without impairing the activities or difficulty to the glandular secretions. Apricots may be taken, or the apricot pit, or seed (if it is roasted) can be taken. Nutmeg may be taken as well, although in small amounts. Almonds should be taken as well.

To that which would be added to the body, manage the diet to refrain from deep-fried foods, soda pop (or carbonated drinks), and any bread with preservatives within the same, or any other such preservatives in food. This should right the body rather quickly; begin the process, you see.

Take the hair or the fingernail (one or the other) and have them analyzed for minerals. The body is deficient in some essential minerals here, and these could be added as supplements; they may be added as food sources as well.

You may find quail oil to be an essential additive to the body, and also flax seed oil added to the body. Olive oil, on occasion, may be added as a food; a spoonful or so. These oils may be taken periodically. They may not be fattening to the body but would be seen as food to the body. This should be sufficient in attempting to shrink the body itself.

Primarily, the adjustment to the nervous system would begin to set the endocrine system in motion. However, bending and stretching exercises should be engaged in, here. Any who engage in this form of exercise that is Eastern in nature (such as yoga) first challenge the mind, and then as the mind is brought around in control, the body naturally follows. Utilize these exercises. Have a simple routine that would be done each morning. Now, if the body can be encouraged to be inverted by shoulder-stands, this would cause the pressure of the neck, the chin upon the thyroid, and this would be soothing and body-building. Inverting the body for seconds, not minutes, would be good. Use a wall, or put the arms on the floor and the hands on the hips as the back would be rolled over, then raise the legs up to a vertical position. This will be invigorating to all parts of the body itself. Now, to the hormonal structure in the reproductive centers, this would also stimulate the ovaries and there would be increased blood flow to the womb itself, and to the menses cycle. Be not alarmed if it is increased, but take more iron into the body; liquid iron, or capsules of iron, you see. This would be the first stage to improve the body.

Understand the body is susceptible and is clairsentient. You may wear a headband, or a bandanna, or something around the head when you feel pressures in the head or the thoughts of many people come to your mind. Reject any intrusion into the mind in this way, mechanically, whether it is an ornament, a band, a string; this will remind the self not to absorb those thoughts, those feelings of others. You may also fold the hands across the solar plexus, and this, too, would prevent intrusion (or, more exactly, the depletion of your energies) within the body.

If done so, protein powder may be given to boost the blood in the brain. This could be done as a shake or a drink; you may add fruit to the same. Blend it and allow the body to enjoy this. This should perk up the energy flows in the body. The goat weed (or sometimes called horny goat weed) may be taken as well to stimulate the systems within the body. The self should feel enthusiastic. You may take other forms of anti-depressants, such as St. John's wort, but in all likelihood it will not be necessary. These are not to affect the mental and emotional states; these would be to speed up the metabolism, as the goat weed would, you see. With increased blood flow through the body by the stretching and bending exercises, with the body shrinking, you may then wish to build the body up, and we would encourage that some form of formal body-building be engaged in. Utilize those exercises that would be specifically to those points in the body; to the middle part, for instance, would require only turning exercises or twisting, you see. But, indeed, the bending and stretching (the yoga) would be sufficient in this. The body will be builded up and will have sufficient strength, energy level, you see.

Be not afraid to eat the meat, or to take the meat juice. When the body becomes fatigued, take the muscle from the beef (no fat should be upon it) and cut it into cubes. Place it in a jar, then place the jar in a pot of boiling water and cook from the second to the third hour. If a pressure cooker is available, place the meat in the jar in a pot of water and cook it in a pressure cooker for forty-five minutes. At the end, allow the jar to cool. Disregard the meat itself, as it is largely useless. Save the juice. This would be very potent medicine indeed! This would be given to the body and would strengthen the body without putting the body through too much effort in digestion.

There can be taken those things that would assist digestion and assimilation. If vegetables or vegetable juices are to be taken, add a little gelatin powder to the same. This would act as a catalyst, and allow the vitamins to be absorbed into and to the cell level itself. You may also expose the entire body to light or light therapy. This would be the ultraviolet ray itself. You may put colored films between the light and yourself - rainbow colors, you see. Be selective, especially into the area of the throat, the chest, and the low abdomen. Exposure to this type of light would be ten to fifteen minutes maximum; five minutes would be sufficient, ten minutes acceptable, and you will immediately feel stronger and the body will be vitalized, you see.

Is the restricted blood flow in my brain the reason why I get a lot of headaches?

This would be part and parcel of the influence here; yes. Very perceptive, you see! Allow the osteopath or chiropractor to manipulate the neck, or at the very least to incur the traction, that would reset the bones in the head, and the skull upon the neck, you see. This will immediately allow the blood flow to increase into the glands and the brain within the head. This, the thalamus and hypothalamus will then affect what is lower, the other glands and the hormonal secretions (those that would be the timing devices in the body).

Yes, as the blood flow is increased here, and as the protein powder would be taken to increase or assist the blood flow here, the headaches should subside. Take the oils, as we have given, especially the olive oil, when there is any indication of difficulty in eliminating (physical congress) and this, too, should assist in the reduction of headache. This is the place, yes.

This would be sufficient to affect the physical and, to some degree, the emotional aspects. Understand the emotions are both the constructive and destructive forces in this (or any) body. The self needs to be jubilant, to be enthusiastic. Soon enough, you will be in complete control of your life.

In the meantime, pack into the self as much in the way of credentials as you can possibly get. You are destined to be somewhat an independent soul, one who is self-reliant, one others would seek to inquire about certain things in their own lives that would relate to yours. You will not be denied love! But be selective at first. And, as such, learn to love the self until truly you love the self so much that your love spills over into the lives of others.

You will find that as you reach out, you will reach in. You may have a few markers, or teachers, or benchmarks along the way (shall we call it) and you will begin to see just who and what you are. You will not maintain yourself in the shadow of anyone. You will be independent and you will have great influence, should you wish to do so. Begin thinking of all the things you wish to do. Formulate a plan here, and allow the self to be filled with enthusiasm to have markers or - let us call them - opportunities; objective points, you see. And as you meet one objective after the next, you will begin to see that your life is on course.

This is a time of extremes. Ye will survive while others deem these times to be chaotic. Your self-assurance and self-reliance will be seen as great gifts, and they will inspire others; again, should you wish to do so (for no man can say this or that must take place). Each possesses its own free will and free choice. Choose the light and life, but it is always your choice.

Douglas James Cottrell, Ph.D.

Douglas James Cottrell, Ph.D. is best known as a trance clairvoyant. He is a spiritual healer, teacher, and published author who demonstrates many abilities studied by Noetic Sciences (the study of consciousness), including clairvoyance, telepathy, remote viewing, prediction, and prophecy.

Douglas is one of a select few able to demonstrate all of these abilities, and even fewer who are considered a reliable information source. He teaches people the world over about spiritual development through the practice of meditation and the application of spiritual principles in daily life.

Douglas's Deep Trance Meditation (D.T.M.) style is often compared to that of Edgar Cayce, Ross Peterson and Paul Solomon, some of the most documented intuitive people of the Twentieth Century. Douglas has been variously called a mystic, a seer, and "the last of the sleeping prophets."

Through the D.T.M., Douglas has authored *Secrets of Life* and *The New Renaissance,* plus numerous digital books available online.

www.douglasjamescottrell.com